HONOURING THE CONTRACT

for Rebecca

HONOURING THE CONTRACT

John E. Martin

VICTORIA UNIVERSITY PRESS

VICTORIA UNIVERSITY PRESS
Victoria University of Wellington
PO Box 600 Wellington
victoria.ac.nz/vup/

Copyright © John E. Martin 2010

First published 2010

National Library of New Zealand Cataloguing-in-Publication Data

Martin, John E.
Honouring the contract / John E. Martin.
Includes bibliographical references and index.
ISBN 978-0-86473-634-5
1. New Zealand—Social policy. 2. New Zealand—Economic policy. I. Title.
361.610993—dc 22

Published with the assistance of the History Group,
Ministry for Culture and Heritage

Printed by Astra Print, Wellington

CONTENTS

PREFACE

This book brings together a number of strands I have been working on from time to time for a long while. In particular the history of the Department of Labour, *Holding the Balance* (1996), left a great deal unsaid about the precursors to the kinds of policies the Liberals introduced around the turn of the twentieth century. Even before that I had a strong interest in labour-related issues in the nineteenth century and these seemed to be pointing in a certain direction. I have always been puzzled by the state's willingness and propensity to intervene and wanted to explore its antecedents as far back as possible.

As I pushed back, being dissatisfied by the usual analysis which starts with the Liberals of the 1890s, I began to think that the state's disposition to intervene was there from the beginning – it was just the form which it took that differed over time. I also became aware that the state's interventions were experimental in nature – always changing in response to changed circumstances, always seeking a solution that worked better. And, as I pushed further back in time to the initial period of colonisation, I began to see that the very project of the New Zealand Company formed part of this framework, and that the nub of the issue was a contract or agreement between state and migrant. The title for the book emerged from this notion – that the state over time and in experimental fashion was concerned with honouring this contract or agreement.

Such a contract was a central idea or motivating force for policy in this country. It helps make sense of a wide range of government activities, all based on the premise of improving or maintaining the standard of living of the New Zealand wage earner. This was the promise held out to migrants, and this was the promise which the state tried to make good for a hundred years or more.

This idea brought together a range of cultural and political influences from Britain, and translated them into a colonial frontier society. The idea of the contract shaped the views of politicians and government bureaucrats in formulating policy. It also shaped the expectations of wage earners, from the first migrants landing on New Zealand's shores, to early settlers scratching a living from deferred payment holdings, to those labouring on railway lines in public works camps, shearers moving between sheds, lumpers going down to the wharves, and young women working in clothing factories.

How did a contract emerge? It came from the expectations and the experience of the early migrants to New Zealand. It linked their cultural backgrounds and political values with their experiences as settlers and colonists. A clause in the contract between the New Zealand Company and its labouring migrants in the 1840s became a springboard for a more general commitment to wage-earning migrants and then to wage earners at large. This clause guaranteed that the Company would provide work for its migrants if they could not find work otherwise. It became the seed for a much broader and symbolic contract between state and wage earner in New Zealand, founded in the migrant experience.

The nature of this contract was shaped by the colonial environment. In Chapter 1, I discuss the interaction of the 'cultural fragment' and 'frontier' perspectives on colonial development, and attempt to tease out how the cultural and political backgrounds of migrants played out in colonial conditions. Central to this discussion is the 'popular instrumental state' by which the contract was promoted and honoured. This form of state is closely linked to the people it governs and for whom it implements policies.

The contract was also shaped by the changing colonial economy and society and by the effectiveness of various policies implemented by the state. Over time the emphasis shifted from land to wage earning in its own right, and then to welfare. Encapsulating these changes and the experimental policy responses, Chapter 2 deals with the 'landed laboratory', Chapter 5 with the 'social laboratory', and Chapter 6 with the 'welfare laboratory'.

The book looks at a wide range of policies: land, collective wage-earner endeavour, employment and the labour market, working conditions and wages, housing, and welfare initiatives. These policies shifted from the enabling and self-help stance of the nineteenth century to a regulating and protective stance in the twentieth century. As the place of the state strengthened, in line with the protective stance, so too did the need for a stronger fiscal base to its policies, which were increasingly expensive. At the same time crucial debates were fought over the rival principles of social insurance versus welfare funding by the state. The resolution in favour of the latter under the Labour government of the late 1930s set the pattern for the welfare state which we still have today.

Poetry was an integral part of the Victorian sensibility. The selections from contemporary verses and prose interspersed amongst the chapters link themes in the book to cultural expressions of the day and give an impression of the way that people perceived such issues. There is a selection from Thomas Hood, the influential early-nineteenth-century English popular poet, and contributions from people who were significant in New Zealand – Edward Jerningham Wakefield, Thomas Bracken, William Pember Reeves and Harry Holland – together with lesser-known versifiers who contributed political and satirical doggerel.

The long genesis of this book makes it difficult to make specific acknowledgements. My experiences in a range of institutions have shaped it – the Stout Research Centre, the Sociology Department of the University of Canterbury, the History Department of Victoria University of Wellington, the Historical Branch of the Department of Internal Affairs, and the History

Group at the Ministry for Culture and Heritage. I have spent a lot of time in the Alexander Turnbull Library and at Archives New Zealand and I greatly appreciate the assistance I received from the staff of both institutions. My grateful thanks go to the Historical Branch for giving me the chance to get the book underway in the late 1990s. I would see this book as a contribution to the themes considered by the British immigration project (which I was involved with) undertaken by the Historical Branch at that time. Many thanks to the History Group for providing a publishing grant that has enabled Victoria University Press to take on the book. I am also very appreciative of Fergus Barrowman's commitment to the project, especially when the book seemed to be disappearing over the horizon, and many thanks to Kyleigh Hodgson of Victoria University Press for knocking the book into shape. The contribution of my family needs to be acknowledged especially in staying away from the only computer in the household when I was battling with never-ending revisions during long evenings.

John E. Martin
July 2010

CHAPTER 1

A 'small nation on the move' – establishing the contract

> Suppose a small number of persons to go out from a densely populated country bristling with old traditions to a new land, carrying with them the memory of freedom and liberty won by a long succession of struggles between various classes extending over hundreds of years, and also taking with them the belief that more freedom and liberty are yet to be attained, and that the struggles are not ended; suppose this band of people find that within what appears to them a practically unlimited area they are free to work out their own destinies, make their own laws, decide their own conditions of existence, is it not clear that their progress will not be exactly parallel with that of the people they leave behind them? The pioneer band will undoubtedly number many who will glory in the idea that they have taken in charge a land free from monopolies and unbound by inherited conditions that conflict with the happiness of the majority of the population.
>
> Julius Vogel, excerpt from 'Social politics in New Zealand'[1]

The New Zealand Company's colonisation project represented the beginnings of a conscious construction of a new 'nation' through an activist state. The Company's inspiration, Edward Gibbon Wakefield, argued that the process of colonisation was one not of 'people merely, but society'; in other words 'a body of men assembled with the intention of emigrating to a distant country are a colony before their departure [and] constitute . . . a small nation on the move'.[2] Likewise, Thomas Cholmondley, in his thoughtful reflections *Ultima Thule* (1854), wrote that 'emigration is the drifting of atoms. Colonisation is the regular movement of an organised body'.[3] And as *The Times* of London commented on the arrival of migrants for the Canterbury settlement and their founding of a newspaper: 'A slice of England, cut from top to bottom, was despatched to the Antipodes . . . Between deck and keel were the elements of a college, the contents of a public library, the machinery for a bank, yea the constituent parts of a constitutional government'.[4] At the heart of the endeavour lay a social contract – a bargain or understanding about the fundamental nature

of emigration, colonisation and its opportunities. Those who would leave
Britain's shores would in return be assisted in what they had set out to achieve.

Frontier and fragment

Julius Vogel, the archetypal business politician and colonial booster, combined
his ambitions with just such a vision of New Zealand's development. A strong
British inheritance meshed with the belief that there was an opportunity in New
Zealand to transcend the bounds of the old society in experimental fashion. He
noted 'that a fragment of a people going from an old to a new country is likely
to progress more rapidly in the attainment of popular conditions than the main
body left behind.' Colonists had unparalleled opportunities to control their own
destiny and fashion their own society, unfettered by monopoly and inherited
class-based constraints. Such sentiments suggest the faith and optimism which
underpinned colonisation and the colonial state.

Cholmondley suggested that 'a new country . . . gives a new form and a
new connection to the life and dealings of before-existing nations'.[5] He said
that in New Zealand 'we may avoid our old national mistakes, and escape
their retribution', and that once the New Zealand Company had finished its
work the country itself had to carry on the business 'not only of extension and
increase, but of civilisation'. A key to this would be the transformation of the
unsettled migrant to a colonist firmly rooted in the land, whereby 'men become
citizens. A body of men becomes a state'. The state would act as a civilising
agency in forging the new world society. The two authors envisaged tremendous
possibilities emerging from the interaction between the philosophies, ideas and
values of the old world and the material conditions of the new country.

This interaction has been much discussed by historians and in the
historiography this has distilled out into the two perspectives of the frontier
and the cultural fragment, depending on whether the emphasis is put more on
the material conditions of the new society or the influences of the originating
society. These perspectives and the way that they can be combined assist in our
understanding of a range of state policies discussed in this book.

The American historian Frederick Jackson Turner provided the classic
frontier perspective.[6] He argued that the 'wilderness masters the colonist'
and strips away civilisation; in confronting the environment settlers built a
new and fundamentally different society. The frontier fused, nationalised and
Americanised various ethnic and national groups; it dictated that infrastructural
improvement, tariffs and land became the focus of national politics; and it
promoted individualism, democracy and a 'practical, inventive turn of mind'.
Most importantly, the availability of land provided continued opportunities
and meant that economic power was the basis of political power.

The frontier perspective has been influential in Australian history. Russel
Ward used the frontier as a powerful explanation of national unity, nationalism
and democracy, giving it a collectivist twist by suggesting that the typical

frontiersman was not a small farmer but a wage worker – the bush worker whose mateship forged a new democratic society.[7] Others have also explored the impact of the Australian frontier, with the qualifications that its expansion was limited relative to the American frontier and that industrialisation and urbanisation challenged its influence.[8] Geoffrey Blainey transposed the 'frontier' into the moulding influence of distance on Australia, an approach which he suggested incorporated not only geographical considerations but also the relationship of Australia with the old world.[9]

'The State? I am the State!' Labour makes its claim. Graphic, *27 April 1901*

The cultural fragment approach has also been useful in explaining Australia's history. Louis Hartz argued that Australia was determined in its character by Britain's stage of development as migration took place. He suggested that the culture conveyed by waves of migration was formative of the society, creating a 'radical fragment' in which a labour spirit and collectivist democracy triumphed.[10]

Richard Rosecrance, in the same spirit, charted the formative influences in Australia of the Reform Act of 1832, factory legislation, the new poor law, Chartism, and the failure of trade unionism. He suggested that a certain 'admixture of "philosophical radicalism" mitigated the working-class ethos of convicts, gold diggers, Chartists, and trade-unionists'.[11] By the mid nineteenth century Australian states had made gains far beyond Britain – in the form of responsible self-government, manhood suffrage, the secret ballot, an eight-hour day and land reform. But once established the radical fragment became fixed and institutionalised; a radical 'myth' which shaped a nationalist legend of mateship. This myth atrophied and blunted socialist politics and philosophies that remained forceful in Europe.

A.W. Martin tried to take Hartz's insights further and make them more dynamic. The lasting link with Britain continued to play an influence both directly through new infusions of migrants and indirectly through political and cultural transmission.[12] Australian society was less collectivist and more individualistic than Hartz had suggested. J.B. Hirst likewise looked at the continued adaptation of British institutions to the colonial context.[13] He made the valuable point that in the colonial context, British institutions originating in the needs of wage earning groups became 'nationalised' and catered to the population as a whole. He suggested that the cultural influence was more radical than collectivist in the 'mutual seeking of self-improvement', which was neither simply individualistic nor collectivist but in between. His analysis of egalitarianism in the colonial period suggests it took the form of equality of opportunity and was consistent with the preservation of unequal results and a hierarchical society.

The basic distinction between cultural influences and local conditions has been fundamental to discussions in New Zealand history also. Edward Gibbon Wakefield's own views are themselves not too far removed from the cultural fragment perspective. And early New Zealand historians elaborated on these cultural linkages.

Alexander Brady in *Democracy in the Dominions* directly applied Hartz's theory to New Zealand (alongside other dominions).[14] He argued that Britain's political influence – individual, civic and political rights, voluntary associations, free debate and a gradualist approach – was expressed in the dominions through the filter of frontier conditions, creating strong democratic and egalitarian orientations. Likewise, W.H. Oliver stressed New Zealand's 'Englishness', its links with 'Home', and its continuity in reformist policies. The Liberals engaged in an 'intelligent improvisation' against a background of overseas doctrine.[15]

MINE, HA! HA! NOW TO STORM THE CASTLE!

THE HON. J. MCKENZIE BRINGS DOWN THE HOUSE.

The 'landed laboratory'. Minister of Lands Jock McKenzie overcomes Opposition leader William Rolleston. McKenzie's initiatives came at the end of a long line of politicians who pursued land reform. This stretched back to Rolleston himself in the early 1880s, a range of provincial politicians in the 1860s and 1870s, and to Edward Gibbon Wakefield's 'working settler' land legislation of 1854. Graphic, *20 August 1892*

There was a strenuous rejection of this cultural fragment approach as New Zealand history emerged as a mainstream discipline after the Second World War. Historians now stressed local conditions. This is evident in the most influential general history of the period, that of Keith Sinclair, which itself was strongly influenced by the earlier work of William Pember Reeves. It is also evident in Michael Turnbull's debunking of the utopian ambitions of Wakefieldian systematic colonisation.[16] In a later work, Sinclair suggests that clearing the bush and breaking in the land (rather than a geographical frontier as in America) was central to building a nation.[17]

As Keith Pickens suggests, such challenges to the fragment thesis took the form of dismantling the pretensions of the Wakefield scheme, and the assertion of geography and an emerging 'colonial tradition' over organised settlement plans.[18]

The frontier approach consolidated in the latter half of the twentieth century through the weight of Sinclair's nationalistic contribution. This resulted in a turning inwards to the study of crucial internal factors contributing to national development, the most important of which were race relations and the Liberal reforms at the turn of the twentieth century.[19] The focus on the Liberals brought with it a neglect of the bulk of the nineteenth century. After a period in which the role of the Liberals in forging New Zealand's distinctive national character was studied, historians began to take a more critical look at the Liberal project and its achievements, but remained locked within a consensus that neglected both overseas (particularly British) influences and the period prior to the 1890s. The effects of this have been felt in labour history as in other areas.[20] Between the apparently 'misguided' Wakefieldian colonisation project and the Liberal reforms of the 1890s is a void filled only by an over-generalised picture of exploitation and poverty for working people and a lack of democracy.

Meanwhile, some have continued to argue for a cultural fragment perspective. The clearest example is Rollo Arnold in his *Farthest Promised Land* and a number of articles.[21] There has been study of the cultural impact of migration, most specifically the way in which wage-earning migrants shaped New Zealand. Tony Simpson's *The Immigrants* explores the reasons behind the 'political revolution' of 1890 which, according to him, set the stage for the modern welfare state and consolidated humanitarian and co-operative values that he believed had been imported into New Zealand by nineteenth-century working class migrants with Chartist backgrounds.[22] For Simpson these values had their origins in a 'moral economy' going back before industrialisation to the eighteenth century, in a yeoman, artisan golden age. But Simpson does not substantiate the Chartist character of those who migrated, nor does he examine evidence for a popular political culture in nineteenth-century New Zealand. He assumes that the Liberal government's social democratic reforms related back to Chartism and simply resulted from an upwelling of support as old world evils arose and were stamped out.

Erik Olssen advances a similar argument, better grounded in research into the working-class Dunedin suburb of Caversham. He argues that artisan radicalism, brought by 1870s migrants, provided a basis for a democratic, egalitarian society here.

> Migration . . . had allowed the colonists to fashion from the new environment their dreams about a paradise for working men, and especially skilled working men. They controlled the labour process, they could move when and where they wanted, they had abundant opportunities for self-employment, they could own their own homes and sections, and because of these triumphs they captured significant political power and forged an egalitarian culture.[23]

He identifies a flourishing of artisan culture and politics after 1890 and links it with their belief that a new experimental social laboratory could be constructed in New Zealand.

Miles Fairburn, in *The Ideal Society and its Enemies*, radically and trenchantly asserts that the colonial frontier largely destroyed social bonds, and concedes little role for the state.[24] More recently he has modified his approach to emphasise the impact of imported culture.[25] The country's remoteness, late settlement, short history and small size, he suggests, heightened this impact and diminished the country's ability to create an independent culture based on its frontier conditions. In his mind New Zealand's distinctiveness paradoxically rests on the lack of an independent basis for culture rather than its development. Despite these interesting observations, he does not explore the implications of the impact of the major contributing emigrant society, Britain, in the nineteenth century.

Recent general histories of New Zealand have drawn upon the frontier and fragment perspectives but have not taken the debate much further. They are more concerned with 'myths' than realities. James Belich's *Making Peoples* characterises the colonising impulse as little more than a trick played by 'colonising crusaders' and pokes fun at the myths of this antipodean paradise.[26] He suggests that a 'colonial populism', derived from British 'folk utopias' and reinforced by frontier conditions, was important, but this point is not developed. And his insistence on putting the so-called 'progress industries' and manufacturing ahead of farming moves the discussion away from notions of the frontier. Michael King's *Penguin History of New Zealand* also talks about 'the myths that shaped New Zealand cultures and provided them with cohesion and coherence'.[27]

Reliance upon notions of 'myths' motivating migrants and settlers is not a satisfactory way of dealing with the political and cultural motives that the fragment perspective emphasises. It devalues these motives as founded on little more than propaganda and debunks them rather than understanding them in context.

Migrant values and experiences were critical to the formation of New Zealand society, but came from a broader spectrum than suggested above and were better integrated in the Wakefieldian vision than often thought. To one side were individualistic radical values of democracy and opportunity; to the other were more collectivist and social democratic Chartist values.

Both the cultural fragment and frontier perspectives when used in isolation suffer the disadvantage of a rather static approach. The cultural fragment approach seeks to define the essential permanent character of new world societies in terms of the period in which settlement took place. Once the fragment is established its nature becomes relatively fixed. In the frontier perspective the character of a new world society is shaped by its determinant material conditions. Change results largely from the extension of the frontier or its consolidation.

The interaction of cultural inheritance and local material conditions introduces a strong dynamic element. Some of the Australian literature adopts such an approach. Pickens' review of the two traditions in New Zealand also suggests their fruitful combination. An initial period of strong influence of the environment would be followed by the consolidation of tradition.[28]

In this book we look at the interaction of the two. The strength of the frontier thesis is as a powerful economic shaping force – in the availability of land and the creation and evolution of the labour market and waged labour force. The fragment thesis guides thinking particularly in the discussion of state policy. What we call the social contract was a crucial expression of the way that British influences translated themselves into the colonial environment. But the interaction was not simply the shaping and adjustment of state policy to material conditions. State policy itself had real effects in shaping the material conditions for labour. The relationship was truly interactive and it produced an enduring experimentalism in policy.

A continued cultural influence from the originating society was transmitted by successive waves of migrants and by increasing contact with the outside world by newspapers, literature, and the telegraph and telephone. Fairburn emphasises the rapidity with which New Zealand became integrated into a 'metropolitan' culture.[29] But, having said this, over time New Zealand's consolidating character itself became increasingly important in shaping its development. Each wave of migrants in turn made a lesser impact as New Zealand's own population grew and as its own sense of cultural direction and identity developed.

The popular instrumental state

This colonial experimentalism, based on the interaction of political and philosophical values with local material conditions, was expressed through a specific form of state – what we shall term the popular instrumental state. It was largely through the state that the social, political and cultural strands carried across from Britain operated, and it was through the state that responses to the frontier environment were formulated. Migrants, largely wage earners, brought values and cultural and organisational forms with them and adapted and developed them to suit a new world in which the state took an active, constructive role. Inherited political ideals were transformed and made practical through the medium of the state.

George Nadel suggests that Australians regarded their state historically as an instrument to enable national unity and cohesion in a country where most had access to land and had a stake or interest in the country.[30] While Nadel emphasises education, Terry Irving focuses on the necessity for a strong government which 'must be responsible for the balance of interests in society . . . to provide work for the unemployed, to regulate immigration, to place small men on the land, to encourage manufacturing'.[31] Irving refers to the 'democratic' interest of the more respectable, skilled working man who desired independence, particularly through access to land in addition to wages, and whose labour was a means to acquire land and capital. This was the basis for a vision of 'the people' which would unify all interests in the community and which would be expressed in self-government and full democracy.

In Australia self-government and the extension of democracy provided the conditions for a liberal dominance in Parliament. Popular support was gained

New Zealand's 'Santa Claus' – the 'social laboratory'. Liberal Premier John Ballance readjusts the balance between capital and labour. Observer and Free Lance, *24 December 1892*

by radical rhetoric and leadership of popular movements, and by electoral reform and progressive land legislation. Liberalism sought to civilise a frontier society by organising it through the state, and to undercut the influence of radicalism. Solutions to old world problems of class warfare, unemployment and land monopoly could be addressed through the democratic mechanism and benevolent state legislation.

Stuart Macintyre takes the discussion of Australian liberalism further. Rather than being a pale derivative reflection of liberalism elsewhere, it took a specific and vital form in the colonial context.[32] He suggests that, given the absence of a 'history' to conserve, liberals had the freedom to 'invent the future', and this they did by forging institutions as they did roads.

In the New Zealand context, David Hamer takes a close look at liberalism.[33] All politicians rejected old world ideological distinctions and wanted to be known as 'liberal'. This rejection and insistence reflected the distinctive character of colonial liberalism. It was pragmatic and based on a willingness to use the state. Although New Zealand inherited the British mid-century laissez faire political philosophy it lacked the accompanying independent local working-class institutions. Thus the state played an active role in creating and maintaining such institutions, modelled on the British ones but adapted to the local environment.[34] There was a subtle interplay of cultural influence and local circumstance, mediated by the colonial liberal state.

Hamer argues that 'Vogelism' foreshadowed liberalism and consequently received much support from working men for its generation of employment by means of public works. Vogelism transcended sectional differences through its developmental synthesis of centralism and provincialism. Grey's version of liberalism in the late 1870s and that of the 1890s were not too different (apart from the shift from free trade to protection). Moreover, the Stout-Vogel government of the mid 1880s and the Liberals of the 1890s shared, in Hamer's words, a 'pragmatic, experimental reform, a doctrinaire gloss at the rhetorical level, and loan-based developmentalism.'[35]

Although we are suggesting the state in colonial society acted as an instrument, it should not be thought that it was an instrument of a particular group – a ruling class or a ruling bureaucracy. We are not arguing for a perspective of social control, which allows little room for independent action by subject groups governed by the state and upon whom policies were imposed from above.[36] The state was not a pervasive external agent of social control. It acted within a migrant society that was 'making' itself, with the state playing a central role.

The colonial state did not act simply in the interests of powerful, propertied groups, whether they were pastoralists, runholders, farmers, merchants or financiers. Such powerful groups themselves accepted the premise of a social contract and the vital role of the state. They also adhered to vital goals shared with other groups, such as closer land settlement, an extended franchise, enhancement of opportunity and self-improvement.

The nascent state in New Zealand was able to respond rapidly to meet popular demands and produce bold, sweeping reforms. It was not constrained by a federal system, a powerful upper legislative house or a countervailing legal system. Conservatism lacked concerted doctrines and an independent institutional base – there was little organised opposition to the colonial liberal vision.[37]

Colonial liberalism incorporated political ideology and material interests and public and private motives without difficulty.[38] Booster developmentalism and high-flown ideals could be fruitfully combined, as they were in the person of Vogel; in fact, boosterism was an important collective mechanism fostering the realisation of individual self-reliance and self-improvement – key motivating forces for many poorer migrants. Working men endorsed this combination of 'self-interest and sentiment'.

The interests of wage earners were included alongside the interests of others, especially when they meshed in with wider settler and developmental interests. Colonial liberalism was given a radical tinge from below, as working men turned broader colonial goals in a more egalitarian direction. The individualistic radical values of democracy and opportunity were combined with more collectivist and social democratic Chartist values. There was a 'mutual seeking of self-improvement' which gave rise to a distinctive egalitarianism.[39]

State activism grew naturally in the colonial setting, as Robert Stout described: '[I]n starting a new colony there is no co-operation amongst the immigrants. The Government is their co-operative association . . . The Government must perforce do many things that in older countries are left to private enterprise.'[40] Moreover, the state belonged to the people it governed. '[A]s the government of the colony is in the hands of the people of the colony, there necessarily is developed this feeling of the power, the wisdom, and the benevolence of the association called Government.' Rather than being seen as an enemy of the people, the state became its 'benign father', protecting them against evils. 'The colonists worship the State and believe that the Legislature and Government can save them from many untoward evils.'

The state reflected and articulated the interests of a range of groups in society without those interests being highly organised. 'Civil society' was for a long time undeveloped because of a lack of mediating layers of institutions and organisations. As Siegfried suggested,

> the Government is often the only bond which unites them . . . [and] is thus brought by the force of circumstances to perform functions, which in the old countries would lie within the province of private initiative . . . the people soon begin to consider the State as a special providence which is *bound* to help it.[41]

He observed that 'when a colonial finds himself face to face with some difficulty, it is almost always to the State that he first appeals'.

> Though we are here that land's antipodes,
> To shield our toils her institutions bloom
> In all their beauty o'er the destinies
> Of these lov'd Islands, our adopted home.
>
> A verse from a poem in tribute to Governor Sir George Grey on his departure, from the Artizans' Mutual Improvement Association, Nelson.[42]

The social contract

Bearing in mind the above comments, we shall explore the creation and evolution of a 'social contract' between the state and wage earners. This contract had a long genesis, stretching back to the 1840s. It first arose in the context of migrants being solicited for New Zealand and was then applied to the growing settler population in New Zealand. The contract was based on the promotion and protection of the interests of wage earners. It had strong moral and collective dimensions embedded in notions of creating a better world. The contract was first focused on the provision of land; it then shifted more directly to the protection of the wage earner, and then to the welfare state.

This book will look at a wide range of policies relevant to labour – facilitating access to land, enforcement of the wage contract, assistance to voluntary organisations, immigration and employment policy, industrial relations and workplace conditions, and old-age pensions and other welfare measures as they were underpinned by issues of state revenue.[43]

At its heart the social contract entailed an evolving set of experimental policies with the objective of enhancing the standard of living of working people. Wage earners expected opportunities and advancement in a society free of class barriers. When they were blocked or denied the state would be called upon to deal with the situation. As American commentator Victor Clark suggested at the turn of the twentieth century, the wage earner in New Zealand had 'faith that the State can in some way make it possible for every man to earn a "living wage". It is toward this end that [the country is] experimentally proceeding'.[44]

The social contract was dependent upon the early democratising of institutions and the broadening of political representation and participation. New Zealand historians tend to look for democratic impulses amongst the miner influx in the 1860s from Australia and further afield. But the evidence for this is flimsy. The impulse came earlier and was much broader. It sprang from the founding of the society itself, through colonisation largely by wage earners who brought with them powerful radical and Chartist influences.

The form the contract took changed over time. New Zealand became known as a 'social laboratory' for the world at the turn of the twentieth century. The term was originally coined by Lord Asquith in England in 1896, when he said of New Zealand that 'We look at our [self-governing] colonies and we find in them . . . what I may describe as the laboratory in which political and social experiments are every day being made for the information and instruction of the older countries of the world.'[45] In this book I extend this term back to the colonial period and forward to the welfare state, suggesting that over the entire hundred years state policy was notably experimental. Effort was first directed into a 'landed laboratory' of experimental policies concerning land settlement. From the 1880s the state took account of more strongly differentiated wage-earner concerns in the form of a 'social laboratory'. And as state-provided welfare became increasingly central, the contract provided the underpinnings of social security, to preserve an enviable standard of living now gained through a 'welfare laboratory'.

The contract required a strong interventionist state which would act as an enabling 'civilising' agency in a frontier society and then as a 'regulating' agency in a society shifting from a rural to an urban economy. There was a shift from facilitating individual endeavour and opportunity, supported by 'contractual' arrangements to encourage independence, to the progressive extension of state powers in order to preserve the existing society. The emphasis moved from self-reliance and risk to protection and security.

We now look at these three successive forms of experimental policy. New Zealand's constitution as a society of immigrants largely from Britain was founded upon a principle of a 'landed laboratory', in which all had access to land, and which was to be spared landed monopoly. Following the New Zealand Company's acceptance that wage-earning emigrants would have to be located on the land as 'working settlers', the state embarked on a huge experiment, shaped by Wakefield's theory of systematic colonisation (modified by local conditions). Land would be purchased or otherwise appropriated from

The 'welfare laboratory' – Labour Prime Minister M.J. Savage admires his 'applied Christianity' social security in the mirror. Auckland Star, *20 August 1938*

the Maori, opened up, sold or leased, and developed so that a prosperous and independent yeomanry rooted to the soil would form the basis of a democratic and egalitarian society of opportunity.

William Pember Reeves argued that 'if there had been no land question in New Zealand, there might have been no Liberal Party', but his statement in fact applied to politicians of all persuasions, at both the provincial and general government levels, throughout the nineteenth century.[46] All were essentially liberal and engaged in experimental policies when it came to land. Alongside John Ballance and John McKenzie we should include Harry Atkinson, William Rolleston and many other politicians.

The separate provinces developed distinctive land systems that demonstrated in their various ways the enduring centrality of the working settler interest by recognising the need for closer settlement. The means varied from cheap land to controlled release of land through a 'sufficient price'. It developed into deferred payment, village settlements and homestead settlements, and to the introduction of state leasehold together with attempts to prevent monopolistic practices such as gridironing and dummyism. All were means to the end of settling wage-earning migrants on the land.

A rebuilding of the social contract was required towards the end of the nineteenth century in the wake of the depression of the 1880s. The depression acted as a vital pivot point for the recasting of the relationship of labour and the state. The previous strategy of limited direct state intervention for wage earners was questioned. Voluntary self-help measures for labour, supplemented by paternalistic protection and 'enabling' labour legislation no longer sufficed. There was a shift from land policy to a 'social laboratory' as wage earners' distinct interests were expressed more directly, with the wage being progressively separated from the land. People could no longer gain a living from the land or fall back on smallholdings in times of need. This shift was accelerated by the Liberals in the 1890s. Their reformist policies were an amalgam of practical considerations in a colonial society and an overarching moral stance reacting against 'old world' evils – encapsulated in Métin's phrase 'socialism without doctrines'.[47]

This experimental image was part of New Zealand's distinctive national identity at the turn of the twentieth century, based on an egalitarian, decent minimum standard of living.[48] Beckoning into the future lay the progressive, democratic 'new world' led by New Zealand, which was, in the words of Frank Parsons, an American Progressive, the 'birth place of the twentieth century'. Considerable state intervention was underpinned by a belief that the state and the people were an organic corporate whole. The Liberals believed that they transcended sectional interests and could build on the concept of the 'people', the community as a whole, in which the state embodied the national community. This view had links with Fabian and New Liberal thinking in Britain, and rested upon an 'idealist' foundation of the creation of an ethical citizenry and the reconstruction of society appropriate to a social democracy.[49]

Preservation of an already achieved standard of living now became paramount. The state committed itself to maintaining the living standards of wage earners already in New Zealand, by restricting immigration, passing a range of labour laws, establishing a Department of Labour, and erecting protectionist tariff barriers to shield local industry. Within the workforce, class warfare would be avoided and social harmony preserved by providing good wages and working conditions and a fair return on capital, while preventing the arbitrary exertion of power by employers (or trade unions). The state would also promote stability and security of good wages, provide shelter and make provision for old age.

New Zealand's concept of egalitarianism began to change from equality of opportunity, implying an enabling state function, to redistributive justice, or a controlling state function.[50] The process was slow but was completed with the victory of the Labour Party in 1935. The Liberals combined elements of both approaches – advances to settlers on the one hand and labour legislation and the arbitration system on the other. Meanwhile the social laboratory provided a 'popular vocabulary for social reform' in the transitional period between nineteenth-century individualistic solutions and the more collective, bureaucratic 'welfare laboratory' of the mid twentieth century that was its eventual destination.

The construction of New Zealand's welfare state was at the heart of the recast social contract. The state developed away from its colonial liberal form as a philosophy of protection replaced that of encouraging opportunities. Francis Castles refers to a distinctive antipodean 'exceptionalism' and the 'wage earners' welfare state' in Australia and New Zealand at this time.[51]

This welfare state was an historic compromise between interest groups at the turn of the century that defined the country's strategic policy direction for the following sixty or seventy years. It was a defensive form of 'social protection' that sought to preserve and protect an existing standard of living. Although the welfare state developed early, it was weakly developed and selectively centred upon wage earners, the labour market and the family wage rather than the citizenry at large.[52] Policies protected an enviable standard of living, not only through welfare payments but also through wage determination, employment promotion, immigration and protectionism.

Following the election of a Labour government in 1935, a tax-funded social security system was established. This was consolidated during the Second World War and in the following prosperous decades. Labour's resolution of how to fund the state's burgeoning welfare responsibilities closed an intense debate concerning the desired nature of the society which stretched well back into the nineteenth century. Mounting the welfare state upon general taxation rather than social insurance made New Zealand internationally distinctive.

To trace the emergence of this kind of welfare state we must go back to the colonisation of New Zealand itself. We need to understand how a social contract concerning an improved place for wage earners in a new world society was created and evolved. For these shaping influences we need to look to Britain.

CHAPTER 2

The landed laboratory in a 'People's Farm'

Draw near if you would understand,
The Rights of Man art in the Land,
Let feudal Lords say all they can;
A Nation is the People's Farm,
They build, they plant, 'tis their strong arm,
That till the clod, defend their clan

Broadside ballad, 'The Wrongs of Man' (1816?)[1]

New Zealand offered an ideal colonial setting for experimenting with settlement on the land.[2] New Zealanders consciously developed models of access to the land and claimed that their form of landed society provided an egalitarian and prosperous society looking towards the future rather than the past. This image of a landed society of the future was carried over from Britain. It was based on a participatory democracy of family farmers linked to a controlled urban world lacking the worst aspects of industrialism. Brooking suggests that a moralistic, religious-based critique of monopoly and gross inequality in New Zealand was reinforced by a secular desire for rough social and economic equality carried over from British rural 'yeoman' and radical urban artisan traditions.[3]

Fairburn argues instead that New Zealand was a 'natural' arcadia with minimal 'atomised' social relationships for migrants from the old world.[4] This arcadia comprised a land of 'natural' abundance, independence and competency for working men, a naturally ordered simple associational framework, and freedom from 'status anxiety' for the 'uneasy' middle class. It was both a myth adhered to by colonists and the reality of New Zealand as a frontier society, according to Fairburn. New Zealand society was a solution to the British social problems of class-based paternalism, poverty, social disorder and status pressures. Emigrants could leave this behind.

But emigrants not only left social relationships behind, they created new social relationships influenced by the values and philosophies they brought with them. Working-class, artisan and middle-class migrants arrived here, infused by Chartist, Radical and Liberal philosophies that contained common underlying elements concerning new kinds of social relationships based on land and a new

26

The loathed workhouse was the worst manifestation of the poor law. The Stockport workhouse was attacked in 1842. Illustrated London News, *20 August 1842*

role for the state. New Zealand represented an arcadian opportunity rather than a reality. It was the capacity to shape and transform social relationships through the land, rather than the immediate reality of frontier New Zealand that provided a compelling image. This was not a backwards glance to a peasant 'golden age' and a few marginal utopian separatist communities, but a practical expression of a British reform movement. The key was availability of land.

Apart from the various means by which Maori lost land, both by sale and unjust methods, the vital place of land policy in nineteenth-century New Zealand is often underrated.[5] Promoting wage earners' access to land through closer settlement (smaller holdings and more intensive use of the land) was by far the single most important strand of state policy at that time. Politics focused on the availability of land, its development into productive use, and the necessary infrastructure to support that development. There was much debate over the rate of disposal of land and the most effective means of encouraging settlement, but not over the very principle that closer settlement should take place.

As Vogel observed, in defending Ballance's village settlements: 'As long as I can remember the history of the colony there has been a desire to see the settlement of land promoted; all parties and Ministries have had that desire, but the difficulty has been to know what to do'.[6]

Stonebreaking in the labour yard, East London. Illustrated London News, *15 February 1868*

Spitalfields soup kitchen, London. Illustrated London News, *9 March 1867*

With breeches thread-bare and worn,
With b— blistered and red,
An overseer sat, in a stringy bark hut,
Smoking his favorite weed –
Puff! puff! puff!
Oh! when shall I rise from this state?
And still with a voice of dolorous pitch
He sang the song of his fate.

Verse from 'The Overseer's Lament' adapted from Hood's 'Song of the Shirt'[7]

This satirical lament reflects on the predicament of the pastoralist's overseer, being unable to rise out of his situation. Freely available land was intended to deal with this problem. Closer settlement was incorporated into the very heart of land policy, to the extent that it was taken for granted. The debate concerned how to promote closer settlement when extensive pastoralism was so important to New Zealand's economy.

Similar debates were evident in other countries colonised earlier by Britain, such as the United States and Australia.[8] There too closer settlement and smaller-scale agriculture was encouraged over pastoralism so that those of little means had access to land. And, as in New Zealand, policies were modified rather than rejected when reality failed to match the ideal model.

In New Zealand closer settlement was the guiding principle. In the early 1850s it was a simple matter of making the land cheap, although even this was questioned because cheap land also allowed in the speculator. The provinces of Canterbury and Otago in their different ways attempted to maintain a higher 'sufficient price'. Then, in the later 1850s and 1860s, the issue became one of putting aside land for the specific purpose of special settlements of smallholdings, and/or placing conditions on the purchase of land to restrict the size of holdings and to ensure occupation and improvement. By the 1870s deferred payment as a general means of purchasing land freehold was increasingly pushed, alongside special or village settlements. This assisted working settlers with little capital to get onto the land.

In the 1880s, as the influence of Henry George (the American land reformer who promoted a value-based land tax) was felt, emphasis on the freehold faded, and the idea that land should be held through leasehold from the state as the people's 'representative' became popular. Lurking in the background, more radical measures such as repurchase or outright nationalisation of land were also advocated. At the end of the century Jock McKenzie's lease-in-perpetuity and the triumph of the freehold resolved the matter, but by then the focus of policy was being displaced away from the land and towards wage earners in their own right.

First we should look at the context of colonisation in Britain to understand the forces shaping such land policies.

Emigration, Wakefield and the New Zealand Company

> Bear, bear me to a land,
> Where hirelings cannot land
> The law-protected band
> Of rude marauding fraud;
> Where Heaven's blessings sweep
> The universal main,
> And millions do not weep
> To feed a robber's gain;
> Where Famine's iron maw
> Ne'er hurries to the grave,
> Ne'er crushes 'neath its law,
> Ne'er buries 'neath its wave.
>
> Verse of poem written by George Binns, Chartist agitator,
> while on board *Bombay* for New Zealand, 1842[9]

The early decades of nineteenth-century Britain were formative for a Liberal, Radical and Chartist culture orientated towards reform. Rapid industrialisation, attacks on the poor law, rising social protest and the consolidating force of radical politics created a ferment that caused many to ponder solutions to poverty, widening inequalities and possible class warfare, and lack of political representation. Luddites attacked stocking frames early in the century, while handloom-weavers, experiencing unemployment and distress, attacked power looms. Repression followed upon political gatherings.

Rather than attacking the machines of the new industrial age, Radicals demanded parliamentary reform. They sought to bring together workers and other groups badly affected by the post-Napoleonic War depression, advocating manhood suffrage, a reformed Parliament eliminating political corruption, and reduced taxes. During the 1820s the struggle for reform moved to centre stage, bringing together many groups, from Whig aristocrats to trade unionists and Owenites. Many saw the alternative as widespread political violence. Repeal of the anti-combination Acts (preventing trade union organisation) in 1824 encouraged the emergence of artisan and other trade unions. In 1830 agricultural labourers attacked threshing machines and burned stacks in the south and east of the country. In 1832 the Reform Act substantially extended the franchise and redistributed electorates to deal with 'rotten boroughs'. At the same time, in depression conditions, the 'ten hour' movement gathered strength and unions agitated for a new Factory Act, passed in 1833. Owen's socialist vision of a new industrial order took hold and the co-operative movement grew dramatically.

The new poor law of 1834 abolished the old system of outdoor relief and instituted workhouses. Adverse reaction came from many sources, from Tory to Radical. In 1836 the newly formed London Workingmen's Association created

This Salvation Army poster encapsulates the Victorian conception of the ills of the old world and the potential solutions found in land and in the colonies. General [William] Booth, In Darkest England and the Way Out, *1890*

Chartist meeting, Kennington Common, London. Illustrated London News, *15 April 1848*

a nucleus for the emerging Chartist movement. In 1837 it presented a petition including the famous 'six Points', which were formally adopted the following year as the 'People's Charter'.

Towards the end of the decade wages were low and unemployment high as the country headed for the 'Hungry Forties'. In 1839, the Chartist movement swelled and took on more threatening proportions, and in November of that year the ill-fated Newport rising took place. Repression and imprisonment followed. Chartists began to turn towards settlement on the land and emigration.[10]

English radicalism and Chartism had a strong rural tradition based on the redistribution of land. Landed monopoly was seen as being at the root of other inequalities. The decline in security and the devaluation of skill experienced by many wage earners and artisans was ascribed to the lack of access to land. Land offered a source of skill, security, independence and status. Agrarian equality amongst small producers would guarantee political liberty. Such ideas culminated in the great Chartist Land Plan of the late 1840s in which workers subscribed to a scheme through which they would be settled on smallholdings in villages.

It was in this environment that Edward Gibbon Wakefield formulated his theories of political economy and systematic colonisation.[11] Wakefield was the primary developer of an alternative approach to colonisation espoused by those of a Radical persuasion. He broke with the existing view popularised by Wilmot Horton and characterised as the 'shovelling out of paupers', and suggested that emigration should be devoted to building new societies which would fruitfully combine labour, capital and land. This conception of emigration replaced the notion of compulsion to leave with one of choice. It was argued that the opportunities offered by emigration would attract a substantial cross-section of society. Compelling reasons were proffered for leaving an 'old world' and forging a new one.

Chartist procession, Blackfriars Bridge, London. Illustrated London News, *15 April 1848*

Wakefield's thinking on colonisation was a vital unifying bond amongst an influential group of Radicals known as the Colonial Reformers. He was also at the very centre of the development of the concept of 'responsible government' for the colonies. He and other Colonial Reformers argued for positive planned emigration, for self-government, and for a property-owning democracy in the colonies.

These Radical reformers, and others who became notable contributors to New Zealand's colonisation and development, tended to come from a particularly dynamic class that was a vital component of early nineteenth-century English society – what Wakefield himself called the 'uneasy' middle class. This class was characterised by individualised ambition, frustrated by continued low status within a strongly stratified society. Its position in society was expressed by Philosophic Radicalism, a key influence on Colonial Reformers.[12]

The New Zealand Company represented the organisational realisation of Wakefield's theory. It was 'predominantly Whig with a strong admixture of Radicalism', with Wakefield himself, Lord Durham, Sir William Molesworth, Charles Buller, John Stuart Mill and others counted amongst the Radicals who pressed for colonial self-government and for extension of the franchise.[13] Politically its philosophy was expressed in the seven-point Radical Charter prepared by H.S. Chapman (a New Zealand colonist and Supreme Court judge) for noted Radical John Roebuck. (This document was a remarkable parallel with the Chartist six-point charter of a few years later.) Wakefield and the New Zealand Company were thus firmly anchored in a British reform movement that stretched from middle-class liberalism to Radicalism to Chartism.

The New Zealand Company's colonisation plans contained within them the germ of a social contract that would later guide policy.[14] The state would

Snig's End estate, Gloucestershire, 1850 – one of the Chartist Land Plan settlements to resettle urban workers on smallholdings. Illustrated London News, *23 February 1850*

Reform Act meeting, Hyde Park, 1867. Illustrated London News, *18 May 1867*

'Plug' riots in northern industrial centres – attack on military in Preston, 1842.
Illustrated London News, *20 August 1842*

Open air meeting of Preston strikers. Illustrated London News, *12 November 1853*

take a stronger role than it did in the old world – it would control the disposal of waste lands, determine the price of land, and act as a civilising agency for the developing colony. More than this, it would act directly in the interests of wage earners as a recognised group contributing to the formation of a new society. For it was wage earners who inevitably predominated as emigrants and upon which colonisation depended. The New Zealand Company migrants were wage-earning groups, largely farm and general labourers, building trades workers and clothing workers.[15] Research suggests that they made an informed choice about their destination and what it could offer, and actively sought a better life through improved opportunities, rather than simply being pushed by adverse economic circumstances.

Land was at the core of Wakefield's theory of systematic colonisation. His scheme moved beyond the Chartist 'Land Plan' land settlement schemes in Britain towards settlement by means of emigration to colonies where land was freely available and where social and economic structures were less constraining. In the colonies wage earners could become independent and gain a 'competency', free from old-world paternalistic dependence.[16] In New Zealand this concept of independence straddling wage earner and small farmer would be expressed in the apposite term 'working settler'.

Wage labour was equally central to systematic colonisation. The usual criticism advanced against Wakefield's theory was that it was a futile importation of an English class-based system in the face of the pragmatic realities of a frontier society. But his 'sufficient price' for land did not (as commonly thought) require the permanent subjugation of labour and exclusion from land. Instead the sufficient price was intended as a dynamic mechanism facilitating the mobility of labour and its move onto the land after merely a short period. Land purchases would both provide the fund for further emigration and create a need for additional migrants to replace wage earners who had moved onto the land. In Wakefield's mind, this process was at the heart of a better form of society that provided high wages and opportunities for social mobility, and this indeed is what came to pass in New Zealand in comparison to the originating society of Britain.

Edward Gibbon Wakefield, whose concept of colonisation entailed the creation of a new society. Edward Wakefield, New Zealand After Fifty Years, 1889

Two matters were crucial to the success of the project. First, the worker-employer relationship should be treated as a contractual arrangement between equals and not a hierarchical one. Second, the wage earner should enjoy high wages and a good standard of living. The wage was intended as a way of obtaining propertied independence. This conceptual link between labour and property was reflected in the strong continuity between Chartism and middle-class Radicalism, or, to put it into the context of the social groups concerned, between the insecure and dependent labourer and artisan, and the uneasy middle class.[17]

Chartist coat of arms. Liverpool Public Libraries (Roy Palmer, A Ballad History of England, *1979, p. 119)*

In the late 1830s the Chartist impulse began to turn to emigration and to the land as the movement lost its political momentum. Thousands of Chartists went to America, Australia and New Zealand, taking their beliefs with them – 'Transplanted, I fear, to other lands, cast out by England to build up Australia, New Zealand, Canada and, mainly the United States', according to a contemporary.[18] Chartist methods and understandings were 'handed on and became part of the international working-class movement'. Strong links developed between the British and United States land reform movements of the 1840s. Emigrant Chartists provided a catalytic effect on land reform and on the American labour movement, out of all proportion to their numbers. The New Zealand Company certainly did not discourage those of a Chartist persuasion from applying as emigrants, and even advertised in their newspapers.[19] The New Zealand Company ships were fertile fields for those with a vision of a new world and a commitment to an improved place for labour.

Chartism was followed in the 1850s by 'popular liberalism' which brought together Chartist strands and liberalism. Popular liberalism provided an inclusive and overarching rationale for the reform movement at large, drawing artisan and working class support, by putting forward a 'social contract' between the people and the state, with the promise of rights of citizenship.[20] This would limit state powers and intervention, and enable a democracy of property-owning producers. It emphasised independence, civil and religious liberty, political reform, self-help, free trade and retrenchment of the state. Popular liberalism came from a longstanding plebeian tradition that defined 'the people' in populist terms as all those excluded from privilege and aristocratic monopoly.

Rather than working class radicals being liberalised, the process was more one of a weakening of the commitment of middle-class radicals to liberal economics. Middle- and working-class radicals drew closer together and skilled workers became more politicised, resulting in a common radical 'idiom' undercutting class differences. An emerging concept of the identity of the 'British' nation sustained radicalism in the latter half of the century and opened the way for the new liberalism of the 1880s and the move from a laissez-faire view of the state towards an interventionist one.

With this inclusion of labour in politics, more respectable forms of 'new model' collective mutualism grew dramatically – friendly societies, the co-operative movement and craft trade unions for groups of skilled workers such as engineers and carpenters. Such unions eschewed the strike weapon and concentrated upon improving wages and hours by control over the market for their skills.[21] In the 1860s and 1870s such unions met with considerable success. By the early 1870s 'new unionism' was extending organisation deeper into the British working class, to miners, to lesser skilled workers in industry and on the docks, and to farm labourers through Joseph Arch's trade union. Defeat for the farm labourers, and before long other groups of workers, in the mid-1870s depression led to consideration of emigration schemes, land reform and further extension of the franchise.

In Britain the 1867 Reform Act gave the vote to male householders, extending the franchise to the respectable artisan, who was now deemed to be part of the political nation. The British state redefined its stance towards trade unionism with the removal of anti-combination criminal legislation, and increasingly recognised and gave a legal status to working-class forms of organisation such as trade unions, friendly societies, building societies, and co-operative retailing.

The successive waves of emigrants to New Zealand brought with them these powerful values, political orientations and forms of organisation – Chartist influences, notions of popular liberalism and enlarged democracy, a role for the state defined by a contract with its citizens, and many forms of co-operative organisation to assist wage earners directly. These shaping influences arrived in New Zealand with a crucial change. Rather than being blocked by the state, a democracy of property-owning producers could be facilitated by the state. The state was not the instrument or creature of powerful and entrenched conservative forces as in Britain. It could be built in a new form to serve desired ends.

Some emigrants

The backgrounds of emigrants from Britain, together with their experiences once in the colony, illustrate the ways in which immigration influenced the development of the New Zealand state. In the 1840s there were identifiably Chartist migrants, such as Robert Carpenter, William Vincent and George Binns, along with others who had been active in the trade union movement, such as Rowland Davis, and working class emigrants, such as Isaac Hill and

J.P. Robinson, who promoted radical causes. There were also Radicals and sympathisers of Chartism, such as Supreme Court judge H.S. Chapman, printer Samuel Revans, journalist Richard Wakelin, and builder and contractor Charles Rooking Carter. Such emigrants brought with them ways of furthering the interests of wage earners that could be given full rein in colonial society.

Amongst the 'socialist' Chartists on the *Birman*, which arrived in Wellington in 1842, was Robert Carpenter, a Bath bookbinder originally from London. Bath was a 'hotbed' of Chartism. He reputedly participated in the demonstrations of 1839. Carpenter was described by the ship's surgeon as 'a Chartist and atheist [who] wishes to have every thing his own way'.[22] He became active in Wellington politics in the 1840s and joined Edward Jerningham Wakefield's Radical Reform Party in the 1850s, being elected to the Provincial Council in 1856 and continuing to foster Chartist aims. He became a bookseller in Wellington.

William Vincent arrived in Wellington in 1840.[23] His brother was the famed Chartist Henry Vincent, who had been imprisoned in 1839 for participation in the Newport riots. William had been apprenticed to John Cleave, a radical republican newspaper printer in London, and E.G. Wakefield and H.S. Chapman sponsored his emigration to New Zealand because of his radical affiliations. He participated in workingmen's local politics and the local constitutional association and was the first Wellington Oddfellows Grand Master.

George Binns, who arrived in Nelson in 1842, was a bookseller with a background in the Mechanics' Institute.[24] His bookshop in Sunderland, England, was the town's centre for radical agitation. It is his poem that prefaces a section in this chapter. He founded the Sunderland Chartist Association in 1838 and travelled through the Durham coalfield as a skilled orator, sharing platforms with well-known Chartist leaders Feargus O'Connor and Robert Lowery. He stood trial in 1840 for making seditious speeches and was sentenced to six months' gaol. Thousands celebrated his release. He was then elected to the executive of the National Chartist Association, and was arrested again for holding meetings.

Robert Holt Carpenter, Chartist bookbinder who became a bookseller in Wellington. ATL, PA3-0342

Rowland Davis, who arrived in Wellington in 1840, had a background of agitation for the Reform Bill and the abolition of slavery, and had organised various trade unions in London.[25] He was president of an engineers, smiths and machinists union. In New Zealand Davis became a publican, and his hotels were frequently used as meeting places for a range of working-class activities. He was prominent in representing working-class interests, being involved in the formation of the Working Men's Association in late 1840 and standing for the 'working class' party in the election of 1842. He assisted in the formation of the Britannia Lodge of the Oddfellows in 1845. He was also keen on land reform and was involved in Wellington's Land Association and in the constitutional association in the late 1840s.

After moving to Lyttelton in 1851 he became involved in the constitutional movement there and in 1853 assisted in the formation of the Working Man's Freehold Land Association. He stood for the Canterbury Provincial Council on a radical land reform platform and was elected to the council in the period 1856–64. He formed the first friendly society in Canterbury (the Lyttelton Oddfellows, in 1851), and became the secretary of the Canterbury Oddfellows in the early 1850s and later deputy Grand Master. He was also a founding member of the Christchurch Mechanics' Institute in 1859.

Isaac Hill, a machine fitter from Aston, Birmingham, came to Nelson in 1842 – to better his condition, according to his diary.[26] He helped to found the first Quaker society in New Zealand, and was also involved in the Rechabites. Hill promoted the organisation of carpenters and became involved in the constitutional association and the Nelson Political Union which followed. He also agitated for compensation for the New Zealand Company labourers (see below), belonged to the Working Man's Freehold Land Society, and was secretary of the Working Man's Sheep Association in the early 1850s. He helped found the Nelson School Society and in the early 1860s he was a founding director of Nelson's Permanent Building Society.

Rowland Davis, London trade union organiser, publican, and founder of friendly societies and co-operative organisations. Johannes C. Andersen, Old Christchurch, 1949, p. 200

J.P. Robinson, a Birmingham wood-turner and close supporter of John Bright, arrived in Nelson in 1843. He had been involved in the Birmingham Mechanics' Institute, and participated in the political agitation leading up to the Reform Act of 1832.[27] He persisted with radical causes here, promoting the case of the unemployed New Zealand Company labourers, and participating in the Working Man's Land Association. When Edward Stafford resigned to become the country's Premier in 1856, Robinson was elected Nelson's Provincial Superintendent on a platform of low land prices, a property tax and electoral reform. He tried to introduce deferred payment (credit lands) into Nelson province along the lines of the Auckland province.

Amongst the middle-class Radical emigrants was Henry S. Chapman, an archetypal member of Wakefield's 'uneasy' middle class. Chapman wrote pamphlets on colonial reform, published the New Zealand Company's *New Zealand Journal* in 1840 and emigrated to New Zealand in 1843, where he was appointed a Supreme Court judge. He was a republican Philosophic Radical who had been deeply involved in the movement to give Canada responsible self-government. A friend of John Stuart Mill and John Roebuck (the eminent advocate of representative government and prominent Bath Radical), he was a leading advocate of the Radical cause, writing in Roebuck's *Pamphlets for the People* on democratic reform. He extolled the virtues of smallholdings and an extended franchise, arguing that 'colonization would be unworthy of notice were it not a means to improve the condition of the industrious classes' and that migrant proportions of capital and labour must 'secure the comfort of the labourer' by means of adequate wages.[28] After moving to Australia in the early 1850s he introduced the secret ballot in Victoria.

Samuel Revans, a militant radical apprentice printer and republican democrat, worked with Chapman in

J.P. Robinson, Birmingham radical who became Nelson's Provincial Superintendent and encouraged land reform. Guy H. Scholefield, (ed), New Zealand Parliamentary Record, 1840–1949, *1950*

H.S. Chapman, author of the Radical Charter, republican Philosophic Radical, Supreme Court judge in New Zealand, *and architect of the secret ballot in Victoria, Australia.* Parliamentary Library, New Zealand Portraits, vol 1

Samuel Revans, radical apprentice printer and republican democrat who became involved in Chartism, and was associated with the New Zealand Company and colonial politics. Parliamentary Library, New Zealand Portraits, vol 1

Canada.[29] On returning to Britain he became involved in Chartist activities and worked with Henry Vincent, John Roebuck and Richard Cobden. He also frequented Radical groups and had contact with members of the New Zealand Company. Upon emigrating to Wellington in 1840 he printed the New Zealand Company's *Gazette*. He later became active in the constitutional association and was elected to the Provincial Council and General Assembly in the 1850s.

Richard Wakelin, who arrived in New Zealand in 1850, was a confirmed democrat and temperance advocate who started a radical newspaper and was involved in the Chartist movement.[30] In New Zealand he was a longstanding advocate of small farms and assisted working settlers in the Wairarapa.

Charles Rae, a painter actively involved in Chartism in 1830s, migrated to Canterbury in 1851 disillusioned by the failure of reform in Britain and wanting 'to assist in the founding of a young nation'.[31] He promoted working men's organisation and radicalism in Canterbury for nearly half a century. On his arrival he participated in the Christchurch Colonists' Society and advocated a Mechanics' Institute for the town. When one was finally formed in 1859 he became its secretary. He was an inveterate contributor to newspapers, promoting radical politics and reforms and the importance of education for working-class participation in politics. In the 1880s he was an active member of the Freethought Association. He represented the Christchurch Working Men's Political Association at the first national Trades and Labour Congress in 1885. In 1889 he became president of the local Knights of Labour, the first secretary of the Amalgamated Society of Railway Servants (ASRS), and the editor of a small radical newspaper.

Charles Rooking Carter's career exemplified that of an aspiring upwardly mobile member of the 'uneasy' middle class.[32] His father had been a builder who had fallen on hard times. Carter was apprenticed as a carpenter, joined the local Mechanics' Library and read avidly about New Zealand. While sympathising with the Chartist cause he disapproved of the physical force variety and described himself as a 'Radical Reformer'. He moved to Newcastle, a centre of Chartism, and began to 'improve' himself, reading of Robert Owen and French socialists amongst others.

During the 1840s in London, working as a carpenter, he became involved in trade unionism. In a similar vein to Wakefield he published his thoughts on emigration. Carter witnessed the Chartist agitation of 1848, endorsed a modified Chartist platform and reported on the uprising in Paris in 1848 for a newspaper. He continued to write on emigration, criticising O'Connor's Chartist Land Plan and arguing that the only feasible alternative was the colonies. There followed a proposal for a small farms settlement in the Wairarapa based on deferred payment, a strikingly prophetic statement of what would come about with his assistance.

The self-improving Charles Rooking Carter whose experiences traversed Chartism, Radicalism, colonial politics and boosterism. Parliamentary Library, New Zealand Portraits, vol 1

Carter emigrated to Wellington in 1850, set up a construction business, and became a leading builder and contractor in the region. He also practised as a surveyor, architect and valuer. He was involved in the founding of the Wairarapa Small Farms Association and Wellington's first building society, and was active in Isaac Featherston's 'Constitutional' Party in provincial politics. He owned land in the Wairarapa and represented the district in both the Provincial Council and the General Assembly.

Carter's life encapsulates many of the values and experiences, albeit in a somewhat exaggerated form, that other artisan and middle-class emigrants of the period must have felt. His starting point, his political and cultural background, and his trajectory of self-improvement through migration were common to many emigrants. He represented a blending of Radicalism and Chartism, a case study of the 'uneasy' middle class, the perceived solution of emigration, the emphasis on independence and a competency, the opportunities available in New Zealand, and the translation of British radical values into the New Zealand context.

Following the labourers of the New Zealand Company, in the first half of the 1860s there was a massive flow associated with the gold rushes. At the same time provincial immigration schemes got into their stride. This was followed by an even larger flow of assisted migrants in the 1870s associated with Vogel's development policies.

These emigration flows included many others bringing with them formative values and philosophies drawn from their experiences in Britain. We can cite radical democrat and trade unionist David Pinkerton, Radical Bill Earnshaw and trade unionists such as David Fisher, Charles Thorn, Andrew Collins and Harry Warner.

We could also mention the better-known emigrants, discussed by Hamer and others, who went on to contribute to the Liberal 'social laboratory' of the turn of the century.[33] The cadre of Liberal politicians who were to become pivotal in determining New Zealand's development entered politics during the 1870s and 1880s. They included in their ranks many who migrated during the gold rush and Vogel years, and they were shaped by their British background of the middle decades of the century. They included John Ballance, Richard John Seddon, Robert Stout, Jock McKenzie, William Hall-Jones, W.J. Steward and W.L. Rees. They came with an image of New Zealand as a new-world utopia which left behind old-world problems.

David Pinkerton, bootmaker and son of a corn merchant, arrived in Dunedin in 1861 from Scotland for the gold rushes.[34] His radical democratic views derived from the artisan radicalism of Edinburgh. He allied himself with Grey's Liberalism in the late 1870s, supported female suffrage, was a member of the Freethought Association along with Stout, and a member of the Foresters friendly society. He became involved in trade unionism in the 1880s, and was a foremost leader of the bootmakers and then the tailoresses before being elected to Parliament as a Liberal in 1890. He was involved in developing the labour legislation of the period, and pushed hard for radical land policies. After he lost his seat in 1896, Seddon appointed him to the Legislative Council.

William ('Plain Bill') Earnshaw was born in Manchester in 1852 and trained as a mechanic. He had a strong Radical background – his father was also a Radical, who was at Peterloo and included Henry 'Orator' Hunt and Robert Owen among his friends.[35] As a boy William Earnshaw worked for Ernest Jones, the renowned Chartist leader who pressed for the Land Plan. He witnessed the hanging of three Irish nationalists and the Lancashire cotton famine of the early 1860s. Earnshaw worked his way across America and Australia and came to New Zealand in 1878, to the Addington and then the Hillside railway workshops as a brassfounder. Earnshaw was involved in the ASRS and was one of the Dunedin 'labour' candidates elected as a Liberal to Parliament in 1890.

David Patrick Fisher, the son of a printer, migrated with his family to Australia in the late 1850s, and then followed his brother, George (also a printer and journalist and later elected to Parliament and Mayor of Wellington) to New Zealand in the 1860s.[36] He worked as a compositor and organised the Auckland branch of the Typographical Association in 1886. He organised various Wellington unions associated with the Trades and Labour Council in 1888 and became President of the Council that year. He also held offices in a number of Wellington unions, was President of the Maritime Council, and became a member of the Sweating Commission in 1890. In the 1890s he worked closely with the Liberals on labour measures and was credited with persuading the government to observe Labour Day as a public holiday.

Charles John Thorn, carpenter and son of a bricklayer, migrated to New Zealand with his family in 1875, having previously joined the 'new model' carpenters' union in London.[37] He epitomised the British artisan migrant of the 1870s. A devout Primitive Methodist, he was a strong believer in self-improvement and in on-the-job co-operation and bargaining characteristic of the new model unions. He became a builder and undertaker in Dunedin and joined the Carpenters' Union in 1876. In 1881 he helped found the Otago Trades and Labour Council and became its first president. He presided over the first Trades and Labour Congress in 1885 and was subsequently treated as one of the founding fathers of trade unionism in New Zealand.

Andrew Collins was apprenticed as a baker in London in 1865 and became

Charles Thorn, carpenter and trade unionist who presided over the first Trades and Labour Congress in 1885. Bert Roth and Janny Hammond, Toil and Trouble, *1981, p. 19*

involved in unionism.[38] He came to New Zealand in the early 1870s and worked as a baker. After several attempts to form bakers' unions, he finally succeeded in 1888. He became president of the union and assisted in the formation of the Wellington Trades and Labour Council, holding various offices in the Council.

Harry Warner, a London carpenter, joined the General Union of Carpenters in 1871.[39] He became a union delegate and representative, and was also secretary of the local Liberal Association, the Radical Club, and John Bright's Working Men's Club. He joined the Amalgamated Society of Carpenters and Joiners in 1880 and represented the union. On his arrival in New Zealand in 1885 he became involved in the strike of *Otago Daily Times* compositors. He soon became secretary of the Carpenters' Union in Dunedin and he organised the Building Trades' Union. He left Dunedin for Wellington in 1892, where he became an organiser for the Carpenters' Union and the Building Trades Labourers' Union.

Other migrants made their humble contributions. Agricultural labourers, following the collapse of agricultural trade unionism in England in the 1870s, brought with them a vision of the remaking of their rural world, for example.[40] *The Times* regarded such 'political' emigration as transferring the agricultural discontent to New Zealand.[41] A substantial number of agricultural union officials and organisers came out to New Zealand in the 1870s, including George Allington, agricultural labourer and delegate of Arch's National Union, who led

200 agricultural labourers to New Zealand. A Primitive Methodist lay preacher and one of twelve foundation members of the executive committee of the National Union, he had worked as an itinerant organiser. He wanted to obtain voting rights for agricultural labourers, as well as raising wages: 'an increase in wages is not all we want; we want, and we intend to have, the franchise, and we intend sending working men to represent our interests' to Parliament.[42]

In New Zealand Allington obtained the franchise, his wages were dramatically higher and the food and housing much superior. He soon settled on the land but retained his commitment to trade union organisation. In similar fashion, Alfred Simmons led 500 agricultural labourers from Kent and Sussex to New Zealand after a lockout of the Labourers' Union by farmers in the late 1870s. One such labourer and union organiser wrote back extolling the place of working men in New Zealand, having moved from 'the land of starvation to the land of living and liberty'.[43]

Having sketched in the linkages for some emigrants between their British backgrounds and their New Zealand experiences, we will now look at the nature of the landed laboratory in more detail.

New Zealand Company emigrants

The New Zealand Company settlements opened up the way for the creation of a social contract between labour and the state, based on land. The Company came to an explicit understanding with the emigrants it brought to its settlements: in addition to general promises of enduring employment at good wages, it specifically guaranteed 'at all times to give them employment in the service of the Company, if from any cause, they should be unable to obtain it elsewhere'.[44] This was spelled out in its 'Regulations for labourers' for those seeking free passage, and underlined in bold and italicised letters in its posters to attract prospective emigrants. Those working for the Company itself had contracts of employment for two years, agreeing to payment of substantial wages with half paid to their wives back in England prior to their own migration. The New Zealand Company did indeed provide a great deal of employment at reasonable wages immediately upon the arrival of emigrants.

But as difficulties emerged in the early 1840s, labourers in the settlements of Wellington, Nelson and New Plymouth argued that the Company had breached its contract with them by not providing adequate work. In Nelson:

> We the working men of Nelson earnestly request you to take our case
> into your serious consideration . . . now the Company's 16th Regulation
> guarantees to us Employment provided that we cannot meet with it
> elsewhere it does not guarantee subsistance [sic] but expresses the word
> Employment distinctly. . . . Now Captain Wakefield if you do not
> stretch forth your hand to the working class of Nelson you will never
> have a Colony . . . If you refuse to stand by the working men of Nelson
> you Sign its Death warrant & seal its doom as a Colony . . . before we

left England we were told that if we could not get work no where else
they [sic] Company would give us one guinea per week with rations, and
this we consider our lawful rights.[45]

It went on: 'Instead of finding Elysian fields & Groves adorn'd with every beauty
of nature they have found unsightly & barren Hills & Mountains covered over
with fern.' The petition closed, 'we remain yours in Peace Law and Order.'

Under pressure the Company kept to its pledge and provided relief work
for all who needed it at wages that were well above what private employers
would pay. The Company continued with this policy even though it had to
withdraw from its pledge in 1843; it recognised that it had no choice but to
fill the gap. The relief works proved to be a disaster for the Company. Large
sums were spent on relief and little work obtained in return. As it became
clear that the problem was not a temporary one, such works became financially
unsustainable, and attempts were made to cut back on wages paid and increase
the work done. This precipitated protests by labouring emigrants against the
Company.[46]

Contrary to accounts presenting the protests as a violent revolt, these
incidents were relatively peaceful attempts to make the Company honour its
agreement. By 1844 the Company had exhausted its funds and had to yield
to advice that the only solution was to allow labourers to take up land.[47] The
alternative was mass emigration from New Zealand – a horrific conclusion to
be avoided at all costs.

Some historians, as part of their discrediting of the Wakefieldian project,
believe that a mass exodus of the disillusioned did indeed occur, but this is
largely a myth based upon erroneous statistics.[48] In fact a relatively small
percentage of labouring migrants left again.

The Company tried to find alternative employment and began to move
labourers onto the land from the mid 1840s. This was carefully documented
in the Company's own statistics.[49] In Nelson by 1845 more than 200 labourers
and the same number of artisans,
mechanics and other wage earners
(40 percent of the total in these
groups) worked smallholdings of
an average size of 5 acres and kept a
large number of fowls and pigs and
some cows. Some 245 farm labourers
(about one-quarter) remained without land. In Wellington, more than
300 heads of families who came out
as free-passage labourers cultivated
the land by 1847. Many artisans
and mechanics also cultivated

15. On the arrival of the Emigrants in the
Colony, they will be received by an officer who will
supply their immediate wants, assist them in reaching
the place of their destination, be ready to advise with
them in case of difficulty, and at all times to give
them employment in the service of the Company, if
from any cause, they should be unable to obtain it
elsewhere. The emigrants will, however, be at perfect
liberty to engage themselves to any one willing to employ them, and will make their own bargain for wages.

By Order of the Board,

JOHN WARD, Secretary.

*The New Zealand Company promised to
give its labouring migrants employment if
they could not find it elsewhere. ArchNZ,
CO208/291*

smallholdings. It was estimated that only 150 labourers (less than half) were dependent upon wages.

A rather remarkable consequence of the New Zealand Company's failure to honour its contract, and the subsequent labourers' protests, was that labourers' demands for land grants in compensation were seriously considered once representative political institutions were established in the early 1850s. Edward Gibbon Wakefield himself, in the first General Assembly in Auckland in 1854, extracted a commitment that the labourers of Wellington, Nelson and New Plymouth would be able to apply for compensation to a commission.[50] In 1857, after a commission upon which Wakefield's son Edward Jerningham Wakefield sat, the Wellington Provincial Council passed a Compensation Act that provided up to 13,000 acres of land to be given for the non-fulfilment of New Zealand Company promises. In Nelson province a concerted campaign during the 1850s resulted in a select committee in 1857, and in 1859 a commission, another select committee and a provincial Compensation Act awarding land. However the legislation was disallowed by the General Assembly.

The experience of the New Zealand Company established a precedent for what would follow. Settlement forged a link between emigrant labour and the nascent state based on the employment relationship; the kernel of a contract between labour and the state had been established, and the state would from this time acknowledge a responsibility for finding relief work for those who could not find work themselves.

But for much of the nineteenth century the primary solution for the needs of migrant labour was held to be in the land. The New Zealand Company settlements in their times of trouble had established this linkage. The fostering of opportunities for the working settler, together with closer settlement, became the primary objects of state policy, and the British agrarian impulse was taken out of a society in which moving onto the land was but a dream and transposed into a country where land was systematically made available by the state. Land policy took centre stage.

Provincial land systems

Following the 1840s wave of colonisation, expansion of settlement slowed to a halt as land dried up. Governor George Grey attempted to encourage closer settlement by way of regulations, believing that there should not be 'difficulties in the way of the poor in their efforts to secure lands for themselves and their families'. He also promulgated an ordinance in the late 1840s to encourage village settlements and powers of local self-government, as he had proposed in South Australia.[51] A number of 'hundreds' (traditional rural territorial units) were subsequently established in the Auckland area to this end.

In the early 1850s Grey became a strong critic of high land prices, in particular Canterbury's £3 an acre. He attacked Canterbury for 'imposing onerous and prohibitive conditions on the acquisition of land by the working classes'.[52] In the

English Parliament in 1851 Earl Grey attempted to strengthen the Governor's powers in dealing with New Zealand Company land. Resistance from Canterbury settlement supporters, however, meant that prices in existing Company settlements were unaffected. Earl Grey suggested to Governor Grey that it was in the settlers' own hands to agitate to lower land prices.

In March 1853, knowing that New Zealand would soon have its own Parliament that might have different ideas, Governor Grey made his move. Claiming that he was responding to 'working settler' demands, he turned the sufficient price policy on its head and issued general regulations which reduced the price of land dramatically, to 10s an acre for agricultural land and 5s an acre for pastoral land.

Sir George Grey. His land regulations issued in 1853 shaped land policy thenceforth. Parliamentary Library, New Zealand Portraits, vol 2

The drop in price caused a veritable explosion of land sales, particularly in Auckland, Wellington and Nelson, as pent-up demand was allowed full rein. Prior to the regulations fewer than 10,000 acres were sold outside of Canterbury. For the remainder of that year in Auckland, Wellington and Nelson nearly 150,000 acres were sold. In 1854 the total (including Canterbury) increased to nearly 300,000 acres. But many soon questioned whether the move favoured working settlers as claimed.[53] It seemed that land speculators were best able to take advantage of the cheap land.

Working men agitated for land to be specifically reserved for them, with the Wairarapa Small Farms Association in Wellington and the Auckland Working Man's Freehold Land Association in the forefront. The Small Farms Association – although initially supportive of cheap land for all (and through Joseph Masters actually involved in the drafting of Grey's regulations) – negotiated with Grey for special exemption from the regulations.[54] More than 5,000 acres of town and suburban land and 10,000 acres of rural land was purchased from Wairarapa Maori and allocated to the association, and from 1854 it began to settle people on the land. Rural holdings were limited to 100 acres and suburban holdings to 40 acres. The small farm settlements of Masterton and Greytown were to provide a model for subsequent similar endeavours that would stretch to the end of the century.

The Auckland Land Association similarly lobbied Grey but was not successful. Some proposed restrictions to favour settlers over pastoralists and to provide specifically for blocks of smallholdings on deferred payment. 'Anti-monopolist', a member of the Land Association, said that he had hailed Grey's regulations at first but then realised that they would get nowhere in competing with the monopolists who have 'pounced like cormorants' on the best land. Grey must interpose himself 'between the class of crushing monopolisers, and the well meaning bona fide cultivators [who were] the bone and sinew of the land' but who were struggling to accumulate capital from their earnings.[55] Grey assured them that he had their interests at heart but deflected them by pointing to an ordinance encouraging 'land and building societies'. Subsequently in Auckland and other settlements a great many land and building societies were indeed to provide a vehicle for promoting working settler needs (see Chapter 3).

Edward Gibbon Wakefield himself arrived in New Zealand in 1853 as the regulations were promulgated. He made what has been described as a remarkable 'attempt to fashion a radically democratic state on an economic basis of small-scale intensive farming' by radically changing the land regulations.[56] Appalled at Grey's unilateral action, he made the situation of working settlers his rallying cry. He shifted the rationale for the sufficient price from the issue of continuing to provide labour for capitalist farmers and others to the prevention of land monopoly. The twin imperatives of free access and encouragement of closer settlement had to be reconciled. The quality of land varied – large tracts of it were only suited to extensive pastoralism if they were to be used at all, and the better land suited to agriculture could not all be devoted to smallholdings. The issue was one of a balance between small and large holdings.

Wakefield used the issue of access to land (and as discussed above, compensation for labourers) to mobilise working settlers and to weld together a party supported by working men. This resulted in his election to the Wellington Provincial Council and the General Assembly, and gave rise to a petition to Grey to give labouring emigrants compensation. He persuaded working settlers that, contrary to their expectations of the regulations, much of the land would disappear into the hands of larger property owners.[57] Wakefield also met with Auckland working men and developed an alliance with Auckland members of the General Assembly. As part of that province's reaction to the land regulations, during the first session of the General Assembly a large petition of Auckland inhabitants was presented. This spoke of the 'evils' arising from 'exposing' waste lands to 'speculation and monopoly' without providing 'fair proportion . . . for real Working Settlers desiring to occupy the lands themselves, and improve it by their own exertions'.[58] It was signed by 415 individuals, including a number of Auckland's Provincial Council members, 104 settlers, 62 farmers, 52 labourers, and 37 artisans and other wage-earners.

In the General Assembly Wakefield almost succeeded in radically altering the waste lands legislation, intended to ratify Grey's regulations, which was passing through the House. He proposed instead that at least one-third of all lands should be put aside specifically for 'working settlers' in blocks of not more than 5,000 acres, to be divided into holdings of not more than 200 acres.[59] His initiative was in the end defeated and Grey's regulations were taken into the Waste Lands Act 1854.

Nonetheless a concession was won: the powers to make land regulations were given over to the provinces. This led to distinctive provincial land sale systems in which the interests of the pastoralists and, to some extent, working settlers could be catered for. The struggle moved to the provincial council chambers and to contests between provincial superintendents and provincial councils. It was no simple matter dealing with the range of interests that varied between provinces.

From the outset the land issue dominated provincial politics. Land sales were the prime source of provincial revenue, but more importantly land was fundamental to achieving the vision of the new society. Closer settlement featured in the provincial deliberations, indicating that runholding oligarchies did not dominate provincial land policies.

The commitment to closer settlement was complicated by a number of factors. The first was the economy's emerging dependence on extensive pastoralism. Pastoralists demanded that their rights to use land (as opposed to simply owning it) were acknowledged, and that their investment in and improvement of land was recognised, if not compensated for. Secondly, the injunction to sell land to provide revenue tended to draw in that much-feared but rather spectral body of speculators and monopolists who threatened closer settlement. Third, while all could agree on the virtue of closer settlement, it was far from clear how to ensure the exclusion of speculators and monopolists while maintaining a market in land and encouraging working settlers and labourers onto the land.

A number of contrasting strategies were adopted by provinces, involving a range of prices, attempts to define 'bona fide' settlers, and different tenures. We now examine the various land policies as they evolved in the major provinces of Auckland, Wellington, Canterbury and Otago.[60] They indicate the wide range of evolving experimental policies, all aimed at settling those of little means on the land.

Auckland

Wakefield's working settler provisions, discussed in the General Assembly, made an important contribution to Auckland's land policy.[61] Because of the scarcity of land in the province, Auckland's politics were shaped by the assumption that land should be plentiful and cheap. The province was unable to expand southwards into areas controlled by the King movement. There was little sympathy for Wakefield's 'sufficient price' or concentrated settlement in this situation. Beyond this the issues were who should benefit from the cheap land and whether speculators might exclude others.

Grey's supporter, Lieutenant-Colonel R.H. Wynyard, was elected as Superintendent in 1853. Wynyard's political group formed the nucleus of a party that gathered working men's support – strongly evident in the military pensioner settlements dominated by working men and largely enfranchised under the household qualification (see Chapter 3). William Griffin (one of those who had signed the Auckland petition to the General Assembly) was a leader of the working men's movement in Auckland. He had been associated with English political radicalism, was regarded as a Chartist, led the Auckland 'eight-hours' agitation of the 1850s, and later contributed to the Working Men's Protection Society.[62]

Frederick Whitaker, himself sympathetic to Chartist principles and an advocate of manhood suffrage, soon joined the Provincial Council and in a strongly populist move picked up Wakefield's working settler regulations (claiming them as his own), and had them passed. He argued that Grey's regulations were not effective in promoting bona fide settlement of land.[63] After a great deal of struggle within the Provincial Council, further regulations were implemented. These also incorporated the interests of working settlers by enabling allotments on deferred payment (subject to improvement conditions) so that people could get onto the land.

The Auckland Waste Land Act 1858 set the pattern of Auckland's land policy. It created a form of deferred payment in 'credit lands' for working settler immigrants. It also provided a system of 40-acre land grants to immigrants. The 40-acre land grant system became the major means of disposal of land, with an estimated 14,500 immigrants taking up land grants and nearly 450,000 acres allocated between 1859 and 1869.[64] This legislation, influenced by early nineteenth-century American land settlement schemes, was watched with keen interest elsewhere in the country.[65] But when many immigrants were attracted by land grants, Auckland found itself in considerable difficulty both in obtaining sufficient land from Maori and in making it available to immigrants.[66]

Such concerns led the General Assembly to abolish Crown pre-emption in land and facilitate direct purchase of land from Maori by passing the Native Lands Act 1862. This legislation reflected the influence of Auckland members. Robert Graham, instrumental in the legislation, became Auckland's Superintendent at the end of that year.

The 40-acre system had a crucial failing – it did not require occupation or improvement. Many of those who went on to the 40-acre holdings gave up the unequal struggle and the land

Emigration to New Zealand.

FREE GIFT of a 40 ACRE FARM.

Messrs. ALEX. F. RIDGWAY & SONS,
General Agents to the Provincial Government of Auckland,
ARE AUTHORISED TO GIVE THE FOLLOWING NOTICE:—

EVERY industrious Man or Woman of good character, and not, through age, infirmity, or other cause, unlikely to form a useful Colonist, will, on approval, receive a FREE GIFT of FORTY ACRES of GOOD LAND, in the Province of AUCKLAND, New Zealand, together with Forty Acres MORE for each Person 18 years, and Twenty Acres for each Child 5 and under 18 years of age, whom he may take with him to the Colony.

Auckland's 40-acre grant system was a key enticement to emigrants. Whitwell, 'Forty acre system'

Frederick Whitaker, lawyer, promoter of
Wakefield's working settler regulations,
electoral reformer and advocate of
manhood suffrage. Parliamentary Library,
New Zealand Portraits, vol 1

William Griffin was involved in a range of
activities to assist working men in Auckland
– trade unions, land associations, the
eight-hours movement and the unemployed.
NZH, *11 November 1890*

was sold and aggregated into larger holdings.[67] Many others never took up their land orders. Direct purchase from Maori bypassed the system, as did the formation of military settlements along the Waikato River, which were based upon 50-acre land grants.

In 1866–7, with labour in abundant supply and the province in depression, Frederick Whitaker and John Williamson as successive Superintendents proposed a new land order system based on capital brought in rather than labour.[68] The Auckland Waste Lands Act 1867 enabled grants to be made to those with capital on condition of occupation and improvement. Within a year the 40-acre system was brought to an end because of the lack of land and the private market in Maori land.

In 1870, in a renewed effort to encourage bona fide settlement by those of little means, the Auckland Waste Lands Act – the so-called 'homestead' Act, directly influenced by the American Homestead Act of 1862 – was passed. Selectors could take possession of the land – holdings of 40 acres per individual or 200 acres per family – by virtue of occupation, applying formally for the land after six months. For purchase, settlers had to occupy the land for three years and cultivate one-fifth of it. But it appears that absentee ownership remained an issue.

In 1874, after exhortations to do more to promote settlement and following the Otago example (see below), another Waste Lands Act introduced deferred payment in the form of special settlements alongside the homestead system. Under both approaches settlers could now select larger holdings.[69] The evolution of Auckland's land policy during the provincial period covered a range of strategies, underpinned by a durable emphasis on setting aside special lands for 'bona fide' migrant settlement.

Wellington

The story of Wellington provincial land policy, apart from the early innovative Wairarapa Small Farms Association, is dominated by Isaac Featherston as Superintendent and the perpetuation of Grey's land regulations in somewhat amended form. However, the seemingly placid application of the land regulations was punctuated at intervals by storms of controversy as advocates of deferred payment and small farm settlements attempted to take charge in the Provincial Council. Featherston's actions generally confirmed that cheaper land largely advantaged those with capital but he also recognised the demands of the working settlers and was instrumental in the establishment of the Wairarapa small farm settlements.

In 1855 Featherston promulgated additional land regulations that facilitated pastoralism (controlling speculation by a tax), and encouraged additional small farm settlements.[70] In 1856–7 the newly created Radical Reform Party, promoting the interests of smaller settlers more obviously than did Featherston, challenged the regulations and took control of the Provincial Council. It proposed new regulations modelled on the Auckland approach. The Reformers whipped up public feeling, saying that Featherston's policies ignored the interests of small settlers and would make the country a 'giant sheep-walk' without people.[71]

> May honour, truth and honesty,
> For ever shield our cause;
> Let all unite to humble those
> Who basely break our Laws.
> The fearless spirit of your Sires
> Will help you safely through the storm,
> And lead you on to victory,
> And RADICAL REFORM!!!

> Verse from 'Unfurl the Flag', song sung at Radical Reform banquet[72]

Meanwhile working settlers had decided they would have to establish their own schemes, and formed a co-operative 'land on deferred payments' society (discussed in Chapter 3). Eventually the Radical Reform Party collapsed and Featherston resumed his hold on power.

In 1865 a reconstituted Constitutional Reform Party took power, demanding radical new land regulations which reserved land to encourage small farms, increased the price of land to prevent monopoly, and limited access to bona fide settlers. These policies were largely blocked.[73] By 1868 party divisions melted away into a confusion of groupings and Featherston again resumed control. A number of small farms associations were formed in the Manawatu and Wanganui districts at that time as land became available.

Small Farms Association.

THE Members of this Association are hereby notified that the Land for the two Townships in the Wairarapa has been purchased, and is now being surveyed, and laid off in one acre allotments. So soon as the survey is completed, due notice will be given, and the day for the final choice fixed. Each Member is requested to pay to the Commissioner of Crown Lands the price of his Suburban Section of Forty Acres, within one month from this date.

Printed Forms will be supplied upon application to Mr. MASTERS, Lambton-quay, or to Mr. ALLEN, Auctioneer, Lambton-quay.

By order of the Committee,
W. ALLEN,
Chairman.

February 3, 1854.

The Wairarapa Small Farms Association was a notable early land association catering for working settlers. Joseph Masters and William Allen, along with C.R. Carter, were involved. NZS, 8 February 1854

Isaac Featherston, Wellington Provincial Superintendent. Parliamentary Library, New Zealand Portraits, vol 1

A key obstacle to continued settlement in Wellington province was the failure to secure the Manawatu. In 1870 the Wellington Waste Lands Act was passed to allow special settlements to be declared, thus facilitating settlement of the Manawatu block, including substantial areas for small farms associations and sale on deferred payment.[74] Pastoralism had consolidated and land sales and provincial revenues had been dwindling; closer settlement was decided upon as a remedy. The long-awaited sale of Manawatu land went through at the end of 1870 but provincial politics succumbed to the grip of depression and retrenchment.

When William Fitzherbert as Superintendent decided in 1873 to raise the price of all agricultural land to £2 per acre, opposition from the small-farming interest and others was sufficient to prevent it.[75] By 1874 the effectiveness of Wellington's policies on closer settlement were being questioned but events were overtaken by the issue of the abolition of the provinces. Thus, Wellington's policies in practice largely gave expression to Grey's regulations but their application did not go uncontested and the interests of working settlers were an integral part of the province's politics.

Canterbury

Canterbury is regarded as the quintessential home of the pastoralist oligarchy. The threat posed by Grey's low land prices aroused little controversy itself since it was taken for granted by those in power that this would not apply in the province – the issue was how high the price should be to prevent monopoly.

But even in this province the working settler interest claimed a substantial place and pastoralist domination of land policy was by no means clear.[76] In the early years the formulation of land regulations involved a sustained battle between pastoralists and settlers.

> Shall I tell you how the Stockmen,
> Crafty Squatters, subtle Shepherds . . .
> Came together down to Christchurch,
> Entered the Provincial Council,
> Made orations in the Council,
> Begged, implored, and prayed the Council,
> Coaxed the unsuspecting Council,
> Hoaxed the simple minded Council,
> Did the very wily Statesmen,
> Humbugged, diddled, all the members,
> And departed, laughing, chuckling,
> With their thumbs up to their noses . . .
>
> Crosbie Ward's 'Song of the Squatters' (part)[77]

Superintendent J.E. FitzGerald argued that pastoral use should not 'stand in the way of permanent settlement of the country by the Cultivator of the soil', but until the land was required for agriculture the utmost encouragement should be given for pastoral use.[78] While the ultimate objective was cultivation it was argued that temporary leasehold occupation by pastoralists aided that end rather than retarding it.

The province's regulations (finalised in 1855) stipulated a high price for land and free selection prior to survey as in Australia and America. Canterbury claimed this was a superior way of reconciling the interests of agriculture and pastoralism. Agriculture was able to spread on the plains, speculation was limited by the price, and pastoralists were given secure leasehold. Pastoralists were well aware of the potential for land reform that had already been unleashed in the Australian state of Victoria, and were wary of the radical movement that might be forged locally if they did not bend. Thus the interests of working settlers were taken into account to some extent in the province's land policy.

Attention focused on pastoralist abuse of the regulations that limited closer settlement, in particular by taking advantage of pre-emptive rights for improvements (first option to purchase land on which improvements had been made). In 1858 'spotting' of land (purchase of strategic small areas) was tackled by the Waste Lands Regulations Amendment Ordinance. This required pastoralists to purchase the entire area under consideration rather than just a strategic 20 acres. Bearing in mind that pastoralists had been pressing for pre-emptive rights over their entire runs, this could be regarded as something of a victory for closer settlement. However, the accidental exemption of larger runs protected many runholders. In the 1860s, attempts were made to tighten up on pre-emptive rights. In 1864 the Waste Lands Act enabled increased pastoral rents, but only on condition that the land regulations would not be altered until 1880.

Opposition to pastoralist pre-emptive rights reached a peak in the latter half of the 1860s and resulted in proposals to create expansive agricultural blocks and a Waste Lands Bill in the Provincial Council that terminated these rights. One of the foremost runholders, John Hall, managed to turn the bill around in the General Assembly to validate existing rights instead.[79] Nonetheless, the resulting Waste Lands Act 1867 terminated future pre-emptive rights and tightened up on existing rights. (All Canterbury runholder pre-emptive rights were eventually abolished in 1880 by the Land Act 1877.)

Agitation continued into the 1870s for policies such as a homestead system, reduced land prices, the resumption of leasehold land and its sale on deferred payment, and the setting aside of land for special settlements.[80] William Rolleston, after previously resisting the introduction of deferred payment, changed his views and argued that the traditional free selection and improvement pre-emptive rights obstructed settlement and the small settler. Rolleston's Waste Lands Act 1873 represented a renewed attempt to deal with gridironing and spotting. The evolution of land policy in Canterbury, then, reflected the importance of pastoralism but also made some concessions to closer settlement.

Otago

The story of land policy in Otago clearly indicates its contested nature and the strength of the working settler interest.[81] Even prior to Grey's land regulations of 1853 Otago had established its own 'hundreds' system in which blocks were allocated for closer settlement. Purchasers were required to improve their land to ensure occupation and cultivation. The province persisted with its hundreds approach and an insistence upon improvement conditions, never accepting the Canterbury 'free selection' principle.

Superintendent William Cargill from the beginning argued that Otago's system of treating all equally under conditions ensuring occupancy and improvement was better than Auckland's 'class legislation' system of reserving one-third of the land specifically for working people. The regulations issued in 1856 declared additional hundreds.

Matters of price and the efficacy of the improvement conditions were to characterise the debate for fifteen years or more. By the 1860s it was evident that the improvement conditions had proved ineffective.[82] Smaller farmers were unhappy at the lack of their enforcement and exerted considerable pressure for new hundreds, while pastoralists wanted more secure tenure. James Macandrew, elected as Superintendent in 1860, proposed penal provisions to ensure improvement, suspended sales, and had the existing blocks broken up into 80-acre holdings. The price of land was increased to £1 and new North Otago hundreds were created for closer settlement.

In 1862 Superintendent J.L.C. Richardson proposed a radical departure from the previous direction of land policy – creating deferred payment special settlements, along the lines of the Auckland provincial system to open up land to the 'labouring classes' – but this was rejected.[83] Richardson then withheld most of the land in North Otago to prevent it falling into the hands of speculators, and passed the Unimproved Land Ordinance 1862, which imposed a tax on unimproved land. This was disallowed by the General Assembly. In 1863 under the new Superintendent John Hyde Harris, a compromise was reached, as expressed in the Otago Waste Lands Act (no. 2) 1863, which stipulated a price of £1 and improvement conditions but also included a 2s per acre tax on unimproved lands.

The 1863 legislation did not satisfy the various interests of Otago settlers, in particular a 'liberal' group in the Council (including Julius Vogel, W.H. Reynolds and James Macandrew) which pushed for free selection. In 1864 Harris pressed for greater income from pastoral leases, together with improved access to pastoral land for settlement, in anticipation of the impending expiry of pastoral licences. In 1865 Otago free selection advocates blocked such a measure in the General Assembly, while under Superintendent Thomas Dick the ineffective improvement clauses and tax of the 1863 Act were dropped. Pastoral tenure was extended in the Otago Waste Lands Act 1866, which, while increasing rentals, replaced pastoral licenses with more secure leases and included compensation for improvements or for incorporation of land into hundreds. Runholders, although critical of the legislation, took up the leases with enthusiasm.

The gold-mining interest in Central Otago complicated matters. Until the late 1860s goldfields lands were regulated by a separate system created under legislation in the General Assembly.[84] Miners were not in favour of closer settlement schemes granting freehold tenure, preferring leasehold arrangements that maintained their rights of access to land for mining purposes. The Gold Fields Act 1866 allowed land to be taken out of pastoral runs for blocks of 5,000 acres of agricultural lease land (and in principle allowed the declaration of hundreds in areas subject to the Act). Far from resolving the land question this kept the issue on the agenda as agitation to declare new hundreds mounted.

In 1867 Macandrew was elected Superintendent again with the support of a growing and obstreperous radical element. Donald Reid and his supporters (including John McKenzie, later in the forefront of national reform of land policy) began to constitute a distinct party that pushed for closer settlement through deferred payment. This proved to be a decisive development that was to shape both Otago's and New Zealand's approach to land. Pastoralists remained unhappy with the hundreds policy, and in 1868 provincial politics was torn apart over the land issue. In this year a select committee was appointed to investigate petitions for hundreds under both the Otago

Waste Lands and the Gold Fields Acts, while a Tuapeka Land League was formed to agitate for access to land. The pastoralists then had the Otago Hundreds Regulation Act 1869 passed to limit the extent of hundreds.[85] The legislation also began the process of merging Otago's separate land systems. In the early 1870s a number of miners' associations were formed to protect their interests against both pastoralists and agriculturalists.

The restrictions on creating new hundreds caused a storm of protest, and they were loosened in an amending Act of 1870, but the pastoralists won new concessions as well.[86] They were now able to take up 640-acre agricultural leases on their own holdings. Under Reid, however, although the province increasingly faced financial difficulties,

Donald Reid, Otago politician who promoted land settlement on deferred payment. Parliamentary Library, New Zealand Portraits, vol 2

its government refused to declare additional hundreds that might give it much-needed revenue. The influx of labouring migrants with few resources in the early 1870s strengthened support for deferred payment. Reid's party eventually passed the Waste Lands Act 1872 that introduced deferred payment, but his attempts to liberalise the Act's provisions were blocked in the General Assembly by the Legislative Council until 1875.[87]

The provinces were abolished in 1876. The issue now was to amalgamate their disparate land systems into a national system.

'The many acre'd sharks' – land policy from the 1870s

In 1870 New Zealand adopted the Torrens system – a national system of registration of title (rather than deeds) to land. This expressed a radical approach to the transfer of land. In doing so it followed Australia and other British-derived new-world colonies.[88] The demand for such a public, open and guaranteed system derived from the widespread concern over the impact of private conveyancing in Britain and its association with aristocratic landholding and monopoly. There was considerable agitation for a free market or trade in land free of strict settlement and entailing practices. Estates would be broken down silently and remorselessly, it was thought, if land was treated as a commodity in a public and open system of compulsory registration of title. Such demands, developing out of the Anti-Corn Law League and pushed by those such as Richard Cobden and John Bright, were an integral aspect of radical politics in Britain from the 1830s onwards and attracted support from all classes.[89]

It took some time before the Torrens system was established here. Initially an 1841 ordinance set up government registration of Crown grants of land based on deeds. This proved difficult to work and a range of provincial systems were developed. Meanwhile Henry Sewell, William Fox and others advocated the more radical system of registration of title. Sewell wrote an influential pamphlet on the subject in 1844 recommending a system akin to the Torrens system, while Fox in the mid 1840s came into contact with the writings of Robert Wilson (later on the British commission of enquiry into such matters in 1857) and published on the issue in New Zealand. In 1848 he wrote to the New Zealand Company recommending such a system.

Introduction of the Torrens system was discussed once again in the late 1850s following its introduction in South Australia, and its general spirit agreed to, but it was in the end turned down in favour of another system of government registration of title provided for by the Land Registry Act 1860. This proved disastrous, particularly because of the long delays in its implementation. Meanwhile the many struggles to create open and public land boards for the disposal of waste lands displayed similar concerns.

In 1870, after persistent efforts by Sewell, Fox and others, the Land Transfer Act was passed, instituting the Torrens registration system. Fox deemed it vital to have secure proof of land ownership and to ease transfer of land, particularly for a society 'where the highest ambition of most people appears to be to obtain a homestead for themselves, on almost any terms'.[90] John Hall endorsed the bill: 'the possession of land was more generally distributed, and its transfer more frequent [than in England]. It was held to a greater extent by what were often called the poorer classes, so that the evils connected with its transfer were more generally felt'. The Torrens system was rapidly instituted from that time.

With the abolition of the provinces the focus of land and settlement policy shifted to the central state. Vogel's public works and immigration policy of the early 1870s created a new wave of assisted immigrants and swelled the unpropertied labour-force. Land policy was reinvigorated. A renewal of the colonising endeavour through immigration required close scrutiny of the land laws.

There was little point in bringing in migrants unless work and land were available, as one commentator pointed out. Immigration must be geared towards permanent settlement said FitzGerald – 'the land must be opened for the people' in the form of deferred payment.[91] To create a workforce permanently dependent upon public works would be disastrous. Rolleston warned of the impending disaster of 'a nomad population full of discontent; there would be class animosities and class hatreds rising up; there would be poverty and distress'.[92] As another put it, New Zealand wanted an independent yeomanry on the land and not labour crowded into factories: 'it is in the immediate interest of the rich to guard against the creation in the Colony of a large body of landless poor, and of huge cities inhabited by festering masses of discontented people. To them such a state of things means critical danger.'[93]

Many believed that the government should not itself employ thousands of migrants but should open up the land as fast as possible and carry on the necessary public works opening up the country and encouraging occupation of the land. With much of the better and more accessible land already settled, eyes were increasingly cast towards the larger holdings. A more direct attack on land monopoly was now considered, to prevent large-scale pastoralists from frustrating New Zealand's expansionist push. By now price had ceased to be a major issue. It was generally agreed that land should be divided into classes and applied for according to quality rather than auctioned.[94] Ex-Premier Edward Stafford wondered whether the state should repurchase such estates with compensation. He was 'prepared to walk over the heads of the whole of the existing land laws of New Zealand' to ensure continued access to land. In parts of the South Island it was 'almost impossible for working men to obtain a place for the sole of their foot.'[95]

In the early 1870s provinces began to reconsider their land policies and renewed a commitment to opening up access to those of little means. As we have seen, deferred payment and special and village settlements were adopted as the major means, while gridironing (buying the freehold of key areas to make the surrounding land less attractive to other purchasers) was attacked in Canterbury. Auckland launched its homestead scheme.

In 1876 Premier Harry Atkinson introduced a Land Bill to bring the various provincial land systems together. It was also intended to introduce deferred payment tenure and 'suburban' smallholdings for labourers generally throughout the colony, a matter that Donald Reid from Otago had been attempting to achieve for some time.[96] Atkinson argued that the legislation was beyond party matters; there was a need to assist the many immigrants who found the inflated land prices and the extent of capital required to move onto the land an insuperable barrier to land ownership. Grey's government passed the legislation as the Land Act 1877.[97] Grey, Stout and Ballance tried to amend the bill to attack Canterbury runholders, while Reid tried to make pastoral land available for auction for deferred payment and to prevent 'dummyism' (employing someone to act as a front for the true purchaser) in deferred payment, but the legislation was not greatly altered.

Deferred payment was still seen as the best option, with the new Land Act establishing it as the major secondary tenure. The measure was extolled as creating many hundreds of 'smiling homesteads' where only sheep had grazed before.[98] The Act also established a Department of Lands and Survey that was to be a major vehicle of land policy. At the same time the Crown Lands Sale Act 1877 created a uniform land sale system. Grey also attempted to apply the Auckland homestead system throughout the country but the Legislative Council struck out these provisions.

In the late 1870s the major thrust of land policy turned towards state leasehold as it was thought that only the state should control the land. Philosophically, the focus became the resumption of large estates or even some vague idea of land nationalisation. People now argued that deferred payment was imperfect and did not necessarily help prevent land aggregation and monopoly. It had worked well in Otago where this policy had originated, but even there settlers experienced problems in improving and paying off their land. By means of dummyism and purchase wealthier people could easily aggregate land.[99]

> I met with Bryce and Ballance, and
> They took me by the hand,
> Says they 'Poor Man;' why don't you get
> A little bit of land.
> Och thin, says I, 'tis what I want,
> But what's the chance for me,
> When all the many acre'd sharks
> Have said it shall not be.
>
> I came out here because they said,
> An honest man was bound,
> If he'd work hard and sober keep,
> To get a bit of ground.
> If Parliament's returned by Sharks,
> Without a hope I stand.
> Say's they poor man, there's more as thinks
> That you should have your land.

Two verses from a piece of doggerel from the election contest of 1879[100]

The land tax of 1879 signalled this shift. Grey had become a convert to J.S. Mill's ideas on taxation and the unearned increment. His major plank was a land tax, to 'save the country from that gigantic evil of an aristocracy with enormous tracts of land, unfairly acquired in many instances . . . [They] will be compelled to part with those great tracts, to break them up, and let others occupy them'.[101] Ballance, influenced by Mill and Henry George, argued likewise. He also proposed closer land settlement, a novel 'agricultural state bank' that would provide loans drawn from the trust funds of savings banks, village settlements alongside railways, and the replacement of auctions with ballots for deferred payment land. The land tax was shortlived, however, and was replaced by a property tax in the 1880s (see Chapter 6).

During the 1880s governments continued to promote closer settlement, made special provision for small settlers, and discouraged land aggregation. In 1879 William Rolleston, as Minister of Lands, relaxed the conditions of deferred payment in the hope of increasing its adoption, and introduced village settlements adjacent to main railway lines and roads, wanting to settle migrants and avoid the problems of a floating population. This was a policy he had pioneered as Canterbury's Superintendent. Premier Hall recognised the political importance of the issue: '"bursting up large estates", & the obstruction they constitute to the progress of settlement is a popular & a growing cry.'[102] The government would need to respond because it added fuel to the fire of Grey's demagoguery. Rolleston amended the Land Act 1877 in 1879 to assist deferred payment settlers and encourage village settlements and special settlements throughout the country. The scheme was successful in Canterbury, if not elsewhere; some 18 settlements had been established there by 1886. The settlements were largely in good farming areas and close to towns, so that settlers had access to both work and markets. By 1899 nearly 1,500 selectors had been settled on close to 10,000 acres.[103] With the expiry of Otago pastoral leases in the early 1880s, the government also

William Rolleston, runholder, Canterbury Provincial Superintendent, and land reformer. Parliamentary Library, New Zealand Portraits, vol 1

resurveyed and subdivided suitable smaller runs for deferred payment holdings and established leases for only ten years on larger runs.

Rolleston's views on land became increasingly radicalised by seeing at first hand the failure of policies in Canterbury, and he came to believe that Canterbury's freehold approach resulted in aggregation and monopoly.[104] His choice was between a 'tenantry of the money-lenders' or a 'tenantry under the Crown' and he preferred the latter.

As Minister of Lands in 1882 he acted with support from the 'liberal' opposition in Parliament, and in defiance of much of the government and ex-Premier Hall, to amend the Land Act. This bold move assisted deferred payment settlers, together with those with perpetual leases limited to 640 acres, who were struggling. Some supporters wanted to go further in land policy and provide for free homesteads, but even Rolleston's move proved too radical for Parliament and caused a furore.

The Legislative Council insisted on the right to purchase in the Land Act. This largely neutralised the leasehold concept (and shifted it back towards deferred payment) but the provisions still proved of considerable assistance to the small settler. Rolleston renewed his plea for a proper perpetual lease in 1883. His initiative – which he described as 'staving off the evils which are holding the old country on the brink of revolution' – was rejected.[105] The same year he put forward the even more radical Railway Improved Lands Bill, which proposed recouping for the state an 'unearned increment', but this was rejected.

By now younger liberals were taking up the challenge. Jock McKenzie and others pushed for more control over dummyism in deferred payment; investigations followed. One such investigation in 1883 concluded that there was 'widespread and systematic evasion of the law' regarding deferred payment land in Otago and as a result the Land Boards Enquiry Act was passed, to general approbation.[106] Another investigation in 1885, limited only to Robert Campbell's Waitaki runs, likewise found that the spirit of the land legislation was being evaded and that its intention in preventing land monopoly was being defeated. A third investigation in 1890 reiterated concern over enforcement but concluded that dummyism was largely an Otago problem.

While McKenzie certainly kept the issue of dummyism to the forefront and some licenses were cancelled, the lack of significant convictions suggests that the function of the enquiries was more to prevent the practice becoming widespread than to punish offenders.[107] The evidence for widespread abuse was not very compelling. Runholder John Hall, for example, vigorously defended his practices. (The celebrated evidence provided for Canterbury by McKenzie in 1898 indicates equally that the vast majority of those who took up land purchased small holdings only.) The most prominent applicants for land took up only about one-quarter of the land in total.

The coming to power of the Stout-Vogel government in 1884, with John Ballance as Minister for Lands, resulted in a consolidation of Rolleston's

Jock McKenzie, critic of 'dummyism' and Liberal architect of land reform. William Gisborne, New Zealand Rulers and Statesmen, *1897*

policies. Ballance's major concern was to prevent the aggregation of land on deferred payment and this led him to promote state control over land. He was in any case severely constrained by Vogel, an opponent of nationalisation, and realistically concluded that the ministry was not 'liberal' enough and that public opinion was not yet sufficiently advanced for a full land reform programme.[108] He would only go as far as the repurchase of larger tracts and did not advocate a comprehensive attack on the freehold.

This move towards a greater role for the state was tempered by a continued belief in self-reliance and a substantial dose of self-advancement.

Grey's radical land legislation is halted by 'Constable' Hall at the door of Parliament. Parliamentary Library, political cartoons, 1879–80

Ballance and Stout's rhetoric concerning nationalisation of land was tempered by the practical reality of a self-improving frontier society in which people had to feel that they had a secure stake in the country. Indeed some working men's advocates such as the Working Men's Rights League felt that the state was taking too large a role. Too much state interference was 'a source of great evil in that it encourages anything but a manly & self reliant feeling in the hearts of those who would like to settle'.[109]

Ballance's Land Act 1885, which went through with Rolleston's support, consolidated the previous legislation, encouraged leasehold, and established a range of new tenures and forms of settlement. It continued to provide for deferred payment, perpetual lease and village settlements, and created a new type of holding – the small grazing run of up to 5,000 acres.

An attempt was made to extend Auckland's homestead system to the entire country through the Act. Stout tried to remove the Legislative Council's 1882 purchasing section from the bill but the Council reinstated it and in response took out the homestead provisions. The government meekly capitulated to the former but managed to retain homesteads in the eventual Act. This system, which had been extended from Auckland to the West Coast in 1877, was now made generally available throughout the country but it was never really taken up outside Auckland.[110]

The focus on land reform resulted in a range of other proposals in 1886. There was further discussion on the homestead system, one MP introduced a

Land Association Bill, and Macandrew urged land grants for the poor.[111] But the major initiative was Ballance's village-homestead settlement scheme. This was a relief measure to disperse the unemployed into the country districts, and to get a 'large class of people who at present find it difficult, or almost impossible, to acquire land at all' to obtain smallholdings.[112] By now the depression had given rise to serious unemployment, particularly in Canterbury and Auckland, and there was much discussion of what to do about the problem.[113]

Under the village-homestead scheme settlers would in part provide for themselves from their land but also work for wages on nearby farms. Land could be taken up on freehold, deferred payment or, from 1886, a full perpetual lease without right of purchase. The government would advance money for settlers to build houses, and to clear and begin cultivation of the land. Key government immigration officials were appointed to supervise these settlements, indicating the intimate connection the initiative had with Vogel's assisted immigration project.

The scheme, which largely catered to labourers, was substantial but never realised Ballance's dream. A total of 75 settlements comprising 1,200 holdings and close to 30,000 acres were established – 20 in Auckland, 22 in Canterbury and 14 in Otago. The scheme was terminated when Atkinson came back into power in late 1887. Atkinson believed, probably accurately, that rather than establishing independent communities the scheme created a 'rural proletariat dependent on public works employment'.[114] The scheme experienced real problems in Auckland. Many of the selected settlers were unsuitable or lacked the skills and resources to develop and cultivate their land; often the blocks were too inaccessible to be viable; holdings were too small to be economic; and there was a lack of alternative employment. Some settlers failed even to claim their holdings; others forfeited or abandoned them because it was too tough. The scheme was, however, a moderate success in Canterbury, where the settlements were self-supporting and able to rely upon a well-developed farming economy with markets for produce and strong demands for seasonal labour.

Ballance's failure to follow through on land nationalisation disappointed some. However he did attempt to limit the amount of land alienated by the state through sale. Some wanted the outright repurchase of larger holdings at this time. In 1885 Grey introduced a Land for Settlements Bill that gave the state powers of repurchase.[115] This was reintroduced annually until 1888, without success. In 1887 Ballance introduced a Land Acquisition Bill that enabled groups of settlers to petition the government to break up estates through compulsory repurchase if owners refused to sell. This got no further than a first reading before the government fell.

Atkinson's government would not tolerate repurchase. However, within the limits of a government struggling to keep its hold on power, it did ease conditions for deferred payment and perpetual leaseholders, allowed settlers to choose their tenure, and introduced legislation encouraging closer settlement.[116]

In 1889 deferred payment settlers' repayment and rent commitments were reduced by legislation which allowed land revaluation. But in 1888 Atkinson's Fair Rent Bill was rejected by the Legislative Council and his Special Settlers Relief Bill was dropped after its first reading.

By the end of the decade pressures for further reforms mounted as a result of serious unemployment and the mounting emigration to Australia known as the 'exodus'. Ballance hammered away at the Atkinson government's failure to promote land settlement more effectively.[117] McKenzie vigorously attacked the Minister of Lands, G.F. Richardson, for relaxing residence and improvement conditions and bringing in size restrictions on land, which in his view consolidated land monopoly.

> Did God create the rolling downs.
> That they should only be
> Grazed on by sheep while men in towns
> sink down in poverty?
>
> No! God when he made New Zealand
> With all its hills and space,
> Meant it for to be a free land,
> The home of a free race.

Verses from 'The Great Land Sale', in Jubilee Farms (1888)[118]

Putting people on the land and encouraging them to improve the land had been a top priority in New Zealand since the 1840s. But many schemes failed due to settlers' lack of capital and inability to invest to make land productive. The high interest rates and shortage of credit crippled them. Government policy usually aimed at penalising those who did not improve the land; the means of making improvements were left to the settler. The Liberals would recognise this issue in the 1890s with their Advances to Settlers legislation and also would introduce a land and income tax to encourage the breaking up of large estates (discussed in Chapter 6).

Such policies, however, came at a time when the broad thrust of policy began to move away from land and towards other initiatives in which the state had already been engaged for some time – co-operative organisation and wage-earning employment. Such policies recognised that a wage-earning population was here to stay. The changing emphasis prepared the way for the fundamental shift towards the social laboratory and the beginnings of the welfare state that began to take place towards the end of the nineteenth century.

CHAPTER 3

'The road to wealth is wide'? Enabling the contract

We greet you stranger, to this land
Where slaves have never trod –
The breeze which sweeps our mountains
Is the breath of freedom's god.
If you've a hand to help us
In the work we've got to do
(The building of a nation grand)
Then, friend, we welcome you.

No wretched dens, nor crowded lanes,
Where squalid starvelings hide,
Disgrace our pure untainted plains –
The road to wealth is wide.
The blessings which great Heaven bestows
On man are here to spare,
Come join us, true and noble souls. We offer you a share.

Thomas Bracken's 'The Emigrant's Welcome' (first and last verse)[1]

Thomas Bracken – who also wrote the poem 'God defend New Zealand' that became the words for the national anthem – welcomed new migrants. He believed that they could contribute to the building of a new nation based on freedom and opportunity, uncontaminated by old-world evils. Opportunities were plentiful and people could join together in a collective endeavour to bring about a 'nation grand'. While much of the effort in the early decades of colonisation went into rural settlement, not all could go onto the land and not all sought this opportunity. Labouring migrants had to find other ways to make a living based on the wage.

'Stranger in a strange land' – co-operative organisation

Having migrated to the new country, working men began to come together to further their interests in a society which lacked strong and well-established organisational structures. Various forms of co-operative organisation brought from Britain assisted them. These included friendly societies, savings banks, and other forms of co-operative organisation, together with the lesser-known land and building societies.

In the 1850s a substantial co-operative movement began to emerge. Those in power encouraged and supported these co-operative institutions by passing a range of enabling and regulating legislation. In the mid to late 1860s – as wage earners began to shift their attention away from land and as the economy experienced some difficulty – the state made a concerted effort to provide a legal framework for a range of co-operative activities. Into the 1880s, as living standards were threatened by depression conditions, unemployment

Thomas Bracken, poet, liberal politician and author of 'God defend New Zealand'. Lays of the Land of the Maori and Moa, *1884*

and lowered wages, labour began to take the stage. Trade union organisation developed apace, the franchise was extended and working men began to agitate and enter the political arena themselves.

In Britain the decline of Chartism and the rise of moderate co-operative forms of organisation in the 1850s is often viewed by historians as a narrowing and limiting of utopian and revolutionary perspectives. Such organisations provided security, stability and a respectable status within a working-class community rather than challenging the established order.[2]

In New Zealand the aim of co-operative organisation was more to elevate the migrants' individual positions by means of 'self-help' than it was defensive mutual aid. As migrant carpenter Isaac Hill (whom we have already met) confided to his diary:

> What a punishment to me being poor is for I cannot associate with the upper class of society many of whom I perceive could give me much instruction on subjects of which I am almost ignorant – it is not so much the money itself but the enjoyment useful knowledge that can be purchased with it.[3]

While Samuel Smiles' *Self-Help* was the best-used volume in the country's libraries and athenaeums, it was the practical example of other migrants that provided a powerful motivating force.[4] The migration experience and the flood of promotional reports giving advice for intending migrants provided strong support for the self-help ethos. The fruits of success, in the form of land, capital, political power and status, would soon come in this fluid and mobile society, according to the literature.

There was evidently a need for co-operative forms of support. As Alfred Saunders, ardent temperance reformer of the just-formed Nelson Rechabites, wrote:

> If a provident society were *desirable* at home, where the working man was surrounded by friends and relatives, always willing to render him any assistance in time of need, surely it must be considered *necessary* when he becomes 'a stranger in a strange land', surrounded only by those who know or care but little about him.[5] [emphasis in original]

Friendly societies

In Britain friendly societies were the first means of organisation of wage earners, going back to the eighteenth century. They were the pioneers of the self-help movement. Other types of organisation, such as trade unions and the co-operative movement, tended to follow. In response to the contribution made by friendly societies in Britain, the state legislated for a code of practice and an administrative apparatus that was subsequently applied to other similar organisations. The Registrar of Friendly Societies in Britain was described as 'the embodiment of the goodwill and protection of the state, in all that goes beyond police, the poor law, justice and the school' for the working man.[6]

The New Zealand Company migrants and others who followed brought with them the British philosophy of co-operative and mutual assistance and established similar institutions here straight away. British friendly society members carried with them official dispensations or authority to establish branches upon their arrival here. Some societies were even formed on board ship during the voyage.[7] Emigrants on board the *Mary Anne* bound for Nelson in 1842 met to form a 'benefit club' or 'friendly association' in the interests of the 'industrious classes' to create a fund 'founded on the principles of mutual aid and friendly combination' to provide for disability, sickness, age, infirmity or death.[8]

The first society to organise extensively was the Manchester Unity Independent Order of Oddfellows, from 1842 in Wellington and Nelson, 1844 in Auckland, 1848 in Dunedin and 1851 in Canterbury.[9] The Ancient Order of Foresters was first established in Christchurch in 1852.

Thomas McKenzie, a printer working for Samuel Revans' *Gazette*, was the first corresponding secretary for the Oddfellows in New Zealand, based in Wellington. They met at Rowland Davis' Aurora Tavern at the time. McKenzie was also a founder of the Mechanics' Institute, was active

FRIENDLY SOCIETY.

To the Editor of the Nelson Examiner.

Sir—At the request of the committee appointed on board the emigrant ship *Mary Anne*, for the purpose of framing regulations for a Benefit Society, or Friendly Association, in this settlement, I beg to direct the attention of your readers to the advertisement respecting this subject which is inserted in your paper of this day.

Friendly societies were formed on the emigrant ships sailing to New Zealand, as on the Mary Anne *which arrived in Nelson in 1842.* NE, *12 March 1842*

in the constitutional association, helped establish the Town and Country Land Association of the 1840s, assisted with the Wairarapa Small Farms Association, and later on was manager of the Wellington Building Society for several years. With William Vincent (whom we have already met) he became the co-owner of the *Wellington Independent* newspaper. He continued to be a notable figure in the Oddfellows.

Some regarded friendly societies as a Chartist threat – an attitude that was common in Britain in the 1830s. On the *Martha Ridgway*, sailing to Wellington in 1840, the ship's doctor threatened the Oddfellows organiser for his activities. But for most the friendly society movement was a valuable part of the local community. On its first anniversary in 1843, the Nelson Benefit Society processed through town to church with music and banners, before returning to its 'club house' for a dinner attended by a number of dignitaries. The newspaper pronounced its satisfaction at the foundation of 'an institution by the working classes, the object of which was to foster a spirit of self-reliance'. In Dunedin the Oddfellows were said to have been the first civil form of organisation in the town in 1848.

Then cheered the carriers,
and Druids grave,
Hibernian warriors,
and Lumpers brave:
Then burst their bellows,
the bold Oddfellows,
And shook the willows,
O'er Avon's wave.

Verse from poem penned for the West Coast Railway League Demonstration,
Hagley Park, Christchurch[10]

Friendly societies soon became firmly rooted in New Zealand, offering a backstop of support in a mobile and unstable society.[11] Those who had to move in search of work could transfer their membership and remain part of the network. They encouraged thrift, investment in public buildings, and involvement in the cultural life of the community. Throughout the nineteenth century friendly societies were in the forefront of the many local community events.

During the 1850s and 1860s societies expanded out from the major centres and into the smaller settlements being established at that time. The Nelson Oddfellows were particularly active and by 1860 seven lodges were established in the district.[12] In the 1860s, the Oddfellows had 81 lodges in New Zealand, with the West Coast, Otago and the Thames-Coromandel figuring large as a result of the gold rushes. Average contributions were substantially higher in New Zealand than in Britain, reflecting the higher wages and standard of living.

Thomson and Fairburn argue that the proportion of the population who joined friendly societies was much lower here than in England or Australia.[13]

James Henry Marriott, optician and instrument maker, who had also been a London Times *reporter for a time, arrived in Wellington in 1842. He was, along with Thomas McKenzie and Rowland Davis, the founder of the first lodge of Oddfellows in Wellington. Parliamentary Library, New Zealand Portraits, vol 2*

A MEETING of the Members of the Order of Odd Fellows, will take place on Monday Evening next, at R. Davis's, the Aurora, on business of importance; and all Brothers are requested to attend.

The Oddfellows met at Rowland Davis' Aurora Tavern, Wellington. WS, 28 December 1842

Independent Order of Odd-Fellows.

THE First Lodge of the Independent Order of Odd-Fellows, M.U., will be held on Wednesday, Nov. 26th, at half past 7 precisely, at R. Davis's, the Canterbury Hotel, Lyttelton.
N.B. The attendance of Members is requested.

Rowland Davis presided over the first meeting of Oddfellows in his Canterbury Hotel in Lyttelton in 1851. LT, 15 November 1851

While the friendly societies were not as pervasive as in Britain, they were certainly powerful and well organised by New Zealand standards. One is hard-pressed to find other organisations of equivalent size or with the same influence over government. To put this in context, by the early 1870s there were perhaps 8,000 members in registered societies (and many more unregistered), compared with about 16,000 skilled mechanics and artisans and 5,000 employed in manufacturing.[14]

The societies had a close relationship to government, which saw them as the most important manifestation of the much-touted self-reliance and thrift practised by working men. The state soon began to regulate their activities. As in Britain, this was on the basis of 'benevolent oversight by encouraging their development by giving them a legal status, and by protecting the rights and privileges of members'.[15] Financial problems and fraud had become a problem in Britain; there was concern that this would arise in New Zealand too.

Legislation encouraging friendly societies was on the agenda from the first days of the General Assembly. Following considerable expansion in the number of societies, and after urging by the Nelson Oddfellows, the government passed the Friendly Societies Act in 1856. Deriving from English legislation, the Act gave societies a legal basis so that they could provide relief for sickness, old age and other provident and benevolent purposes.[16] Registration was required with the Supreme

The friendly societies were a vital part of the social order in colonial society. In 1859 a new Oddfellows Hall was built in Wellington. Illustrated London News, *5 November 1859*

Court, rules had to be certified by a barrister and trustees had to file annual returns. Protection against fraud was provided, while limits were put on the extent of benefit payments.

Some societies wanted further legal protection.[17] Against a background in Britain of controversial interventions in their affairs, together with rising concern over their financial soundness, new legislation was passed in New Zealand in 1867. This created the position of Registrar of Friendly Societies, and required annual returns, including quinquennial statements of sickness and mortality. Societies providing old-age annuities could be registered only if their tables of contributions were properly certified as being adequate to cover benefits paid. This derived from the English legislation that created two grades of society – societies that had their tables certified by an actuary and others that simply had their rules registered. But the 1867 legislation was not implemented, as the government did not want to risk being accused of gross interference at a time when self-improvement and self-reliance were highly valued.

With an unstable labour market and a youthful workforce following the gold rushes, it is understandable that the emphasis was on the sickness benefit and not the death benefit, let alone the provision of annuities. Memberships were young, small and rapidly changing, so long-term actuarial considerations would have been impossible to contemplate. The issue of certification of tables raised by the 1867 Act could not be confronted for the simple reason that not even life assurance companies had actuaries available.[18]

The friendly society movement was coming to a crossroads by the 1870s. Government intervention and attempts to put societies on a more secure

Masthead of the Ancient Order of Foresters, another friendly society well established in New Zealand. ArchNZ, IA1, 78/12306

footing had met with limited success, and yet more migrants were arriving and more societies were being formed as the country entered a new expansionary phase. Politicians became increasingly concerned to regulate societies. By the early 1870s a total of 127 societies were registered, largely Oddfellow and Forester lodges.[19] The rapidly increasing value of societies' freehold property and high rates of interest in the economy provided a misleading picture of their prosperity, and disguised their unrealistic flat rate contributions and the emerging problem of aging members within many societies. Some within the movement became conscious that they were not operating on sound actuarial principles. The more responsible societies, such as the Oddfellows, were greatly concerned, but as in England the movement was divided over strengthened government regulation.[20]

Following pressure to implement the 1867 Act, a government actuary was appointed in 1874.[21] But the government's efforts to ensure registration under the Act met only partial success. Friction soon developed between the actuary and lodges over the need to revise societies' contributions and rules. The government was not getting the complete and accurate returns that it needed. The Registrar argued that the Act was inadequate and that the penalties provided were derisory. He wanted compulsory registration, returns and valuations, while keeping the adoption of his recommended tables of contributions voluntary.

Rolleston, himself a member of a friendly society, demanded that the returns of societies be tabled in Parliament. He extolled the benefits of friendly societies and urged the active support of government and regulation, as in England, to put them on a sound footing. C.C. Bowen, Minister of Justice, for the government agreed: 'the condition of these friendly societies was a matter of the most urgent importance, he might say, to the whole State.'[22]

A subsequent draft bill of 1876, which was modelled upon the English 1875 Act and created a new government registration agency, was circulated to all friendly societies.[23] It proposed that valuers and auditors be appointed by the state rather than societies and that society accounts be compulsorily audited. Some societies opposed this but Bowen argued that if they wanted the

Premier Richard John Seddon in full regalia as Grand Master of the Freemasons, 1898–1900. The association of the state and friendly societies was close in nineteenth-century New Zealand. Seddon joined the Freemasons in 1870. Drummond, Life and Work of Seddon, *1906, after p. 352*

protection of registration they had to accept some supervision and interference. The government had to be confident that sound practices were being followed. However, in the end the government backed off, and its regulating role was reduced beyond even that intended by the 1867 Act. The revised bill stated that the government was merely to supply actuarial tables for the information of the societies, and certification was required only for deferred annuities (superannuation), a matter which societies had not yet confronted. The bill was then delayed by amendments and a wait for further developments in England. Meanwhile a number of friendly societies continued to chafe at the existing impositions of government.

Colonial Secretary Daniel Pollen introduced a revised bill in 1877 and this time it went through with little discussion.[24] The government had retreated substantially. Registration was to be voluntary and societies themselves could appoint valuers and auditors. The rules of registered societies were to be approved by the Registrar, and they had to provide annual and quinquennial returns and were to be valued every five years. George Leslie, Oddfellow Grand Master for Otago, and another Oddfellow member from Dunedin became the first valuers under the 1877 Act. Leslie was to become Registrar himself at the turn of the century.

Reform was slow. It took some time for the 1877 Act to be fully brought into operation and for the Registrar and other officials to be appointed.[25] Many societies refused to accept their dire prognosis and it was some time before most societies registered and provided returns. By 1880 those registered under the Act comprised less than half the total – 142 out of the 299 lodges.[26] Some 256 lodges supplied returns; their membership was 18,212.

The Registrar's annual reports, published from 1878, documented the shaky nature of many societies.[27] The Registrar pushed for higher contributions graduated by age, and for more adequate rates of interest on society investments. His role, however, was largely an educative and facilitating one.

In 1882 the Act was consolidated and the five-yearly valuations changed. Societies now had the choice of having a valuation done or simply sending in a statement of contributions and benefits for the Registrar's actuary to value and report on. The debate concerned whether valuations should be required of societies and whether societies or the government should pay the cost. Many societies were determined to remain independent of government; they wanted to pay for valuations themselves. Some societies failed to adopt the government-recommended tables and experienced much financial difficulty, but the movement continued to grow, and the strongest and most numerous society, the Oddfellows, adopted a graduated scale for new members in 1885.

Revised tables of contributions were produced for New Zealand conditions and the regulations were finally gazetted in 1886. The English tables of sickness and mortality were used in spite of the widespread belief that conditions in New Zealand were healthier and mortality lower. It was argued that the difference was the result of the younger age structure in New Zealand and that in view of the longer-term aging membership it was more realistic to adopt the English tables.

The ambivalence of friendly societies towards any form of government assistance persisted into the twentieth century and proved their downfall, as the state sought more direct methods of providing for the welfare of its citizens. The viability of friendly societies would in the end founder not on the actuarial concerns expressed in the nineteenth century, but on the competition provided by the state. For the societies' eventual fate we must await Chapter 6.

Trustee savings banks and co-operative retailing

In the early years of settlement it was difficult to save. Because of the lack of financial institutions security could not be provided for funds and interest was not paid. But thrift was an integral part of self-help. In 1846 a group of concerned Wellington citizens including Colonel William Wakefield established a savings bank to assist the working-class saver.[28] (Wakefield's grandmother, Priscilla Wakefield, was probably the first to establish such an institution in Britain.) The same year the Governor issued an ordinance to encourage such institutions.[29] As a result the Auckland Savings Bank was formed. By the early 1860s it was a substantial institution, holding money for artisans, tradesmen, clerks and shop employees, together with domestic servants and other female employees. Similar institutions were formed in New Plymouth and in Canterbury in the 1850s.

An adaptation of savings banks were co-operative loan societies. In Christchurch, for example, a Tradesman's and Mechanics Loan Society, influenced by similar English institutions, was established in association with the Foresters friendly society.[30] Initially small loans of about £10 were made, later rising to up to £50 as the society proved itself, and several thousand pounds were lent each year during the 1860s. Substantial dividends were issued annually.

These savings banks were developed on the British model with local influential citizens lending their names as trustees.[31] But while the British banks were given government subsidies in order to pay high interest rates and attract savings, in New Zealand the government merely guaranteed deposits and prescribed rules for returns in order to keep them solvent. In 1858 the Savings Bank Act strengthened the state's guarantor role. The government would make up deficiencies between the rate of interest paid on deposits (fixed at 5 percent) and the rate obtained from

WELLINGTON SAVINGS BANK.

NOTICE IS HEREBY GIVEN, That on or after the FIRST MAY next, DEPOSITS will be received at the UNION BANK OF AUSTRALIA, on account of this Institution. Temporary Rules and Regulations will be prepared and shortly published, for the information of Depositors, until the necessary arrangements are completed, and Trustees appointed.

A. M'DONALD,
Provl. Manager.

The Wellington Savings Bank was established in 1846. WS, 2 May 1846

By 1847 Auckland had established a savings bank. New Zealander, *8 May 1847*

the bank's investments, and would guarantee payment of depositors up to £1,000 if trustees could not meet the demand.

In 1867, influenced by Britain, the government founded its Post Office Savings Bank (POSB).[32] There was a strong attraction in opening a savings institution associated with the Post Office, because it could offer many more branches and much longer opening hours than the trustee savings banks, which were small-scale part-time institutions whose hours were extremely limited. The POSB had a detrimental effect on the trustee savings banks; indeed legislation soon enabled their takeover.[33] The amending Act of 1869 made this very explicit. The move was controversial, illustrating the collision of the more traditional self-help view and direct intervention by the state. Many politicians now believed that trustee banks should not be allowed to compete, should not benefit from government assistance, and should even be closed compulsorily. In 1870 a Savings Bank Bill, if passed, would have closed all savings banks and prevented any further being formed.[34] The Legislative Council, many of whose members were themselves trustees of savings banks, prevented this from happening. The POSB developed rapidly from its foundation and soon grew much larger than the trustee banks. By the early 1870s, trustee banks were no longer prospering and some merged with the Post Office. Others have continued to the present day.

Another form of co-operative organisation brought here from Britain was the co-operative store. Retailing by such means had been extremely successful in the stable, cohesive, urban working-class communities of Britain. Social mobility, geographical isolation and the lack of large urban centres hindered such developments here, but they still established a significant presence.

In the 1840s the New Zealand Company itself aided the establishment of a co-operative store in the Riwaka valley near Nelson, supplying labouring

Nelson had a co-operative store in Waimea Street in the early 1860s. NE, *28 July 1863*

and settler migrants in the district with basic provisions.[35] In 1846, in the face of high bread prices, a co-operative Union Baking Company was planned for Auckland, and in 1851, with the aid of the Oddfellows, a co-operative bakers' association was established there (with up to £200 in £1 shares) to provide cheap bread at a time of poverty. Another co-operative store was established in Nelson in the early 1860s, selling flour, bread, meat and a range of groceries.

The government in 1867 passed the Industrial and Provident Societies Act to assist 'Workingmen's Co-operative Societies with limited liability' by providing a partnership framework, as had been done in England.[36] This Act legalised co-operative shareholding. Such societies were to be registered with the Registrar of Friendly Societies. About a dozen societies subsequently registered under the Act in the four major and a number of minor centres.

The Wellington Co-operative Society, for example, (also registered under the Friendly Societies Act) was established in 1869. Its object was fairly standard among co-operative societies: 'to carry on in common the trade of General Dealers and Manufacturers, both wholesale and retail'.[37] It was based on shares of £1 paid at a rate of at least 4s a month, with an entrance fee of 6d and a deposit of 1s per share. Members were limited to 100 shares. In the early 1870s there was also a Wellington Co-operative Bakery, the largest bread bakery in town. At the same time a Lyttelton Industrial Co-operative Society operated with 80 or so members holding about 300 shares of £1, paid at 1s per week with an entrance fee of 2s. Dividends were to be paid to members in proportion to their purchases.

In Dunedin an Otago Provident Society was established in 1869 under the friendly society legislation.[38] It existed well into the 1870s and probably ran the Dunedin co-operative store of the same period. Other similar institutions established in the 1870s included the Friends of Labour Loan and Investment Society (founded in Christchurch, with working-man's politician S.P. Andrews as chairman of its directors), the Wanganui Pioneer Co-operative Society and the Mahurangi Co-operative, all formed in 1876; an Otago Co-operative Store and a Canterbury Co-operative, registered

CHEAP BREAD!
PROPOSED PUBLIC BAKERY.

A PUBLIC MEETING will be held this afternoon, at 5 o'clock, in the Hall of the Auckland Mechanics' Institute, to consider the propriety of forming a Public Company for the supply of CHEAP BREAD. Heads of families, and all parties interested in this movement are invited to attend.

Auckland suffered depression in 1851. As a result people proposed to form a co-operative bakery to provide cheaper bread. In response Auckland's bakers advertised their own cheap bread. New Zealander, *7 June 1851*

WELLINGTON CO-OPERATIVE SO-CIETY (LIMITED).

Registered under "The Provident and Industrial Society's Act."

The only Co-operative Society in Wellington.

THE COMMITTEE of the above Society take this opportunity of thanking the public for the very liberal support they have received since opening their Store in Manners-street, and have great pleasure in informing them that, having made a considerable addition to their stock, they have determined to sell the same at a
CONSIDERABLE REDUCTION
on former prices.
    Only first-class articles kept, and full weight guaranteed.
    By order of the Committee,
        SAMUEL WOODWARD,
            Secretary.

The Wellington Co-operative Society operated its store in Manners Street and dealt in various goods. EP, *12 October 1870*

Co-operative societies continued to be popular through the nineteenth century. Stamps for the Pahiatua Working-Men and Settlers' Co-operative Society, 1894, Petone Industrial and Provident Co-operative Society, 1899, and Masterton Industrial Co-operative Society, 1900 are shown above. ArchNZ, CO-W, 2, box 13

as companies in 1877; and the Southbridge and Kawakawa Co-operative companies, established in 1878.

The government continued to encourage the formation of co-operative societies by improved legislation in the Industrial and Provident Act of 1877, and substantial numbers of societies were registered in the 1880s and 1890s as working people attempted to improve their lot during the depression. Most did not last long, however. As in the USA, the British model of co-operative retailing did not flourish in New Zealand. A more competitive environment for commercial retailers than in the old world, combined with the higher standard of living, made it hard for these societies.[39]

Land and building societies

We now look at a little-known institution in some detail.[40] Land and building societies were an extremely important form of co-operative assistance; in fact the most important after the friendly societies. This was despite strong suspicion of such organisations amongst the early colonists because of the bad reputation of earlier speculative builder-organised building societies in Britain. Unlike the British societies, the land and building societies here were founded on the principles of a savings bank and secure lending via mortgages.[41] They were sufficiently numerous and large that they ranked amongst New Zealand's significant financial institutions in the nineteenth century. In the early decades they provided crucial help for those of little means to acquire land. Their emphasis then moved to housing, in which they played a similar role. Residential housing investment was the most important private sector investment at that time (apart from investment in land).[42] One writer remarked in the 1870s that 'any steady man [could] soon obtain his own house' with the aid of a building society.[43]

For a period in the nineteenth century, these societies may have made a greater contribution in New Zealand than anywhere else.[44] In a colony that was desperately short of credit, especially for the less wealthy who did not have easy access to the trading banks, they played a vital role. Stout suggests that in the mid 1880s they had an estimated £500,000 in capital for lending and receiving on deposit. Together with the POSB and trustee savings banks, such institutions controlled about 40 percent of the country's financial assets.

Land and building societies drew upon the very popular British terminating building society move-

THE WELLINGTON LAND ASSO-CIATION.

THE object of the above association is to increase the prosperity of the artizans, mechanics, and working classes of this Colony, by enabling them to possess land which secured at this early period of the existence of this settlement, cannot fail to be attended with certain, rapid, and great increase in value at no distant date.

The Wakefield system of colonization, though very comprehensive, is not sufficiently so to secure the mechanic and artizan at an early period an interest in, and thereby a local attachment to, the soil, an object deemed by the founders of this association of the utmost importance to the prosperity of this Colony.

The Wellington Land Association declares its objectives. WS, 6 March 1841

ment (in which societies dissolved when their contributing members obtained housing) that had become well established by the early nineteenth century. The movement grew very rapidly in the 1840s. The standard mid nineteenth-century British manual on such societies turned its attention towards emigration and colonisation.[45] It argued that Wakefield's system should be extended by 'colonising' on the co-operative principle, both overseas and at home, through mutual benefit societies.

Such societies were influenced by the freehold land society movement, which in turn had its roots in Chartism.[46] The freehold land societies provided a strategy to increase the numbers of those eligible to vote (as 40-shilling freeholders) and were central to the popular politics in Britain at the time. They brought together artisans and the radical middle class and expressed a philosophy for co-operative mutual improvement within an agrarian framework.

In New Zealand the freehold land society concept blended into the land and building society concept because working men already had the franchise (see below). As one proposal to form such a society pointed out, 'as every one knows that in New Zealand, blest with a very liberal constitution, and enjoying all but universal suffrage, – where every man 21 years of age, and not being an alien, may easily become franchised – there can exist no necessity to establish "great vote-creating societies"' as the freehold land societies.[47]

Land and building societies were usually founded by activist radical artisans or mechanics with the support of wealthier local liberal- or radical-inclined businessmen and politicians. Often such societies were managed on a day-to-day basis by an auctioneer or land agent whose business overlapped with their commitment to the society. In some instances such societies came together with other forms of co-operation, as in the Auckland Odd Fellows' Settlement Society.[48] This society proposed to obtain land from the government at 10s an acre and make it available to shareholding members, with a certain proportion reserved for public recreation, churches and schools.

The earliest such institutions were recorded in Wellington. In February 1841, in an announcement 'To the Working Classes', the Wellington Land Company or Association was formed, to invest the surplus from wages to purchase town acres.[49] The object was to supplement the Wakefield system by securing 'the mechanic and artizan at an early period an interest in, and thereby a local attachment to, the soil'. The organisation probably merged with the Port Nicholson Association for the Purchase of Country Lands, formed later that year. Its prospectus urged an institution so that the 'surplus earnings of the industrial classes' were not squandered. It suggested a land association to obtain 'homesteads' on 'moderate and easy terms' and to invest 'hoarded labour', the accumulated 'capital' of the working classes.

While the Land Association had been formed for the needs of town workers, people also saw a need for labourers to purchase land and create an independent freehold yeomanry. These organisations likely developed into the Working Man's Land Association in Wellington, which existed through much of the 1840s and worked on the principle of members pooling their savings to buy blocks that would then be divided amongst them.

Similar institutions followed elsewhere. In Nelson in 1850 a Building and Land Purchasing Association was established.[50] This soon became the Working Man's Freehold Land Society, directly influenced by the English freehold land society movement. Nelson also had an interesting local adaptation of the idea in the Working Man's Sheep Association, formed to invest in a large flock of sheep. The association leased land and employed a shepherd. By 1855 it had purchased nearly 1,700 acres and ran 1,600 sheep.

In 1850 a United Sheep Association was formed in Dunedin. The association aimed to include labourers as well as settlers of greater means, through subscriptions of 5s a week leading to a share valued at £12 10s for 20 sheep. A flock of 800 sheep was proposed. Influenced by the success of the Nelson sheep association, Otago settlers also organised a Sheep Investment Company in 1855, based on £1 shares and 2s a fortnight, that planned to run more than 10,000 sheep and obtain more than £4,000 from wool after five years. A similar society to provide shares for working men in a sheep run in South

Cancelled share no. 1, Nelson Building, Land, and Investment Society, 1859. ArchNZ, NP26/7

Canterbury was proposed in 1864 but it is unclear whether it got off the ground.

F.D. Bell described such organisations as of great benefit to the working classes, both in saving and in buying property. They were 'infinitely more advantageous in a new country where wage and profits and the interest of money were so much higher' and where it was much

NELSON WORKING MAN'S SHEEP ASSOCIATION.

[From the *Nelson Examiner*, July 10.]

The first annual meeting of the Shareholders in the above Association was held in Bridge-street School-room on Wednesday evening, the 30th June, and was well attended. Mr. J. P. Robinson having been called to the chair, the Secretary, Mr. I. M. Hill, read the following Report and the Financial Accounts for the past year :—

Meeting concerning the Nelson Working Man's Sheep Association, involving J.P. Robinson and Isaac Hill. NZS, 7 August 1852

easier for working men to save.[51] As a result of the considerable interest in such societies Governor Grey had the Legislative Council pass the Regulation of Building and Land Societies Ordinance in 1851. The ordinance made it lawful to establish co-operative societies by subscriptions of up to 20s per month in the form of shares (a maximum of 5) up to £150 per share, for the erection or purchase of dwellings and the purchase of freehold land or the leasing of land.

Such property was to be secured by mortgage to the society until full repayment was made. A number of societies subsequently formed in the major centres, while in Auckland the ordinance was liberalised to allow members to hold more shares of higher value.[52]

The British terminating building society began to emerge in New Zealand, as did further land societies, as a result of the stimulation given to land sales by Grey's 1853 land regulations. In Auckland in 1853 a Working Man's Freehold Land Association (later the Auckland Land Association) was formed specifically for the purchase of smallholdings.[53] With Grey's encouragement and with the success of the first land association, a second Auckland Land Association was soon formed. Another land association was formed in Onehunga that year, together with many others subsequently because of the acute shortage of land. By 1870

Sir George Grey. W. Leslie, Parliamentary Portraits, *1887*

PROJECTED LAND ASSOCIATION.

A PUBLIC MEETING of the Shareholders, and others interested in this Association, will be held in the Hall of the Auckland Mechanics' Institute, on FRIDAY evening, at ½ past 7 for 8 o'clock, when the present Preliminary Committee will resign office, and it will therefore be necessary for those who may have by that time become Shareholders, to elect a Committee and Officers, for such period as may be deemed expedient.

WM. GRIFFIN,
Sec. pro tem.

Auckland Land Association No. 4.

THE Rules and Regulations of this Society having been duly approved by the Revising Officer, and deposited with the Clerk of the Magistrate, in compliance with the Building and Land Society's Ordinance, Sess. 11, No. xi, members are requested to call upon the undersigned and subscribe the Rules.

A Meeting of the Members will be held in the Hall of the Auckland Mechanics' Institute (TO-MORROW) EVENING, at 8 o'clock, for the Election of Officers.

Proposed Land Association meeting, Auckland, organised by William Griffin.
New Zealander, *3 September 1951*

Auckland Land Association no. 4.
Southern Cross, *20 August 1858*

Auckland Land Associations no. 6 and no. 7 were recorded, together with an Onehunga Land Society and a Northern Land Association.

Wellington kept up its momentum. In 1851 a building society was established to purchase town lands.[54] This was closely associated with C.R. Carter and William Allen, who would help found the Wairarapa Small Farms Association two years later. Allen in particular was to remain central to Wellington's societies over following decades. A second building society was established in 1856, through which a loan account was also successfully established, as a form of savings bank.

In 1859 a Land on Deferred Payments Society was formed in Wellington. This became the basis for an enduring co-operative initiative.[55] Alongside its subscriptions it operated a very substantial deposit account, which largely supplanted the operations of the local savings bank because of the high interest rate offered. Such deposit accounts became an important feature of land and building society operations. Friendly societies often invested funds in such accounts (and took out shares in building societies). During the 1860s land and building societies also overlapped with loan and investment companies, which were another unrecognised but important source of finance.

Similar developments took place in Canterbury. Discussions were held in 1851 to form a 'Heathcote Building Society' but this seems not to have got off the ground.[56] This was followed in 1852 by the Lyttelton and Christchurch Building and Investment Society. A Working Man's Freehold Land Association was formed in Christchurch in 1853, after Rowland Davis had described the society he had been involved with in Wellington. That year the Lyttelton Loan Society was also formed to enable small loans.

There was a flourishing of land and building societies in Canterbury from the late 1850s. A Canterbury Land, Building and Investment Society was formed in 1857 and a Christchurch institution of the same name began in 1859.[57] (The latter was replaced by the 'no. 2' organisation in 1868.) In 1861 a Working Men's Building Society was formed. There were also the Lyttelton Land Societies no. 1

(formed in 1862) and no. 2 (formed in 1865). The Canterbury and Lyttelton Freehold Land Societies were formed in early 1866, when closer land settlement had become a key issue in the province. The Canterbury Freehold Land Society was created specifically to purchase blocks of country land and to ballot sections of 5 acres within each block. It bore the strong influence of recent migrants who had been involved in similar English organisations. A Kaiapoi Land, Building and Investment Society was formed in 1867.

Otago too maintained a substantial crop of co-operative land and building societies.[58] In April 1850 the Dunedin Property Investment Company was formed to act as both a savings bank and a loan society, and it soon became a thriving institution. A year after its formation the company had advanced substantial sums for the purchase and improvement of land and for house construction. The Otago Property Investment Company followed in 1853, and the Otago Building and Land Society in 1858. In 1860 a Dunedin Building and Land Society was formed. These and later organisations that were established in smaller Otago centres following the gold rushes became vital institutions in the province. By 1873 there were 14 such organisations in Otago and Southland.

Many other provincial centres had their own societies by this time, promoted by local radical leaders. In Wanganui, for example, John Ballance was a founder-director of the local land and building society. He also urged the formation of small farms associations.

The government took a keen interest in fostering and regulating such societies to promote and protect the interests of shareholders. The 1856 Building Societies Act consolidated the earlier ordinance, and in 1865 the Act was amended so that societies could invest their funds. The legislation was consolidated into the Building and Land Societies Act 1866, which prescribed the operations of societies in more detail. While the restrictions on payments and share capital remained, societies could now purchase land and erect buildings for their operations, and could borrow money on debentures. Officers had to give a bond or sureties for their performance. An amending Act of 1869 extended their borrowing powers.

The first systematic official statistics in 1867 on such institutions indicated their strength within the financial sector. A total of 27 societies existed, with 7,454 shareholders and 28,970 shares (of which 60 percent were unrealised). This number of shareholders was greater than those in friendly societies and represented close to one-tenth of the adult male population. Annual contributions comprised nearly £250,000, which is comparable with the year's sales of waste lands of somewhat under £300,000 and was more than one-tenth of total public revenue that year.[59] Canterbury led the way with seven societies and more than 4,000 shareholders (who contributed much larger sums than elsewhere), but individual shareholders did not hold large numbers of shares. In terms of shares, Otago and Nelson ranked with Canterbury, while Wellington was well ahead.

*Wellington Land on Deferred Payments
Society. NZS, 13 February 1864*

In 1870 the government appointed a commission of enquiry because of rising concern at the operations of such societies.[60] This found some 33 societies with more than 4,000 shareholders, all established in the 1860s and most operating on the by now traditional terminating principle. The Wellington Mutual Investment Society no. 2 was the largest, followed closely by the Wellington Mutual Investment Society no. 1. Other large societies existed in Nelson, Christchurch and Dunedin. The money involved in their operations was considerable indeed: their annual income was about £140,000 and the amount out on loan more than £500,000. To put this into context, the nominal share capital of all registered joint stock companies that year in New Zealand amounted to only about half this amount (after a decade of development of companies following the Joint Stock Companies Act 1860), and deposits in the POSB and other savings banks less than one-third.

The commission concluded that the business of land and building societies was risky, even though they had performed favourably up to that time. The societies lacked reliable calculations regarding their operations and there was little protection against 'delusive schemes'. The commissioners felt that the common system of selling shares by auction was iniquitous, and recommended legislation that prevented auctions or tenders for shares, controlled the borrowing powers of such societies, provided for an inspector to issue certificates, and required annual reports to be filed with the government.

Change had to await legislation in 1876. Societies, following the boom conditions of the early 1870s, wanted to expand their operations to attract additional capital. The manager of the Canterbury Investment and Loan Association wanted the legislation to allow wider share issues, greater borrowing powers, and the formation of permanent societies. His association had loaned the large sum of £160,000, 'a very large proportion of this having been advanced to persons of the industrial class, to become the owners of their own dwellings, and thus fixed, as it were, to the soil.' They could have loaned much more if they had been able to attract more funds; instead they were forced to suspend operations for a time because of the lack of capital. However, the association did not want the government to interfere directly; it was 'an evil for any Government to assume a paternal character and to undertake the management of the people's affairs'.[61] The Southland Building, Land and Investment Society ambitiously asked for powers to purchase blocks up to 10,000 acres, to subdivide into small farms and erect houses upon.

The Building Societies Act 1876, which had been circulated to building societies and largely drew positive comment, loosened conditions substantially. Societies now had wider investment powers, clearly specified borrowing powers and were able to receive deposits. Registrars of Companies now also became Registrars of Building Societies, terminating and permanent societies were explicitly defined, and societies were formally incorporated.

The number of societies, shareholders and shares increased considerably in the 1870s. In 1878 there were 48 societies and 9,492 shareholders, with well over 80,000 shares.[62] The position of societies consolidated in the 1880s. While there were fewer shareholders the amount invested and loaned increased. In 1885 there were 49 societies, together with 4,700 investing shareholders who held shares worth approximately £500,000. Societies advanced nearly £1 million and held about £350,000 in deposits. By now a new breed of permanent building society, founded in the 1870s and 1880s to provide access to housing rather than land, was beginning to dominate.

As Vogel remarked, 'to working men, these societies have proved of immense advantage, enabling them to secure a freehold or erect a building on easy terms'.[63] These unrecognised institutions were central to the improving ethos of the colonial wage earner and provided a vital bridge between wages, land and housing, which was such an integral part of the social contract in early decades.

Early trade unionism

Despite the wish to leave behind class warfare, working men found it necessary to employ old-world methods to protect wages and hours of work in the early days of settlement.[64] Migration brought with it an assertive wage-earning orientation that was soon expressed in trade union organisation and, at times, strikes. But the nature of a frontier society and its unstable, localised and primitive labour markets made it difficult to sustain such initiatives. Strikes were usually aimed at the limited objectives of wages and hours – either improving them on a rising labour market or resisting cuts when times were slack.

In the early years it proved very difficult for trade unions to maintain any kind of continuity; they came and went according to the fluctuations of the labour market. The earliest recorded trade unions emerged in the optimistic first years of the Wakefield settlements in the early 1840s. In Wellington, for example, a Union Benefit Society was established in May 1840 and in December that year a Working Men's Association was formed to establish a library and to run a labour exchange.[65] In 1842 the first trade union in the country, for carpenters, was formed in

HOUSE OF CALL of the Benevolent Society of Carpenters and Joiners, held at Mr. JENKINS's, the New Zealander, Wellington, where gentlemen and builders can be supplied with good workmen.
May 24, 1842.

The beginnings of trade unionism in Wellington. The Benevolent Society of Carpenters and Joiners operates a labour exchange. WS, 25 May 1842

Wellington (possibly preceded in 1840 by an earlier organisation of carpenters). In the same year carpenters in Nelson organised to push up wages to 12s a day. It was no accident that carpenters were amongst the first to be organised, as there was a huge demand for dwellings and other buildings in these early years.

There was sporadic wage-earner organisation in the 1850s in the main centres, often associated with attempts to preserve an eight-hour working day. Carpenters and other building trades workers were most active. These early efforts fell by the wayside as a shortage of labour rapidly turned into a surplus and wages fell dramatically.[66] Many of the early disturbances involved public works or the rural sector. Manual labourers, amongst whom formal combination was largely absent, used the 'wildcat' strike weapon frequently. Such localised spontaneous strikes by farm and station hands, harvesting and threshing hands, and, in particular, shearers were frequent.[67] The 1860s witnessed an increased assertiveness by shearers and the latter part of the decade was particularly disturbed as runholders attempted to reduce rates. The artisans, with a monopoly of skill, did not need to organise or strike. They tended to adopt less confrontational methods and were well integrated into co-operative institutions.

During the 1860s, as the labour market stabilised and a division of labour developed, the first trade unions that maintained a continuing presence were formed – the printers in Dunedin and Wellington in 1862, and in Auckland in 1864, engineers in Auckland in 1863, and the tailors and bakers in Dunedin in 1865 and 1869.[68] These early unions based on the more skilled crafts were strongly influenced by Britain; some were indeed branches of the British unions. One of their major functions was, like the friendly societies, to act as benefit societies to protect against unemployment, accident, illness or death. But the presence of trade unions was fleeting and limited compared to other co-operative forms of organisation at this time, which were actively encouraged by the state.

Favourable labour market conditions in the first half of the 1870s resulted in a much wider range of skilled groups becoming organised, together with

Time statement of employers and journeymen tailors of Wellington, 1873, ArchNZ, IM4/1/1, 74/1604

the emergence of the first unskilled trade unions. The earlier unions consolidated and were extended to other centres, while other trades – carpenters, bootmakers, bricklayers, drapers and butchers – organised, as did the seamen. There was also some organisation of watersiders in Auckland and Lyttelton.[69]

CAUTION.

ALL MASONS of New Zealand and Australian colonies are cautioned that the MASONS of AUCKLAND have STRUCK WORK for the customary rate of wages of the above town (namely, 12s. per day), at the Supreme Court-house, now in course of erection by Messrs. Amos and Taylor.

Notice of strike of Auckland masons,
Southern Cross, 3 July 1866

A 'strike mania' was evident as the balance of the labour market swung the wage earners' way and workers sought gains and staked their claims through localised quick strike action.[70] Workers sought increased wage rates, reduced hours and union recognition. There were strikes by carpenters, shipwrights, tailors, bootmakers, butchers, bakers, shearers, watersiders, labourers, seamen and miners.

To contend with industrial disturbances, employers could use measures inherited from English law – the anti-conspiracy provisions or the Masters and Servants Act. They could also try to enforce contracts in the courts.

In England under common law, trade unions at this time were regarded as 'illegal conspiracies' acting 'in restraint of trade' by means of intimidation and coercion. England's Combination Act 1825 was adopted in New Zealand.[71] It was used by the Bay of Islands Coal Company when its Kawakawa mine was affected by a strike early in 1871.[72] When strikebreakers were intimidated by strikers, the company directors sought help from the Armed Constabulary. The Commissioner sent a contingent of ten men under arms and they arrested nine strikers who were charged with conspiring to intimidate others. They were eventually discharged after an agreement was signed to allow work to recommence. Three of the strikebreakers who refused to continue to work were less fortunate. They were charged with breaking their contract and were imprisoned for a month with hard labour.

The development of the railways soon attracted significant industrial disputes, as did the expansion of government generally. In 1872 the railway works of British contractor Brogdens were plagued by disputes relating to wages and the eight-hour day in places such as Picton, Waikato, Napier, Oamaru, Invercargill and Wellington.[73] In the same year Canterbury's railway workers successfully resisted a cut in wages, enlisting the aid of sympathetic MPs and Rolleston, the province's superintendent and 'working man's friend'.[74]

In 1876 Christchurch railwaymen again struck, this time over the eight-hour day and overtime. Late in 1879 there was a telegraph operators' strike in response to an extension of their working hours. The government regarded the strikes of this period, and reports of associated intimidation, with considerable alarm. The reaction of the Post Office was similar to that of the Railways – union organisation would not be tolerated – and the organisers were blacklisted. But as was noted at that time:

> The working classes . . . have nothing like the proportionate majority in this colony [and] there is not that deep-seated antagonism between the labouring and the wealthier classes . . . Here the labourers have as yet no common political purposes to achieve. Their interests and industries are almost wholly circumscribed by particular localities.[75]

In 1878 Stout passed the first legislation concerning worker combination – the Trade Union Act. He argued that labour was a commodity that should be free to co-operate, associate and organise to secure the best price in the market.[76] This was consistent with his Spencerian Liberal principles of removing restrictions and enforcing contracts, and also with his wish to encourage voluntary co-operation. Legislation was needed to avoid class antagonism; redressing the balance between capital and labour by giving trade unions the capacity for independent action analogous to the ballot.

The Act followed the 1871 English Trade Union Act closely, but with one crucial difference – it was not accompanied by legislation that constrained strike and picket activity. The New Zealand measure passed with little observable dissension even if some wanted this constraint included. It allowed seven or more workers to register as a 'trade union' along the lines of a friendly society. The Act was clearly designed to allow trade combination in the broad sense of the term. The legislation, as in England, specifically avoided sanctioning employment agreements between employer and worker, while registered trade unions were precluded from becoming corporate bodies. The intent was simply to remove the previous criminal and unlawful anti-combination provisions, and to provide a basic framework of protection for union funds.

The Act was a symbolic gesture of some importance in asserting the principle of free combination and enabling co-operative organisation, but few unions registered under it. It proved most useful to trade unions that wanted to operate benefit societies.

The franchise

Wage earners had the franchise from an early date, as the right to vote was central to the kind of egalitarian society colonists wanted to create, and to emerging concepts of citizenship and national identity.[77] The independence of workers and the opportunities to own property implied that they should also participate in the political process from a position of equality as citizens. As 'a working man who has no claim' proclaimed 'to the working men of Canterbury' in exhorting them to vote – 'Remember that God helps those who help themselves'.[78] It was the political correlate of the economic opportunities offered in the landed laboratory. Participation in politics was integral to realising a decent standard of living from the land and from the wage. If the state was to be the instrument of the people, then the people should be represented in the state. The broadening of the franchise from the 1850s to the 1890s, the introduction of the secret ballot in 1870, the introduction of manhood suffrage in 1879, and the increasing political participation by working men (and then women), went hand-in-hand with the growing powers of the state.

It is commonly believed that nineteenth-century New Zealand politics was undemocratic.[79] Lipson's *Politics of Equality*, upon which such conclusions are usually based, divides the numbers of registered voters by the total European population for the period 1853–79 and produces proportions somewhat below 20 percent, to support an argument that 'participation in politics remained a class privilege'.[80] But this was far from the case. We should not be blinded by the association of voting with property; this did not exclude the common man from voting and was seen as appropriate because it was associated with having a stake in the country. New Zealand did not have such an obvious manhood suffrage as the Australian states, but it was 'de facto' manhood suffrage nonetheless.

RULES AND REGULATIONS

OF THE

OTAGO

Typographical Association.

Established 1873.

REVISED AND ADOPTED, 4th OCTOBER, 1873.

Unitas, Justitia, Amicitia, Industria.

Rules and Regulations of the Otago Typographical Association, 1873. ArchNZ, IA1, 74/464

Pressure for full manhood suffrage began early. From the late 1840s colonists demanded it, particularly in Wellington and Nelson where constitutional associations were active.[81] Governor Grey's constitutional proposals of 1848 contained a virtually universal franchise for the two-thirds of the assembly members who were to be elected.[82] Meetings in Nelson culminated in the great 'reform' meeting of December 1850, which sought suffrage for all adult males with six months' residence in New Zealand, the secret ballot, triennial parliaments, and an elected upper House.[83] Further meetings in Wellington agreed upon universal male suffrage for those in the country a year. A restrictive qualification would give the vote only to a small number, 'creating an oligarchy to whose rule the bulk of the people would not submit'.[84] A lower property qualification would yield full male suffrage in effect, because of the widespread ownership of property. 'Is it not better, then, to

PUBLIC MEETING
OF WORKING MEN
WILL BE HELD AT THE
BRITANNIA Saloon, on
WEDNESDAY EVENING,
Aug. 3, to commence at
SIX O'CLOCK.

Working men were involved in elections for the Wellington Provincial Council in 1853. ATL, B-K, 63-012

designate things by their right names, and when you give what amounts to universal suffrage, to call it so?'

The argument was couched in terms of the advantages that New Zealand brought to wage earners. They became independent, property-owning and respectable, and should not be treated like English labourers, whose condition was so 'mean' that they were deemed to have no 'will' of their own and thus be subject to undue influence by others. There was no justification in New Zealand to exclude 'the domestic, the labourer, and the mechanic [who] are quite as independent as their employers'.[85]

The British Secretary of State Earl Grey, in response to this agitation, included an almost universal franchise in the constitutional proposals for New Zealand, upon which Governor Grey based his draft Constitution of August 1851 and draft bill of February 1852.[86] Supporter of manhood suffrage F.D. Bell (of Grey's nominee Legislative Council) urged that the 'household' qualification be dropped to £5 for both town and country and that the term 'household' be replaced by 'tenement' to reflect the living conditions of wage earners. Those such as the working settlers of Nelson 'who were living in mud hovels were the thews and sinews of the colony', he said. His recommendations were adopted.

The Constitution Act, passed in 1852, was little altered. It stipulated a franchise with a property qualification because of a belief that voting rights should be associated with having a stake in the country.[87] But the qualification was so low that most skilled workers and labourers were not excluded. Full male suffrage existed in all but name.

The threshold for householders was extremely low, while that for freehold and leasehold was not onerous either. Males 21 years and over could vote if they had (1) a freehold estate of annual value of £50; (2) a leasehold estate of annual value £10; or (3) as a householder occupied a dwelling worth £10 annually in the town (or £5 annually in the country) and had resided there for six months.

Workers qualified largely through the household provision but substantial numbers also qualified by their freeholds. The inclusive nature of the franchise is suggested by the early electoral rolls.[88] The proportions of mechanics, artisans and labourers who enrolled compared favourably to the proportions of these groups within the population at large. While nearly three-quarters qualified through occupation of a household, another quarter did so through the freehold option. In reality people's failure to register on the electoral rolls was much more of an issue than outright exclusion.

The formal property qualification did function to avoid the issue of whether and how to give Maori the franchise, a matter that exercised the minds of many at that time. Outright full male suffrage would have included Maori unless they were specifically excluded. With the franchise based on individual ownership or holding of land and housing, Maori, who largely owned land in common, did not qualify to vote. The view was that Maori needed to be 'civilised' and their landholdings individualised before being given the privilege of the vote.

The matter was altogether simpler in Australia. Voting rights for the indigenous population was not an issue. When a wave of radical miners arrived in the 1850s full manhood suffrage was granted. Here a sidestep was necessary, through the creation of a separate franchise for miners in 1860 (and for Maori in 1867). The Miners' Representation Act 1860 gave miners the vote based on miners' rights (licenses to mine). This enfranchised all male miners, and was introduced as a pre-emptive measure, following the violent confrontation at the Eureka stockade in Victoria that had been motivated by Chartist sentiments. The miners' franchise would later act as a wedge facilitating full manhood suffrage in the late 1870s.[89] Itinerant miners eventually became settled citizens; the vexed issues of electoral redistribution and the special miners' electorates would widen the discussion of the franchise.

The introduction of the secret ballot in 1870 illustrates not only enduring Chartist influences in New Zealand but also a changing concept of citizenship.[90] The secret ballot debate focused on whether the vote was a right for the enfranchised population or whether it was exercised on behalf of those not enfranchised. Adopting the secret ballot reflected a shift from a right based on commitment to the country (reflected in property and a period of residence) towards an abstract right for all. Those who argued it was a matter of trust wanted votes to be openly exercised, in order that the political support of an individual be publicly identifiable. Those who argued for the secret ballot pointed towards intimidation and interference and suggested that voters were only responsible to themselves in voting. To this opponents of the secret ballot countered that the working men were extremely independent in New Zealand and that they would not allow themselves to be intimidated.

Those with Chartist sympathies, such as Edward Stafford, pushed for the secret ballot. Stafford led Nelson settlers in demanding it in 1850, along with a constitution for New Zealand.[91] He said that 'the electors should be protected and defended in exercising that freedom of choice which the Constitution professes to give them', and that the secret ballot was needed to eliminate intimidation, bribery and corruption of weaker voters during the 'open struggle of the hustings'. But some working people present

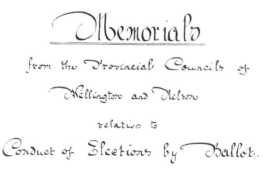

The Provincial Councils of Wellington and Nelson petitioned the House of Representatives in 1858 for the introduction of the secret ballot. ArchNZ, LE1, 1858/241

W.H. Reynolds, politician and advocate of the secret ballot and manhood suffrage. Parliamentary Library, New Zealand Portraits, vol 2

at the Nelson meetings wanted an open vote, to demonstrate just how independent they were in a new country. They conceded, however, that they might need the protection of the secret ballot in the future.

In 1858, with Stafford leading the government, the secret ballot was included with other reforms to electoral practices advanced by the Attorney-General, Frederick Whitaker. The move was supported by memorials from Wellington and Nelson.[92] But others in the General Assembly opposed it and it was not included in the electoral legislation of that year.

In 1867, when Stafford was again Premier, W.H. Reynolds introduced a bill (supported by Stafford) to introduce the secret ballot, following an Otago Provincial Council motion. In the General Assembly William Reeves argued that the secret ballot was 'desired by the working classes in his district, because they believed it would relieve them from a pressure which was already being brought against them'. The bill was defeated in a close vote at its second reading, but Reynolds vowed to continue the fight and visited different parts of the country on the issue. The following year his bill almost made it onto the statute book but it fell at the last hurdle of the Legislative Council. Walter Mantell, in a minority in the Council, pointed out that the trust argument had little validity in New Zealand compared with England because 'there was almost manhood suffrage, everybody represented himself, and he for instance held his own vote in trust for himself'.[93]

Reynolds introduced the bill again in 1869. Premier William Fox 'trusted that they would not be found to be lagging behind the old country' now that England was itself considering the secret ballot.[94] The Legislative Council now favoured the principle but amended the bill and offended the House of Representatives in the process. Again, the bill lapsed. The issue returned to Parliament in the following session after further resolutions from Nelson and Otago Provincial Councils.[95] The Governor's Speech from the Throne opening Parliament included the measure, and Fox's government ensured that the Election by Ballot Act finally passed.

The length of time it took to adopt the secret ballot did not reflect the strength of conservative reaction but rather a genuine hesitancy that such a measure was really necessary in a country where wage earners showed considerable independence and proudly showed this through the open voting process. But the ballot became more necessary when trade unions faced employers and labour began to organise and participate more directly in politics.

With the secret ballot implemented, pressure again began to mount for full manhood suffrage. In England the franchise had been extended to householders in 1867. Whitaker had suggested introducing manhood suffrage in 1866 but Premier Stafford had put him off at a time of turmoil in government.[96] During the session of 1870 a resolution for full manhood suffrage emerged, supported by Premier Fox, arguing 'we all endure nearly equal taxation . . . representation should be co-extensive with taxation'.[97] It would take nearly a decade for this to be achieved. The conservative Hugh Carleton 'feared they should be sucked into the howling maelstrom of radicalism', noting that a 'nightman' had almost beaten the late Speaker of the Legislative Council in an election in Auckland.[98] Manhood suffrage was raised frequently and endorsed widely; indeed a number of governments supported the principle. However, bringing it in was complicated by its de facto existence, the variety of franchises that now existed – that based on property, the miners' franchise and separate elections for the four Maori representatives – and the potential inclusion of Maori.[99] There was also confusion with more general electoral reform.

The large numbers of new migrants in the early 1870s created an 'unsettled' (both literally and metaphorically) interest group. Increasing numbers were denied the vote. They were unlikely to qualify through the freehold for some time and, having to roam far and wide in search of employment, found it difficult to qualify as householders because of the residence provisions.[100] There were those lodging or living in boarding houses, others who did not qualify as householders or by ownership of property, and more who lived an itinerant way of life.

It looked as if full manhood suffrage was not far away. The wedge used was the lodger issue – men who did not qualify under the household qualification. Eugene O'Conor said in 1873 that the 'vast majority' of MPs favoured manhood suffrage – if the government would not do anything others would – and in 1874 Reader Wood commented that 'if we do not concede the principle now as a boon, it will be wrested from us as a right'.[101] In 1873 and again in 1874 Reynolds introduced manhood suffrage bills but there was considerable confusion as to their true intent – to provide a lodgers' franchise, attack the miners' franchise or exclude Maori? Reynolds introduced a similar bill in 1875.[102] While the ministry itself largely voted for the bill, many otherwise liberal MPs who were strongly in favour of suffrage extension did not, and it was defeated. E.J. Wakefield then introduced a bill that speedily passed as the Lodgers' Franchise Act 1875 to deal with the immediate problem of disenfranchised lodgers.

John Hall, runholder, Premier and reluctant promoter of electoral reform. Parliamentary Library, New Zealand Portraits, vol 1

In 1876 Grey introduced a manhood suffrage bill that replaced other franchises in the Constitution Act but continued with the miners' franchise and included Maori.[103] Whitaker, meanwhile, had entered the government on condition that he could promote electoral reform. In 1877 he drafted a huge electoral reform bill (that included elector qualification). Grey persisted with his own measure.[104] Later that session Grey himself became Premier but did not introduce a bill, stating that he preferred to go to the country first.[105] He spent the election touring the country promoting manhood suffrage and was re-elected on a platform of manhood suffrage and triennial parliaments, amongst other policies.

In 1878 Stout introduced the Grey government's Electoral Bill. This was a complex system that retained the various property qualifications and introduced a manhood suffrage by qualification of two years' residence, together with ratepaying qualifications. Whitaker, now in opposition, introduced his much more straightforward Parliamentary Representation Bill (drawn from proposals he had advanced since 1858), based on a residence qualification of six months and the abolition of plural voting.

The debate failed to focus on the principle of extension of the franchise, this now being largely taken for granted. It got bogged down in technical details and the parallel debates on the two bills. The main issue boiled down to whether property should continue to be recognised in plural voting. Grey took a surprisingly pragmatic and conservative stance, suggesting that the time had not yet come for the abolition of plural voting. Grey's bill almost passed after much amendment, but in the end Stout (with Grey's angry support) discharged it, having failed to reach agreement with the Legislative Council on the inclusion of Maori.[106]

Manhood suffrage was finally enacted in 1879 after John Hall (an opponent of manhood suffrage) formed a government with the aid of four 'liberal' defectors, who got him to promise to pass Grey's electoral legislation in exchange for their support. Hall had grudgingly conceded the inevitability of reform, saying that it would not extend the effective franchise greatly in any case and it had the virtue of eliminating 'the trade of the stump orator and

'The working man's friends'. Sir George Grey came into power promising many reforms to land laws and the franchise. John Hall, who replaced him as Premier in 1979, picked up the pieces of the legislation and got the bills passed. Parliamentary Library, political cartoons, 1879–80

demagogue'.[107] Under the Qualifications of Electors Act all adult males who had been resident for twelve months were able to vote. The miners' franchise was abolished but the freehold qualification remained (reduced from £50 to £25) and thus so too did plural voting (although Ballance nearly managed to abolish it while the bill was in Committee).

Ironically the final touch to manhood suffrage was made as a footnote to the consolidation of a country quota. The quota was established in 1881 as a counterbalance to the gathering forces of labour in burgeoning urban centres. Its establishment reflected a continuing emphasis on the settlement ethos and commitment to landed property in New Zealand's concept of citizenship that was supported even by notable Liberals such as Seddon, McKenzie and Ward. It was justified by the well-worn phrase 'the backbone of this colony is in the country'.[108] In 1889 the extent of the country quota came up for negotiation.[109] The existence of a quota was not in doubt (indeed it was to remain until 1945); it was its extent that was a matter of dispute. At the end of an exhausting debate Grey slipped in a clause abolishing plural voting (which allowed those holding freehold property in different electorates to cast votes in those electorates).[110] This was passed with a large majority, probably as a quid pro quo for finally fixing the quota.

The one-man one-vote principle could now easily be extended to women. There had been mention of female suffrage in 1870 and 1874, and in 1879

Ballance had nearly managed to extend the franchise to women, a matter supported by a number of male politicians at that time.[111] Issues associated with franchise qualifications and the inability of its more ardent proponents to agree to compromise hindered progress.

Grimshaw describes these earlier initiatives as expressing abstract liberal reformism – success had to await the rise of female social movements in the 1880s and the temperance movement. Women began petitioning Parliament from 1886 and also lobbied powerful supporters such as Ballance, Stout, Vogel, and later, Hall. In 1887 Colonial Treasurer Vogel introduced a bill enfranchising women on the same basis as men. This received considerable support before being defeated in a close vote late at night when supporters had left the House.

From 1890 women's suffrage was permanently on the parliamentary agenda. The suffrage campaign was broadened and extremely large petitions presented to Parliament. The new Liberal government of 1891 faced a dilemma – it was uncertain whether women's votes would in fact aid their cause, because a number of Ministers, in contrast to Premier Ballance, were actively opposed to female suffrage. Seddon, after tacit encouragement of blocking by the liquor interest, put his hopes in a Legislative Council veto. For some time the delaying tactics were successful. In 1893, to the astonishment of many, the Electoral Bill that had passed smoothly through the House was agreed to in the Legislative Council. Seddon's machinations against the measure had proved too much for two opponents of women's suffrage in the Council to stomach and they had switched sides.

Grimshaw explains this pioneering electoral reform in terms of the lack of conservative forces and a readiness to accept new ideas in a pioneering society; the prior existence of manhood suffrage; the radical political climate in the 1890s after depression; the strength of liberalism and the prevailing liberal tolerance on the part of men; and a self-conscious nationalistic pride in being the social laboratory of the world.[112] The political context also helped: fluidity in party structure; the calibre of leading supporters; and the pressure for state intervention in social issues associated with temperance.

The same year, previously disenfranchised itinerant groups, such as shearers and other rural workers, seamen and travelling salesmen, were able to vote. In 1900 the Electoral Act was amended so that employer influence in isolated rural areas in elections was prevented.[113] These reforms put the seal on nearly fifty years of franchise extension and brought to an end a process that had begun with the political constitution of this country in the early 1850s. Citizenship was disentangled from property, became an abstract right of the individual and was extended to women, at least in exercising a vote if not at that point in representing the people. The matter of Maori political representation had been settled by the permanent status of the four Maori seats in Parliament and the virtual exclusion of Maori from the general roll.

Entry into politics

> In office homes he saw the glow
> Of happy Vogel, Fox, & Co.;
> Say's he, "I'll make a rumpus here;
> This cry will conquer, never fear –
> "The working man!"
>
> . . .
>
> When the House met – from Southern hills
> Came squatters to redress their ills;
> Says he, with many a bitter scoff,
> "I'll show you who is master of –
> The working man!"
>
> Doggerel from 1879 referring to Grey's rise to power – 'The Working Man'
> (3rd and 7th verses)[114]

In the mid 1860s in Canterbury, a Working Man's Political Protection and Mutual Improvement Association was formed.[115] This organisation was associated with the already mentioned Canterbury Freehold Land Society and with S.P. Andrews, the first working man to stand for election to the Canterbury Provincial Council. Its objects were to advance the working classes by participation in politics, closer land settlement and the improvement of its members' 'competency' and 'respectability'. It sought full manhood suffrage and the secret ballot, amongst other things. Later in the decade there were stirrings in Otago, with the Mount Benger Self-Protection and Land League Association and the Tuapeka Land League formed to push for closer settlement.

Labour participation in politics gained momentum into the 1870s. The mass immigration of those who were less likely to be able to take up land transformed the labour market. Labour began to carve out a distinct place politically and trade unionism made its presence felt. The 1870s wave of migrants came from Britain with a different view of wage labour than before; for these people labour was not so much an adjunct to a civilised society as a legitimate interest in its own right. Thus if the wage earner did not enjoy the benefits appropriate to a civilised society then that society was not civilised at all. This gave a strong impetus to state intervention, changed the nature of that intervention, and emphasised the need to keep old-world evils at bay.

The urban environment was beginning to provide the conditions for popular labour politics, as indicated by the high levels of voter registration and working-men's participation in elections in urban centres. The strengthening tradition of public meetings and outdoor gatherings over issues such as immigration, unemployment, tariff reform and public works promoted the organisation of wage earners.

In 1871 Working Men's Protection Societies (probably influenced by the creation of the London Workingmen's Association in 1866, which was concerned with getting working men into Parliament) formed in Auckland and Christchurch to promote the interests of the unemployed, agitate for public works, and to protest against continued immigration.[116] The Auckland organisation also

A PUBLIC MEETING of the WORK-ING MEN'S PROTECTION SOCIETY, to which every·ne is cordially invited, will be held on the Green outside the Drill-shed, This Evening, at 7 sharp. Business of importance, and members will be enrolled.—By order of the Committee.

The Working Men's Protection Society meets, Auckland. Southern Cross, 3 February 1871

agitated for the eight-hour day, against reductions in wages, and to eliminate contractors' wage payments by truck (goods rather than money) in public houses. In 1874 an unemployed working men's association briefly emerged in Christchurch, and the following year some 1,200 in Dunedin petitioned the government to stop further immigration to New Zealand, which was 'already crowded with Unemployed . . . who are now bordering on Starvation.'[117]

By now self-proclaimed working men had begun to enter the provincial councils. S.P. Andrews was elected in Canterbury in 1872 and the following year Henry Carter made it in Wellington.[118] The 1875 general elections threw up some working men's representatives but none got elected. One C. Moody with Chartist principles stood in Wellington as 'a representative of the working class fighting the landed oligarchy', being described by the *Evening Post* as a 'very common place and vulgar political agitator'. In Thames C.A. Cornes, who was described as a 'working man', stood but then withdrew, while ex-Chartist C.F. Mitchell came fourth behind Grey and Vogel.

Abolition of the provinces in 1876 refocused politics towards the general government and made the tone of national politics more radical, as local safety valves expressed through the provincial councils no longer existed.[119] Grey became Premier in 1877 and during the summer of 1877–8 he toured the country in novel fashion, appealing directly to the public for endorsement. He spoke of manhood suffrage, electoral reform, a land tax and the break-up of land monopoly, and rallied many to the cause. Liberal Associations were formed in many centres. Grey embarked on another 'stumping' tour in 1879, drawing accusations of stirring up the 'mob'. He stimulated a flourishing of liberal political organisation and popular involvement in politics not seen before.

An element of the direct political representation of labour began to emerge at the national level. Canterbury was especially active. S.P. Andrews entered the House of Representatives in 1879 alongside Grey, backed by the Liberal Reform Association. Another 'Greyite' working man, Harry

TO THE WORKING MEN OF CANTERBURY.
(Per favor of the 'Lyttelton Times.')

WORKING MEN,—Now is your time if you mean to do any good for yourselves and children. You that have a freehold of the clear value of £50,—you that have a leasehold of £10 yearly, having had it for three years or having three years yet to hold it.—also you fortunate householders that have held your present house for the last six months—Register your claims to vote. Remember that God helps those who help themselves.
I am, yours truly,
A WORKING MAN,
WHO HAS NO CLAIM.
Christchurch, March 12, 1860.

Working men are exhorted to register to vote. LT, 14 March 1860

Allwright, was elected by the working men of Lyttelton.[120] Grey appointed a few 'self-made' men to the Legislative Council.

In the early 1880s the Canterbury Working Men's Political Association organised the labour vote to get their own representatives into Parliament.[121] It had a number of branches in the city and surrounding areas. In 1884 it even attempted to create a colony-wide political association by forming branches and linking with similar organisations. The association developed a concerted platform and insisted that political candidates agreed to a list of thirteen measures; it also stood candidates in two Christchurch electorates.

In Timaru a Political Reform Association was formed for the 1884 election, following a meeting of largely wage-earning electors in the town.[122] It modelled itself on the English Liberal Associations of the 1870s and sought 'the full and just representation of the working classes in Parliament'. The association supported the radical liberal incumbent Richard Turnbull. A farm labourer stood in the Cheviot electorate in North Canterbury, while other working men stood in the Gladstone and Temuka electorates in South Canterbury.

> ### TO THE ELECTORS OF THE CITY OF WELLINGTON.
>
> GENTLEMEN—Believing that the time has arrived when labour as well as capital should be represented in the political institutions of our common country, I have deemed it my duty to present myself to you as a candidate for election to the Provincial Council.
>
> As I have long taken an active interest in the political and local institutions of this and other provinces of New Zealand, I may fairly claim some knowledge of your wants.
>
> If you return me I shall endeavour to obtain such a modification of the Education Act as will admit of denominational schools receiving as a right a fair share of the school revenue, in proportion to their number and usefulness.
>
> I am opposed to the present mixed system of immigration and labour traffic as carried out under the "Brogden" immigration scheme.
>
> I would advocate the building of more healthy schoolhouses, with well paid and properly qualified teachers ; the recognition of eight hours in all Provincial Government contracts, as the legal and customary day's labor of all employers.
>
> I would encourage the establishment of local self-government in all centres of population, and the establishment of free public libraries, in part supported by the province.
>
> I am in favor of all public works being publicly tendered for ; the same conditions of contract to apply to all contractors, imported or otherwise.
>
> Generally, if you return me, I will support all progressive works or measures likely to prove beneficial to the interests of my fellow-colonists.
>
> Yours, &c.,
>
> H. CARTER,
>
> Wellington, 25th January.

Labouring man H. Carter presents himself for election to the Wellington Provincial Council. EP, 25 January 1873

From 1881 there was a surge in voting in Otago, much of it from wage-earning groups.[123] In some Dunedin electorates, manual and skilled workers formed a majority of those voting. By the latter half of the decade in Dunedin voting was more clearly based on sectional and class lines and working-class political organisation began to occur.

By the late 1870s, as unemployment increased (see Chapter 4), agitation by the unemployed became one of the most important forms of representation of the interests of labour.[124] Many had been thrown out of work or could not get seasonal work any more as the rural economy shrank, trade and commerce suffered depression, and public works were cut back. Gatherings by the unemployed were a common phenomenon in the major centres in the depression years of the 1880s. Their protests were used to impress authorities with the size of the problem and to stimulate the provision of relief work and restrict immigration. While the protests were relatively spontaneous and did not usually lead to enduring organisation, at times they were linked to wider movements and in particular to land reform.

The long depression both radicalised and politicised labour. The organisations which sprang up were modelled upon the reformist organisations of post-Chartist Britain from the late 1860s, which sought an alliance with the advanced wing of the Liberal Party to provide representation, and which relied upon powerful arguments of equal rights under the law for both master and man. In 1877 in Auckland a United Labourers' Mutual Aid Society was formed as a result of unemployment, and in 1879 a Working Men's Political Association was formed in Auckland and a Working Men's Rights League in Christchurch.[125] These organisations explicitly sought to promote working-class interests in Parliament, and to agitate against immigration and for a land tax, settlement on the land, and protection for local industries.

A coalition of liberal and labour interests began to emerge in the context of an identifiable 'Liberal' grouping within Parliament that drew greatly upon support from working people. Trades and Labour Councils articulated reformist political platforms and forged links with Liberal MPs. A Trades and Labour Council had existed for some time in Auckland in the mid 1870s; in 1881–4 they were formed in Otago, Auckland and Wellington. The Otago Council was particularly active and pursued very broad objects: to 'better the condition of the working classes'; to maintain the eight-hour day; to give 'moral assistance' in disputes; 'to obviate as far as possible the necessity for strikes' by careful investigation and settlement by arbitration; and to promote 'proper representation' of labour in Parliament.[126]

Such organisations aimed their efforts at Parliament rather than encouraging the exercise of industrial muscle. The Otago Council's rules specifically stated that 'the only hope of the Trades and Labour Council lies in being able to wield political power. If this is lost, then the Council may as well be dissolved.' In 1881 it successfully sponsored Thomas Bracken (the author of the poem at the head of this chapter) and M.W. Green as parliamentary candidates, and in 1884 it supported Stout, W.D. Stewart, Bracken, John Bathgate and others.[127] In 1890 the labour movement endorsed Liberal candidates in a number of electorates; in others either the Liberal or Labour candidate would withdraw by mutual agreement, while in a few there were agreed Liberal-Labour candidates.

During the 1880s trade unionism developed apace in the economically depressed but radicalised environment. Unions for printers, tailors, seamen, miners, bootmakers and watersiders became federated national bodies. Agitation was extended well beyond the skilled craft workers to a range of previously unorganised unskilled groups whose wages suffered far more as

❦MANIFESTO.❦

THE OTAGO TRADES AND LABOUR COUNCIL, after careful and anxious consideration of the political questions now agitating the public mind, and the claims and qualifications of Candidates for the various seats, have resolved to RECOMMEND the WORKING CLASSES to SUPPORT the following CANDIDATES:—

Mr. Robert Stout, Dunedin East.	**Mr. John Bathgate, Roslyn.**
Mr. W. D. Stewart, Dunedin West.	**Mr. William Barron, Caversham.**
Mr. T. Bracken, Dunedin Central.	**Mr. O. J. Hodge, Peninsula.**
Mr. H. S. Fish, Dunedin South.	

The active Otago Trades and Labour Council endorsed candidates for the general elections in 1884. Victoria University, Stout unbound pamphlets, no. 183

a result of economic fluctuations.[128] For a time the shearers were organised throughout the country as a branch of the Australian union. Watersiders, seamen and miners increasingly used the strike weapon, while more generally unions made concerted efforts to elevate wages and impose standard rates through combination.

The government was the largest employer in the country and provided public works employment to soak up unemployment. As a result the government acted as a conducting rod for the grievances of wage earners and was the focus for worker mobilisation and a 'nationalisation' of the issues.[129] The core values of the social contract were being challenged – migrants could not be attracted if fair wages were not paid; people could not live on 6s a day; the government had a responsibility to ensure proper wage levels.

With the onset of depression the government's gathering fiscal crisis resulted in substantial cuts to public works and railway services and a tightening of discipline. The salaries of civil servants were cut by 10 percent in 1880, while government wages were also largely cut (between 10 and 15 percent) in line with the wage cuts in the wider labour market.

The wage cuts provided the impetus for a organised campaign by government employees, together with supportive MPs, on a scale not witnessed before. In September 1881 there was a strike amongst the artisans of the Addington railway workshops. Their focus was the restoration of wages and an eight-hour day. After much pressure, prolonged discussion in Parliament, and a move to make the matter one of confidence in the government, railway labourers' wages were increased slightly.

In the mid 1880s the trade union movement began to step onto the national stage with the first Trades and Labour congresses.[130] These gatherings of labour representatives throughout the country represented a substantial shift in the relationship between trade unions and the state. Premier Robert Stout formally acknowledged and legitimated the role of trade unions, in a fashion reminiscent of British Prime Minister William Gladstone.

Key groups of workers became emboldened as unionism developed apace and strikes became more frequent. These disturbances are outlined below in some detail, not to suggest that the entire country was in ferment but because there is very limited awareness of the extent of such activity prior to the Maritime strike of 1890. Just as we should not see the Liberal legislation of the 1890s appearing out of the blue, it is important not to disregard the longer-term industrial relations context. The Maritime strike was not a sudden violent eruption out of nowhere; it formed part of an enduring attempt by workers to organise and improve wages and working conditions. This discussion of swelling trade union organisation and action belies the usual picture of depression and difficulty. It was not a matter of dark days for labour, but a time of growing power and assertiveness.

In 1883 there was a strike at the Walton Park mine, Dunedin. In 1884 seamen successfully pursued wage increases and an eight-hour day for cargo work through tactics such as picketing, and Lyttelton wharf labourers struck over a reduction of their usual rate; the same year miners at Springfield went on strike. The following year was particularly noted for industrial disputes. Bootmakers successfully struck to force recalcitrant firms to adopt their rates, and there was a strike at the Coalpit Heath Company's mine in Greymouth for increased rates and a changed system of work. A six-month dispute at Denniston on the West Coast, over reduced rates and recognition of the miners' union, ended with the company capitulating and agreeing to re-employ most of the striking miners at the old rates.[131] All the miners at the Kamo mine, Whangarei, went on strike against reduced wages, while the Auckland Seamen's Union battled with the Northern Steamship Company about overtime provisions.

Three of New Zealand's four major ports were extremely disturbed in 1885 as watersiders attempted to impose unionism on the waterfront. At the same time the major shipping companies attempted to cut wages throughout the colony.[132] Wharves in other parts of the country were disturbed by strike action, and there were scenes of disorder involving intimidation and assault as non-unionists were engaged. Stout agreed to act as referee for arbitration in the dispute, but the shipping companies refused to enter into any negotiations or recognise the union. They eventually succeeded in breaking it up.

In response to the strikes and intimidation, the government in 1885 introduced a Threats and Molestation Bill (based on the English Criminal Law Amendment provisions of 1871) into the Legislative Council.[133] This was the first attempt to control trade unions through state powers. The bill was pushed by some MPs such as George McLean, banker, chairman of the Union Steam Ship Company and associated with the Denniston mine. It was designed to prevent violence, threats or intimidation during industrial disputes (subject to up to three months' imprisonment), and specifically included seamen and watersiders amongst other groups of workers. It quickly went through the Council but at the end of the session was not enthusiastically received in the House of Representatives. Seddon suggested it involved 'legislating in the interests of capital as against labour', and that it was 'an insult to the working-

GIANT OF THE PERIOD

'The giant of the period' — the coming political force. Politicians begin to petition the working man in Canterbury for votes, with Superintendent William Rolleston (holding the ladder). The background to this cartoon lay in an industrial dispute in the railway wool store in Christchurch. James Irving from the store, depicted as the giant working man, spoke against cuts to railway worker wages. He was not disciplined by Rolleston, who came into conflict with the Provincial Council. T.S. Cousins, 4 June 1872. Bert Roth and Janny Hammond, Toil and Trouble, *p. 45*

men of New Zealand'.[134] Premier Stout (the author of the 1878 legislation encouraging trade unionism) favoured the measure but said that it needed further consideration; the bill was discharged.

The second New Zealand Trades and Labour Congress, in early 1886, condemned the bill as a 'direct blow aimed at the rights of the labouring classes, and a serious infringement of the liberty of the subject in this colony'.[135] The Congress sent a deputation to Vogel over this matter, amongst other issues. He declaimed knowledge of the bill's contents but acknowledged that it required serious consideration. Premier Stout defended it as providing for individual liberty, and he believed, moreover, that it would have been supported by a majority in the House had he not withdrawn it. He emphasised that if trade unions supported the kind of activities proscribed in the bill it would be a 'great blow . . . struck at trades unionism'.

Strikes continued. Bootmaking was particularly disturbed during the next few years in both Christchurch and Auckland.[136] In 1886 the Kaitangata miners attempted to form a union and change working practices, but they were locked out when they refused to work alongside non-unionists. The company soon found willing free labour, and the confrontation dragged on for five months, punctuated by threatening incidents, until the miners gave in. There were strikes in gold mines on the West Coast the same year, at Ross and at the Welcome mine in Reefton, when the working day was lengthened from eight hours to nine. The miners successfully resisted these increased hours. There was also a strike of compositors on the *Otago Daily Times*, against a 10 percent reduction in wages.

Deepening depression conditions caused a withering of the trade union movement for a time, but before long lesser skilled groups were again organising and the gathering forces of unionism were expressed in moves to federate, considerable co-ordination of disputes, and support from other unions. The lesson for trade unionists seemed to be that they could succeed if they achieved concerted national and 'industrial' organisation.

In 1887, seamen employed by the Northern Steam Shipping Company struck against reduced wages.[137] After a rejected offer of arbitration and a failed approach to the government, the Federated Seamen's Union, led by J.A. Millar, established the rival Jubilee Shipping Company. For a time it looked as if the dispute would escalate into a general Australasian conflagration, but after a year's competition the Northern Company conceded defeat and agreed to employ only union members at union rates. This was to lead to the formation of the Maritime Council in October 1889, a body that brought together the seamen, watersiders, miners and others.

In the face of this challenge and in sustained depression conditions, major employers such as the shipping and mining companies attempted to reassert their traditional powers of control in the workplace.[138] Shag Point Mine came to a standstill in 1889 when the employers fired two union officials and

OBSTACLE RACE FOR THE WORKING-MAN STAKES.

The cartoonist comments on the fate of various politicians touting for the working man's vote as the 1890 election loomed. In the early 1870s Julius Vogel promised public works employment; later that decade Sir George Grey promised reforms to labour. In 1890 prohibitionist Robert Stout came down on the side of labour during the boycott of Whitcombe and Tombs and the Maritime strike. Labour organiser and founder of the Knights of Labour H.W. Farnall was left behind by more militant labour during these industrial disturbances of 1890. He stood in the election but was deserted by working men and not elected. Observer and Free Lance, 6 September 1890

subsequently evicted strikers in company houses. The company backed down when the Maritime Council got involved and organised a boycott. West Coast miners under John Lomas engaged in a test of strength with the Westport Coal Company in late 1889, which by this time controlled the coal mines on the Coast, but the union was forced to concede a reduced hewing rate. The boycott of Whitcombe and Tombs in 1890, following a strike by the Typographical Association, resulted in a confrontation between the Maritime Council and the Railway Commissioners and a threat of a general strike, as the Council's boycott involved the railways.

In parallel with the development of trade unionism a radical movement emerged, based around settlement on the land, industrial development and tariff protection, to fulfil the aspirations of migrants and deal with unemployment.[139]

Land reform societies sprang up in various centres. In Wellington, Timaru and Greymouth there were Land Leagues, in Lyttelton the optimistic-sounding 'Land Ho! Association' and in Gisborne a Land Tenure Reform League. Late in the decade further land reform societies were formed – the Auckland Anti-

Poverty Society in 1888, the Wellington Single Tax Society the following year and the Social Reform Association in Dunedin in 1889–90.

A range of other organisations emerged – workingmen's associations, Liberal Associations, early closing associations, the Canterbury Electors' Association, the Anti-Poverty League, Freethought Associations, the State Bank League, the Industrial Protection League and the Knights of Labour. The Industrial Protection League in particular pulled together a wide range of concerns. In addition to protective tariffs, its objects included a land and income tax, restrictions on immigration, and reconstruction of the labour bureaux to deal with sweating, wages, arbitration and unemployment. The Freethought Associations acted as secular politically radical organisations for left Liberals from artisan or self-made independent backgrounds. Their goal was a more rational, liberal and individualistic society. Anti-squatter sentiment was strong and land reform was high on the agenda.

These organisations directly addressed central issues of longstanding significance, by not only demanding greater state intervention in working conditions, employment, wages and industrial relations, but also advocating a protective tariff, a land tax on the unearned increment, and the opening up of land for settlement (as well as a state bank and cheap rural loans). Their political programme was borrowed from middle-class colonial progressives such as Grey, from English land reformers, and from Fabian socialism with a Christian colour. In the words of J.D. Salmond, 'Utopian Socialism, Liberalism, Land Reform and the Single Tax were all to be found side by side'.[140]

All were agreed upon the principles of land settlement, protection of industry, and protection of workers against exploitation. Many were greatly concerned that the developing monopoly in land, reductions in wages, high unemployment, sweating in industry, class warfare in industrial relations and poverty amongst families had overturned the original social contract constructed during the initial decades of settlement.

As working people began to mobilise, the state began to consider new policies to deal with the situation. The working man had grasped political rights of citizenship and had an expectation of economic citizenship in a desirable standard of living – a matter that could easily be frustrated without greater state intervention.

New Zealand had reached a turning point in the 1880s, with the emergence of a stronger, more differentiated labour interest at a time when the state had adopted a centralised and unitary form, the provinces having been abolished in 1876. The rise of popular political movements reflected both a renewed impetus given to radicalism by the fresh influx of migrants from Britain, and the impact of unemployment, reduced wages and class conflict as the depression took hold. Into the 1880s representation of the working man in Parliament reached the point where policies affecting working people became serious issues of government.

Depression challenged the previous terms of the social contract; the panacea of land and limited state intervention was no longer sufficient. The state began to focus on wage earners' standard of living and a greater extent of intervention, while the liberal franchise and its extension, together with labour's extensive participation in politics and a high level of voting, made state policy increasingly responsive to the popular will. This allowed space for bold, sweeping reforms.

CHAPTER 4

The 'duty of the state'? Extending the contract

With workmen of all trades to swell the brave throng,
Over many a waste shall be Industry strewn;
And the workmen shall earn, all the busy year long,
Fair wage for his work, in a Land of our own!

Tenth verse of E.J. Wakefield's 'A Land of Our Own', 1848[1]

Having looked at how working people brought with them forms of organising from Britain and how they began to express their interests politically, we turn to the state's response to the emerging presence of labour in its own right – policies concerning the employment contract, the workplace and unemployment.

The bounds of and the reasons for state intervention were the bread and butter of the debates in political philosophy at the time. It was not simply a battle between individualism and collectivism.[2] The rationale for policy shifted from a negative view of freedom towards a positive view. The state could enhance or redistribute freedom of the individual, first by preventing moral or physical dangers, then by the enforcement of minimum standards, and then moving to state financial support for the private provision of services and eventually to direct state provision and state monopoly of services.

William Gisborne, head of New Zealand's civil service from 1856 until 1869, discussed the general principles at work as government intervention enlarged, particularly in the protective sphere.[3] Every initiative must be carefully scrutinised, he said, and demonstrate both that an evil is to be redressed by means of intervention and that the means are practical. It was a pragmatic matter but guided by notions of morality – viewed in an eminently 'colonial liberal' manner.

The mildest form of intervention, Gisborne argued, was the offer of government assistance in an enabling sense, as in the co-operative movement, savings banks or life insurance. Then followed negative 'naked prohibition', such as the abolition of child labour in factories. This interfered with individual liberties but for good cause. The 'highest' form of intervention was positive regulation to obviate 'social, moral, or political evils', such as the sanitary provisions of the factory legislation. This Liberal conception of the role of the state envisaged an escalation of intervention according to need, a matter brought to a head by the deepening depression conditions of the 1880s.

Although theoretically inclined liberals were rather rare in New Zealand there were some, such as Stout, who articulated his thinking more than most. His personal intellectual trajectory followed the shift from traditional laissez

Robert Stout, lawyer, Premier and liberal thinker. William Gisborne, New Zealand Rulers and Statesmen, *1897*

faire to interventionist new liberalism.[4] In the end he conceded that there were areas of social life in which state intervention was required, because of the emergence of old-world evils.

Stout in 1870, in examining the problem of the unemployed and whether the government should intervene, made a strong plea for a Spencerian 'liberal' approach. This accepted that human nature made people unequal and that state support and the right to relief only encouraged spendthrift wastrels and drunkards and meant that they had to be supported at the expense of the thrifty and prudent. The former had 'no right to demand from Society when out of work, employment, nor when in want of food, temporary relief.'[5]

A pamphlet he published in 1883 maintained this stance and attacked Atkinson's advocacy of a national insurance scheme (discussed in Chapter 6) in terms that the state, because of its role in advancing the common good, had a duty to support the poor.[6] In considering whether the state or private enterprise should be involved, Atkinson defended state intervention on pragmatic grounds. It was not a matter of abstract debate on the proper functions of government. He pointed out that the government in New Zealand had already gone far beyond what the 'greatest Radical' might have envisaged fifty years ago.[7]

Stout emphasised, in classical liberal style, that the state's role should be limited and should recognise and enable individual liberty. Wherever the state interfered it diminished liberty and weakened individuality. National insurance would burden and enslave the working classes. The aim of democracy was not to work for the common good but to create 'perfect' men and women by training and educating the individual, promoting culture and raising their standard of living. The state should act as a moral guide for the poor. Stout was at that time preoccupied with the fear of a permanent parasitic class of paupers reliant on the middle class.

Stout did qualify this argument, however, in an interesting way. He conceded that 'in new countries – through want of historical associations, through want of habit of organisation amongst residents in new colonies – the State may have to step in and do things that it is not necessary in old countries that Governments should undertake'.[8] This concession opened the way for a much greater role for the state.

Stout maintained his laissez faire views as late as 1886, when he contended, in a parliamentary debate on unemployment, that the government had no duty to find work for the unemployed. His views then began to shift, as they did for many others, when the full weight of depression conditions bore down. A year later, in a sign of change, he acknowledged the necessity for Ballance's village settlement scheme to deal with unemployment.[9] It was the anti-sweating agitation in Dunedin shortly thereafter, and Stout's own role in attempting to find a means of dealing with the problem, that led to his acceptance of state intervention.

As the Liberal government was beginning to launch into its battery of reformist legislation in the 1890s, Stout was entirely at home in describing the extension of state activities that had taken place.[10] But there was still work to be done beyond the vision of Chartists and other early nineteenth-century reformers. The extension of democracy, free government and the abolition of privileges had not necessarily brought with it the expected benefits.

The employment contract

Certain elements of labour legislation were carried over from Britain to regulate the employment contract, and New Zealand also inherited the English common law relating to contract. (In general the English laws as they existed in 1840, when Britain formally claimed New Zealand as a colony, applied to New Zealand, but this was not clarified in law until 1858 with the adoption of the English Laws Act.) It was agreed that the state should remain 'even-handed' between employer and worker and not introduce draconian legislation supportive of employers. The understanding was that, in a civilised new-world society, labour and capital should negotiate fairly in the market place. It was a matter of ensuring the commodity status of labour.

The most obvious response by workers to unsatisfactory wages or conditions was simply to leave their employment, and this was a common and effective tactic in the early days when plenty of other work was available. As wage labour became a more durable presence, enforcement of the employment contract became an issue for the sake of both employers and workers. As the Reverend James Watkin of Waikouaiti complained in the early 1840s, there was a need to prevent 'Masters and agents from practising oppression towards their servants [and] servants breaking their engagements at pleasure'.[11] In Canterbury in 1851, little more than a month after the arrival of the first immigrants, J.R. Godley, the leader of the settlement, had to issue a notice enforcing contracts with employers, because workers were deserting them to work for the Canterbury Association.[12]

Employers and workers seeking redress could take cases to the resident magistrate courts for civil damages for breach of contract either verbal or written. Written contracts might be recorded as an entry in an account book or something similar, which set down the employee's starting date, period of employment and rate of pay, or they might be drawn up as a more formal contract signed by both parties and stamped in order to give it the status of a legal instrument.[13] (Contracts for less than a year did not have to take a written form.) Thus, for example, William Wintersgill agreed to serve the runholders Charles Clifford and Frederick Weld 'as Shepherd or otherwise as their Manager at the station may direct for the sum of Thirty pounds a year & rations. This agreement to be binding for 12 months & to commence from the date of arriving at the station'.[14] Edith Iremonger, recently arrived on the *Waitangi* in 1884, was engaged through the immigration barracks to serve Mrs Davies of West Eyreton as a general servant for £20 a year, to be cancelled at one month's notice.[15]

Enforcement of employment contracts was a commonplace part of nineteenth-century civil litigation.[16] Most such litigation concerned debt, breach of contract and wages due. In 1855 for example, Barbara Shand, employer, took John Wright, farm servant, to court for having left her service, breaking a six-month contract.[17] He was fined £10 10s and costs. On the other side of the ledger, wage earners were themselves prepared and able to use the courts to recover wages. Magistrates were not

NOTICE.

COMPLAINTS having been made that Labourers have broken their Contracts with employers, in order to obtain employment on the Works of the Association, Notice is hereby given, that in case any such complaint be substantiated, the labourers to whom it refers will be immediately dismissed.

JOHN ROBERT GODLEY, AGENT.

Jan. 21, 1851.

The Canterbury Association had trouble from the beginning in keeping its emigrant labourers working for employers. LT, 25 January 1851

Contract of engagement with Edith Iremonger for domestic service, organised by the immigration barracks. Kaiapoi Museum reluctant to deal with employers mistreating their employees. Employees won the majority of cases taken, justifying their confidence and indicating that the courts did not necessarily operate in the favour of employers. Maori workers were also able to use the courts successfully.

The following cases come from the rural sector but there is no reason to think that similar cases did not arise in other parts of the economy. In 1857 a farm servant successfully sued his employer, a sheep farmer, for wrongful dismissal and obtained more than £25. The employer had clearly failed to conform to the contract of employment. The following year John Sidey, employer, was fined £3 1s for assaulting John Gillies, labourer, by striking him on the shoulder with his whip while Gillies was working on the threshing mill. In 1863, in a case heard before the Supreme Court, another farm hand sued a farmer for the balance of wages due. He had been fired after he contested the employment of his two sons and daughter without pay. The jury found for the plaintiff on all issues and he was awarded the full £25 claimed. In 1865, Peter Naylor, shearer, brought a case against the Hakataramea station manager for £11 for shearing 1,100 sheep. He had been fined for bad shearing and not paid. He was awarded £6.

Beyond contract law, the Masters and Servants Act 1823, carried over from England, allowed masters to enforce proper service, and servants to claim wages due, based on a contract between the two parties.[18] The legislation was enforced from the early days of settlement but it was never used as a major means of disciplining the workforce. Early court records include a number of cases under the Act. For example, in 1842 three farm labourers on a year's contract were charged with breach of engagement with their employer during harvest, being absent after a day's holiday and then refusing to work. The court imposed a fine of £5 or one month in prison for each.

Australian states passed their own more draconian Masters and Servants Acts to replace the English one. New Zealand lawmakers also attempted to strengthen the legislation against a backdrop of labour market instability. In 1840 it looked as if the New South Wales legislation might be extended to New Zealand, as a modified form of the Masters and Servants Act entitled 'an Act for

Sir John Cracroft Wilson, Canterbury estate owner and promoter of Masters and Servants legislation. Parliamentary Library, Canterbury Portraits

WHAT MAY COME OF THE MASTERS AND SERVANTS BILL.

Original Question.—"THAT A DISOBEDIENT SERVANT SHALL BE IMPRISONED."   *Mr. Punch's Amendment.*—"THAT A MASTER, IF HE MISCONDUCT HIMSELF, SHALL BE LIABLE TO HARD LABOUR."

Cracroft Wilson, who came from India, found that ways of doing things in New Zealand were very different. Punch in Canterbury, *8 April 1865*

the better regulation of servants, labourers and work people'.[19] In 1856 W. Brodie tried to get legislation through the Auckland Provincial Council, saying that 'employers had been too long servants instead of masters'.[20] His bill, in which servants were liable to go to prison while masters could only be fined, was trenchantly criticised and rejected. The measure was called a 'White Slave' Act and considered not suitable for a free colony that had never been a penal settlement, unlike Australia, and where working men had the power to make just laws.

In the wake of the gold rushes many employers found themselves deserted by their workers and sought a way of binding them to their contracts more effectively. In 1863, in a letter to the *Christchurch Press*, a government contractor asked what redress he had for his workers walking out when they had signed contracts for three months.[21] In 1864 runholder F.T. Walker explored the possibility of a Masters and Servants Act in the Otago Provincial Council; a select committee recommended legislation but the matter was not taken further. Later that same year Sir John Cracroft Wilson, a Canterbury estate owner, introduced a Masters and Servants Bill into the General Assembly.[22] Again there was considerable resistance to the idea. James FitzGerald, liberal politician and the colourful and vitriolic editor of the *Press*, responded that he was completely against breach of contract being treated as a criminal offence; that was a remnant of a barbarous age and a 'great wrong and a great injustice to the working men'. In his view, labour was a commodity like any other and any breach should be a civil offence, for which there were ample remedies in the form of damages.

The bill was again introduced in 1865 by the Attorney-General, Henry Sewell, on Wilson's behalf. While not a government bill it did have substantial support in the House. The bill defined 'servant' widely and provided for imprisonment for up to three months for servants failing to fulfil their contractual obligations and for a range of other offences. Penalties were provided for harbouring or employing already engaged servants. A general provision enabled Justices of the Peace to make a summary judgement about any 'complaint, difference or dispute' between masters and servants, and to make an order or award, cancel the agreement, and impose a fine of up to £30. Servants were able to recover up to £30 in unpaid wages and could be compensated for 'ill-usage' or 'ill-treatment'.

The bill, like others before it, was roundly criticised for its draconian nature. FitzGerald suggested that the bill 'went back into the dark ages' and that it was only appropriate in conditions of slave labour. It was a 'shameful un-English bill' and 'so opposed to the spirit of the age, and so monstrously onesided and oppressive in its details'.[23] The vote on the bill's third reading was tied; the Speaker, David Monro, according to convention cast his vote for the status quo and the measure was lost. Although it was a close-run matter, in the end New Zealand refused to go down the Australian road. People were content for both employers and workers to have recourse to the old English legislation that gave some rudimentary legal backing to civil contracts.

Two kinds of wage earners were strongly bound to their employers by specific legislation – seamen and apprentices. In the early years ships relied upon the British Merchant Shipping Act, which applied only to British ships and subjects. The penalty for desertion was up to twelve weeks' imprisonment with hard labour, together with the forfeiture of wages due, clothes and other personal effects left on board.[24] Those aiding, abetting or harbouring deserters could be fined substantial amounts. The legislation was vigorously enforced, but at that time seamen on the many foreign ships escaped scot-free.

With desertion rampant, the Auckland Provincial Council in 1854 passed legislation to deal with seamen on foreign ships.[25] An attempt was made in Nelson to legislate similarly. In 1858, at the request of Britain, the General Assembly passed the Foreign Seamen's Act to enable prosecution of the numerous offenders. Many instances of prosecution followed, for a variety of offences including desertion, assault, pilfering, drunkenness, and refusing to obey or to

£6 REWARD.

THE above Reward will be paid to any person giving such information as shall lead to the conviction of any party or parties ASSISTING my SEAMEN TO DESERT, or for the APPREHENSION of any Seaman who may have so deserted.

J. CHERRY,
Commander "Sir Allan M'Nab."

Desertion of seamen was a serious problem in New Zealand. NE, 29 September 1855.

work. Prosecutions were taken under this Act and also under the Merchant Shipping Act and the subsequent Shipping and Seamen's Act 1877.

In 1851, for example, against a background of allegations of mistreatment, eighteen seamen from the *Travancore* were prosecuted by its master for refusing to work. The men were in the end delivered into the master's custody and their loss of wages and clothes waived.[26] In 1857 seven deserters from the *Solent*, who had been imprisoned in the Lyttelton gaol while the ship was in harbour, were ferried out to the ship as it left. In spite of the captain pointing a pistol at them they managed to snatch it away and escape from the ship in the harbour master's boat, not to be seen again. There were also cases in which seamen were protected by the legislation. In 1858 when the bankruptcy of a shipping company resulted in a failure to pay seamen's wages on the *Glentanner* the magistrate ruled that all wages must be paid.

New Zealand also carried across British apprenticeship legislation, such as that of 1766 and 1823 enforcing contracts. In 1855, for example, a person harbouring an apprentice who deserted his employer was prosecuted.[27] The magistrate strongly warned others against helping runaway apprentices. They were liable in the same way as those harbouring deserting sailors. This legislation was replaced in 1865 by the Master and Apprentice Act.

The new legislation confirmed the indenture of apprenticeship for a period of no more than five years and specifically extended the British legislation to New Zealand. Its main object was to prevent runaways, or other employers enticing apprentices away, in conditions of labour shortage. Apprentices who left their employ could be gaoled for up to three months.[28] But other provisions balanced the interests of employer and worker. Employers had to look after their apprentices' morals, ensure they attended church, and deposit sums in savings banks on their behalf. Apprentices could not be discharged or transferred without the consent of two Justices of the Peace, who were also to arbitrate on grievances. Masters who ill-treated or ill-used apprentices could be fined up to £10 and apprentices who breached their duty or were disobedient could be sent to gaol for three days.

Apprentices were also protected by the Offences Against the Person Act 1865. This dealt with employers who neglected to provide their apprentices

DESERTERS FROM THE UNITED STATES WHALING SHIP "MILO," IN AKAROA HARBOUR.

NOTICE is hereby given that any Party or Parties aiding either of the two Deserters from the U.S. Ship MILO, will be prosecuted with the utmost rigor of the law.

DESCRIPTION.

David George, 5ft, 7in., light complexion, blue eyes, auburn hair, beard under chin—native of U.S., aged 26.

William May, boy, age 18, hair bright yellow, eyes grey, very much freckled—native of Great Britain.

N.B. This boy is well known in the peninsula. £10 sterling reward will be given for their apprehension.

G. H. SOULE,
Commander.

Akaroa, Jan. 6, 1857.

Detailed descriptions of deserters would be published to aid their apprehension. LT, *7 January 1857*

Articles of apprenticeship for Arthur Johnston with Anderson's engineering, Christchurch, 28 April 1873. CM

or servants with food, clothing or lodging, or who abused them through physical assault. This legislation remained in effect until replaced by the Apprentices Act 1923.

An example of this kind of binding of master and apprentice concerned one Richard Turton, twelve years old and the son of a widow in prison, who was apprenticed in 1852 to Charles Clifford, runholder, for three years as a farm servant.[29] In language inherited from eighteenth-century England or even earlier, he was bound to serve faithfully, be obedient, inflict no damage on his master nor 'waste' his goods or lend unlawfully on his behalf. He was also not to 'fornicate' or be married, nor to play cards, dice or other unlawful games by which his master might suffer loss. He was not to buy or sell, nor haunt taverns or playhouses, nor absent himself from service. His master was to provide him with proper clothing, sufficient meat, drink, lodging, washing and other necessaries.

A later indenture of 1873, between Arthur Johnston and John Anderson of the Canterbury foundry, no longer had the same moral strictures on the apprentice's behaviour nor the requirements regarding board and lodging, but simply stated that Johnston should 'demean and behave himself as a good true and faithful apprentice' should. He was to serve 'faithfully, diligently and honestly' for five years, obey Anderson's lawful commands and not absent himself without leave nor spend or 'waste' his master's 'moneys, effects, goods, tools or chattels'.[30] Anderson was to train him and pay a wage that would increase over the five years.

New Zealand's labour market continued to be regulated by the common law of contract and these specific statutes. In the 1870s the booming economy, the shortage of labour, and the consequent increased assertiveness of wage earners saw a rise in the number of common law cases and in the use of the Masters and Servants Act.[31] Workers continued to experience success in claiming wages due, while employers were also able to enforce contractual obligations.

But as a more developed waged labour force emerged these limited forms of protection of labour no longer sufficed. Vogel's public works schemes brought to a head issues of enforcement of the wage contract. Brogdens, the British contractor engaged by the government for railway construction, had brought into the country some thousands of migrant navvies for the work.[32] The navvies, being unaware of the more favourable conditions in New Zealand, had agreed to work for two years at 5s a day with one-fifth of wages taken until the cost of passage and clothing was repaid. Upon their arrival they discovered that they were working for longer hours and lower wages than others.

Brogdens found to their cost that New Zealand law was inadequate to their purposes of holding their labourers to their draconian contracts, including repayment of the cost of passage to New Zealand. The contractor claimed that the government had assured them that the law of arrest for debt was effective and that they should limit their wages to prevent any disorganisation of the labour market. In a number of cases Brogdens shifted the men onto subcontracting works, which many navvies considered to be a breach of contract. Many went on strike to achieve an eight-hour day and better wages, and large numbers refused to pay their debts and deserted the works. They argued that Brogdens had breached their contract by bringing them to New Zealand under false pretences.

Before long three-quarters or more had gone. It proved impossible to recover the debts even though many were taken to court.[33] There were legal problems with the promissory notes; imprisonment for debt was at the cost of the creditor and it extinguished the liability to further imprisonment if the debt remained unpaid; and men escaped repayment by filing as bankrupts or by simply 'clearing out'. The company made strenuous and repeated efforts to use the Masters and Servants Act to prosecute the navvies and pressed hard for legislation that would strengthen its hold on them.

The government had little sympathy, having itself got into serious dispute with Brogdens over the nature of its contract with them. It argued that immigration was an integral part of the company's scheme and that the company had the responsibility for control of its workforce. The government ceased to pursue prosecutions over promissory notes and in 1874, through the Imprisonment for Debt Abolition Act, it repealed the provisions providing for arrest for debt.

There seemed to be more concern with the obverse situation – the ability of wage earners to recover wages, in particular from contractors who went bankrupt, absconded or avoided their responsibilities by means of subcontracting. The prevalence of contracting and subcontracting in the fluctuating frontier environment and on the many public works made the working man particularly vulnerable.[34] Businesses were often speculative and undercapitalised, there was a dearth of credit, and bankruptcy was common.

The Bankruptcy Act 1867 included the first provisions specifically protecting wage earners amongst other unsecured creditors. The wages and salaries of servants and clerks were protected for up to three months or £50, and the wages of artisans and labourers for up to one month. Wage earners could 'prove' debts beyond that. However, wage earners were not protected in cases of limited liability companies, nor when a contractor had not yet been paid and in which there was no 'lien' from which wages could be paid.[35] The Contractors Debts Act, based on a Victorian Act and passed in 1871 when Vogel's public works were taking off, was intended to remedy this situation. It provided a lien for wages due and dealt with subcontractors on the same terms. The Debtors and Creditors Act of 1875 replaced the Bankruptcy Act; it extended protection of servants and clerks to six months' wages or £100.

Dissatisfaction with legislation protecting wages heightened as the depression began to bite and bankruptcies mounted. In 1882 one MP attempted unsuccessfully to improve the Contractors Debts Act by extending it to piecework and labouring subcontracts; another private member's failed Bankruptcy Bill included provisions that doubled the period and amount that wage earners could claim from bankrupts.[36] The following year the government re-enacted the Bankruptcy Act and extended the wage provisions. All kinds of workers – artisans, labourers and those on piecework – were explicitly included, and wage earners could claim amounts greater than £100 if they could 'prove' the debt.

Protection through a lien remained important, particularly as public works contracting expanded during the depression years. Large petitions were sent to the government in 1883 but an attempt to pass such an Act, including provisions to attach wages prior to going to court, failed.[37] In 1884 A.J. Cadman successfully pushed through the Workmen's Wages Act, which repealed the 1871 Contractors Debts Act. It gave workmen (including those on piece-rate) the power to take out orders of attachment for wages and the first claim for up to 21 days' wages. It also stated that where employed by a contractor, wage earners were to have priority.

Premier Harry Atkinson. William Gisborne, New Zealand Rulers and Statesmen, 1897

In the late 1880s a number of MPs resurrected the lien issue as a result of the many depression bankruptcies. Private members' bills were introduced in 1888 and 1889. Atkinson's government drafted a Workmen's Lien Bill but it was not introduced.[38] Hislop followed this up with a Building Lien Bill in 1890, that had been discussed with the Otago Trades and Labour Council. Construction workers were a substantial part of the workforce and especially vulnerable to economic fluctuations and the activities of unscrupulous speculators. Their vulnerability had been of concern for some time. Although the bill was conceded as important, the government dropped it in favour of other labour bills for consideration the following session.

The Liberals recognised the importance of such measures, passing the Contractors' and Workmen's Lien Act of 1892. This gave priority to payment of wages in cases of debt or bankruptcy. Workmen could take out a lien against the land and property on which they were employed, while the legislation obliged the property owner to withhold a quarter of the sum of the contract for a month, to ensure that the contractor paid his men in full or to allow the men to take out an attachment on it. William Pember Reeves, who was then Minister of Labour, commented that this legislation was effective and helped reduce the affliction of speculators tendering at a cut price and then fleeing and leaving workmen without redress.[39] Reeves renewed efforts to protect those working for contractors, observing that the 1884 Workmen's Wages Act had deterred dishonest contractors for some time but that there had been a resurgence of such practices. A consolidated Workmen's Wages Act in 1893 extended protection of wages by including subcontractors and strengthening penalties and methods of obtaining wages due. At the same time the Liberal government introduced co-operative contracting on public works in order to eliminate the problem of subcontracting.

The modest forms of employment protection by virtue of common-law contracts had now been supplemented by substantial provisions protecting wages, particularly when wage earners were working for contractors or on public works. This reflected the centrality of these kinds of employment in the frontier setting and the inherent vulnerability of such workmen in depression conditions.

Workplace legislation

With the emergence of a more settled, urban and to some extent industrial workforce in the 1870s, politicians became concerned that old-world problems such as degraded working conditions, especially for women and children, would appear. This was a serious threat to the promise held out to migrants. The small but expanding number of factories attracted attention. There was concern that women and children might be found in coal mines, now being developed, and that the introduction of steam power in mines and factories posed new dangers. Eyes were cast back to English legislation, and to the state of Victoria in Australia, where manufacturing was more advanced.

The government was prepared to act (although historians tend to believe that little was done) but, as on a range of reforming issues, it took the initiative against little obvious organised opposition and in concert with little identifiable support. This makes its context difficult to gauge. It was left to individual MPs to press for measures almost in advance of the issues arising. We also have to be aware that some MPs went along with reformist proposals cynically – 'They can lead the public to believe that they are prepared to assist in carrying through

James Bradshaw, politician and labour reformer. Parliamentary Library, New Zealand Portraits, vol 2

measures proposed in the interests of the labouring class or the smaller settlers, and hostile to their own . . . laughing in their sleeves all the time at their constituents' – knowing that the Legislative Council would nonetheless defeat the legislation.[40]

Relative to the slow and small-scale development of mechanised workplaces in industry, we should acknowledge that the legislation enacted was significant, but mostly as a symbolic assertion that any threat of such old-world evils would not be countenanced. Moreover, the extent of enforcement was greater than is usually thought, at least in the area of greatest moral concern – that of women and children in factories.

From the 1870s, as steam power was adopted by industry and coal mines were opened, safety legislation was enacted. The explosion of a boiler at a quartz mine prompted a Royal Commission of Enquiry and the passage of the Inspection of Machinery Act in 1874.[41] This enabled inspection and certification of boilers and steam-driven and water-powered machinery, and its fencing and guarding, as well as preventing the employment of young persons around machinery.

The same year, 1874, the Regulation of Mines Act was passed.[42] Donald Reid, who drafted the bill, urged the government to act along the lines of the English legislation. The Act provided for inspectors, prevented the employment of women and young persons below ground, and stated that any accident would *prima facie* be regarded as owner negligence or defect in management, ventilation or machinery, and further that compensation for injury or death should be paid. The Act was not properly implemented, however, until a serious explosion at the Kaitangata mine killed 34 men in 1879. The legislation was then replaced by the Coal Mines Act 1886, which improved safety and ventilation regulations. Inspection was aided by the appointment of 'workman' inspectors, paid for by the miners themselves, to accompany the government inspectors and make independent examinations. These inspectors were probably first appointed following a report of 1887 into accidents.[43] Special regulations encouraging active miner involvement in safety issues were also gazetted.

In 1882 the first legislation providing workers with compensation for injury was passed.[44] Prior to this the English Fatal Accidents Act 1846 applied to New Zealand. This had allowed dependents to sue for the death of a breadwinner but suffered the considerable disadvantage that the negligence of others such as foremen or managers was excluded (known as the 'doctrine of common employment' or 'common servant rule'). The 1846 legislation was replaced by the Deaths by Accident Compensation Act in 1880, which gave a general capacity to sue whoever was responsible for the negligence that led to the accident.

The Employers' Liability Bill was introduced in 1882 by M.W. Green and received substantial support from the government, including advice on drafting. The bill was rapidly passed, with Bathgate suggesting that, 'if the House threw out the Bill the doors of the legislature would be knocked at by the working-classes

J.L.C. Richardson, Otago Provincial Superintendent and land and labour reformer. Parliamentary Library, New Zealand Portraits, vol 2

session after session until they got their demand granted'.[45] The Act provided compensation of up to three years' earnings for personal injury related to machinery or negligence by employers or those in the same employ. It included those employed by the government. Workmen had to take an action under common law in order to prove that injury was due to 'actionable negligence or other misconduct or default'. While workers were able to contract out of the Act, this legislation made the first dent in the doctrine of common employment (not completely abrogated until the Law Reform Act 1936).

Concern to protect workers against accidents remained. Vogel attempted to introduce state insurance for accidents in 1884 but the Legislative Council blocked it because some of its members were directors of insurance companies.[46] W.D. Stewart tried to amend the employers' liability legislation in 1888 and in 1890 to extend protection for workers.

Much of this early legislative endeavour concerned safety, but broader concern over working conditions also came to the fore in the 1880s, despite depression conditions. Politicians such as Premier Atkinson, whose ministries encompassed much of the 1880s, accepted the role of the state in ameliorating the situation. His position on the levels of need for intervention echoed that of the head of the civil service William Gisborne.

In 1888 Atkinson notably argued that, because industries had become established under the protective tariff that he had introduced, the government

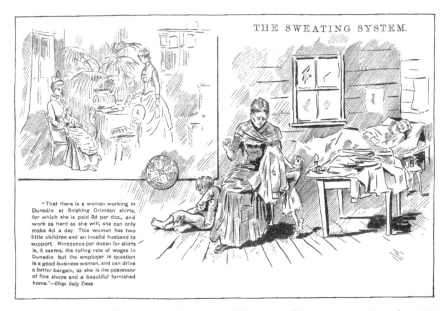

How the sweating problem in Dunedin was seen. Observer and Free Lance, *3 November 1888*

had a responsibility to regulate these industries and see that employers provided employment, that working conditions were regulated, and that workers were housed properly. 'As soon as factories begin to be established we shall have to determine that they shall have proper accommodation for the housing of their workpeople' and be located in the country so that there was sufficient air and gardens for workers.[47] This association of protectionism and state intervention in improving the state of labour foreshadowed the principles established under the Liberals.

Some attempts were made to improve the living conditions of those on farms and stations. Stout raised the matter in Otago Provincial Council in 1875 but legislation was not forthcoming.[48] A decade later Stout, now Premier, ordered the government's sheep inspectors in 1886 to include reports on the numbers of shearers and their accommodation. Unfortunately the returns of this survey cannot be traced and no legislative action was taken.

In 1873 the Employment of Females Act was passed to regulate the hours of females in factories. The measure was largely anticipatory in nature, as there were few females in what was a very small manufacturing sector at that time. Stafford nonetheless emphasised that it was 'the duty of the State' to interfere with the 'liberty of the subject' in this instance.[49] Women, lacking political rights and representation, defenceless, and properly fitted for their role as mothers, needed protection.

The legislation was introduced by James Bradshaw, a liberal reformer who espoused the interests of Otago miners, promoted closer land settlement, and urged the regulation of shop hours and an eight-hour day. The Act prevented

HUSBAND.—HIS HALF HOLIDAY.

WIFE.—WHERE IS HER'S?

The half-holiday movement closing shops was intended to protect female shop assistants; the cartoonist reminds people of women in the home. Observer, *29 August 1885*

females from working more than eight hours a day, gave them certain holidays, and appointed inspectors. It is widely believed, following comments by reformist critics at the time, that the Act was a 'dead letter', but as manufacturing grew from the late 1870s, the police took their duties as factory inspectors seriously and enforced the legislation more rigorously. There were official investigations, prosecutions and parliamentary reports.[50]

In the mid 1880s the Act attracted considerable attention as the movement against sweating began to gain momentum. At the 1885 Trades and Labour Congress Henry Hogg demanded more effective enforcement and annual parliamentary returns of inspection, while stating that 'there is no doubt the Act has benefited in a large degree a majority of the female employees, but still there is always the unscrupulous class to contend with'.[51] The government gave instructions to enforce the Act strictly and convictions reached a peak in these years. Bradshaw and others pressed determinedly on – they kept the issue in front of Parliament and attempted to broaden the legislation to include shops and even offices – but without success. In 1887 Premier Stout attempted to strengthen inspection but this was rejected by the Legislative Council, while in 1889 other improvements were discussed but were overtaken by the wider political events of 1890.

Restriction of shop opening hours had been long discussed but proved very difficult to implement. Early closing associations were evident in many centres from the early days of settlement, shop hours being a perennial concern for the liberal and philanthropically minded. In 1850 in Wellington, for example, the following notice was published. 'We the undersigned retail storekeepers, at the request of those in our employment, Agree . . . to close our respective places of business at 7 o'clock, p.m. Saturdays excepted, during the Winter Months'.[52] As one longstanding advocate put it, rather dramatically, in 1880, he was espousing the cause of the

> spindle-shanked shopmen . . . condemned to toil, within doors, amid a deleterious atmosphere, from 8 a.m. till 10 and 11 p.m., and in many cases, till midnight on Saturday . . . We can trace the seeds of disease and death in the very lineaments of their palid [sic] cheeks, trembling frames, and tottering gaits, as they wend their weary ways to their homes, after fourteen and even sixteen hours of continuous labour.[53]

Regulation caused deep cleavages in the retail community, which was riven by competing interests dividing town and country, different parts of towns, suburbs and town centres, trades, and large and small shops.[54] Once a movement got going and some merchants and shopkeepers became involved, a public campaign would be launched to bring in others less willing. This would often include boycotting of shops or attempts to persuade the public to shop only within approved hours. Although frequently successful in the short term, such campaigns always collapsed in the end due to the pressures of competition. Often it was the larger shopowners who wished to keep opening hours within sensible limits and restrain the worst elements of competition.

By the 1880s the movement was gaining in strength and MPs began to introduce legislation to regulate shop hours. In 1883 William Hutchison attempted to appoint a commission to enquire into the regulating and shortening of hours in banks, offices, shops and other wholesale and retail businesses.[55] M.W. Green unsuccessfully introduced a bill that made shop closing hours have the force of law if two-thirds or more of shopkeepers signed a memorial to that effect.

By the mid 1880s there were early closing associations in the four main centres but in spite of all the agitation voluntary agreements inevitably collapsed. In 1886 Bradshaw attempted to include seating for shop workers in his amendment of the factory

---

NOTICE

To the Inhabitants of Auckland and its Vicinity.

WE, the Undersigned, Merchants and Storekeepers of Auckland, having observed with pleasure the Early Shop-shutting movements at home, and considering that the hours of attendance at business in Auckland are by far too protracted, do hereby engage ourselves to close our places of business in the Evening as follows, viz.: Every evening during the week, except Saturday, at 7 o'clock, P. M.; and on Saturdays, at 9 o'clock, P.M., commencing on Monday next, the 1st May.

Gibson & Mitchell.	R. & D. Graham.
Gundry & McDonald.	J. Coney.
James Stuart.	Thos. S. Forsaith.
Joseph McCan.	W. Hughes.
Abraham Mears.	W. Clayton Hayes.
W. H. Monk.	Henry Hadlow.
Brown & Campbell.	Florence Gardiner.
Thos. C. Hallamore.	Rod. McKenzie.
W. S. Grahame.	Nicholas Simms.
David Nathan.	Richard J. Hunt.
Wm. McKenzie.	John Williamson.
James Mackey.	John Macfarlane.
John Woodhouse.	George Taylor.
William Gorrie.	

Auckland, April 28, 1848.

Early closing here was influenced by the movement in Britain. Shops would agree to common hours and publish their arrangements. Southern Cross, *29 April 1848*

legislation, and the following year Stout attempted the same.[56] John Joyce introduced the first specific Shop-hours Bill in 1887 on the grounds of the effects of long opening hours on women's health. Although the bill was rejected, Parliament was petitioned, surveys were undertaken by newspapers in support of the movement, and public pressure began to mount. Efforts to introduce such legislation were maintained under Atkinson's government. Hutchison in 1888 attempted to extend the eight-hour day to females in shops, and W.D. Stewart suggested amending the factory legislation to include retail workers and stipulate an eight-hour day, while Joyce continued to introduce Shop-hours bills.

SATURDAY HALF-HOLIDAY.
___
THE FIRST
PUBLIC MEETING
OF THE
EARLY CLOSING ASSOCIATION,
Will take place at
SPENSLEY'S HALL,
ON THURSDAY, NOVEMBER 2, 1871,
At 7.30 p.m.
___
HIS WORSHIP THE MAYOR
Will take the Chair.   11-1 5959
___
THE COMMITTEE
OF THE
EARLY   CLOSING   ASSOCIATION
will meet at
WHITE'S   HOTEL,
At 7.30 p.m.,
ON   WEDNESDAY,   NOVEMBER   1.
11-1 5960

Later on the early closing movement began to press for a Saturday half-holiday. Press, *1 November 1871*

But these expressions of concern remained the realm of the middle-class reformer concerned at the prospect of old-world evils being visited upon colonial society, and were largely expressed in the arena of Parliament. There was little organisation of factory workers, and in particular women, into trade unions at that time. As noted in Chapter 3 it was the unskilled male manual worker who engaged directly with the state through the unemployed protest movement. Such protest became a major threat to the social contract because of its direct association with immigration and the promise of plentiful work.

Relieving the unemployed

I will represent the people
When they wish to agitate;
And interview our ministers,
And workmen's cases state.
In the choicest of Queen's English,
I'll each argument commence,
And then I'll swill a pot of beer
At Tom and Bill's hexspense.
I'm considered influential,
And, of course am overjoyed
To officiate as spokesman
For the Dunedin Unemployed.

Second verse of the satirical 'One of the Unemployed'[57]

WORKING MEN

ATTEND a Public Meeting at the Odd Fellows' Hall, Lichfield Street, Christchurch, on SATURDAY EVENING, September 3, to consider the depression of Labour ; also, to find some means to relieve the distress prevailing amongst the unemployed and others in Christchurch.
On behalf of the unemployed,
W. H. BARNES.
Chair to be taken at 7 o'clock precisely.

At times of recession unemployed would meet. W.H. Barnes was a well-known organiser of the unemployed in Christchurch. In the 1860s he organised the Working Men's Association. LT, 31 August 1859

The labour market of the colonial economy was highly unstable, casual and seasonal, with underemployment as a feature. Periods of depression and immigration affected the labour market greatly; there were marked fluctuations in supply and demand locally and labour supply was difficult to organise. Underemployment became defined as 'unemployment' and a problem to be dealt with when it was sufficiently severe and stretched beyond customary bounds. Public works and unemployment relief policies – which were closely associated – became central features of the labour market in hard times.[58] The public sector, especially at these times, was vital to the economy as a whole, and it was particularly crucial in setting the conditions of employment, hours and wages, in addition to providing many thousands of jobs.

Following the New Zealand Company's attempts to provide its labourers with work in the 1840s (see Chapter 2), authorities recognised that it was right and proper for them to relieve unemployment. Provincial and national governments routinely provided unemployment relief by means of public works, which would be activated during the winter slack time and tailed off during the summer when farmers wanted labour for harvest. Specific relief works would be commenced in response to serious unemployment and agitation by the unemployed. This institutionalised the expectation of a government response in times of distress and made protest by the unemployed commonplace.

The connection between migration and the provision of work was made directly and forcefully. As the Dunedin unemployed proclaimed in 1885:

> We the undersigned . . . having been miserably betrayed by false representations of New Zealand by emigration agents, lectures and printed pamphlets, threw up situations, broke up homes and left loving friends, are now facing the bitter reality of parading the streets, hungry and ill-shod, with no prospect of a better future.[59]

One observer suggested that every shipload of immigrants was 'met by a howl of something very much like rebuke from the working classes. They are deemed interlopers. Dismal stories of unemployed hundreds are dinned into their ears.'[60]

By encouraging immigration, it was argued, the government should bear responsibility for the consequences, including relieving the resulting unemployment, shutting down assisted migration, and protecting local industries. The unemployed maintained that they:

did not come to ask this work as alms or charity. They thought they
had a right to approach [the Minister] . . . because they think that the
Government of the country has interfered with the labor market, and so
prevented them from getting that employment which they would have
had only for the undue influx of immigration.[61]

A massive Dunedin petition of March 1880 put it similarly: the government
had a 'duty to provide for the surplus Labor which they have brought into the
Colony.'

Wellington's Provincial Superintendent Isaac Featherston made this
abundantly clear at a time when the province's public works were to be cut:
'the Government is morally bound to give employment on the Public Works to
all who require it, and especially to afford such employment to the Immigrants
it has introduced.'[62] William Fitzherbert, Provincial Secretary, when challenged
on the existence of a guarantee of employment, reaffirmed that 'the Government
recognised that they were under a moral obligation to give employment to those
immigrants whom they had been instrumental in bringing into the Colony'.

In 1864 William Gisborne instructed immigration agents working
for the general government immigration scheme to publicise the fact that
immigrants would obtain accommodation and that the government would
'find employment for them during at least six months'.[63] And again, in 1870,
when Canterbury's provincial government had to enquire into the problem of
unemployment, the connection with migrants was a paramount consideration.
The unemployed were investigated to establish when and under what terms
they had come to New Zealand. One employer surveyed commented that if
employment could not be found, 'much loss, misery, vice and disorder
would be the consequence' and that the government was 'bound' to come
to the rescue and fulfil 'one of the most onerous and responsible of
all the duties that can attach to the exercise of public authority.'[64]

The bulk of wage earners (many of whom were recent migrants)
were unskilled and therefore vulnerable to underemployment and
unemployment. Skilled workers, by comparison, largely existed outside this
labour market and were able through craft unionism to regulate entry and
maintain employment. Unskilled workers lacked trade unions; instead
they could exert leverage only as a

WORKING MEN'S RIGHTS LEAGUE

—

M ASS MEETING

RE IMMIGRATION QUESTION,

To be held in the Arcade

THIS (SATURDAY) EVENING.

—

Chair to be taken at 7 30.

—

WORKING MEN,

BE SURE TO ROLL UP:!

*Working men felt concerned at the extent of
immigration when hard times threatened.*
EP, *9 August 1879*

Christchurch unemployed petitioned the Governor in 1880 for additional employment and a Royal Commission to investigate the situation. ArchNZ, IM4/1/2, 80/754

Unemployment was severe in the South Island in the early 1880s. Many wanted to go to the North Island for land. ArchNZ, IM4/1/2, 83/667 result of the fluctuations of supply and demand. When times were bad the unemployed appealed to the government to assist by means of mass agitation.

Vogel's 1870s immigration scheme was touted as a renewal of the spirit of colonisation that had been characteristic of the 1840s. Stafford specifically pointed to the similarity of Vogel's and Wakefield's schemes: 'Land, labour, and capital – that cry is older than many of the members who sit around me [and] are the three elements which are necessary for the creation and progress of any new country.'[65] Fox observed that few now 'still cherish on the altar of their hearts that sacred fire of colonization' as war intervened, settlements progressed and people grew comfortable.[66] He sounded the clarion call – 'the time has come when we should again recommence the great work of colonizing New Zealand . . . the object of the Government proposals is, if possible, to re-illume that sacred fire.'

The policy met with widespread support and was seen as the means of lifting the country out of recession. By the late 1860s the provinces were struggling financially and it was becoming apparent that the only way to break the deadlock was by national means.

Vogel's immigration and public works scheme precipitated a much greater involvement by government in the labour market.[67] The government's plan was to disperse immigrants into the countryside and employ them on massive public works schemes, which included building railways throughout the country and roading in the North Island. Stafford was concerned that migrants not simply be dumped on the country, and reminded Parliament

William Powell, unemployed organiser and on the Royal Commission on unemployment in Canterbury in 1885. Lightning Sketches, *Christchurch, [late 1880s?]*

PUBLIC NOTICE.
LABOUR EXCHANGE.

Employers of Labour and the Working Classes are hereby informed that an unpaid Board of Advice in connection with the Government Labour Exchange, Dunedin, has been formed for the purpose of extending its usefulness as a medium of communication between employers of, and applicants for, labour throughout the Provincial District. The Board will meet fortnightly for taking the state of the Labour Market into consideration, and so advising and assisting the Secretary in carrying out the objects of the Exchange as may appear most expedient. Forms of application can be obtained at the principal Post Offices, Telegraph Offices, Railway Stations, and Police Offices, and be posted free of charge to the Immigration Officer, Dunedin, who will supply the class of labour applied for, if available, with the least possible delay.

Persons wanting employment are invited to communicate personally or by letter with the Immigration Officer.

JOHN HISLOP,
Chairman.

From 1870 Otago established a labour exchange to assist with the labour market. ArchNZ, IM4/1/2

that provision of work was part of the contract that had characterised the colonisation of New Zealand. The government was also going to have to ensure that immigrants could become self-supporting and not 'receptacles' for the 'refuse population of large towns and cities'.[68] Without work, many migrants would soon leave again. Rolleston similarly argued that the government had 'interfered with the ordinary labour-market of the country by the introduction of immigrants' and that it should therefore deal with the consequences.[69]

> Billie Taylor was a stout old fellow
> Who never had worked and wouldn't now.
> The Government, he looked upon it
> As a sort of milch cow.
>
> Billie's chum formed a deputation
> And wrote out all he'd got to say
> Proving to his own satisfaction
> No man can live on six shillings a day.
>
> 'This here Government ain't fit for
> Them who isn't fond of work,
> We'll upset it and provide one
> Who will help a man to shirk.
>
> What they calls that law of nature,
> Which we thinks a precious cheat,
> That a man who will not labor
> Likewise also shall not eat.'
>
> This they carried 'midst loud cheering,
> Which ought to put his Honor [the Superintendent] in a funk,
> And then the greater part of the meeting
> Finished the day by getting drunk.
>
>   Selected verses of 'Billie Taylor', about a well-known Wellington agitator,
>   satirising his efforts to obtain relief work[70]

A very substantial public sector workforce rapidly developed, initially for construction works and then to operate the railways. This made the government the largest employer in the country and meant that (as discussed in Chapter 3) its own employment and wage-setting policies became the focus of attention.[71] Into the 1870s a workforce of several thousand was employed on public works and by the late 1870s, as railway lines were opened, the numbers of operating staff expanded rapidly.

Governments had always carefully monitored the labour market to regulate the immigration flow according to the needs of the economy and in response to unemployment. Public officials now began to co-ordinate the labour market as part of their responsibilities.

This began with provincial initiatives. By the late 1860s provinces had to confront an emerging problem. The economy went into a serious recession and public works were cut back. In 1870 there were serious demonstrations by the unemployed in Canterbury and Otago and investigations were made into the problem.[72] Employers petitioned the Otago Provincial Council to establish a labour bureau as part of its responsibility to migrants. The *Otago Witness* complained: 'Government has nothing to do with the emigrant after he has landed, but it is precisely at that point that he requires assistance. In these colonies he is left to shift for himself . . . there is no feature in our social system which more urgently demands attention.'[73] The provincial government in response established the first official labour bureau in the country, providing the forerunner of concerted efforts to control the labour market from the 1890s onwards through the Department of Labour. The bureau was later taken later over by the general government.

Immigration officers in the major provincial centres became vital co-ordinators of local labour markets in the 1870s and 1880s, both providing employment and organising relief works. Barracks and labour depots were established for immigrants to stay in while work was sought, and in some cases fares were paid for travel to employment. The officers placed advertisements in newspapers giving employers information about 'hiring days' and about immigrants and their occupations. They also collected information on the demand for labour by occupation, wages paid and retail prices of basic commodities, to send to the Agent General in London. This became ammunition to persuade others to emigrate.

In the early 1870s the labour market was very much in favour of the working man, as demand for all kinds of labour increased drama-tically due to Vogel's public works schemes. Wages rose substantially and the flood of incoming migrants was able to take advantage of this. By the late 1870s, as the impact of the immigration drive was felt and the

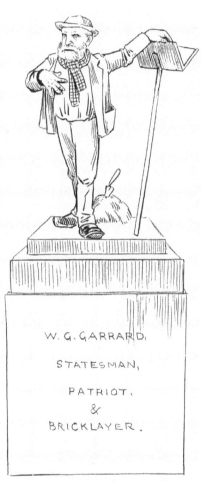

Facetious monument to William Garrard, organiser of the Auckland unemployed in the 1880s. Observer and Free Lance, *16 April 1887*

balance of the labour market tipped in favour of employers, some wanted to expand the state's role further and looked at the possibility of labour agents being licensed by the government. W.H. Reynolds wanted unpaid Boards appointed in each centre to act as a 'medium' between employer and worker. There was concern that commercial labour agents, who had a long history in the colony, were exploiting the unemployed.[74]

Premier Atkinson became increasingly alarmed at the state of the labour market and the emergence of unemployment. By the end of the 1870s the government was forced to introduce relief railway construction on a large scale, employing up to 2,500 workers.[75] But in the early 1880s, large-scale relief works were wound down as the government felt that its intervention unbalanced the labour market and induced dependence amongst the unemployed. Direct organisation of the unemployed on relief works was to be replaced by letting small contracts. As men were laid off the government made sure that the labour market could absorb the influx and that government relief work was not affecting wage rates in the private sector. But it was conceded that 'although the Government are not bound to make work for the unemployed, it is now universally agreed that it is one of their functions to relieve destitution.'[76] Unemployment relief was increasingly provided by local authorities, with immigration officers acting as organisers and co-ordinators.

A cry for land went up amongst the unemployed at this time. Thousands needed to be settled on huge blocks of land. It was said: 'It seems to me the only place suitable to gather all the unemployed of New Zealand, and save them from idleness'. If warnings were not heeded, 'such a cry of distress will arise as will require more spoon meal than mere Public Works or passages to settlers'.[77]

> Land of mountains in the ocean
> Plainly shows what it should be.
> Strongly marked is Nature's motion
> Of a great land for the free.
> But now the country reels and groans
> Beneath the burden of its loans.
> And sheep on ev'ry side we see
> Where happy homes ought for to be;
> While working men, honest and true,
> Walk about with no work to do.

Verse cited in *Jubilee Farms* (1888)[78]

Canterbury working men, denied access to land and experiencing serious unemployment, demanded that the government pass legislation so that they could settle many thousands in areas opened up for settlement in Taranaki, such as the 'Waimate Plains'. In 1879 a 'Waimate Plains' Co-operative Land Company was formed in Christchurch.[79] Rolleston, not wanting to ship the unemployed north, did not encourage the movement and the planned

AND THE

REMEDY.

During the depression there was much concern at the extent of unemployment. Pamphlet by Gavin M. Park, 1886

settlement failed to get off the ground. In line with his self-reliance philosophy he considered that it was better to encourage co-operative societies to purchase land than for the government itself to repurchase estates or to create village settlements. Others argued that such organisations merely pushed the price up. It appears also that there were strong differences between those who favoured individualist deferred payment and others who wanted co-operative settlement associated with public works.

The broader role of public works in employment maintenance remained through continued expenditure on more 'reproductive' public works (works not just to relieve the unemployed) through the letting of private contracts, particularly for railway construction in the South Island. Some 2–3,000 men continued to be employed by both the government and private contractors on railway construction during the 1880s.[80] Atkinson explicitly tied the need for additional loans to continued employment for up to 3,000 labourers.

The Stout-Vogel government expanded public works, particularly in Canterbury and Otago, to try to borrow its way out of the depression. This was accompanied by heightened and widespread agitation to force the government to provide relief. The numbers employed rose to almost 4,000 in 1886.[81] Relief work spread to the North Island and the government began to pay to shift the unemployed around the country.[82]

Agitation also led to the appointment of a Royal Commission on unemployment in Canterbury in 1885, and in the same year Ballance introduced the homestead village settlement scheme for the urban unemployed (discussed in Chapter 2). In the wake of the commission and Ballance's scheme, settlement of the unemployed on the land by

MR J. E. MARCH will receive applications at the Immigration Office from persons out of employ, or others who are desirous of settling on land, and give them full information as to the localities and terms of the land which the Government offer.

JOHN H. BAKER,
Commissioner Crown Lands.
Land Office, Christchurch,
March 4, 1886.   7594

Canterbury Immigration Officer J.E. March helped organise the unemployed onto the land. LT, 5 March 1886

co-operative means again received public attention.[83] Rolleston publicised the advantages of co-operative land associations and extolled the activities of the Canterbury Co-operative Freehold Land Association, whose object was to purchase or acquire blocks of land.

Grey gave voice to the importance of the social contract in dealing with unemployment. In his view it was 'the duty of the State at large, under such circumstances, to provide labour for the people thrown out of employment' and this should be for fair wages.[84] William Pember Reeves argued similarly that the unemployed should get work at market rates: 'The unemployed do not occupy the position of paupers who are waiting for charity. They are demanding that which has been promised them from the first. They are entitled to get the work at a price that is commensurate with the general price of labour.'[85]

But with retrenchment a necessary priority, this was extremely difficult. Public works were cut right back when Atkinson was re-elected in late 1887. The government's inability to honour the social contract resulted in working men voting with their feet and leaving for Australia in what became known as the 'exodus'; from the mid 1880s substantial numbers left the country.[86] This was a fundamental challenge to the colonists' utopian vision of New Zealand society – an issue which would soon be addressed by extending government intervention.

The colonial state undertook a range of measures in the interests of labour. From the outset it protected labour and its commodity status and refused to entertain draconian measures favouring employers. Over the decades the 'duty of the state' began to extend beyond such enabling legislation to more protective measures, and to unemployment relief as the social contract was threatened by depression. The state began to regulate the wage relationship more strongly and established extensive public works schemes. Meanwhile, New Zealand's viability as a migrant-founded society was threatened by the exodus of workers to Australia, which became a galvanising issue for a reassertion of the social contract in a new form.

There would be renewed efforts to ameliorate unemployment, both by strengthened tariff protection for manufacturing and by a new government agency intervening in the labour market. Land legislation and village settlements would be revisited to facilitate the movement of small settlers and workers onto the land. The place of the wage earner would be acknowledged by extended legal recognition of trade union organisation and protective labour legislation to eliminate sweating. These policies would come together in a powerful and concerted form with the Liberal government of 1891. The developing association of the emerging labour movement with liberalism in the 1880s became a close relationship with the government in the 1890s.

CHAPTER 5

The social laboratory – rebuilding the contract

Though young they are heirs of the ages,
Though few they are freemen and peers,
Plain workers – yet sure of the wages
Slow Destiny pays with the years.
Though least they and latest their nation,
Yet this they have won without sword,
That Woman with Man shall have station,
And Labour be lord.

W.P. Reeves – 'New Zealand' (fourth verse)[1]

Following the late-nineteenth century depression and the exhaustion of efforts to secure closer settlement on the land, the methods used to deliver the promised good life to immigrants, and increasingly to settled residents, changed dramatically as New Zealand left its colonial origins. This was signalled in the shift from a 'landed laboratory' to a 'social laboratory' around the turn of the century. Reeves' poem 'New Zealand' starkly stated that 'labour' would reign in egalitarian and democratic New Zealand. But how was labour to be lord? For this to occur a renewed effort was required of the state to rebuild the social contract.

Atkinson commenced this project in the late 1880s and it was accelerated and completed by the Liberals in the 1890s and beyond. The renewed contract moved beyond land and towards a recognition of the interests of wage labour specifically. Now the state made a fundamental commitment to maintain and improve the living standards of those wage earners already in the country. Immigration receded in importance and as the older commitments faded the state considered new elements of living standards – stability and security of the wage, provision of shelter, and provision for old age. The state made a concerted effort to protect the wage earner against exploitation and unemployment by passing a range of labour legislation and establishing a Department of Labour, while land policy shifted dramatically as the focus became the landless wage earner and eventually turned into state assistance with housing instead.

THE POLITICAL JUPITER AND THE LESSER DEITIES.

Would the election of 1890 resurrect the high-flown ideals of Grey from the late 1870s? The cartoonist thinks not – but he was wrong. Observer and Free Lance, *4 October 1890*

The concept of egalitarianism began to change, from the state enabling an equality of opportunity to the state regulating a redistribution towards the needy.[2] Policy shifted in emphasis, from maximising opportunities in order to improve status, towards protecting and securing an existing position. The process was a slow and incomplete one, and the Liberals (1891–1912) combined elements of both approaches, as manifest in advances to settlers on the one hand and labour legislation and the arbitration system on the other. The shift became consolidated only with the victory of Labour at the polls in 1935 and the establishment of social security (see Chapter 6).

In 1891 the Liberals came to power against the background of more than a decade of depression, continual protest by the unemployed, the politically damaging exodus and the Maritime strike. They adopted a wide range of policies to address the exodus and to protect workers' standard of living. These policies included statutory protection of the wage earner, dealing with the unemployed, a refusal to reopen assisted immigration (which had been shut down during the depression), the tightening of anti-asiatic immigrant measures, a renewal of closer settlement initiatives and attacks on larger estates, and strengthened protectionism through tariffs.

The Liberals were strongly influenced by the image of a new-world ideal society that was seen to exist before the advent of large-scale industry and cities. New Zealand offered a society in which individuals should be able to get on through qualities of industriousness and frugality, but this promise was being denied. Old-world evils of landed monopoly, poverty and sweating threatened; a greater degree of state intervention was required than older laissez faire liberalism felt was appropriate.[3] The Liberals, in developing the powers of the state, attempted to transcend sectional interests and class-based politics and build on the concept of the 'people', the community as a whole, in which the state embodied the national community. While deriving in part from the currents of New Liberalism in Britain, this approach also drew strength from previous colonial liberal interventions.

In various ways the image of old-world evils was such a powerful influence on policy that it obscured the fact that New Zealand was substantially different from Britain. The city was regarded as the repository of these evils, but substantial urban centres hardly existed in New Zealand by the standards of other nations, and had not significantly increased as a proportion of the population in the latter part of the nineteenth century.[4] Considering urban populations as 5,000 people or more, the urban population remained relatively static at around only a quarter of the total population between the censuses of 1874 and 1901. The British Fabian concept of an 'industrial army' strongly influenced the thinking of Reeves, Edward Tregear and the Department of Labour even though the labour force was dispersed through the country in a multitude of small workplaces, often outside urban settings. Concern over the pauperised and marginal unemployed population (called the 'residuum' in Britain) translated into the alarm felt over unemployed protest and a 'moral panic' over the shiftless and unemployed swagger. The British anti-sweating movement was applied here to an economy with very little industry. But it was small matter that the New Zealand economy and society was very different – it was the fear of what might happen, rather than the reality, that motivated policy. A few indications of an emerging problem were sufficient to justify draconian solutions.

From land to labour settlements to workers' dwellings

Was settlement on the land still the ultimate solution, or should the state find other means of honouring the contract? By the 1880s what previously had been a single issue of settlement of working people on the land began to separate into two strands. It took two or more decades for this to be fully expressed. Meanwhile New Zealand was influenced by the British utopian 'back to the land' movement, as translated into the more practical expressions of village settlements, the state farm and workers' hamlets.

The government began to provide small subsistence holdings for wage earners, not to settle them on the land so much as to deal with unemployment and to provide labour for farmers, public works and other employers in the countryside. Then the holdings provided shrank and were located closer to the towns and cities as land became seen even more as a supplementary backup to the wage. Eventually the association of land and labour was broken at the turn of the century when the concept of 'workmen's villages' was transformed into that of 'workers' dwellings'. Before long New Zealand would base its claims regarding its enviable standard of living upon a high level of home ownership rather than the ability to own land.[5]

John Ballance, Liberal Premier and promoter of land reform. William Gisborne, New Zealand Rulers and Statesmen, 1897

The election of 1890, although dominated by land reform, presented a confused picture.[6] Atkinson seemed radical – he resurrected Rolleston's perpetual lease without right of purchase and suggested that the state could compulsorily resume land. McKenzie, although advocating a land tax in preference to the property tax, was surprisingly cautious in his pronouncements, while Ballance revived his land acquisition proposals in the context of a sweeping land reform programme, talking about the nationalisation of remaining crown lands, a graduated land tax and no further freehold land sales.

HOW TO STOP THE EXODUS OF WORKING MEN.

Premier Atkinson should get rid of the property tax and rejuvenate industry to stop the exodus from New Zealand. Observer and Free Lance, *17 August 1889*

The result of the election remained uncertain until Parliament assembled. The Liberals became the government after defeating Atkinson in the House early in 1891 and brought in reforms that were the denouement of land policy.[7] The matter at issue was the leasehold – would it be a perpetual lease, as Rolleston argued for in the 1880s and as Georgites and single taxers demanded, or would it be something less, as McKenzie and those who attempted to straddle the leasehold/freehold divide advocated?

The weight of several decades of agitation and the many experiments concerning land disposal and closer settlement culminated in two pieces of legislation. McKenzie's 1892 Land Act resolved the tenure controversy by a clever sleight of hand – the lease-in-perpetuity – that drove down the middle of the leasehold and freehold proponents. While technically a form of lease it was freehold in all but name. The freehold had won the long battle.

The Land for Settlements Act, passed in the same year, enabled voluntary repurchase of estates by the government. McKenzie kept the pressure on to make this compulsory and this was achieved in 1894, alongside another piece of legislation that did much to open up Maori land in the North Island for purchase. The compulsory repurchase provisions were not greatly used. Many large landowners were willing to subdivide and sell either to the government or on the private market. However, this measure, along with the land tax (see below), was a hugely successful political move. This was evident in the purchase of the Cheviot estate by the government.

As industrial conflict worsened in 1890 concern was expressed that New Zealand should avoid the class warfare of Britain. Observer and Free Lance, *26 July 1890*

Seddon precariously straddles the freehold/leasehold divide. Observer and Free Lance, *23 September 1905*

Ballance's village settlement concept of the 1880s was transmuted into two distinct policies. First, in the late 1880s the concept of the 'village' became translated into the 'labour settlement', in which plots of up to 50 acres, close to towns, were intended to provide supplementary backup to the wage when the worker was unemployed. However, it proved difficult to find cheap land adjacent to the towns, and only 52 people were settled on 1,500 acres on this basis.[8] Second, in 1894 the Liberals replaced village settlements with the improved farm settlement scheme, providing lots of 10 to 100 acres. This finally recognised that the areas of land allocated previously had simply been too small and that in many districts no outside work was available to sustain smallholders.

This concept of backing up the wage on the land was also expressed in the Department of Labour's state farm in the 1890s.[9] In the original plan the unemployed were to be provided with work on a number of farms established by the government – a reflection of international interest in 'labour colonies'. One such farm was established on the outskirts of Levin, but it was never large enough to make a significant impact on the many unemployed and was vociferously attacked by the Opposition in Parliament before being wound up.

Also in the 1890s, Secretary of Labour Edward Tregear and the Department of Labour assisted in establishing worker allotments in hamlets close to cities. The idea was that the workers would commute into town for wage work but still be able to sustain themselves from their allotments when unemployed. In 1896 the Land for Settlements Act was amended specifically to allow the government to assist workmen into homes in or near towns. Progress was slow but hamlets were eventually established in Christchurch, Wellington and later in Auckland. By the early years of the twentieth century the policy was no longer actively pursued but there had been some moderate practical achievement. In terms of the general shift, workmen's hamlets were but another step towards severance from the land.

The break from the land came with the passage of the Workers' Dwellings Act in 1905. This pioneer state-provided worker housing scheme, administered by the Department of Labour, arose from the Liberal government's commitment to protecting living standards.[10] Tregear had specifically highlighted the effect of rising rents upon wages and argued that the arbitration system needed to be supplemented by worker housing. At the same time there was concern, particularly in Auckland, about slums, overcrowding and insanitary conditions as the country feared an outbreak of the bubonic plague. Drawing upon the British approach, the workers' dwelling scheme was to be self-financing – there would be no subsidy, and the government should not make a loss on the scheme. The theory was that the provision of good-quality government housing would, by adding to the housing stock, force down private-sector rents and thus reduce the cost of living. Workers would not need increased wages, thereby benefitting employers and lessening inner-city overcrowding. This

Why not advertise New Zealand as a country in which people can get 3 acres and are presented with a cow? Graphic, *28 January 1893*

approach was to characterise the state's house construction policy into the mid twentieth century.

The government's requirement both to recover the cost and build dwellings of reasonable quality meant that the scheme catered to the better-off, to the skilled artisan 'aristocracy' of labour. Some 643 houses were built in the period 1906–19. Before long there was pressure to convert the scheme into mainstream home ownership; in 1910 the freeholding of the houses by tenants was made much more attractive. The workers' dwelling scheme was reactivated after the First World War but, because of postwar shortages of materials, only 395 houses were built between 1919 and 1923 (with a further 107 purchased). The scheme had made a moderate impact, but more importantly it provided a model for the first Labour government to follow from the late 1930s.

The Advances to Settlers Act 1894, initially intended to aid a move onto the land, ended up assisting more workers into housing than the workers' dwelling scheme ever did. New Zealand historically relied upon high levels of borrowing to finance development. But government policy, as we have seen in Chapter 3, favoured savers rather than borrowers. The high interest rates and lack of access to credit that had characterised the deflationary long depression, and continued for some time afterwards, provoked popular discontent and caused widespread

'Bhoys, this is the castle that Dick built for me'. Government policy moves away from the land and towards settling workers in their own cottages. Observer and Free Lance, *31 October 1896*

agitation amongst farmers and wage earners. By the 1880s a powerful movement for cheap credit had arisen in the country and financial institutions were attacked for their monopolistic exploitation. Cheap credit became a central issue in the 1893 election, as the Liberals' land and taxation policies (which favoured the leasehold and not the mortgaged freehold) exacerbated the situation, while Crown tenants lacked the security for attracting private sector financing.[11] These problems were in the minds of Ballance, McKenzie and Seddon when they developed the lease-in-perpetuity, which offered more security for loans.

In the decades around the turn of the century the government began to provide cheap credit and its policies reduced interest rates. Mortgage interest rates, which had been 8 percent or higher prior to 1880, fell to 7 percent by 1890 and then to 5 percent by 1900, due to the government subsidising lending.[12] The traditional view is that this government intervention was made necessary by the failure of private mortgage provisions, high interest rates and a shortage of credit. More recently, however, it has been argued that the shortage was itself largely created by the Liberal land and tax policies, and that the government then filled the gap that it had unwittingly created. In any case, advances to settlers played a crucial role in making housing available to workers.

"WHEN   A   LITTLE   FARM   WE   KEEP."

This cartoonist used the Department of Labour's state farm as a metaphor for the fiscal underpinnings of Liberal policies. Graphic, 21 January 1893

In the first decade of the twentieth century, the advances to settlers policy was extended to homeowners to provide longer-term mortgages at interest rates below market levels. The subsidisation of borrowers was funded by taxpayers, in meeting the cost of government borrowing internationally for deficits, and also by those saving, who now received low or even negative returns. Saving was discouraged and the demand for credit tended to exceed available funds, while government debt could be financed internally at below market rates.

Thus the nineteenth-century emphasis on thrift and self-reliance (supported by appropriate savings institutions) was abandoned, to be replaced by state provision of lending facilities. The route towards property, that had been mapped out by accumulated savings from high wages, was supplanted by borrowing at low interest rates. The functional role of employment also shifted, from maximising opportunities to improve one's status, towards providing the means of paying off loans and gaining security for the wage earner by home ownership.

In 1906 Ward passed the Advances to Workers Act, enabling government to lend to workers at favourable rates so they could build their own homes. Many more houses were built as a result than under the workers' dwellings scheme. Ward strongly encouraged the lending policy over direct construction of housing.[13] In the period before the First World War more than 10,000 loans, totalling nearly £3 million, were authorised. The rate of loan takeup declined during the war but increased again during the housing boom of the 1920s. The government continued to favour loans over direct construction of housing. In 1923 the scheme was liberalised and was greatly taken advantage of in the latter half of the 1920s, before the numbers of loans declined to a very low level during the depression. By the end of the 1920s, nearly 40,000 loans for more than £21 million had been made under the scheme.

Government policy had emphatically shifted from land and savings to housing and borrowings in this period. Access to housing replaced access to land. This was associated

The success of the Advances to Settlers scheme created business for lawyers. Observer and Free Lance, *31 August 1901*

with the increasing urbanisation of the wage earner and a growing recognition that the wage-earner status was relatively permanent.

The government's massive lending in the early decades of the century led to almost half of all wage- and salary-earning households owning their own homes by the 1920s. This was perhaps the highest rate of ownership in the western world. The Reform government consciously advanced the workers' property-owning democracy to counter the threat of radical labour organisation 'by setting up the State as an alternative and competing instrument of material self-advancement'.[14]

The Labour government's approach in the late 1930s would duplicate that of the Liberals, in expanding the housing stock through both loans and direct construction. What distinguished Labour's scheme was the volume of housing constructed. Over time, subsidy of rentals intruded into the market model, but in disguised fashion, until rentals were explicitly related to incomes in the 1960s. From this time on, state-provided housing was much more clearly related to welfare than to assistance for the broader labour market.

Halt to immigration

In the wake of the gold rushes of the early 1860s people began to see a threat to the kind of society they envisaged for this country. The most obvious indication of this was the mounting resistance to the immigration of Chinese. But it was also reflected in a wish to keep other undesirables out. The government wanted to prevent New Zealand becoming 'a cesspool for the convict population'.

In 1863 Parliament passed the Foreign Offenders' Apprehension Act to deport offenders crossing the Tasman. A bill to prevent criminals coming

THE COMING MAN'S ARRIVAL.

MR. PUNCH, AS CHIEF OF THE BOARD OF COMMERCE, RECEIVING THE AMBASSADOR OF HIS CELESTIAL MAJESTY THE
BROTHER OF THE SUN ON HIS MISSION TO OPEN NEGOCIATIONS WITH OTAGO.

Otago takes notice of the arrival of Chinese immigrants. Dunedin Punch, *28 October 1865*

over from Australia failed to get through the Legislative Council; some saw
the measure as excessive and extreme.[15] In 1867 the Introduction of Convicts
Prevention Act provided substantial powers of arrest and penalties, including
deportation and fines, for those bringing convicts in or harbouring them while
in New Zealand. The deportation legislation of 1863 was eventually (in 1879)
seen as ultra vires, and the government asked Britain to legislate instead.[16]
In 1881 Britain passed the Fugitive Offenders Act to allow offenders to be
returned to the country where their offence was committed.

At the same time, as some shiploads of freed New Caledonian French
prisoners arrived in 1880, New Zealand wanted Britain to act on its behalf
to prevent 'liberated Communists and convicts' arriving in the country.[17]
It also reacted against Britain's proposal to enable the transfer of prisoners
within the Empire for health reasons. This was seen as threatening a revival of
transportation. New Zealand was not to become a 'receptacle of the criminal
class' of another country.[18]

By the end of the 1870s the Vogel boom years had gone. In the latter half
of 1879 the government was forced to stop all assisted immigration apart from
single women, and in February 1880 New Zealand's assisted immigration
scheme effectively ceased.[19] A period of forty years of settlement premised
upon government-encouraged immigration had come to an end. This

YOU WANTEM KEPPEGEE.

*First Working Man : Bloomin' muffs, those Chows.   Hanged if I'd pay
£100 to land in Wellington.*
*Second Working Man : Strikes me Bill it's we working men that are the
muffs.   Don't they make us pay their poll tax ?   Arn't we their best customers ?*

Chinese were apparently happy to pay the poll tax while New Zealand workers complain.
New Zealand Free Lance, *5 January 1907*

signalled the beginnings of a fundamental shift. The social contract would
now focus on those here more than those arriving. Due to the perceived
association of immigration with unemployment and wage cuts, assisted
immigration would not regain much of a role for more than fifty years, and
even then it was contingent on economic prosperity and full employment
and was very vulnerable to the pressure exerted by interest groups. Large-scale
migration promoted by the state was no longer seen as a necessary dynamic
for the economy.

The impact of migrants on the country diminished in relative terms
as the resident population increased. In the 1840s immigration had been
incontrovertibly at the core of an emerging new society. During the height
of the Otago gold rushes in 1863, the immigrants of that year formed more
than one-quarter of the already resident European population; by the peak of
assisted immigration in 1874 the proportion was still about one-eighth; but
in 1893 when immigration reached another peak (by this time not assisted by
government) this represented only a few percent of the resident population.[20]
The relative impact of immigration was to decline even further in the twentieth
century. Furthermore, by the turn of the century the numbers of New Zealand-
born residents (although a very much younger population) substantially
exceeded those born overseas.

FAIR EXCHANGE IS NO ROBBERY.

During the exodus of the late 1880s New Zealanders left for Australia while Chinese arrived in New Zealand. New Zealand Punch, *12 May 1888*

This shift of emphasis away from immigration was reflected in the mounting hostility to arrivals from China. These policies are usually cast in terms of racism, but they do also reflect the kind of society sought in New Zealand and the extent to which groups fitted in.[21] Such policies derived from the cohesive community drawn from British migrant wage earners and founded upon settler citizenship. There was a belief, whether justifiable or not, that certain groups were a threat to employment and the standard of living, and that they were not assimilable into New Zealand's predominantly British-based culture.

The deterioration of the economy in the 1880s brought to the fore working men's and miners' antagonism towards the entry of Chinese, or 'asiatics'.[22] Victoria, New South Wales and Queensland had previously legislated to restrict Chinese immigration. A bill along the lines of the Queensland Act was introduced in 1879 but did not pass. Stout did not support it, arguing that New Zealand simply required good colonists; place of birth was not important. Richard John Seddon came forward at this time as the champion of white miners against the 'horde'. A more draconian private member's bill that prohibited entry outright was dropped by the government in 1880.

The issue was discussed with Australian States at an inter-colonial conference, where it was agreed that uniform legislation based on the Queensland poll tax legislation was required to restrict the Chinese influx.[23] In 1881 the New Zealand government passed the Chinese Immigrants Act. This introduced a £10 poll tax and a limit of one Chinese person per 10 tons of ship tonnage, and was to remain until 1944. The measure was explicitly justified in terms of protecting British civilisation and maintaining workers' standard of living, and was passed in spite of protests that the measure represented a surrender to working-class agitation.

Opposition to the Chinese hardened during the 1880s, and in 1888, following a panic in Australia over increased numbers, the government here restricted entry further by raising the limit to one person per 100 tons of shipping.[24] The House of Representatives and especially the protagonists of the working class argued in favour, while the Legislative Council opposed restrictions on grounds of racial equality.

There was a strengthening of anti-Asiatic immigration legislation under the Liberals. Reeves argued that the days of easily available land and labour shortages had gone, and that 'small industrious communities' such as New Zealand needed to be protected by the careful selection of immigrants that would assimilate into society. His argument is worth quoting at some length, for it spells out with great clarity the prevailing attitude.

Reeves saw the Chinese as having no commitment to New Zealand society – 'the men came, to be strangers and sojourners in the land, without families, without capital, without knowledge of the English language or English ways'.[25] They threatened competition, 'at once unclean, unnatural and unfair'. While industrious their civilisation suffered from 'arrested development', they were 'utterly unfit to use political rights in a democracy' and had 'no conception of government and public duty as these are understood in Europe'. He concluded that 'no fair national minimum of comfort and sanitation for labour is possible in any land where the Chinaman is freely admitted to compete in the labour market . . . the right of Australians and

William Pember Reeves – Liberal politician, poet and architect of labour reforms. W. Leslie, Parliamentary Portraits, 1887

New Zealanders to keep their soil for men fit to be free and self-governing is clear enough'. Reeves' general opposition to other undesirable immigrants came from similar motives. They tended to 'lower the standard of health and comfort'. He equated their exclusion with the prevention of unrestricted competition, sweating or child labour, and believed that such safeguards were essential so that 'destitution, crime, disease, and Asiatic labour' did not undo the work of colonial progressives. In his mind the threat to New Zealand's enviable status was stark indeed.

In 1896 Seddon introduced legislation (the Asiatic Restriction Bill) so draconian that it drew strong protest from the Legislative Council.[26] This legislation was intended to extend the anti-Chinese provisions to other 'coloured' aliens. The Act was passed but Britain refused to assent to it because of its overt racism; the British government preferred exclusion to be made on the basis of undesirable qualities of the person rather than overtly by race or 'colour'. Seddon, after considerable temporising, passed the Immigration Restriction Act 1899, based on the South African Natal Act, instead. The Act required all immigrants, except for those of British or Irish birth or parentage, to pass a language test. It allowed continental European migrants to enter, having passed the test, but largely prevented others.

In 1920 the government passed the Immigration Restriction Amendment Act, which substituted a discretionary permit system (for those not of 'British birth or parentage') for the language test. This discretionary and selective entry permit system was the mainstay of immigration policy until the mid 1980s, and has been described as New Zealand's equivalent of the 'white Australia' policy.[27]

Labour reforms

The Liberal government of the 1890s is better known for its progressive labour legislation than for its restriction of Chinese immigration. These labour reforms set the pattern of regulation of wages, working conditions and employment in the twentieth century, and they have been described extensively by historians, including the present author in his history of the Department of Labour, *Holding the Balance*, and associated articles. Rather than providing a detailed account of the reforms here, I will just highlight their significance to this discussion.

By 1890 – just before the Liberals assumed power – many of the issues of labour reform emerging out of the 1880s (and discussed in Chapters 3 and 4) had crystallised.[28] This year was a significant but little-recognised turning point in state policy. The Atkinson government did not lack the will to tackle labour issues; Atkinson consulted with the Maritime Council and introduced reforming legislation that at least anticipated and was in some respects more radical than the soon-to-be-introduced Liberal legislation of the 1890s.

The work of the Sweating Commission in 1890 reinforced concerns already promoted by MPs, particularly concerning workplace legislation, and shifted the legislative endeavour from private members' bills to overt government sponsorship of measures to improve the workers' lot. Cabinet Minister T.W. Hislop, an 'ex-Greyite' Liberal and 'a Radical in the Tory army', was in charge of the labour bills, which received priority by the Atkinson government.[29] In

Gumdiggers and the Truck Act. Observer and Free Lance, *8 August 1891*

addition to the crucial Factories and Shops Bill, the government had prepared a Shipping and Seamen's Act Amendment Bill, an Employers' Liability Bill and a bill dealing with 'truck'. Hislop also introduced a Building Lien Bill (see Chapter 4) but this was dropped in favour of the others. Many petitions supported the labour bills, and a deputation of labour leaders, including John A. Millar, leader of the Maritime Council, and John Lomas, West Coast miners' leader, met with Atkinson to discuss them.

But Atkinson was in poor health and his government was too weak to pass its radical labour legislation, especially with a Liberal Opposition that wished to hamstring the government in spite of its labour bills. The government's promise concerning the labour bills was honoured insofar as it could be. The Employers' Liability Bill was rapidly passed in the House but was blocked in the Legislative Council. The Shipping and Seamen's Act Amendment Bill, which protected the wages of seamen falling ill in port (seamen could claim up to three months' wages, until their recovery, if they were left behind through illness), also passed through the House but was blocked in the Council. It eventually scraped through.

For the first time there was a serious attempt to pass anti-truck legislation, half a century after such protection against exploitative trading to workers was introduced in Britain.[30] The Truck Bill specifically included those employed by government contractors on railway and road work, where the practice was common. The pioneering nature of the economy and the importance of truck in public works made it particularly difficult to legislate against.

> Buy up old stores for next to shice,
> And bring them on the ground;
> And put on them a tidy price,
> Say twelve bob in the pound.
>
> And when your man won't make a draw
> Of cash their grub to buy,
> Just give 'em orders on your store;
> You will if you are fly.
>
> And when the Saturday comes round
> For their fortnightly pay,
> Just bring them to the shanty round
> and keep out of the way.

Verses from 'How to Make a Contract Pay'[31]

Truck – the provision of food, other supplies and tools by employers as payment for work – was necessary for isolated farms and stations, bush felling, timber mills and public works out in the countryside, as workers were unable to travel to purchase necessities elsewhere. However, the practice was open to exploitation, and it understandably provoked great friction between employer and worker because of the monopoly of supply and alleged exorbitant prices.

THE POLITICAL TRUCE—GOVERNMENT AND OPPOSITION ARMIES FRATERNISE.

Ballance's Liberal Party fought Atkinson's exhausted conservative government to a standstill in 1890 – and as a result prevented much of its reformist labour legislation. Warring Generals Atkinson (left) and Ballance shake hands on a political truce. Observer and Free Lance, *23 August 1890*

Truck had been of concern since the early 1870s when large-scale contracting of public works took off.

The Trades and Labour Congresses of the mid 1880s drew attention to the practice, and abuses by public works contractors in the late 1880s prompted action. The Truck Bill was passed in the House in 1890 after stubborn opposition, but like the other bills it was killed in the Legislative Council.

The Factories and Shops Bill of 1890, applying to enterprises with half a dozen employees, was intended to repeal the Employment of Females Act. It signalled the beginning of a shift in factory legislation from the simple regulation of hours of females to the broader regulation of workplace conditions of all workers. The bill also regulated the hours of work in shops. It virtually created a new department and inspectorate and was much strengthened by the Labour Bills Committee. The legislation was even made applicable to one-person workplaces.[32] Debate finally began on the bill late in the session, but it was doomed; a few days later the session of Parliament came to an end.

The Liberals did not greatly emphasise labour reforms in their 1890 election campaign. Ballance himself was far more interested in land legislation. The major concern of the election was to re-establish stable and effective government. On the other hand, most of the urban candidates on Atkinson's side seemed to recognise the labour interest and supported the government's labour bills of the previous session.[33]

The long depression, the exodus, and the failure of charitable aid and temporary government relief to deal with the problem of unemployment caused many to rethink possible solutions. Reeves, strongly influenced by 'state socialist' and Fabian thinking, drew heavily upon the image of an 'industrial army'.[34] In Britain there had been a strong reaction against unconditional relief and towards the reform and regimentation of the unemployed. This was associated with revived interest in 'home colonisation' schemes, whereby the unemployed would be 'returned' to the land. Here too politicians moved towards the active organisation of the unemployed as part and parcel of the wider organisation of the labour market and, at least for Reeves, the organisation of society itself into an 'industrial army'.

Reeves, in the new Cabinet position of Minister of Labour, established the Department of Labour in 1891. This step was the direct result of the deep concern felt over the exodus of workers to Australia. The department was to deal with the unemployed and thereby keep people in the country; its activities built upon previous policies outlined in Chapter 4.[35] The department's labour bureaux sought to shift labour around the countryside and smooth out fluctuations in the labour market. As before, much of the work was to be provided by the government, and the co-operative contract system for public works, established under Minister of Public Works Seddon, institutionalised the relationship between the unemployed and the state. By these means the government also eliminated subcontracting, which had depressed wages well below a living wage. Co-operative contract rates were set at what were considered fair wages.

> Out of work! In lordly palace,
> With the millionaire's rent roll;
> Look for God's sake at your fellows,
> At the poor down-trodden soul,
> Who with muscle and with bone
> Seeketh work, but findeth none. . . .
>
> Out of Work! O would the wealthy
> But dispense with liberal hand,
> Then the cry of Communistic
> Would be heard less in the land.
> Would the wealthy learn to know
> Wealth has duties here below.

'Out of Work' (selected verses)[36]

From the mid 1890s onwards economic conditions improved considerably and the unemployment problem dissipated. The Department of Labour now largely acted as a labour agent for the Public Works Department, in a return to the approach of the 1870s, but now applying to a largely resident labour-force rather than to migrant newcomers.

There was a resurgence of unemployment in 1908–9 and concerns in the early days of the First World War, but there was little need to change the well-established nineteenth-century solutions of public works relief. The government considered the possibility of unemployment insurance and better developed labour exchanges but this was rejected (see Chapter 6). By the 1920s, with the collapse of the postwar boom, questions were raised about the means of financing relief and greater responsibility was given to local authorities but the system carried on much as before. The government continued to insist on providing relief work for wages rather than monetary relief. This national commitment to provide unemployment relief through public works persisted into the depression years of the 1930s.

The Liberals also picked up on the labour bills thwarted in the parliamentary session of 1890. The reformist legislation passed in the next decade or so would provide the framework for New Zealand's workforce for the next half-century or more. Their origins, as we have seen, lay in the concerns of the latter part of the nineteenth century.

Reeves took over Atkinson's Employers' Liability Bill and had it passed in 1891. It clarified the definition of workman, explicitly extended protection to seamen, improved the Act's administration and allowed a greater extent of compensation in certain cases. Under the Act, workers could continue to be employed while knowing of defects or negligence without forfeiting their rights, but on the other hand they had to inform their employers of such matters to be entitled to compensation; the Act also specified that they could not claim compensation for injury sustained by their own negligence. The same year, with little opposition, Reeves also passed the Truck Act, based on the 1890 bill.

Reeves separated out the factory and shop legislation and introduced them as separate measures. The Factories Act 1891, passed after amendment by the Legislative Council, was a compromise measure applying to workplaces employing three or more workers and was very much in line with the 1890 bill. The Factories Act 1894 provided the most comprehensive regulation, since it included the smallest possible workplaces by reducing the definition of 'factory' to two employed (including the employer). It also regulated 'sweated' outwork, and shearing sheds, following a specially commissioned national survey of shearers' accommodation that had shown the need for regulation.[37] This Act provided the basic framework for New Zealand's factory legislation thenceforth.

Shops were more difficult to deal with. The 1891 bill based on the early closing principle was blocked and a much milder Shops and Shop-assistants Act was passed in 1892, which provided for a half-day holiday, restriction of hours of females and children, and seating, but avoided the central issue of early closing. The half-day holiday proved a minefield and it was not until 1895 that a formula was arrived at that was reasonably acceptable to most parties.

The moral drive to protect women and children became less central as concerns over sweating receded and the Department of Labour uncovered little

William Pember Reeves' radical credentials. 'The working man as I found him – a slave. The working man as he is now – a free man'. Observer and Free Lance, *12 May 1894*

evidence of its existence. The department extended its powers to deal with the conditions under which the vast majority of (male) workers laboured, that were on the whole far worse than those for females.

In the early 1890s there were moves in Britain to abrogate the doctrine of common employment and prohibit contracting out. This meant limited employer liability for accidents. While the moves were ultimately unsuccessful they led to the passage of more comprehensive workmen's compensation legislation.[38] Following the Brunner mine disaster of 1896, Secretary of Labour Edward Tregear argued for a similar approach here, advocating an insurance fund to be contributed to by both government and employers, and administered by employers. This was against a background of scrutiny of private benefit societies provided by employers for their workers. The proposed scheme followed the German approach that involved self-regulation of industry and would not allow employers to evade their personal liabilities by paying premiums to private insurance companies to insure their workforces. This practice had led in some instances to employers deducting the cost of insurance from wages.

The Workers' Compensation for Accident Act was passed in 1900. The Act applied to workers earning not more than £5 a week, and to all forms of work apart from agriculture (unlike the British Act which covered only work seen as dangerous). In 1908 the Act was completely revised and the Employer Liability Act was formally repealed.[39] The Workers' Compensation for Accident Act remained the basis of New Zealand's legislation in this field until the Accident Compensation Act of 1972.

Concern for the working conditions of all workers was reflected in the consolidated Factories Act 1901. For the first time male hours of work were limited, and occupational safety and health provisions were improved. The factory legislation was now cast in a form that would persist until the second half of the twentieth century. Apart from very gradual reductions in the hours for males and females towards the forty-hour week (attained in 1936) there would be little change. New Zealand's industrial workplaces were now comprehensively regulated.

Improvement of conditions in manufacturing workplaces now lay in the hands of the inspectorate. The Department of Labour appointed increasing numbers of factory inspectors and extended its network into the smallest and most inaccessible workplaces as the organisation itself and the industrial sector grew.[40] With the establishment of a professional inspectorate and legislation that covered all factories, a flexible compliance-based strategy, that was well suited to New Zealand's small-scale, dispersed and diverse manufacturing workplaces, became strongly entrenched.

The waged standard of living

The Liberals were also known, of course, for the creation of the distinctive compulsory arbitration system that governed New Zealand's industrial relations for nearly a century. While the passage of the Industrial Conciliation and Arbitration Act in 1894 was prompted initially to prevent class warfare from emerging, its longer-term impact, through regulation of wages, was on New Zealanders' standard of living. At this point we need to look backwards to the place of the wage in achieving a standard of living in New Zealand in the nineteenth century.

By the turn of the twentieth century, the wage in its own right came to the forefront as the benchmark for the social contract. This had a long genesis going back to the earliest efforts of the New Zealand Company to entice migrants with promises of good wages and claims of one of the highest standards of living in the world. The standard of living was the ultimate test of whether migrant hopes and aspirations were realised and whether the country really was a land of opportunity.[41]

Some thought state regulation was getting out of hand. Graphic, *16 October 1897*

The prolific literature of the mid nineteenth century seeking to attract migrants by emphasising such benefits has often been noted. The many emigrant letters back to Britain are full of reports of high wages, plentiful, good and cheap food and short working hours, and from the earliest years it was asserted that the country offered superior living standards. The New Zealand Company itself encouraged and printed letters from labouring migrants back home that proclaimed these virtues.[42] The Company asked: 'Why should you stay here [in Britain] to work for wages which will hardly find you and your families in bare food, and sometimes to be out of work altogether?' Far better to migrate and work for good wages, and then own land and employ others. Thomas Kempton, an agricultural labourer who came out in 1840, wrote unsolicited that

> a poor man if industrious and sober he can save more money in three months than he can in 12 months in England . . . 8 hours a day is the time for labour and a man need not run after a Master, for the master will be after him, and pay him well for his work and neither Tax nor Tithe, we can eat the sucking-pig ourselves.[43]

Kempton became a successful settler in Greytown, one of the Wairarapa settlements associated with the Small Farms Association.

This perception was durable. The 1870s immigrants found themselves in 'a land of Goshen'.[44] They were paid good wages of eight shillings for an eight-hour day, and were soon able to save a few hundred pounds to buy their own house and become masters rather than servants. 'Happy toilers! Here is realised their dream of prosperity – "eight hours' work, eight hours' sleep, eight hours' play, and eight shillings a day".'[45] A good standard of living was found amongst all classes and working-class homes were models of neatness. What the land reform movement sought in Britain had been achieved here; New Zealand was an 'earthly paradise'. And even in the depths of depression in 1887 one politician still felt able to say:

> this colony is almost a paradise for the working-man . . . I say that there is no place on God's earth where the working-man is so well off as here. He has got his eight hours a day to work, and he gets, on the average, 8s. a day for that work. And, then, land is easily acquired in small blocks – land which will grow anything. His vegetables and meat are cheap; education is given to him for nothing; he has the suffrage – I might say, universal suffrage.[46]

An associated claim was that New Zealand provided healthier conditions than Britain, as a result of the good climate and the high standard of living and wages.[47] In the 1850s A.S. Thomson provided statistics, which were subsequently widely used, demonstrating that New Zealand's climate was healthy. In 1882 Alfred K. Newman came to the conclusion that New Zealand had the lowest death rates of any country. This conclusion was backed up by the work of George Leslie, assistant actuary for the Government Life Insurance Department and leading friendly society statistician. The low death rate in New Zealand was attributed to the high degree of equality, the absence of urban poor and overcrowded slums, good nutrition, selective migration, a temperate climate, and a large proportion of the population engaged in outdoor work such as agriculture rather than unhealthy factory work or mining. Modern demographic analyses conclude, for very similar reasons, that New Zealand had the lowest mortality on record in the nineteenth century and that this was especially noticeable in low infant mortality rates.

The collection of official statistics in New Zealand was guided by the wish to demonstrate not only that a civilised society was in the making but also that migrants could enjoy a superior standard of living. The Population Census was used to document the country's progress, while from the early 1870s the government commissioned its immigration officers to conduct specific surveys of wages and prices around the country in order to provide information to attract migrants.[48]

The earliest substantial (and much cited) estimate in 1866 of New Zealand's standard of living concluded that New Zealand's annual income per head was £78, compared to Britain's £25.[49] After adjustment for the substantially higher cost of living here (perhaps twice as high) and the distortion resulting from the gold rushes, the standard of living was still at least one and a half times that of Britain and higher than that of Australia. Such a level was to remain through the 1870s and 1880s in spite of depression. Indeed in this sense New Zealand remained a wealthy country until the turn of the twentieth century, and while the wealth was not entirely evenly distributed it was an egalitarian society compared to the USA or Britain, or even Australia.

But what of wage earners themselves? The fact that New Zealand had a high average standard of living but also lacked the extremes of other countries strongly suggests that wage earners were well-off. Ordinary labourers were paid up to 8s a day in the 1850s, about 6–7s in the 1860s and close to 8s again in the 1870s.[50] Rates fell to 6–7s during the depression (at a time of deflation) before rising to 8s or more after the turn of the century. Skilled rates were more stable, at about 10s a day throughout the nineteenth century.

This standard of living was supplemented by the support offered by co-operative means. A high proportion of wage earners were members of friendly societies and other similar organisations. More than half of the families in a Department of Labour survey of 1893 paid life insurance, friendly and trade society, or building society dues.[51] Another survey of 1910 suggested that about half of all families belonged to friendly societies.

In England, wage rates were far lower, particularly for the unskilled manual workers.[52] Unskilled wage rates were about three to four times higher in New Zealand during the colonisation period, and they were still more than twice as high as England's by the turn of the century. But in New Zealand there was a markedly lower differential for skill.

On the other hand, certain crucial elements in the cost of living, such as rent and clothing, were significantly higher.[53] The high cost of clothing in particular was of concern. Food was generally cheaper but tea, coffee and sugar were about the same price. Tom Mann in 1902 suggested that the decreased purchasing power of New Zealand currency required an increment of 25 percent over and above English wages to compensate.

The seasonal and unstable nature of the colonial economy also lowered the effective standard of living. The many itinerants in the workforce, a large proportion of whom were not married, incurred additional costs such as board and lodging, travel, washing, cooking, gathering firewood and water, and other activities around the household. Underemployment and unemployment were common, and substantially reduced annual earnings, particularly for lesser-skilled labourers and the large numbers employed in the building trades.[54] The average unskilled general farm hand not 'found' and on day rates lived a marginal existence. While shearers made a better living, their high earnings were not sustained throughout the year and costs were high for travelling, equipment and lost time due to bad weather. Despite these qualifications there is no doubt that New Zealand's wage earners on the whole enjoyed a good standard of living.

Eight hours

One element of this standard of living was the ability to earn a good wage in fewer hours than was the case in England. Attempts were made to establish and maintain an eight-hour day from the first years of the colony. The eight-hours movement flourished from the mid 1880s and was incorporated into the labour movement's pantheon in the 1890s, when the idealised origins of the eight-hours system became a metaphor for the goals of the labour movement in a new world society.[55]

The Australasian eight-hour movement was spawned by Chartism. The first issue raised by labourers and artisans landing on New Zealand's shores was the hours of work; this led to New Zealand's claim that it was the first to adopt the eight-hour day. The eight-hour day became a key selling point to migrants: 'the Immigration Agents sent Home took this motto: that in this colony the eight-hours system prevailed, and there was eight hours' work, eight hours play, and eight shillings a day.'[56]

The precise provenance of the eight-hour day is a little hazy but this is less important than its association with the arrival of the early emigrants. The existence of competing retrospective claims for the different settlements reflects the fact that diverse emigrants travelled with similar expectations. It is interesting that it was actually employers, such as Samuel Parnell, Thomas Burns and William Valpy, who were instrumental in establishing an eight-hour day. This illustrates the broad support for such initiatives.

At best the eight-hour day existed as a 'colonial custom' in certain parts of the economy, in particular in the craft sector. In a labour market desperately short of skills, artisans were able to impose their own conditions, but the eight-hour day could easily slip away in harder times. In many other sectors of the economy eight hours was never worked. Such was the case in farming, domestic work and in many other forms of work associated with the frontier and resource extraction industries.[57] In industry, males in woollen factories worked nine hours a day because of the need to work machinery longer, while thousands of men in the bush and timber mills worked ten hours.

Samuel Parnell, widely regarded as the founder of the eight-hour day in New Zealand. NZH, 11 November 1890

Efforts to maintain an eight-hour day became a vital part of the assertion of a better new world, if not its touchstone. In an early notable example

Samuel Parnell centre, flanked by others of the Wellington Eight Hour Committee. During the 1880s 'eight-hour' demonstrations were held in the major centres. The one in Wellington in 1890, in the wake of the Maritime strike, was led by Parnell on a dray as the father of the eight-hour day. ATL, PAColl-2324 (Graphic, 6 December 1890)

in 1874, engineers and engine drivers at the Thames goldfield successfully sought amendment of the Regulation of Mines Bill to bring in an eight-hour day.[58] The Act as passed indeed limited the hours of those in charge of steam machinery to eight.

In the 1880s, as pressure tightened to reduce wages and increase hours, the eight-hour movement gained new momentum, particularly with the cuts imposed on the railways. While some proponents thought that it should be legislated for in general, most simply regarded it as a salutary reminder and symbolic statement of the general conditions that workers should be able to enjoy in this country. At this time the eight-hour day alongside a fair wage of eight 'bob' a day became central to an 'invention of a tradition' (in Hobsbawm's phrase) for labour.

M.W. Green, supported by Thomas Bracken, introduced the first eight-hours bill into Parliament in 1882, following a mass demonstration in Auckland, a large public meeting in Dunedin and agitation in Australian states (such demonstrations were to continue through much of the decade).[59] The bill stipulated that eight hours should constitute a day's work, and forty-eight hours a week's work, in all kinds of occupations. Its symbolic character was evident in the fact that no penalties were provided for failure to comply. It passed through the House in simplified form, but was stopped in the Legislative Council. Thus began more than a decade of attempts to provide statutory endorsement for a dearly held colonial custom.

Time and again, in spite of widespread agreement that indeed eight hours should be the custom, four central arguments were raised against such

A METAMORPHOSIS.

Firth's Auckland Roller Mills were well-known for their eight-hour system. With Firth having his mill taken over by the New Zealand Loan and Mercantile Agency Company people feared that the eight hours would be lost. Observer and Free Lance, *17 August 1889* a legislative statement. The first was that the bill could not possibly mean anything in practice; it was simply a gesture and if it did have effects then it should be resisted because of damaging effects on trade and industry: 'that is the practical outcome of attempts to tinker with the inexorable laws of political economy'.[60] Secondly, it was argued that eight hours was already a well-established colonial custom and that it was unnecessary and a restraint on the freedom of labour to impose such conditions through legislation. The third argument was that many forms of work, particularly in the rural sector but also in retail and domestic service, were not amenable to regulation. On a number of occasions attempts were made to exclude rural labour from the bill. Customary expectations were regarded as more flexible and sufficient. The fourth was that the working man had no need for such protection, being perfectly capable of looking after himself. Colonial self-reliance and independence would ensure this.

Following further failures in 1883 and in the first session of 1884, the eight-hour day became an issue in the election later that year.[61] Bradshaw then introduced a bill stating that eight hours would apply 'unless where there is a contract in writing to the contrary'. The bill was taken more seriously on this occasion. New Premier Stout, together with Seddon, supported the principle, arguing that laws followed and were the solidification and expression of custom, so a declaratory Act that kept the custom alive and educated public opinion was useful. Nonetheless, the bill narrowly lost on its second reading.

Bradshaw, endorsed by Stout, persisted with the eight-hours bill in subsequent sessions but Parliament refused to pass it. In a significant shift away from his usual laissez faire view, Stout said that the state must protect those who needed protecting; in the struggle between capital and labour the former was the stronger. During the life of the Stout-Vogel government the bill became a kind of moral touchstone denoting where an MP stood with respect to working people.[62] In the latter part of the decade further bills were introduced by Grey and R.M. Taylor, but they stood little chance of success under Atkinson's government.

In the wake of industrial defeat in the Maritime strike in 1890, the labour movement came together in a symbolic assertion of its strength and paraded through the streets to mark 'Labour Day'. Such events commemorated the growth of trade unionism and the assertion of an eight-hour day. Samuel Parnell, recognised now as the father of the eight-hour day, led the procession through the streets of Wellington on a dray.

> He worked with head – with heart and hand
> From early youth to age,
> And in a new unfettered land
> He taught this precept sage.
> 'Eight hours for work, eight hours for play
> And eight for sleep excel.'

This was the charter for each day
of our wise king, Parnell!

Verse in Alexander Stuart poem in memoriam for Parnell[63]

Labour Day became institutionalised and embodied in statute in 1899 but the eight-hour day itself remained only a customary touchstone. The legislative quest for the eight-hour day, as in other countries such as America and Australia, was displaced into the operations of the arbitration system and the development of factory legislation.[64] It was not to become formally prescribed by legislation until 1936, by which time the agitation had been transformed into the movement for a living or family wage.

Arbitration and the living wage

In the 1880s the eight-hour movement, in combination with the substantial workforce employed on public works and in the public sector, encouraged a commitment to a 'fair wage'. Although the concept of a living wage was not formally articulated at this point, it was this concept which motivated public works policy and underpinned the struggles over wages and conditions on the railways.[65] The increasing involvement by the government in protecting the wage earner against the depredations of contractors, by bankruptcy and lien provisions, and then by the co-operative contracting system from the 1890s, also helped.

As the waged labour-force became established it was dominated by the many unskilled males and a low differential for skill. Unskilled and skilled hours and rates of pay were not greatly different and the participation rates of women and children were low, in contrast to the USA for example.[66] The low skill differential – a noted antipodean phenomenon from the turn of the century – is usually explained by the egalitarian society and centralised wage fixing, but it actually existed much earlier. The high demand for unskilled labour in an undeveloped economy was boosted by the dominance and profitability of the primary sector, therefore raising its price. The perennial labour shortages kept the wage floor up and promoted compensatory payment to the unskilled for the unavoidable insecurity and underemployment associated with the kinds of work they did.

As the nineteenth century came to an end, the skill differential lessened further.[67] In the mid 1870s skilled wages had been more than a third higher than unskilled wages; by the first decade of the twentieth century the differential had reduced to one-fifth. Basic wage differentials were somewhat higher as they were based on minimums only. In the first decade of the 1900s, the Arbitration Court fixed 1s an hour or 8s a day for the unskilled, with a margin of 2–3s a day for skilled workers, suggesting a differential of 25–35 percent. There was further convergence during the First World War as unskilled labour commanded a premium. The 1919 standard wage pronouncement fixed a basic wage differential between unskilled and skilled labour of 26 percent.

The Labour Unionist : Now that I have given you a tremendous majority, Mr Seddon, I have a little request to make. I want a six hours' day.

Trade unions get stroppy under the reforming Liberals. Observer and Free Lance, 23 December 1905

The observations of the American commentator Clark around the turn of the twentieth century are particularly acute.[68] He concluded that in New Zealand, in contrast to the USA, 'a large portion of the working-people are still transplanted British workmen, retaining many of their old ideals and traditions and not thrown into active competition with other nationalities or submitted to new industrial methods.'[69] This resulted in a distinctive homogeneous egalitarianism ('homogenous in race, language and trade traditions', in his words) with a lack of strong wage differentials or stratification between skilled and unskilled workers, which had its roots in Britain prior to the late nineteenth-century emergence of political labour and socialist theory.

This wage compression was felt strongly in seasonal industries such as waterfront work and shearing, and was consolidated through the arbitration system. Indeed the Arbitration Court, reflecting the traditional practice, specifically recognised the need to compensate seasonal workers for their unstable employment. It added a margin of close to 40 percent on top of the unskilled rate for seasonal occupations. Watersiders were paid a premium of a quarter or more on top of the unskilled rate; this lifted their wages to those of skilled workers.[70]

Living standards were rising at the same time, particularly around the turn of the century. A key indicator was the declining percentage of expenditure required for food, from about 55 percent of total outgoings in the 1870s to 45–50 percent by 1900, and to 35–40 percent by 1910. The cost of food was among the lowest in the world, largely because of the very low cost of meat. The overall cost of living, as measured by food and rent combined, was also near the lowest internationally. People had a growing surplus of income after paying for necessaries; consumption per head in 1910 was nearly twice what it was in the late 1880s.[71]

New Zealanders boasted that they had the highest standard of living in the world.[72] Parsons' *Story of New Zealand*, published in 1904, suggested that New Zealand did have the highest net wealth and average annual income, and the second highest wages for skilled labour (behind the USA). A South African study of 1914 suggested that New Zealand had the highest real wages for skilled artisans compared to a wide range of other countries; 60 percent higher than such wages in the United Kingdom. The lack of a pronounced wage differential widened the gap between New Zealand and other countries, because the high standard of living was widely dispersed.

From the turn of the twentieth century the arbitration system protected this enviable standard of living through the notion of a 'fair wage'. The Arbitration Court levelled up and standardised wages; an approach that had previously been articulated by the Sweating Commission in 1890.[73] As in Australia, there was general agreement that a fair wage related to the more prosperous period prior to the late nineteenth-century depression, but the arbitration system itself provided no guidance on how to fix the extent of the wage. There was a greater sense of definition of what a fair wage was not; 'sweated' wages would not be countenanced.

The arbitration system was originally developed as a means of containing industrial class conflict.[74] The Maritime strike which broke out in August 1890 was the most serious industrial conflict that New Zealand had experienced (although by international standards it was short, remarkably peaceful and involved only a small proportion of the workforce), but it rapidly exposed the inherent weakness of the trade unions. Public opinion, politicians and the labour movement turned towards compulsory state arbitration as employers refused to negotiate with the strikers and harshly rammed home their victory over the trade unions. The largely symbolic threat of class warfare was enough to precipitate immediate state action, and resulted in a somersault in government policy.

The government traditionally had stood aside from strikes that did not affect its own role as employer or involve civil disorder. The Threats and Molestation Bill of the mid 1880s (see Chapter 3) was a harbinger of state intervention in industrial relations; it was reintroduced during the Maritime strike but was rejected in Parliament as 'inopportune'.[75] W.D. Stewart then introduced into

THE NECESSARIES OF LIFE.

As Arbitration Court awards increase wages the necessaries of life seem even further away for working people. Observer and Free Lance, *9 November 1907*

Parliament a Strikes and Board of Conciliation Bill that provided for conciliation. This was more in tune with contemporary sentiment. Arbitration of industrial disputes had aroused considerable interest, and Stewart argued that it was vital in order to avoid the epidemic of strikes that was afflicting other countries. He notably suggested the bill could easily provide for compulsory instead of voluntary conciliation, opening the way for the Liberals' subsequent legislation on the matter. The bill specified that once proceedings were entered upon voluntarily, the process became mandatory and a binding 'award' would be made.

Many politicians at the time of the Maritime strike, including Liberals such as Grey and Ballance, found compulsion iniquitous and viewed it as unenforceable. Others on the conservative side of the spectrum, such as Hall, favoured the initiative but argued that it needed further discussion. James Fulton, the former Chairman of the Sweating Commission, suggested perceptively that 'where unions were strong and well-organized they did not demand or need these Courts, but where they were weak they wanted them to lean on'. T.W. Hislop, for the government, convinced Stewart to withdraw the bill in the meantime.

Led by Reeves, the Liberals subsequently passed the Industrial Conciliation and Arbitration (ICA) Act in 1894, and New Zealand became the first country to institute a compulsory state arbitration system. Reeves intended the legislation to 'put an end to . . . the evils of industrial war' and put in its place civilised methods of settling disputes.[76]

While the intent of the legislation was to prevent class warfare, it soon became a means of wage fixing. The touchstone of eight-hours legislation in the 1880s was translated into a state mechanism for fixing fair wages for breadwinners. In the process the longstanding conceptual separation in policy of the labour market and needy groups requiring relief became a separation of state-determined wage fixing from state payments for welfare purposes.

The ICA Act replaced the market wage contract with a 'status' relationship in which the state played a key determining role.[77] A Court of Appeal ruling of 1900 made it abundantly clear that the ICA Act abrogated contracts regarding labour. The nineteenth-century approach of protecting and regulating common-law contracts of employment was replaced at a stroke by a state-controlled system defining the relationship between employers and workers outside of the market, at least in principle. Of course market forces made their presence felt in a number of ways, but now they were filtered through the legal relationship established by the state. The most important impact of the market was the ever-present conundrum of how to fix wages by edict. This eventually led to both the cost of living and the profitability (or prosperity) of industry being taken into account by the Arbitration Court.

In the first decade of the twentieth century, following the first round of awards (which redressed depression wage cuts on the basis of what a fair employer would pay), the Arbitration Court began to consider more general principles of wage fixing. Trade unions now had to argue for increases on the basis of changes in the cost of living. Notions of an adequate 'living wage' (blending into a 'family wage') for male breadwinners rather than simply differentials between male and female wages began to arise.[78] But, unlike in Australia, the principles upon which decisions were made were not discussed overtly. Judges remained cautious and hesitant to promulgate general principles. We have to look at the Court's deliberations in some detail to trace the emergence of a living wage. A number of judges of the Court wrestled with the issue over time.

Justice J.S. Williams, the first judge appointed to the Arbitration Court, suggested that the Court should consider both industry conditions and changes in the standard of living when deciding on a fair wage.[79] In practice, industry conditions were the major criteria until 1907, in spite of Justice J.C. Martin in 1900 implicitly arguing that wage fixing should follow a living wage principle. Justice T. Cooper seemed for a time to suggest profit sharing as a possible consideration. He declined to award wage increases in gold mining and other industries in 1901–2 because of the depressed nature of these sectors, but he denied that this was his intent. In 1904 and 1906 Justice F.R. Chapman rejected this approach (followed shortly thereafter by Justice W.A. Sim) but he also conceded that industry prosperity might be a general factor.

By 1907 the grounds for wage determination began to incorporate the cost of living. As commentators pointed out at the time, the commitment to a living wage was the logical positive correlate of the antagonism towards sweating.[80] Sweating wages were not enough to live on decently; a living wage was. Furthermore, the benchmark against which this was to be measured was a colonial one, which was considerably higher than British or European benchmarks since it was based on a higher standard of living. The Arbitration Court's self-defined role was to maintain a customary colonial standard, and to raise wages if possible, in the context of the prosperity of industry.

The philosophy underlying the burgeoning arbitration system was much contested as it reached a crisis point. Secretary of Labour Tregear, responding to the Court's rejection of profit-sharing proposals, advanced the notion of legally fixing a minimum wage, and the Court began to play a role in fixing standard rates for unskilled workers.[81] From 1911 it fixed rates for skilled workers and by 1914 standard unskilled and skilled rates had been adopted in various industries.

Around 1907 Tregear was becoming increasingly concerned that the intent of the arbitration system was being thwarted by the escalating cost of living, especially in the form of rising rents. An appraisal was made of the increase in the cost of living since the ICA Act came into operation.[82] This prompted those such as John Barr of the Legislative Council and Dr J.G. Findlay, Attorney-General, to declare some basic principles. Barr urged that awards be fixed on the basis of a living wage – based on a standard of living giving the necessaries of life over the course of the year – including intermittent and casual work.

His view was that men had a right to a living wage irrespective of whether the industry was profitable.

Findlay – Seddon's philosophical mentor and a major intellectual Liberal theoretician – referred to the state as a third party representing the community incarnate. In exchange for state interference on behalf of the community, wage earners must have justice applied in the form of a decent living wage obtained through the arbitration system: 'a competent man can be paid such wages as will keep him from degradation and maintain him in that position in which we, as a civilised people, wish to see our workers as a whole.'[83]

These statements coincided with the most significant revision of the tariff since 1888, both to remove the remaining duties on necessaries of life and to strengthen protection.[84] They also coincided with the famous 'Harvester' judgement on the living wage by Australian Judge Higgins. This judgement strengthened the views of proponents here, although it was overshadowed by the attention paid to the strike provisions in the ICA Act. Justice Sim indicated that he agreed with Higgins' discussion of the doctrine of the living wage but he did not view the Arbitration Court as a mechanism for redistributing wealth. Instead the Court could do no more than provide for a minimum wage in order to prevent sweating. Sim defined this as a 'living wage' for the unskilled worker (usually related to the building industry), roughly equivalent to 1s an hour or 8s a day, with a 2–3s a day customary differential for skill.

The Australian living wage was pitched higher, being based upon an average across unskilled and skilled groups. It was also associated with moves to strengthen protection through tariffs, just as the earlier Victorian tariffs had been associated with moves against sweating in local industries. But the New Zealand 'living wage' was really an unskilled basic minimum wage, and was not based on any systematic empirical foundation. The traditional 8s a day, a correlate of the eight-hour day, was regarded by the Court as a basic wage for the unskilled; it became institutionalised in the arbitration system in the first decade of the century.

In 1908 Dr Findlay pronounced on the living wage. In response to mounting criticism of the ICA Act, he emphasised its role in eliminating sweating and in allowing workers to obtain a living wage. The Court had 'steadily become a State regulator of fair wages in each industry', he said, but it had no means of assessing a standard wage. Findlay thought that the wage should be based on the 'needs' of the worker, 'the needs which society, through the Arbitration Court taking an enlightened view of the means available, of the worker's position and welfare, and of social interests, deems necessary or proper.'[85] Such a wage was not bare subsistence but a living wage giving decency and self-respect.

In the same year Judge Sim commented that, for those casually engaged by the day on farms, 'anything less than 7s. per day is not a living wage where the worker has to maintain a wife and children'.[86] However, this should be regarded as an exceptional case since the vast majority of farm workers lived-in with their employers and were thus outside the parameters of a living wage. The Arbitration Court deemed that workers who received board and lodging, tied cottages at a cheap rent, or cheap farm produce were not to be protected.

It might seem that New Zealand was poised to make a path-breaking statement similar to Higgins' Harvester judgement, but this did not happen. As industrial disputes escalated there was less consideration of such issues by the Court. Nonetheless, in the next two decades the rather vague concept of a living wage was consolidated as wage-fixing processes became increasingly centralised and related to the cost of living. The government, following the example of Australia and amid mounting concern, once again tried to assess the impact of the rising cost of living on wages. In 1910–11 the Department of Labour conducted a survey of household budgets to

WEEK OR MONTH ENDING		, 191 ,		
		£	s.	d.
INCOME.				
From earnings of husband	...			
„ „ other receipts	...	...		
TOTAL	...	...		
EXPENDITURE.				
Rent ...	...	...		
Food—Bread ...	...	...		
Meat ...	...	...		
Vegetables and fruit	...			
Milk ...	...	...		
Butter, cheese, &c.				
Sugar ...	...	...		
Tea, coffee, &c. ...				
Other food	...	...		
Other groceries (not food)				
Non-alcoholic beverages ...				
Alcoholic beverages	...			
Tobacco, cigars, cigarettes				
Clothing, drapery, boots, &c.	...			
Fuel and light ...	...			
Fares, railway, tram, 'bus, &c.	...			
† Insurance, fire, life, &c.				
† Contributions to benefit societies, &c.				
† Education: Fees, school materials,&c.				
Medical attendance, medicine, &c.				
† Rates and taxes	...	...		
Sport, amusements, club fees, &c. ...				
Sundry expenditure	...	...		
TOTAL	...	...		

Cost of Living survey booklet, Department of Labour, 1910. Parliamentary Library, New Zealand pamphlets, vol 4

provide a statistical basis for assessing wage demands. This provided the core statistics for the Royal Commission of 1912 on the cost of living. In 1912 the department proposed amendments to the ICA Act, including a provision that the Court's wage-fixing function include a minimum wage where practicable 'to enable the workers, with their families, to live in reasonable comfort'.[87] While this was not taken up, the First World War led to the formulation of a general wage order system. Overt consideration of a living wage receded for a time as the emphasis shifted to basic unskilled rates and their relativity with skilled rates.

Consideration of a living wage associated with the rising cost of living was forced during the war and was associated with increased compression of unskilled and skilled wage rates. In 1915 the phrase 'a reasonable living-wage' was used as a justification for raising wage rates in a number of awards.[88] The Arbitration Court adopted a war bonus policy from 1916 that was underpinned by the living wage concept. This was exemplified in the Northern builders' labourers award that was used as a launching pad for the policy. The war bonus of 10 percent was a means of getting around the inability to amend awards during their currency. It was founded upon the Court's belief that unskilled labourers' rates were insufficient for a 'reasonable living-wage', which should be at least 1s 3d an hour or £2 12 a week. In addition to carrying across these provisions to other labourers' awards, the Court urged employers generally to accept this approach in order to 'preserve industrial peace'.

In 1918, in support of a living wage concept, the Court actually formally stated that an industry should close down in preference to paying sweated wages.[89] In the Inangahua gold-miners award the judge stated that the present wages could not provide 'a reasonable standard of living' and gave a substantial bonus in spite of the industry suffering badly from poor international prices for gold.

Wider concepts of fairness for wage earners became more salient during and after the First World War as the increased cost of living made an impact and the government sought to retain the support of the people for the war effort. The prices of necessary commodities and rents were fixed or controlled.[90] There was much greater state intervention in and control of the economy and a substantial elaboration of the role of the Arbitration Court. The Board of Trade – with J.W. Collins from the Department of Labour, who had previously been heavily involved in the cost of living exercise of 1910–11, as its first head – and the National Efficiency Board concerned themselves with the movement of prices, the availability of consumer goods and manpower issues.[91]

Postwar reconstruction took into account the interests of labour and a concept of fairness related to wage earners' standard of living. This was combined with an emerging concept of the national or public interest. Together these shifts prepared some vital philosophical ground for the eventual construction of the welfare state.

After the war, continued inflation kept pressure on the arbitration system and the government began to cast around for a solution.[92] For a time it looked as if wage fixing would be brought into close association with wider economic planning. Findlay wanted to extend the Board of Trade's functions to include wage fixing in addition to control over industries. The Department of Labour argued that the Arbitration Court should be reconstituted as a court of laymen and associated with the Board of Trade in order to bring wages into line with the changing cost of living.

The Board of Trade was in principle strengthened greatly under a 1919 Act, supported strongly by Findlay and by the leader of the Opposition, Joseph Ward. Prime Minister Massey emphasised how the government had kept duties off the necessaries of life, awarded war bonuses, regulated rents, fixed prices and controlled the supply of commodities. The Board was now widely empowered to act to promote the prosperity of industries and the welfare of the country. This included the issuing of its own regulations for subsequent approval by Parliament. As Findlay observed, the Act gave the Board 'practically unlimited power to mould and fashion our industrial and economic system'. But Findlay's optimistic vision of control over New Zealand's economy did not come to

Family wage, New Zealand Worker, *23 October 1929*

pass.[93] Massey as Minister of Industries and Commerce allowed little freedom of movement and the Board reverted to a commonplace government department. The retrenchment of the early 1920s sounded its death knell.

As the war ended, the government (in the most significant change since 1908) modified the Arbitration Court's role so that it could amend awards during their currency. In doing so it was required to take into account both conditions affecting industry and increases in the cost of living. This was a crucial change that led eventually to the general wage order system and created an element of judgement of the national interest that was to become central in the period from the Second World War.

The complexities of dealing with the cost of living for each award led the Court immediately the war had finished to fix basic wage rates for unskilled, semi-skilled and skilled workers.[94] Its statement of April 1919 constituted the first standard wage pronouncement. This was based on the continuation of the original 8s a day basic wage for the unskilled as adjusted for by rising prices, thus keeping faith with the principle of a living wage.

Late in 1920 the Court's powers to amend awards were restricted; amendment of awards during their currency became discretionary and was only permitted after taking account of conditions affecting the industry and changes in the cost of living. Significantly and for the first time the Court had to be satisfied that amendment was 'just and equitable to the employers and the workers' in the industry and that the industry would not be 'unduly imperilled' by the effect of the change on the cost of production. The Labour Party did manage to extract a significant concession by including provision for a 'fair living-wage' in any such awards, but from this time conditions affecting industry began to take precedence over the cost of living. This was evident in the wage pronouncement of December 1920 which stated that wages would not necessarily be increased in line with the cost of living because the state of the economy had to be taken into account.[95] In May 1921 the Court awarded no increase at all, in spite of statistics indicating that the cost of living was still rising. Later that year shearers' rates were cut because of declining wool prices.

The amendment of the ICA Act in early 1922 gave the Court the capacity to issue general wage orders, having regard to the cost of living and the 'economic and financial conditions affecting trade and industry'. It was to be guided by what it thought was 'just and equitable, having regard to a fair standard of living'. Two reductions in wage rates were made that year in the light of the declining cost of living.[96]

Amid these discussions of wage cutting Judge F.V. Frazer acknowledged that, compared with the notion of a 'bare living wage . . . the modern view is more enlightened, and is based in a realization of the dignity of the worker as a man, a citizen, and the head of a family'.[97] The Australian Basic Wage Commission of 1920 had set a fair living wage relating to a man with a wife and three children under fourteen years. But it was generally agreed in Australia and New Zealand that such a wage was unsustainable and that the average number of dependent children was considerably less. Here the judge declared the average family to have two children.

This was the first formal articulation of the principle of the living wage in the form of a 'family' wage specifically, but the concept was not incorporated into wage fixing. Instead the judge advocated calculating a family wage on the basis of no dependent children. For children families should rely upon the family allowance – a much-discussed welfare policy initiative of the 1920s (see Chapter 6).

In 1925 a Royal Commission on the basic wage was proposed by the labour movement. The Alliance of Labour sent a deputation to the government demanding an enquiry into the cost of living and the Labour Party included it in its manifesto of that year. This debate prompted Judge Frazer to comment that the basic male wage should be 'regarded as sufficient to maintain himself, a wife, and two children. He is to be regarded as a social unit, rather than as an economic unit.'[98]

Quite why Frazer made such a statement when he had previously indicated otherwise is uncertain, although it may be significant that this was not included in his formal pronouncement. The statement probably signalled a reversion to the approach taken at the turn of the century: male wage earners should be paid at a market rate during times of prosperity; in times of depression wage rates should not be depressed below the amount required to maintain the social unit of the family. In any case the issue was immediately bypassed by the introduction of family allowances in 1926.

In 1927 James McCombs introduced a Minimum Wage Bill into Parliament, but it was unsuccessful.[99] Judge Frazer that year departed from the cost-of-living approach and placed emphasis on the previous prosperity of farmers in awarding an increase to freezing workers; in doing so he emphasised the living-wage approach as a backstop. This unleashed concerted attacks on the Court by farmers.

In 1929 the trade unions attempted to follow up on this opening provided to them and presented their own family budgets in order to argue for a much higher family wage. Frazer, however, refused to grant an increase to watersiders. He said that the principle of a 'family wage' had never been formally adopted and was only a guide with many inherent problems. The National Industrial Conference of 1928 did not shift positions that had become increasingly entrenched as economic conditions deteriorated. Any further advances in protecting workers' standard of living were supplanted by more immediate imperatives as depression loomed. The early 1930s were to see a shift of attention from labour market remedies to welfare assistance.

Thus, even though the living or family wage was not formalised within the arbitration system there is no doubt that such a concept informed the evolution of the arbitration system in the early twentieth century – standardised wages, assessment relative to the cost of living, and the use of the basic wage of an unskilled labourer as the benchmark. The family allowance began this process, by providing an alternative source of assistance for families that was separate from the wage earner.

The Arbitration Court – following its ruminations of the 1920s and the ICA Amendment Act of 1936 which fixed a basic wage for a family with three children – had withdrawn from consideration of the family wage by the 1950s.[100] While making a general wage order in 1951 that dealt with the removal and reduction of subsidies and the increased cost of living, the Court ruled that it should not fix wages on the basis of the family unit of five. (The Federation of Labour had argued that the Court should follow the prescription of the basic wage legislation of 1936.) This was because of the existence of the Minimum Wage Act 1945 stipulating minimum wages for women and the introduction of a universal family benefit. It passed the matter on to the government for it to determine via the family benefit. The ICA Act 1954 then dropped consideration of the basic wage altogether.

At the same time the Federation of Labour pressed for equal pay from the late 1940s. The eventual institution of equal pay in the public service in the early 1960s, followed by the Equal Pay Act in 1972, reinforced perceptions that the wage was paid to the individual independent of family circumstance.[101] As was argued by the Federation in 1947, the issue of equal pay should be divorced from family and other benefits.

These developments in wage fixing went hand in hand with measures protecting employment and working conditions for those already here: the exclusion of undesirable immigrants, the introduction of protective tariffs, increased government intervention in the labour market, and protective labour legislation. The key objectives of these policies were greater security and stability of employment for breadwinners, together with wages sufficient for a family to maintain New Zealand's customary standard of living.

But, as we have begun to note, from the turn of the twentieth century there was a gradual shift away from intervention in the labour market to address poverty and support for the elderly. Those outside the labour market could no longer be neglected and marginalised as a residual part of society requiring little attention in a land of opportunity. Just as the labour market required the intervention of the state so too did those falling by the wayside. At the same time as the arbitration system was extended to the workforce, pensions were provided first to the elderly and then to other groups. This would lead to the welfare state.

CHAPTER 6

The welfare laboratory and the social contract

O the war-drums of Labour are throbbing
Their call from the depths of the years,
And they'll end the young children's wild sobbing
And sorrow of sad mothers' tears.

They shall take all the earth and its treasure,
They shall tear down the banners of Wrong,
They shall hold all their wealth in full measure,
And gladden the world with their song.

Harry Holland, verses 6 and 7 from 'They Shall Take and Hold',
Red Roses on the Highways[1]

Holland's vision of the triumph of labour in the early twentieth century was a more assertive one than Reeves' (see beginning of Chapter 5). Instead of being assisted paternally by the Liberals, it was now time for labour to wrest control for itself and ensure that the people received the fruits of their toil. This would take place through the Labour Party attaining power at the end of 1935, although Holland himself would not live to see this come about, and the kind of party Labour became in order to be elected was not the socialist vision Holland had in mind. Nonetheless, Labour came to power with a strongly redistributive orientation and a determination to create an economy and a welfare state that would provide security for the wage earner.

The trajectory of Labour's rise to power and its interventions in the economy and the expansion of the state are familiar to most and much examined by historians. What is less adequately considered is precisely how Labour was able to construct a welfare state and why it was so distinctive. In this chapter, I explore the fiscal basis of New Zealand's social security system, shaped as it was by New Zealand's origins in a colonial society, the separation of poor relief from the labour market, and an emerging concept of citizenship based on the social contract.[2]

Historically there was a protracted battle between contributory and non-contributory forms of welfare. The contributory principle was well established in the nineteenth century through the many friendly societies and other benefit societies which protected their members against misfortune. Assistance for those outside the labour market comprised only relief for the poor at the margins.

When it came to greater state intervention in welfare there was a split between labour market and residual relief policies, in the form of Atkinson's contributory National Insurance scheme of the 1880s and Seddon's much more limited old-age pension from 1898. New Zealand was feeling its way towards a very distinctive form of welfare provision. In the end the country plumped for non-contributory benefits funded out of general taxation, based on the principle of the old-age pension. This differentiated New Zealand's welfare state from many others that adopted the contributory principle.

Welfare and citizenship

> No parish money, or loaf,
> No pauper badges for me,
> A son of the soil, by right of toil
> Entitled to my fee.
> No alms I ask – give me my task:
> Here are the arm, the leg,
> The strength, the sinews of a Man,
> To work, and not to beg.
>
> Verse 9 of 'The Lay of the Labourer', Thomas Hood (1799–1845)[3]

Charity

Pauperism and charity were anathema in a self-reliant, hardworking New Zealand. Public works measures for dealing with unemployment – historically New Zealand's major form of labour market relief – could be conceded as a right to assistance in terms of the social contract, but poor relief should not be treated so. As Rolleston said:

> Does anyone suppose that [relief for unemployed migrants] is a form of want which is to be dealt with as a matter of charity or benevolence, or that the recipients of aid should be dealt with as paupers? It is a form of want that has to be dealt with as a matter of right.[4]

New Zealand was founded on an aversion to the English poor law and a determination that alternatives could be found. The movement against the poor law has been described as the 'midwife' of Chartism; other radical movements of the time felt similarly hostile to this form of welfare.[5] The poor law and a pauperised population represented the worst manifestations of the old world that migrants strove to get away from. Contemporaries were convinced that New Zealand did not have a poor law, even if historians thought otherwise.[6] The provision of relief was not associated with a penal loss of citizenship rights as in England. English agricultural labourers' union and emigration organiser Alfred Simmons advised intending migrants that there was no poor law here:

'There are no Paupers in New Zealand.'

Seddon claimed in Britain that there were no paupers in New Zealand. The cartoonist looks towards charitable aid. ArchNZ, Seddon collection, 3, 62, The Spectator, c. mid 1897

'We almost felt disposed to settle down in the public roadway and return devout thanks to heaven when we heard tell of it . . . May ages roll over the colony ere it be found requisite to establish a system for the relief of their poor!'[7]

A range of attempts to provide for the poor in New Zealand were shaped by this antipathy to the poor law, including the emphasis on the family, development of a system of 'charitable aid', and proposals for benefits and pensions. As well as the obvious forms of 'welfare' policy in the nineteenth century, land and labour policy was instrumental in aiding the poor by various means – making land available for settlement, public works relief, control over immigration, and a general concern for the standard of living.[8] These are matters dealt with in previous chapters.

Charitable aid in nineteenth-century New Zealand was a residual and grudging response outside of the labour market, intended as a haven for women, children and the elderly. The poor were by these means marginalised or hidden rather than confronted or coercively controlled. It was possible to provide limited relief because male breadwinners were dealt with through labour market mechanisms. In order to sustain the image of 'God's own country' it was necessary to sideline the less fortunate in the land of opportunity.

The very term 'charitable aid' was an effort to avoid the connotations of the British approach. There was no formal entitlement to charitable aid (unlike the poor law) nor did principles exist upon which claims might be made – it was entirely discretionary. The discretionary and restrictive nature of relief was a means of separating relief from the labour market and avoiding the English poor law principle of supplementing the labour market. This kept wage earners from dependence on relief by making it less attractive than the most basic means of earning a living. The crucial shift at the turn of the twentieth century in England was the recognition that the state would instead provide welfare without demanding such penalties in return.[9] Here the shift was a different one – from marginalisation of welfare to an integration of welfare and labour market measures.

The Destitute Persons Ordinance, promulgated in 1846, placed the onus for relief upon the immediate family and near relatives and not on the government or the community.[10] It was intended to enforce family support of the poor, even allowing the poor to bring court actions to extract relief from families. The Destitute Persons Act 1877 extended this by allowing the government to claw back from relatives any expense it incurred in relief. The family itself was to bear responsibility.

The combined voluntary and poor law hospital system that existed in Britain did not develop here, because of a lack of well-established philanthropic sources of funding and the hostility to the poor law. Instead government hospitals providing both health and welfare services were founded in the main centres from the mid 1840s.[11] They catered to the poorer classes and artisans in the same institution. The poor received treatment free or at a reduced rate on a discretionary basis as part of the exercise of hospitals' charitable functions. Doctors would provide their services free. Wealthier people were expected to pay on a fee-for-service basis in their own homes.

Hospitals also distributed charitable aid in the form of 'outdoor' relief to those in their homes – the major form of relief in New Zealand. English 'indoor' relief in workhouses would not be countenanced. By such means the poor who were outside the labour market were dealt with, if family support proved insufficient.

David Thomson argues that New Zealand broke with British forms of welfare by providing minimal state relief and insisting that the needy (primarily the elderly) rely upon family, neighbours and the community.[12] Friendly and other benefit societies, life insurance and savings were insufficient to provide for old age, he argues. Philanthropic charity and government assistance, in the form of charitable aid or pensions, were also inadequate. He concludes that the ownership of property, backed up by family assistance, was crucial to welfare.

Thomson suggests that the inadequacy of formal state and voluntary provisions implies that informal family provisions must have taken their place, but there is not a great deal of evidence for this. His discussion of the Destitute Persons Ordinance (retained well into the twentieth century) includes limited examination of the extent to which the legislation was enforced and only covers the period from the late nineteenth century.[13] Some indirect evidence is provided by implication, in the widespread extent of property ownership, but

POVERTY A DISQUALIFICATION, IF NOT AN ABSOLUTE CRIME.

Saint Reeves guards New Zealand's working man's paradise against undesirable immigrants.
Observer and Free Lance, *13 October 1894*

it remains to be demonstrated that property was used to relieve family-related poverty and distress for the elderly.

Colonists' aversion towards the poor law and their emphasis on self-reliance seems to be taken too literally here. Avoidance of the poor law did not mean a lack of assistance but rather a redefinition of the terms on which it was given. Self-reliance in the New Zealand context did not involve an extreme form of family or household 'individualism'; it was a recognition of a collective endeavour endorsed and enabled by the state. Self-reliance did not imply a minimal state; rather the form of intervention taken by the state was shaped by such beliefs.

To some extent also Thomson may be setting up a false problem. The extent of poverty based on monetary incomes may well have been limited until late in the century, even if many experienced harsh and difficult living and working conditions, as there were few elderly people in the colony until then. The crucial forms of assistance were not monetary. As we have seen, newly arrived immigrants, working labourers and settlers received assistance in the form of land, were aided in the labour market, and took advantage of opportunities available in the colonial economy. Monetary pensions for the elderly were not particularly relevant. Moreover, as in Australia the provision of so-called 'voluntary' assistance when it was given was in fact underpinned by state finance. The vast bulk of income for hospitals came first from central government, followed by local and hospital authorities. Voluntary contributions comprised only 10–15 percent of the total, ranking equally with patients' own payments.

With the abolition of the provinces the central government began to consider how it should deal with poverty. Its financial support of hospitals and charitable aid had to expand greatly, while depression increasingly affected the country and the problem of a pauper class loomed.[14] In 1877 Donald Reid's Charitable Institutions Bill precipitated what was probably the most extended debate ever in this country on the principles of aid to the poor. Should a compulsory poor rate be levied or should the system remain based on voluntary discretionary charity provided by local institutions and supplemented by subsidies from the government? The government decided upon the latter – hence the bill – but Rolleston and others, including Fox, wanted the state to give relief to the deserving poor as a right, and did not see this as degrading the poor to pauperism. Rolleston specifically argued that it was 'a matter of duty' for the nation – the state had to act and was bound to provide for those in distress.[15]

To many, 'relief as of right' reeked of the English poor law and could not be tolerated. Stout criticised any proposed increase in state interference. Grey thought it would create a pauper class. Bowen, a minister in the government, spoke against the measure too: 'God help the country which looks on a poor-law as a charter of rights! We have seen something of what a poor-law has done for England'.[16] He believed in self-reliance supplemented by philanthropy: 'what will really tend to decrease pauperism is national education, with a fair rate of wages'. And so the debate remained trapped in nineteenth-century confines. Voluntary charity was identified with dependence and pauperism, while provision as of right was identified with the poor law. Over following years various schemes were considered but nothing eventuated.[17]

Grey, despite his own clarion call, failed to deal with the matter when his supporters won control over the House during the session of 1877. He withdrew the bill. But his proposed land tax included an extremely significant kernel of what the future would hold: it stated that smallholders as well as larger landowners should pay the tax. Spreading the contribution in this way was an expression of citizenship that would create a 'guarantee fund' to support the

We have had the experience on "one" Board of three generations in a family being brought up on charitable aid. It is a disgrace to a country like this that such a state of things should exist.—*A delegate on the Charitable Aids Conference.*

WHERE IS THE BREADWINNER ?

Charitable aid was seen as residual assistance divorced from the labour market. New Zealand Free Lance, *30 July 1904*

destitute, including smallholders themselves if in need. This was the conceptual nucleus of the later Liberal project of funding an old-age pension from taxation.

Hall introduced bills in 1880 and 1881 that attempted to bring in a principle of a right to relief through the levying of local rates but many reacted vehemently against what they saw as the introduction of the English poor law.[18] Schemes based on land endowments were also considered.

The deepening depression during the 1880s meant that something had to be done. In 1885 Vogel introduced the Hospitals and Charitable Institutions Bill, which would shape relief into the twentieth century. This retained the previously established principle of local support supplemented by a central government subsidy, but it also provided for a comprehensive and uniform system of hospitals and relief based on ad hoc local boards, funded half from local sources and half by government subsidy. The Act consolidated the emerging principle of substantial government financial aid if not a right to relief.

Old Age

Emerging concern for the elderly led to a shift from residual forms of relief to assistance as a central right of citizenship. By the 1880s the demographic bulge of males resulting from immigration, particularly of miners in the 1860s, was entering older age brackets, and the elderly, particularly widows and bachelors, were increasingly visible.[19] Charitable aid was inadequate and friendly societies refused to make provision for the elderly. In England friendly societies excluded those over 60; in New Zealand there was no such explicit rule but old-age benefits were not paid. The Oddfellows ceased sick pay at 65 years of age.

The Oddfellows had considered annuities for some time. They had investigated a weekly payment of 10s at 65 years of age in 1877, but this required a more than doubling of even the proposed higher graduated contributions that would have made societies financially viable. The scheme was rejected. In the early 1880s the Oddfellows adopted rules for Otago lodges to establish such funds, but no lodges responded.[20] Contributions were unattractively high and there was very limited interest. Members believed that they would die before being able to take up the annuity and at that time the number of members aged over 65 years was extremely small (0.25 percent of total membership).

The year of 1882 was a startling one, signalling important shifts of attitude to land and welfare, at a time when depression challenged fundamental values. Just after Rolleston had astounded Parliament with his perpetual lease, Premier Atkinson came up with a compulsory contributory (flat tax) National Insurance proposal to cover sickness and old age. The scheme was based on the ideas of Canon Blackley in England and was drawn up by F.W. Frankland, an eminent international actuarial practitioner.[21]

Atkinson was more interested in a contributory scheme than in charitable aid, which could be construed as a version of the poor law. He made the scheme a feature of his speeches that year. All would pay and all would have the right to benefit from it 'in accordance with the ideas of equality which we hold in this part of the world'.[22] It ranked alongside the constitution, taxation and land tenure; in other words, it was integrated with fundamental issues concerning the country's future.

Atkinson defended state intervention and was determined to avoid the poor law, but private thrift was inadequate. Friendly societies would never be able to cope with 'national poverty' since they took in a select population, excluded women and did not provide for old age. Frankland, writing for the *New Zealand Times* newspaper, orchestrated support for the bold scheme.[23]

The relationship of the scheme to friendly societies was crucial. As Frankland wrote to Atkinson, friendly societies

> referred to the National Insurance scheme as 'certain to crush all friendly societies out of existence'. Mr Leslie [Oddfellow actuarial expert] said to me . . . that he thought the friendly societies could never survive as mere medical clubs, neither could they as burial clubs. They will try to insist on retaining the sick business.[24]

Atkinson denied that the scheme would compete with and destroy the societies. He considered absorbing societies into the scheme and offered the option of exemption from contributions to members of societies who were provided for.

The societies had moved to kill Blackley's proposed scheme in England, but they seemed bewildered and less certain of their ground here.[25] Canterbury and Otago societies supported the scheme, but the Otago society later changed its mind. The Nelson Oddfellows, on the other hand, opposed the scheme from the start, probably because their parent body in Britain was implacably opposed to state pensions. A hostile demonstration in Dunedin, fostered by politicians and others concerned for the friendly societies, in the end proved an important factor in Atkinson abandoning the proposal.

Actuarially, the scheme was likely to have been sound but administratively it was problematic. It would have required

Harry Atkinson, Premier and promoter of a National Insurance scheme. W. Leslie, Parliamentary Portraits, *1887*

The "Wellington Advertiser" Supplement.

No. 46.—THE LAST STRAW BREAKS THE CAMELS' BACK.

Premier Atkinson's compulsory National Insurance scheme is seen as the last straw for the taxpayer. ATL, William Hutchison, Wellington Advertiser Supplement, *22 July 1882, A-095-045*

a large organisation and a comprehensive register of the population, employer co-operation with payments and extensive surveillance of beneficiaries by travelling inspectors similar to friendly society 'district visitors'. Politically, the scheme was considered laughable and completely unacceptable. Older-style liberals intensely disliked such state interference, sure that it would sap self-reliance. Grey and others argued that access to land or a land tax was the proper solution to poverty. Stout argued that the state should interfere less rather than more, and that National Insurance would burden and enslave the working classes.[26]

The proposal disappeared as an apparently harebrained 'faddish' aberration, but the initiative might have been regarded differently in retrospect if New Zealand's welfare system had indeed taken a contributory form. It became something of a touchstone in the early twentieth century, when contributory insurance was once again examined very seriously.

Settlers become honourable citizens

The old-age pension of 1898 is often taken as a benchmark development towards the welfare state. This is true, but there was also considerable continuity with nineteenth-century solutions.[27] The future significance of the pension lay in its direct payment by the state from the government's consolidated account. This marked a movement towards a public and bureaucratic form of welfare in which the notion of a 'benefit' began to shift from a contributory private right to a public taxpayer or citizen's right. The association of savings and benefits underpinned by insurance, so strongly emphasised by nineteenth-century politicians, was challenged and the ground was shifted towards the payment of taxes. The existence of the pension, and of subsequent additional benefits, created a commitment to providing welfare out of taxation and made it increasingly difficult to pose alternative methods of funding over time.

On the other hand, looking backwards, the pension continued a central government-funded form of relief consistent with traditional charitable aid in that it was discretionary on moral grounds. There was not the rupture that occurred in England between the parochial poor-law system and the central-state-provided pension of the early years of the twentieth century.

In the 1890s the notion of state-provided old-age pensions was being discussed internationally. There was extensive debate in Britain, while Germany and Denmark provided examples of such pensions. In New Zealand a parliamentary select committee was established in 1894 to consider the issue. It regarded a contributory scheme as unworkable. Many would not be able to contribute consistently because of the precarious nature of the labour market and the lack of steady employment. The labour movement itself urged a non-contributory pension. The committee recommended a non-contributory state-provided pension of 8s a week at 65 years for those who had resided in New Zealand for twenty years.[28] This immediately set the battle ground for the future.

Evidence given by friendly society lobbyist Mark Cohen provided a clear statement of the friendly society position and presaged the route that the state would indeed take. He drew upon the approach taken by friendly societies towards pension proposals made in Britain by Charles Booth and Joseph Chamberlain at that time, by suggesting that the state provide not for all but only for the 'deserving poor'. If the pension was given to all, the friendly societies would 'be subjected to improper and unfair competition'. The deserving should be assisted as of right and not in the form of a charitable dole. The Registrar of Friendly Societies suggested that if elderly friendly-society members experienced poverty the state should fill the gap with a pension of £26 per annum 'to all persons on liberal terms'.

As re-election of his government loomed, and conscious of the increasing numbers of elderly ex-miners on the West Coast, Premier Seddon spotted electoral advantage and suddenly introduced an Old-age Pensions Bill into Parliament.[29] The bill gave no indication of how much it might cost or where the funds would come from other than general taxation, but he was determined to limit the cost of the scheme within current taxation and confine it to the poor elderly.

Seddon, in heartfelt fashion, described the measure as the most important he had ever been involved with. The pension was in the nature of an 'annuity' for 'industrial soldiers' who by their labour had developed the country. He, like the

HIS SUPREME EFFORT.

Seddon passes the Old-age Pensions Act on the foundation of the consolidated fund rather than contributions. Graphic, *6 August 1898*

committee of 1894, emphasised that a compulsory contributory scheme was impossible because of the nature of the labour market.[30]

Opposition leaders pressed a contributory scheme upon the government, arguing that the pension was just another form of degrading charitable aid. A number argued that the scheme should be universal and not carry across the discretionary approach from charitable aid. Captain William Russell and William Rolleston advocated Atkinson's scheme in association with friendly societies, and Rolleston specifically talked of supplementing the annuities provided by friendly societies, trade unions or other bodies by up to 10s a week.[31] A distinction between state 'assistance', which was enabling and preserved individual self-reliance, and intervention, which created a new welfare relationship between the individual and the state, was at the heart of the difference between 'conservative' and 'liberal' politics over the issue.

The Liberals were re-elected and in 1897 Seddon reintroduced the bill, in which the pension was now to be funded from the consolidated account. The bill, although it eventually went through the House of Representatives after tumultous debates and a host of amendments, failed in the Legislative Council. Seddon insisted on the bill's reconsideration the following year and, after a massive stonewall, had the bill finally passed.

The pension provided under the 1898 Act was a meagre and means-tested measure funded from the consolidated account, and backed strongly by the distinction between the deserving and undeserving poor. It provided £18 a year for those 65 years and over who had resided in the country for 25 years, and was reduced for income over £34 per annum and property over £50. The Act's preamble recognised settlers' and wage earners' contributions: 'it is equitable that deserving persons who during the prime of life have helped to bear the public burdens of the colony by the payment of taxes, and to open up its resources by their labour and skill', should receive a pension. This concept of 'honourable citizenship' underpinned the state's initiative and justified its recourse to the consolidated account. Seddon argued that this source of funding would ensure its continued existence and would prevent attacks on the scheme on the basis of only one class contributing by way of taxation. He acknowledged the experimental nature of the pension and the likelihood that conditions would be eased and extensions made, but he certainly did not foresee that it would become the pivotal principle for New Zealand's welfare system.

Contributions?

It took a long time for New Zealand to shake off its belief that the populace could continue to rely upon the vitality of the economy to sustain itself and to realise that state-funded welfare provisions more substantial than charitable aid were required. The notion of contributory pensions certainly did not die, and was given added appeal by the agitation for a universal old-age pension, which no-one thought could be funded out of the consolidated account.

As pressure mounted to make the pension universal, the government in 1904 investigated the cost, but it was regarded as politically impossible.[32] From 1912 the Reform government maintained the Liberal opposition to a universal pension. Many were concerned that extending the pension would lead to the penalisation of thrift and an increasing fiscal burden.

Seddon in 1898 had himself given a commitment to a complementary contributory annuity scheme, seeing it as eminently desirable since it would appeal to the 'great bulk of the people' who were more independent, and would cost the state less.[33] Over time he foresaw that the old-age pension would largely be subsumed by annuities and that there would be a reduction in charitable aid. He envisaged a three-tier system with the 'undeserving' poor relieved by charitable aid, the 'deserving' poor supported by the old-age pension, and the better-off enjoying the benefits of a contributory scheme. Both Seddon and Opposition leader Captain Russell advanced the possibility of a national pension scheme, with the former referring to Atkinson's proposals and suggesting that before he retired he wanted to endow the country with a voluntary contributory scheme (Seddon thought that the problem with Atkinson's scheme was its compulsory nature).

In 1906, Seddon floated the idea of a voluntary contributory old-age annuity scheme with a government subsidy. He staked his reputation on it – it was to be the 'coping stone of his political life'.[34] A complex National Annuities draft bill was produced, the scheme paying 10s a week at 60 years of age. Seddon circulated the friendly societies with it, saying that he wanted to include them as much as possible. He proposed to integrate friendly society benefits into the state-provided scheme by massive subsidisation.

The issue of the uncertain viability of friendly societies persisted into the last decade of the nineteenth century, by which time the Registrar was more assertive about financial reform and it was becoming clearer that although New Zealand suffered lower mortality rates than England its overall sickness rates were similar.[35] By the late 1880s societies paid out £1 million in benefits but received only £0.6 million in contributions and had a mere £0.3 million in accumulated funds. The high sickness rates for older members were a particular threat to societies when combined with low mortality. Societies needed to set an age for cessation of benefits, the Registrar warned.

Thomson emphasises this long-term lack of financial viability to buttress his argument that friendly societies did not form a central part of welfare assistance in New Zealand, although he does concede that their sickness benefits comprised one-third to one-half of all expenditure on charitable aid at around the turn of the century.[36] As in Britain, there were good reasons why the seriousness of the societies' long-term financial position was not properly appreciated, and why even when it was appreciated it was very difficult to do anything. The fierce competition between societies for members forced contributions down and benefits up, and prevented effective action. For many years societies were mostly concerned with meeting the immediate needs of sickness and death of younger members. Their operations were premised on the assumption that many members would die before middle age and serious or chronic sickness – members would essentially work until they died.

But the improved standard of living and increased life expectancy undercut this approach, while on the other side of the ledger spectacular quick-killing diseases were increasingly replaced by chronic lingering ones. Members were living considerably longer and making additional claims on the sickness benefit to keep them in old age. The situation was exacerbated by a reduced birth rate that constricted the pool from which societies drew new members. These changes were not properly understood until the early twentieth century.

By the turn of the century, with New Zealand's population getting older, the issue of longer-term financial viability became increasingly central and the need for annuities became more compelling. Seddon's move represented a new environment for the societies, in which co-operative self-reliance was replaced by direct state assistance. Signs of this shift were already evident in the state's entry into savings banks and Atkinson's insurance proposals of 1882, and were consolidated by the old-age pension in 1898. Societies were deeply divided on the extent and terms of assistance that should be rendered by the state.

Seddon's National Annuities scheme was the first step towards the merging of the societies and the state that was being considered in Britain at the time. In Britain the landmark National Insurance Act of 1911 replaced an earlier non-contributory pension with contributory insurance in association with friendly societies.[37] The British societies, after decades of powerful resistance, finally recognised the inevitability of a state-provided old-age pension, and acknowledged that they could not stand aside from the process. They sought to become a central delivery mechanism for the emerging concept of national health insurance.

Some friendly societies here strongly opposed the suggestion of a state subsidy, and the movement as a whole, taken aback by Seddon's bold move, seemed paralysed. The offer to be involved in developing such a scheme was not taken up.[38] Ward, after constantly promising a scheme, eventually revived the measure in 1909. It was passed into legislation in a substantially simplified form with strong bipartisan support as the National Provident Act 1910.[39] This provided voluntary old-age annuities, together with a maternity allowance, an incapacity allowance and a death benefit. Notably, Attorney-General Findlay underlined that it was but a first step along the road to compulsory contributions, which were the norm in other countries. The Registrar of Friendly Societies, who was to become the National Provident Fund's first Superintendent and a key proponent of social insurance, hailed its establishment as 'a notable step forward in social legislation towards universal provision'.[40] Compulsion was seen as a means to universality; more comprehensive social insurance was firmly on the agenda.

But the National Provident Fund failed to deliver. Contributions were so high that it became the preserve of a better-off minority and suffered many withdrawals from the scheme. The crucial problem was that those in most need were the least likely to become contributors. Its failure pointed the way towards a compulsory scheme.

The friendly societies meanwhile coexisted uneasily alongside the Fund, attracting members and increasing their contributions but increasingly being pulled into the orbit of the state.[41] The government wanted to introduce 'adequacy-of-contributions' clauses for friendly societies in association with its national annuity proposals in 1906, so that friendly societies would become 'approved' financially secure organisations suitable to join with the state. This was rejected by societies at a national conference convened by the Wellington United Friendly Societies' Council, in spite of their endorsement of adequate contributions. The reason appeared to relate to complications over death levies. The government as a result backed off.

A split had developed in the friendly society movement. The Druids, based on American practices, had introduced attractive but less secure, and therefore controversial, separate death benefits based on levies.[42] This move resulted in a large increase in membership, but the levy was unsustainable in the long term in the view of both the Registrar and other societies. Following a parliamentary investigation into friendly societies a new Friendly Societies Act 1909 was eventually passed.[43] This dropped the contentious clauses insisting on financial security in order to get the measure through. The Act retained voluntary registration of societies but it did enhance the powers of the Registrar and actuary while 'encouraging' adequate contributions.[44]

In 1911 societies bowed to the inevitable and accepted the adequate contributions requirement; the Act was amended to this end. It now looked as if New Zealand might follow Britain in incorporating the friendly societies into its emerging welfare measures. In the years that followed the government continued to look at this, particularly as the medical role of societies grew. A.R. Guinness, as a private member, had introduced a National Sick and Accident Insurance Bill in 1911. This was a contributory scheme that would have insured against incapacity due to sickness or accident and provided a death benefit, but it did not get onto the statute book.

Friendly societies had extended their traditional sickness benefit as their membership grew to provide insurance for medical and hospital services and pharmaceuticals.[45] By the 1930s some 34 United Friendly Societies pharmacies catered for 50,000 members. Together with the transformation of the hospital system, at one end this undermined the traditional function of hospital services for the poor and at the other it reduced the incomes of general practitioners reliant upon better-off fee-paying patients. Hospitals increasingly catered to all classes – as was clarified in the Hospitals Act 1909 and as was increasingly required by the use of more expensive specialist

'*The latest freak of the BMA trust*'. *In the early decades of the twentieth century friendly societies and doctors were at loggerheads over their relationship.* Observer and Free Lance, *7 November 1908*

equipment – in spite of doctors' urging that access be restricted to poorer groups.

Doctors were increasingly drawn into what they regarded as an invidious capitation system, in which friendly societies sought tenders for the lowest per capita rates (usually £1 per annum), and better-off people were attracted into the societies for cheap medical services.[46] This gave rise to considerable antagonism by doctors towards societies and pressures to place hospitals on a very different footing.

Integration of provision was on the horizon. Registered friendly society benefits were made exempt from assessable income for the old-age pension. The Registrar began to work on a 'subvention' (subsidy) scheme similar to the one New South Wales had introduced in 1908, which would have brought societies into a closer association with the National Provident Fund.[47]

In 1912 Ward's government, as part of a desperate bid for labour votes, drafted an amending National Provident Fund Bill to subsidise friendly society long-term sickness allowances, funeral benefits, and old-age benefits. When the Reform Party became the government the bill lapsed.[48] New Prime Minister William Massey obtained figures that graphically underlined friendly societies' poor prospects, but also demonstrated how a state subsidy could turn around their fortunes. The Registrar continued to agitate for the British approach of greater integration based on contributions:

> the extension of the 'free' [pension] schemes must undoubtedly create difficulties in the future, apart from the cost – we are in New Zealand

at present going in two directions at once in this reform – the one road leads to the Australian idea of enlarging the area of free schemes, while the other leads to the British idea of dealing with the trouble at the root.[49]

In 1913 a parliamentary 'joint friendly societies committee' was appointed to consider the relationship of societies and the state.[50] The Registrar (also Superintendent of the Fund) again urged the adoption of the British approach. He remarked privately, 'the government is not taking this matter up with a view to helping the Friendly Societies so much as a recognition of the State's responsibility in the wider question of Social Insurance', whether by subsidy or some other means.[51] Harry Ell introduced into Parliament in 1914 a private member's bill that would have integrated National Provident Fund and friendly society contributions and provided a subsidy for friendly society sick allowances. It did not pass.

Developments came to a head during the First World War, at which time the societies were drawn further into the embrace of the state. Increasingly concerned at what they regarded as the unfair competition of the National Provident Fund, in 1915 friendly societies asked the government to provide a subsidy and agree that the societies should administer the Fund.[52] This was rejected and the government's subvention provisions were dropped.

During the war, societies experienced considerable problems in maintaining soldier contributions and in meeting soldier death benefit claims. The state agreed to subsidise by half the cost of death benefits through a reinsurance system, and in 1916 established a fund to this end. It also assisted by covering friendly society contributions for absent servicemen and by providing societies with compensation for half the 'excess' sickness experienced by members after the war as a result of wartime service.[53]

A government-organised conference of 1916, to mediate between the warring societies and doctors, merely strengthened politicians' resolve for the state to take charge. Societies were now drawn into the National Provident Fund by Ward's Finance Act 1916.[54] Societies were able to contribute to the Fund on behalf of members, with a half subsidy from the government, to obtain pensions and maternity allowances. The latter was evidently attractive – maternity allowances to friendly society members soon became a feature of the fund – but the number of members who contributed to Fund annuities was minimal.

As in other countries, welfare policy directions crystallised in the immediate postwar period.[55] The government considered whether to take over the friendly societies in order to establish a universal contributory state medical service along the lines of the British National Health Insurance. This would have absorbed the societies into an extended National Provident Fund that provided medical attendance, medicines and sick pay, but it came to nought. Investigation of voluntary national hospital insurance based on friendly societies also led nowhere. By the 1930s falling incomes for doctors and the looming threat of a state health system induced doctors to promote their own insurance scheme, while pensions for the elderly were to become part of an integrated and comprehensive social security system.

The state's interventions in the business of friendly societies came to an end and societies remained divided over the principle of state subsidisation. Nonetheless, there can be no doubt that the relationship between the two had shifted permanently in favour of the former. Because the friendly societies proved such unwilling collaborators, key policy-makers such as the Registrar of Friendly Societies/Superintendent of the National Provident Fund and the Commissioner of Pensions began to develop proposals for a separate, state-provided, universal contributory national insurance scheme.[56]

In parallel with the debate over old-age annuities there had been discussion of unemployment insurance, with the recession of 1909 encouraging deliberation on new policies to deal with unemployment. The government announced that it was considering a subsidised contributory insurance scheme, and the labour movement, together with the new Labour Party, supported these moves.[57] In Britain in 1911 Lloyd George passed the compulsory contributory National Insurance Act, which covered British workers against sickness and unemployment. Ward gave notice here that such a scheme, possibly associated with the friendly societies, would be considered. The Reform Party quickly got on the bandwagon but when it assumed power in 1912 any development stalled. Matters remained thus until the end of the war.

After the war the Labour Party, and particularly Peter Fraser, advocated unemployment insurance with increasing forcefulness.[58] Fraser argued that it was time that New Zealand followed overseas examples and provided 'sustenance' in the form of a minimum living wage. He worked towards setting up an Unemployment Board and greater government intervention in the labour market. In 1921 he introduced into Parliament the Unemployed Workers' Bill, modelled on a Queensland Act and providing insurance and sustenance payments, to be funded via a government contribution and levies on employers.[59] Although Massey and Gordon Coates, for electoral purposes, made commitments to an unemployment insurance scheme, the government refused to take up Fraser's proposal when it came time to act.

The postwar revolt against taxation and the strong pressure to reduce the fiscal burden of the state (see below) was undoubtedly a major influence on their decision. A public campaign, including a Farmers' Union call for a compulsory contributory scheme, pushed the issue to the fore. The Labour Party also pressured the government to increase and extend pensions, amid rising concern at their costs.[60] The old-age pension had increased substantially and its conditions had been liberalised. The weekly rate was raised to 10s in 1905 and to 15s in 1917.

The government in 1922 asked G. Fache, Commissioner of Pensions, for advice on the burgeoning system of 'free' (that is, non-contributory) pensions.[61] Alongside the old-age pension there were now widows' pensions, military pensions, miners' pensions and epidemic allowances. Fache forcefully recommended compulsory superannuation to render the problem of funding pensions redundant.

> Everything lends itself in New Zealand to the smooth working of such a scheme. The population is still comparatively small; it has already been educated to accept compulsion in many directions, e.g. in regard to education; the social services controlled by the State would render the administration comparatively easy; and . . . the nucleus of the scheme is already in existence in the shape of the National Provident Fund.

G.J. Anderson, Minister of Pensions, endorsed the initiative, and Fache produced proposals in 1924.[62] Fache suggested the progressive introduction of a subsidised contributory scheme for old age, invalidity, widowhood, unemployment, sickness and orphanhood. This would be based on the National Provident Fund and start with those 25 and under. With the eventual inclusion of unemployment insurance, Fache felt able to ask for employer contributions; the contributor, state and employer were to pay equal amounts.

The proposal seemed well received by government and others. Anderson regarded a compulsory contributory scheme, such as that adopted in other countries, as the only means of funding adequate pensions and other benefits.[63] Politicians as diverse as the Liberal educational reformer J.A. Hanan, Thomas Wilford (leader of the Liberal Opposition) and Savage and Holland of the Labour Party called for national insurance. Massey acknowledged that 'we are moving steadily – and quite rightly – towards some scheme of general superannuation'. Anderson continued to work on a scheme.

The proposals provided different methods of contribution up to 35 years of age and excluded those above this age. The issue of contributions by employers and the state remained unsettled. Following the death of Massey, during the 1925 election campaign the new Reform leader Coates promised a scheme for sickness and unemployment based on these proposals.[64]

In 1925 Britain announced its own contributory social insurance scheme, combined with income tax reductions and concessions. This developed the previously incomplete social insurance scheme commenced in 1911. Britain had decided to grasp the nettle and commit itself to social insurance, while overcoming the crucial actuarial problem of how to deal with older people by providing open-ended state financial backup.

Such an approach was far more difficult in New Zealand. It was impossible to make further tax reductions beyond those already being made as a result of postwar political commitments, and there was not an existing compulsory scheme to build on. Such a heavy burden on the state had to be avoided, in the opinion of Fache; it was 'outside the bounds of practicable politics in a young country' such as New Zealand.[65] The only solution was to carry on with the free pensions and limit the contributory scheme to those 25 years and under in employment.

In parallel with these developments, family allowances were now being considered. Such state assistance to bring up children received much attention internationally in the early 1920s.[66] In 1925, the Department of Labour advocated a contributory, graduated taxation scheme under which single men would receive 7s 6d a week less in wages, those with one child would experience no effective change in their wage, and men with more than one child would get an extra 7s 6d for each additional child. This proposal became a hot issue during the 1925 election campaign, with the Labour Party arguing for a scheme funded from general taxation that did not entail wage cuts. Coates adamantly rejected wage cuts and backed away from the contributory tax, while saying that he realised that 'the man on the minimum wage could not bring up a family as it should be brought up. The Government earnestly desired to help him and was considering how it could be accomplished'.[67]

The government capitulated to the Labour Party's view – a contributory approach was resoundingly rejected. The Family Allowances Act 1926 – rapidly passed with little discussion – established a distinctive scheme funded from general taxation, as had happened with the old-age pension.[68] This was another peg upon which an eventual tax-funded welfare system might be launched.

The proposed social insurance scheme, restricted to those 25 years and under, was forced into a corner.[69] It would be two or more decades before it began to 'pay off'; in the meantime the state would incur the rising costs of free pensions. Such a scenario for the future had little appeal to the politicians in spite of their considerable commitment to social insurance in principle. The government did eventually draft a bill, after tinkering with the levels of contributions, age groups and benefits, but its resolve waned.[70] Unemployment insurance was discarded and the insoluble dilemma of the level of contributions of those above the age of 25 years was put to one side by the simple expedient of failing to specify them in the draft bill.

RT HON. J. G. COATES

Gordon Coates, Reform Prime Minister keen on social insurance. J. T. Allen, Parliamentary Portraits, *1936*

An end was finally put to the miserable exercise when Parliament opened for the 1928 session; the proposals were withdrawn in the light of deteriorating economic conditions and rising unemployment.[71] To tell the truth, there was no way that any government would have been able to impose such a scheme on the country, even if it had wanted to, when employers and employees alike would not co-operate and the state's own worsening fiscal situation militated against the move.

Although a social insurance scheme did not eventuate, the debates over state assistance highlighted a drawing together of the state's wage and welfare provisions, particularly with the inclusion of unemployment insurance. The divide between wages and welfare was also bridged by the view that free hospital services should be provided as of right and not as part of a residual charitable function, and by family allowances and the emergence of a concept of a living wage.

New Zealanders were beginning to develop an opposition to contributory schemes that would harden over time. It would become more and more difficult to pose the contributory alternative when non-contributory pensions existed and when people perceived contributions as reducing their income in a way that taxation did not. But this shift implied that the state was able to raise its own revenue to fund pensions, and this was not at all certain.

Fiscal constraints and opportunities

The state's increasingly redistributive role required not only a reorientation of policy but also an enlarged capacity to respond to the claims made upon it. The economic correlate of 'political' democracy, embodied in the phrase 'no taxation without representation', was supplanted by that of 'social' democracy – that taxation embodied social rights and expectations of state intervention and eventually the redistribution of incomes. The colonial state's longstanding capacity to assist the settler was extended and expressed in the welfare state, founded upon a massively increased fiscal capacity.[72]

Long-term changes in the structure of state revenue in the nineteenth century prepared the ground for taxation-based forms of welfare. The following discussion focuses upon central government fiscal policy, although until the mid 1870s, provincial government, funded by land revenue, public works loans and a proportion of customs duties transferred from the central government, should be kept in mind.

Vogel's development scheme of the 1870s and the abolition of the provinces had heralded a considerable expansion of the central state and prepared it for greatly increased powers of intervention. Not only were the perceived bounds of state intervention extending outwards, but the material possibilities were increasing as a result of expanding revenue. The state's increased resources would provide a means of escape from the conundrum of a universal old-age pension when a contributory principle was rejected.

From customs duties to income taxation

For many years customs duties were the major source of revenue for the central government.[73] Other forms of revenue were difficult to collect in a newly founded, unsettled and rapidly changing society. Income tax was discarded as inappropriate; property-based taxes were more typical of developing societies but New Zealand never really developed this source of income.

For a time in the early 1850s, with Grey's regulations freeing up the land market, the sale of land became an important contributor, but following the 'compact' of 1856 the provinces obtained this source of revenue. Customs became the central exchequer's staple. Supplemented by stamp duties from 1866, this source of revenue dominated the nineteenth century. The 1879 land tax made a slight contribution, and the property tax which followed it a little more.

Income tax had been a central issue for British popular radicalism because poorer people were taxed but lacked political representation. 'No taxation without representation' was the catch-cry. Here wage earners had largely gained political representation and did not pay any income tax.

In the early years much of the customs revenue came from a limited number of items regarded as the 'necessaries of life' for working men. Such duties, described as the working man's 'breakfast table' were considerably higher than in Australia. This was justified by the fact that the comfortably-off working man in New Zealand was well able to withstand duties on his bread, tea and coffee, tobacco and tipple.[74] Half of the total customs duties came from alcohol, with another quarter from tobacco, tea, coffee and sugar. In 1858 the government raised the tariff on these basic items, rejecting a huge petition against such an 'oppressive' tariff. Wages were sufficiently high and workers sufficiently well-off not to need such relief: 'Jack was here as good as his master . . . the fact was,

Seddon's free breakfast table did not please all. New Zealand Free Lance, *21 April 1906*

THE REDUCTIONS IN CUSTOMS DUTIES.

I am in favour of a free breakfast table.—*The Premier at Rangiora.*

The Housewife: But me and the kiddies can't eat tobacco, Mr. Seddon.

in the colony we were all gentlemen. It was not necessary in New Zealand to distinguish between class and class.'[75] Confidence in a high standard of living continued to underpin high tariffs on necessities until 1878.

In 1864 tariffs were imposed on a wider range of imported goods to help finance the land wars. In 1866 the customs net was widened, and stamp duties were introduced to relieve the less well-off from the unfair burden of customs duties.[76] However, an attempt to abolish certain duties to give 'some relief to the poorer classes' failed, and there were no reductions in the tariff until the turbulent late 1870s, when a fundamental re-evaluation of the role of the state and its revenue took place.[77]

In 1873 revenue from customs was greatly increased, to deal with the emerging deficit, by being placed on an ad valorem basis. Then, following abolition of the provinces, agitation for tax reform began to surface. In 1875 some MPs, including Grey, attempted to have customs duties, and in particular those on necessities, reduced to help working people. In 1877 Grey argued for a land ('property') tax and the removal of duties on the necessaries of life.[78] He advocated a progressive form of land tax based on acreage. His initial idea was that all would pay – speculators, monopolists and smallholders alike. He saw it as an expression of citizenship to create a contributory common 'guarantee fund' that would support the destitute and proclaimed that 'every human being in New Zealand has the right to claim subsistence, or the means of gaining it, from the State'.[79] This foreshadowed the association of the old-age pension and taxation in the 1890s.

Atkinson argued in contrast that constitutional issues needed to be settled first. As Treasurer in 1877 he sought a 'political rest' from Vogelite development. Changes to the tax system should not be contemplated at that time, he argued. He favoured a comprehensive property tax rather than a land tax, arguing that monopoly in land had not developed to the extent that the state had to act in this way.

Grey came to power in 1877, and promised prosperity, revised tariffs, taxation reform (including a land tax), expanded public works and land settlement policies in 1878.[80] He also made an impassioned plea for the removal of duties on tea, sugar, clothing and other necessaries of life. E.J. Wakefield said that if New Zealand was to have free trade in land and commerce then such should also apply in taxation – all classes must pay a just share. The government should pre-empt any agitation against tariffs by lowering them. 'If we are to wait until the working-classes of this country find the duties upon the necessaries of life so burdensome and so oppressive that they are driven to rise in agitation against them, what sort of a tariff should we have after that?'[81]

Ballance, now Treasurer, issued a manifesto on fiscal reform, noting the considerable discontent over the incidence of taxation and arguing for a fairer distribution.[82] He pronounced that the 'bounty of Nature must be matched by the beneficence of our institutions, and the equity of our public policy.'[83] He was determined to adopt reforms that would 'show a country inviting labour as well as capital' and, moreover, retain such wage-earning migrants by changing the structure of duties to encourage manufacturing, and reducing duties on some necessities. But he believed that, unlike in Britain, the working classes could bear most duties without inconvenience; a 'free breakfast table' was not necessary but the 'huge imposts' on tea and sugar should be reduced. Ballance proposed to remove duties on all raw materials and articles used in trades, retaining them only when genuinely protective of an industry rather than to raise revenue. Duty on grain and flour was indeed removed but other members of the government prevented further reductions, suggesting that duties would be removed when such industries were stronger. (This argument foreshadowed the Liberal position on tariffs articulated later by Reeves.)

Grey introduced the land tax in 1879. This was aimed at larger landowners and explicitly proposed that state revenue should reflect a concept of 'fairness'. Grey acknowledged that the measure was intended both as a land tax and an income tax. Ballance explicitly justified the land tax in terms of the injustice done to those who had to pay the bulk of taxation through duties on the 'necessaries of life'.[84] Large landowners, who benefited from increased land values due to the state's investment in immigration and infrastructure, paid nothing. Such inequality had 'implanted a strong sense of injustice in the minds of the wages class', and the burden had to be adjusted 'according to the capacity of the different classes' to bear it. In contrast to the approach in 1877, land worth £500 or less would be exempt; the bona fide small settler would be excluded. Grey's idea of linking citizenship and welfare was lost.

The land tax proved largely symbolic in the end, reflecting popular beliefs that state revenue should be adjusted to achieve social objectives, rather than becoming a significant source of revenue. Its perceived association with a general property and income tax (that was by then regarded as inevitable) broadened its appeal.[85] Its long-term effect was to open the way for the expansion of state revenue by means of a land and income tax some decades later.

Meanwhile the land tax proved very unpopular amongst farmers, and within a matter of months and with a change of government, Atkinson replaced it with a general property tax of a penny in the pound.[86] He argued that the land tax imposed too great a burden on capital invested in land, retarded development in order to attack abuse by a few, and would not check speculation, and he appealed to a sense of equity in bringing in the more general property tax that spread the load. Atkinson thought that realised wealth in all forms should bear its fair share but incomes should be excluded. An income tax to his mind was too inquisitorial, required elaborate machinery and was open to great inequalities.

Atkinson had consolidated his ideas about the economic impact of government on the people during his time in opposition to Grey, and this led him to advance novel solutions in the early 1880s, when depression threatened the well-being of the country.[87] He advanced his radical National

Premier Atkinson ponders the fiscal options as the country is weighed down by the government's demands for revenue. Parliamentary Library, untitled cartoon collection, 1870s.

Insurance proposal (discussed above) and made a detailed analysis of the fiscal impact of the state, intending to open up debate in preparation for a time when the government's accounts were healthier.[88] But the depression deepened, retrenchment dominated debate, and protectionism increasingly swayed opinion.

Having spent up large, the country had little choice but to swallow the bitter pill of retrenchment during the depression. Through the 1880s fiscal policy was dominated by the consequences of Vogelite loans; the over-riding goals were to avoid deficits and to deal with huge interest payments.[89] Governments fell with regularity, as it proved impossible to deal effectively with this predicament. An income tax seemed politically unattainable as wealthier groups sought to impose retrenchment upon the state itself; meanwhile the property tax proved very unpopular.[90]

As we have seen, New Zealand began to contemplate protection of manufacturing as local industry grew. Into the 1880s the protectionist movement swelled and the state looked at tariffs to create barriers to the import of manufactured goods.[91] With greater industrial development, it began to be argued that the interests of wage earners were better served by higher duties that assisted in the promotion of local industries and employment.

In the Australian state of Victoria protective tariffs were directly associated with preventing the exploitation of wage earners. The understanding was that the state would encourage local industry in exchange for eliminating 'sweated' labour – poor working conditions, long hours and low rates of pay. The so-called 'new' protection shielded manufacturers from outside competition in

MAJOR ATKINSON'S LAST STRAW.—THE PROPOSED ADDITION TO THE PROPERTY TAX.

Atkinson, having halved the property tax in 1882, was forced to increase it again in 1883 as the economy worsened. Observer, *14 July 1883*

exchange for them paying fair and reasonable wages.[92] This approach was consolidated early in the twentieth century by the Harvester judgement and later judgements that directly linked the family wage and protectionism. In New Zealand the link was not so direct, but there was a strengthening association between protectionism and an expectation that New Zealand should offer superior working conditions. This complicated tariff policy. Ballance had introduced an element of protection into his tariff reforms of 1878, while in 1880 some manufacturers advocated protective duties for industry to the Colonial Industries Commission. The commission declined to recommend increased duties, arguing that the tariff was already sufficiently protective and that this had resulted in exceptionally high wages in some industries.[93] William Montgomery (leader of the 'Liberal' opposition) and Seddon spoke in the House that year in favour of protection as a means of protecting living standards and providing work.[94] In 1882 Atkinson raised duties slightly and widened the range of commodities subject to duty.

Protectionism was much discussed during the election of 1884. The New Zealand Protection Association was formed that year and had its platform adopted by the Trades and Labour Congress in Dunedin in 1885.[95] Local protectionist associations were formed throughout the country, and Trades and Labour Councils and the recently formed Manufacturers' Association began to press for a more substantial protective tariff. Atkinson himself now advocated the development of local manufacturing.

The Stout-Vogel government attempted unsuccessfully to increase duties in 1885 and 1887 against the resistance of the retrenchers and free-traders, although Vogel's reasons were avowedly for revenue only.[96] Even though he preferred a land and income tax for reasons of fairness and revenue (but not to attack landed monopoly), Vogel conceded that the property tax would have to stay.

In 1887 the Chambers of Commerce advocated increased duties on tea and sugar, to the extent of half of their value.[97] This was taken up by the parliamentary opposition. On the other hand, the New Zealand Protection Association wanted no tariffs on tea, or cotton clothing, but substantial tariffs of 25 percent on boots, cloth and woollen hosiery.[98] It modelled its proposals on the Victorian tariff (and was influenced by the example of American protectionism). The association placed great emphasis on bettering the position of labour, encouraging immigration and employment, and preventing the exodus to Australia.

The failure of the Stout-Vogel government's duties proposals in 1887 led to the government's fall. Protection remained a prominent issue in the 1887 election but increasingly powerful opponents advanced government retrenchment in association with free trade. A strong conservative 'retrenchment' movement was reflected in the emergence of Political and Financial Reform Associations and the so-called 'skinflints' in Parliament, as those with property felt threatened by proposals for increased taxation.[99] Keith Sinclair argues that such forces led to the formation of a conservative party and a shift from the 'politics of public works' that had characterised the previous decade to the 'politics of class philosophy'. But such a class-based configuration, if it existed at all, was stillborn. The pattern was more one of a temporary polarisation and deviation from the course of liberal politics due to the deepened depression. The coming of the Liberals to power in 1891 rapidly rendered this conservative movement redundant and consolidated the liberal-radical force.

In 1888 the government's increasingly dire financial situation came to a head.[100] The New Zealand Protection Association had re-formed and a conference of the Industrial Protection League issued its agreed tariff to Atkinson. Protection, it was believed, would

Protection for local industry gained force during the 1880s. Observer and Free Lance, *2 July 1887*

THE COMING HORSE.

As Premier Atkinson prepared to introduce protectionist tariffs some felt that this would damage New Zealand's interests, but one politician said that he would support protection even if Satan was in favour. New Zealand Punch *(Dunedin), 5 May 1888*

assist in stemming the exodus as well as promoting local industries and increasing revenue. Atkinson largely conceded to their demands and, with the aid of opposition Liberals and against the strenuous opposition of his own government's free-traders, he increased customs duties to make up the revenue shortfall and to increase protection substantially.[101] Many items were now subject to double the previous rate and protection was specifically given to local clothing and boot manufacturers. Atkinson's tariff revision established a precedent that henceforth New Zealand would adopt a moderate extent of protection for its infant industries.

Some Liberals, including Seddon (who had broken ranks to oppose the tariff on tea and sugar), attacked Atkinson fiercely because of the effect of the tariff on working people.[102] In the end there was no increase in the tariff on sugar. Reeves, by contrast, advanced the emerging Liberal position that put protection first as 'the greatest benefit that a Government can possibly offer to the people of New Zealand'.[103] Thus the debate had shifted towards greater protection for local industry, combined when possible with the removal of duties on tea and sugar as a concession to the labour interest. Such a stance was difficult to challenge without invoking the combined wrath of manufacturer and worker.

Reeves offered an insightful analysis of the reasons for protection.[104] The extreme dependence upon a few primary staple exports and the lack of a diversified economy meant that workers were given few alternatives when

OUR FREE BREAKFAST TABLE.

The free breakfast table seemed as elusive as ever. New Zealand Free Lance, *25 January 1908*

prices plunged and work dried up, forcing an exodus from the colony. Huge borrowings and the inability to extend the taxation of landowners and farmers to fund the loans necessitated a reliance on tariffs for revenue. Farmers, although largely supporting free trade, agreed to this because it avoided additional land taxes. The moderate protective tariff checked the imports of certain goods and built up a range of light consumer industries as well as engineering workshops. It did not keep wages up but was important in generating employment and therefore in keeping unemployment down. (For wages workers had to await the arbitration system.)

This period thus saw a major shift of philosophy in the gathering of state revenue. Revenue from land was no longer sufficient, and it had gone to the provinces in any case. The lack of income taxes and the reliance upon customs was buttressed by the belief that all could afford to pay in a new country offering opportunities and a high standard of living. In the late 1870s there was a re-evaluation of this approach and a shift towards protection as industrial employment swelled and as some appeared to lose out with a wage-earning labour-force coming to the fore. Alongside customs duties, the land tax in a symbolic sense asserted the inherent unfairness of gross inequality in land – a matter that had been of concern since the early days of settlement. Into the 1880s protectionism increased the country's continued dependence upon indirect taxation rather than income taxes. It was to take some time before a new fiscal base could be created, and this would require both massive political change and another deep depression.

We now turn to the introduction of an income tax, long resisted in New Zealand. In the mid 1860s New Zealand had come under pressure from Britain to levy an income tax. Britain criticised the colony for failing to tax its own people to support the land wars.[105] New Zealand's government rejected this on the grounds that revenue would not be adequate because it was politically impossible to tax wage earners. Moreover 'the nomadic character of a large part of its population' and frequent changes in occupation made the tax impractical.[106]

The debate over the respective merits of the property tax versus a land and income tax was the single most important issue of the 1890 election.[107] When they came to power in 1891 the Liberal government introduced the land and income tax with little controversy. Many countries were by now introducing income taxes. A property and income tax had come to be regarded as inevitable, assisting its introduction.

Its underlying objective, in spite of the rhetoric, was not to break up the estates nor to impose a Georgite single tax but to reassert a principle that all should pay a 'fair' share of taxation. This meant that large property owners should pay more and other hitherto exempt groups should begin to pay.

Under the new tax scheme, many fewer landowners (just over half) paid somewhat more in aggregate than under the old property tax regime; in particular land companies paid much more. Most importantly for the future, even though wage earners were initially excluded, the tax instituted a progressive system for the first time in the English-speaking world. As the Commissioner of Taxes phrased it, 'the end sought . . . is to compel contribution to the requirements of the State according to the ability of those who are called upon to contribute thereto'.[108] In the early years of the tax, attention focused on the land tax component and its relationship to other Liberal policies aimed at breaking up large estates, but it was the income tax that would prove vastly more important in the long term.

Just prior to the First World War the income tax net was extended downwards towards wage-earning groups, but for now wage earners remained exempt. This met with general acceptance. Following hard on the heels of

Lloyd George's radical 'war budget on poverty' in Britain (that included the introduction of redistributive income taxation), in New Zealand the income tax had its progressivity strengthened in 1910. Additional tiers were introduced and its graduation was steepened.[109] The introduction of tax exemptions for families with dependents in the Land and Income Assessment Amendment Act 1913 established two principles. The first was that the income tax system could be used directly for purposes of social equity; the second was that income tax could be extended to lower income groups.

The First World War radically reshaped and enlarged state revenue.[110] From 1915 the government expanded its revenue base in order to cope with the extraordinary wartime expenditure. Rates of income tax were increased by a supertax of one-third and the tax was extended to incomes from land (bringing farmers into the net). The land tax and customs duties were increased and new stamp duties imposed.

Income tax graduation was again steepened in 1915. As Minister of Finance Ward noted, 'you cannot take part in a great war without requiring to make provision in the manner of finance to an extent which in normal times would be looked at aghast'.[111] The principle Ward declared was to spread increased taxation over the widest possible area so that its effect was least oppressive, but not to touch the wage earner by lowering the income tax exemption.

New Zealand's income tax threshold remained the highest in the developed world. The Commissioner for Inland Revenue maintained in support of this that the administrative cost of collecting income tax from wage earners exceeded the revenue obtainable. A reduction in the exemption to £150 per annum (as in Britain), which would have brought in virtually all wage earners (130,000 more taxpayers), was rejected.

The failure of Ward's radical 'excess-profits' duty of 1916 forced its replacement in 1917 by a comprehensive progressive land and income tax, supplemented by a huge special war-tax on incomes. This massively increased the tax and steepened its graduation yet again even if wage earners still paid little.

During the First World War years the amount of tax taken, the progressivity of the scale, and the number of taxpayers were all dramatically increased. The state's total revenue more than doubled, largely as a result of income tax, which increased tenfold.[112] Income tax now provided 45 percent and customs less than 30 percent of total tax revenue. Before the war, customs duties had provided 60 percent and income tax less than 10 percent of revenue. The groundwork for a modern income-tax-based state had been prepared, even if wage earners still remained outside the net.

Ward assured the country that taxation would be lowered the moment the war was over but Massey did not immediately honour this after the wartime coalition with Ward broke up.[113] He gave priority to dealing with the massive war debt to balance the budget, as did other countries. Meanwhile, income tax revenue rose even further during the postwar boom – it comprised 65 percent

The Taxation Committee of 1922 was supposed to give the taxpayer some relief from high marginal income tax rates but Doctor Massey was more worried about a deficit. NZH, 20 May 1922

of a considerably increased revenue base by 1921.[114] There was a corresponding explosion in state expenditure. For the first time in New Zealand's history there was a substantial upwards shift in state expenditure as a proportion of its gross national product. By the mid 1920s social services expenditure (on health and hospitals, pensions and education) had increased by nearly 50 percent in real terms since the war, expanding from one-third to virtually one-half of all expenditure (excluding war charges).[115]

As the fragile postwar boom collapsed in the early 1920s the government retrenched government expenditure. Taxpayers, for their part, 'revolted' against the massively increased impositions. There was considerable resistance to expanding welfare provisions any further, based on the pincers of unprecedented postwar debt and a perceived maximum 'taxable capacity'. Schemes of self-financing social insurance came to the fore as we have seen above. Income tax scales were rationalised and some reductions made, but at the same time the government imposed a 20 percent additional tax on incomes to keep revenue up. This meant that total revenue actually increased.

In 1922 the Taxation Committee concluded that 'the limits of taxation that this country can bear have been reached – indeed exceeded'; that the higher graduated rate income tax was 'drying up the sources of revenue'; that income tax on large companies was the highest amongst the British dominions; and that both the income tax and land tax were seriously affecting production.[116] It advocated reduced marginal rates of income tax and a lowering of company tax amongst other things. The 20 percent additional tax on incomes was removed and the basic rate of income tax was reduced.

Low income earners still paid virtually no income tax and the steepness of the scale had declined somewhat from the heady heights of the war.[117] The rate was negligible for those earning just a few hundred pounds, and was still less than 5 percent for those earning just under £1,000, but now the numerous wage earners in the £400–£1,000 band contributed a quarter of tax revenue overall. Virtually half of the state's income tax revenue came from those earning £1,000–£5,000 and the remaining quarter from incomes of more than £5,000. The distribution of assessable incomes of the time demonstrated just how much taxable capacity remained in lower incomes and how little was available from incomes of £1,000 or more. Some 40 percent of the total assessable incomes were less than £400 and another 40 percent were £400–£1,000. The state was obtaining the bulk of its income tax from little more than one-fifth of the potential assessable incomes in the country.

Pressure to reform taxation was maintained. The Royal Commission of 1924 affirmed that a graduated income tax should remain and that the tax base be broadened as much as possible to augment revenue.[118] Concern over those on lower incomes paying even less tax than before, and far less than in Britain or Australia, resulted in a steepening of the lower part of the scale in 1927 so that the 'middle class' on incomes up to £1,500 paid substantially more.

The long-term impact of the tax revolt meant that income tax was reduced by about 60 percent in the latter half of the 1920s compared with its peak in the early 1920s. A resurgence of revenue from customs, due to the dramatic increase in trade, and increased death duties and other taxes (such as stamp duties) bolstered more traditional forms of state revenue and restored the dominant place of customs to government revenue. Customs now provided about 50 percent and income tax only about 20 percent of the state's revenue base.

Lessons had been drawn for the future nevertheless. The income tax had dramatically extended the state's revenue base at a time of need. This could readily be achieved again, while the potential taxable capacity of those on wage-earning incomes had been noted. If economic conditions moved against New Zealand again the state would not be able to rely upon customs revenue as its mainstay.

Depression, taxation and social security

Like the depression of the late nineteenth century, the depression of the early 1930s proved formative for developments in government policy.[119] Most historians look at these years in terms of their impact on people's consciousness and the bringing to power of a Labour government which broke with the past by legislating in favour of wage earners and creating the welfare state. This approach does not sufficiently take account of continuities with the past, or explore the experimental initiatives associated with the 'welfare laboratory'

The government resists pressure to use its surplus for tax reductions, arguing that the 1922 and 1924 tax recommendations have been acted on. NZH, *6 August 1927*

which formed the crucial context for the welfare state. Instead of focusing upon the content of the Labour government's reforms – which are adequately covered elsewhere – here we look at the revenue base for the welfare state, for this was the hidden key to its distinctive nature.

Prior to the election of the Labour government, the decision to create a taxation-based unemployment relief fund in 1930, although little-noticed, ranks alongside that of the old-age pension of 1898 in the shaping of New Zealand's welfare system. In conjunction with the extension downwards of income tax into the bulk of wage earners, it provided a fiscal platform for launching the welfare state. Labour took up these new revenue-gathering powers and capitalised upon them, first with the Social Security Act 1938 and then during the Second World War. By the end of the war the state had been put on a dramatically different footing. The ground was prepared for the long postwar boom, during which the state's revenue powers could be expanded painlessly in conditions of inflation.

Along the way options such as social insurance and enlisting the support of the friendly societies, which had been on the agenda since the 1880s, were discarded. Self-reliance and self-help were replaced by direct state assistance, and a new relationship was forged between state and citizen, based on taxation of the family wage earner.

Unemployment

The deteriorating economic conditions of the late 1920s forced a reconsideration of unemployment policy.[120] The traditional response of public works relief, expanded greatly during the 1920s, became inadequate. In 1927 Fraser attempted to introduce unemployment insurance legislation based on contributory principles, provoking the first serious official consideration of a scheme. The National Industrial Conference of 1928 recommended that a commission be set up to investigate the problem and Prime Minister Coates set up an Unemployment Committee to explore unemployment insurance, while attacking the concept of a monetary 'dole' without work as 'dangerous'.[121] The National Industrial Conference recommended that funds be provided from the consolidated account to deal with unemployment, but economist Horace Belshaw and others advocated unemployment insurance. Coates, however, made no promise to introduce insurance prior to the 1928 election.

During the 1928 election campaign Ward, on behalf of the new United Party, mistakenly promised massive borrowing to deal with unemployment by promoting land settlement and building railways. He also promised an unemployment insurance scheme. United, in alliance with the Labour Party, came to power. In September 1929 the government announced that unemployment insurance would be fully investigated and a scheme introduced. But Fraser introduced his own bill, sceptical of the government's real commitment. Although his bill was rejected, the Labour Bills Committee recommended that the government urgently consider unemployment insurance.[122]

Dealing with unemployment was still couched in terms of social insurance, but it was never contemplated as a fully contributory approach. The difficulty in operationalising schemes even for the more predictable life events of sickness and old age and for more affluent groups in society, indicated that a contributory scheme for highly unpredictable unemployment was not feasible. By this time in Britain it was recognised that provisions beyond the contributory system were required.

In New Zealand any notion of contributory insurance was soon discarded by the Unemployment Committee of 1929–30, which was charged with managing the rising tide of unemployed workers. An insurance scheme was no use in the developing emergency – an immediate response was required. It was impossible in any case to calculate the risk in New Zealand's highly seasonal and vulnerable economy based on infrastructural, extractive, and primary industries.

The Committee stressed that unemployment was not an 'industrial problem', for which employer and worker contributions were justified, but a 'social problem'.[123] It argued that all should contribute on an equal basis and 'share the burden'. Every citizen – employer, worker, farmer or whoever – should take on their shoulders the responsibility for dealing with the problem, by paying for its remedy through their taxes.

SLAYING THE GOLIATH OF UNEMPLOYMENT.

Sir Joseph Ward makes a futile attempt to ward off the Goliath of unemployment with public works. New Zealand Free Lance, *6 February 1929*

This concept of broad social responsibility drew upon earlier notions expressed at the time of the old-age pension legislation. Any such scheme was a collective national enterprise to which individuals both contributed and could draw upon for assistance. This foreshadowed Labour's 'social scheme' of social security of the late 1930s (see below). It was not a matter of ducking responsibility; governments had dealt with unemployment for more than fifty years.[124]

What the Committee meant by its stance was that unemployment was the product of the broad organisation of the New Zealand economy and society based on farming. With the country so dependent upon primary export prices and all members of society deriving benefit from this, so too must they share, in the interests of 'social justice', the responsibility for unemployment resulting from the collapse of primary export prices. It was stressed that the special taxation would make every taxpayer 'feel that the problem of unemployment is one which affects him personally'.[125]

The attacks by Gordon Coates and George Forbes on the British 'dole' have often been interpreted as conservative resistance to unemployment assistance. This was far from the case. The 'dole' was not the original British unemployment insurance but a supplementary backup that took over when unemployment insurance could no longer cope.[126] The pair were objecting not so much to monetary payment per se, as to indiscriminate payment not linked to an insurance scheme. The existence of the dole damaged the credibility of the insurance principle and created an expectation on the part of workers that they had an unconditional right to support from the state. This created a wedge that rapidly destabilised unemployment insurance.

Extension of the income tax scale (as distinct from an alternative unemployment tax) down into the lower income groups was ruled out as uneconomical, as it had been earlier in the 1920s.[127] An administratively simple flat tax would instead be imposed on all incomes, including those exempted from income taxation, augmented by a further flat tax on various groups to represent the principle of equality of contributions. The unemployment fund was to be supplemented by a contribution of up to an additional one-third from the consolidated fund (a proportion accepted in Britain at the time) according to fluctuations in unemployment.

The government largely accepted the Committee's recommendations and in 1930 introduced unemployment legislation that would radically transform the nature of social assistance in this country. For the first time in New Zealand's history the bold step was taken to provide by law a fund for unemployment relief. The measure obtained support from the Reform Party and from key pressure groups such as the Farmers' Union and Employers' Federation. However, the Labour Party wanted the more traditional solution of central government-provided relief work.[128] It also wanted sustenance to be paid, a graduated rather than a flat tax and women to be eligible for relief.

The Unemployment Act 1930 established an Unemployment Board to administer a fund based on a simple flat levy on all adult males. (The supplementary elements of the unemployment fund were dropped.) The government was to contribute £1 from the consolidated account for every £2 in the fund. The level and amount of relief wages would vary according to the family needs of the unemployed and the exigencies of the fund. During the depression the traditional single/married distinction in work-based relief would be developed by varying wages according to the number of children.

The Board got to work, and a range of work-based schemes were introduced and administered by local bodies, most of them in urban centres. As the depression deepened and the numbers of unemployed spiralled upwards, the

STILL MORE TAXATION!!!
Our Government Explores Every Means to Raise Fresh Revenue.

As the government seeks to balance the books it looks at every source of revenue. New Zealand
Free Lance, *8 February 1933*

Board's funds became exhausted early in 1931. Relief rates were reduced, the
scheme was tightened up and rationed work was introduced. This was still
not enough and the government rushed the Unemployment Amendment
Act through Parliament to provide a new 'emergency charge'. The tax now
comprised a reduced annual levy on adult males, together with the new impost
on wages, salaries and other incomes, including those of women.

During these years the state's more general sources of revenue had to be
raised to compensate for dramatically shrinking customs revenue as imports
fell away. The government was determined to balance its budget so as not to
increase the extremely high levels of debt inherited from the First World War,

as covering such debt required 40 percent of government expenditure.[129] In the late 1920s annual tariff revisions (and other taxes, such as primage – a surtax of 10 percent on income tax, from 1930) were introduced. In 1931 the surtax was raised to 30 percent, greater numbers of wage earners were drawn into the net, and new forms of income tax were introduced.

Continued pressure on the unemployment fund resulted in an amendment to the Unemployment Act in 1932; the emergency charge rate was increased drastically and the contribution from the consolidated fund was abolished. Coates wanted the fund to be made completely self-supporting.[130] The size of the fund swelled dramatically and the unemployment tax now provided a greater proportion of taxation revenue (just over 20 percent of the total) than did income tax itself. Some 365,000 males and 95,500 females contributed to the unemployment tax (including nearly 120,000 receiving less than £104 per annum). In short, the emergency conditions had extended taxation down to the mass of wage earners.

In 1933 the exemption for income tax was dropped further to forestall a catastrophic fall in revenue, bringing large numbers of lower income earners into the general income-tax net for the first time. The exemption was now roughly at the level it would maintain into the postwar period. By this time taxation had reached about 24 percent of national income, compared with only 14 percent prior to the depression. Overall tax rates returned to the levels of the First World War, but with taxation on lower incomes well above the previous mark. The government had reached what was regarded as the effective taxable capacity of the higher income earners while substantially increasing the proportion of lower incomes taken and extending the tax net downwards to all wage and salary earners.

By the end of the depression the state had considerably expanded its sources of revenue and had created a platform for expansion. The state's fiscal capacity had not been limited or damaged – it had come out of the depression remarkably well. The government had established the necessary taxation and had kept the books balanced. The highly regressive unemployment tax provided a simple and efficient form of revenue collection that could easily be adapted for different ends.

Social security

As the depression lifted, contributory social insurance came back onto the agenda – indeed it was pointed out that the unemployment tax could easily be adapted to this end.[131] News filtered through of American and Canadian moves to establish social security provisions, and in 1934 hospital boards proposed compulsory health insurance in co-operation with the British Medical Association. Forbes and Coates, on their trip to Britain in 1935, investigated superannuation and health insurance schemes, while a departmental committee looked at ways of implementing a comprehensive superannuation and health insurance scheme.[132] Coates acknowledged that many countries already had such schemes; the crux of the matter was how to finance it, especially for older age groups. Those who argued for a universal non-contributory pension would have to face the fact that it was impractical and would cost a massive 60 percent of existing taxation revenue.

The departmental committee recommended a comprehensive scheme covering a wide range of benefits and health insurance. (Unemployment insurance was to be kept separate.) The benefit and health insurance schemes were to be financed together, with workers and employers probably making equal contributions and the state making up the deficiency due to inadequate older-age contributions (as in Britain). Coates appeared serious in promoting the schemes, and national superannuation and health insurance appeared in his election manifesto.[133]

Labour's overwhelming victory at the polls eliminated the possibility of social insurance, according to the historians. But did it entirely? Was Walter Nash's advocacy of a contributory scheme in 1937–8 an aberrant change of mind induced by the persuasive powers of a British actuary, or was his consideration more serious than this? Nash's role and the persistent championing of the scheme by key government department heads in the face of Labour Party and caucus opposition demands a closer look.

In order to examine the ultimate shape of the funding of social security we have to retrace the intricacies of internal policy developments. The overall development of social security policy is well covered in Hanson's book, *The Politics of Social Security*. The object of this discussion is to draw out the extent to which the contributory insurance principle remained relevant to the debate about, and the fiscal underpinnings of, the emerging social security scheme.

As soon as Labour was elected to office it began to examine a social security scheme, but first, as promised to the electorate, pensions (particularly the old-age pension) had to be increased.[134] This was a forerunner of the battle lines to come. The Pensions Department

HON. WALTER NASH

Walter Nash, architect of the Social Security Act. J.T. Allen, Parliamentary Portraits, *1936*

RT HON. M. J. SAVAGE

M.J. Savage, first Labour Prime Minister.
J.T. Allen, Parliamentary Portraits, *1936*

and Treasury examined a wide range of options for liberalising and increasing pensions. Bernard Ashwin, Assistant Secretary to the Treasury, reacted very strongly against the expenditure implications, warning of what would follow. Other large expenditure proposals loomed, requiring a 40 percent increase in revenue, the source of which was still to be determined. While Cabinet took some cognisance of Treasury's advice, the Labour caucus refused to accept it, and after much conflict the old-age pension was raised.

Treasury's concern was that the country's taxable capacity had been reached, as was evident in the concurrent discussions over taxation reform.[135] While taxation legislation was being consolidated, an interdepartmental committee with a very wide brief looked at the taxation of companies and banks, and at new forms of taxation, as well as the incidence of taxation. There was searching scrutiny of company taxation in particular, which made a very substantial contribution to the total income tax take. The general thrust of the committee's deliberations was to shift taxation towards personal incomes, to render revenue less susceptible to external economic fluctuations.

Deliberations on the full social security scheme then began. A special committee was appointed in September 1936, which included Ashwin and J.S. Reid from Nash's office, together with the heads of the Pensions Department and the National Provident Fund, and the government actuary.[136] Labour had promised a universal old-age pension of 30s a week at age 60 years for men and 55 for women; the cost was gigantic compared with any previous proposals.

Ashwin clearly opposed a taxation-based scheme and its implications for the economy. He questioned Nash on this closely.[137] Nash, probably conveying Prime Minister Savage's view, said that the scheme would be entirely funded through taxation – half in the form of the flat-rate emergency unemployment charge, half by the consolidated account to the extent of previous pension costs. He had in mind an approach similar to that instituted for unemployment relief in 1930. Savage did not hesitate to advocate the imposition of additional taxation, as had been reflected in his motherhood endowment bills of the early 1920s.

The committee emphatically stated that 'the complete scheme as visualised by the Cabinet Committee is beyond the financial capacity of the Dominion'.[138] It would require a tremendous increase (nearly fourfold) in the unemployment charge, and the state's taxation revenue would have to be virtually doubled, to about half the country's aggregate private income.

Desperately searching for some means to continue, Nash asked the committee to explore the extent of existing private schemes for their possible transfer to a state scheme.[139] Meanwhile Sir Walter Kinnear, Controller of the British Ministry of Health's Insurance Department and involved in its schemes of the 1920s, was asked to describe how the British system worked. Kinnear advocated the tried and true social insurance principle that he was familiar with, and highlighted the precariousness of Labour's plans, which lacked any adequate funding base. Kinnear, perhaps unintentionally, also removed any possibility that the friendly societies might be involved in the scheme. He said that there had been problems with societies administering the British health scheme. This would ultimately spell the death knell for the societies.

The committee held out little hope of trading on existing private schemes.[140] Labour would have to reduce its expectations – the task should be to design a financially realistic scheme. As suggested by Reid, the committee introduced an insurance principle by proposing a division of the old-age pension into a means-tested one, funded by the unemployment tax, and a small universal contributory one, subsidised by the state. In this scheme, the contributory pension payment would be progressively raised to eliminate the means-tested one eventually. In this way New Zealand would make the transition towards a compulsory, universal and contributory scheme similar to the British one. The Cabinet committee seemed favourably disposed towards this proposal.[141]

The committee's final report of August 1937 tinkered with the proposals. It discussed how women might fit into the proposed scheme, looked at the impact on friendly societies, and modified the recommendations regarding unemployment and sickness benefits. Nash now followed the direction suggested by the committee and developed an insurance-based scheme in association with the British government actuary, G.H. Maddex. The funding was more obviously based on contributions, and benefits were income-related. Maddex, who was in close touch with Ashwin, took as his brief a means of achieving a transition from the non-contributory to the contributory scheme. He thought that, in order to achieve this the state should subsidise contributions, and should also switch the savings made from the wind-down of the free old-age pension to the contributory scheme.

Maddex worked feverishly in association with Nash, exploring a wide range of possibilities – initially a universal pension of 25s a week, followed by a means-tested one of 30s with a supplementary 10s contributory superannuation.[142] Reid and the actuary S. Beckingsale promoted the contributory principle after Maddex left. Indeed a subcommittee of the departmental committee, formed in late September, suggested a properly contributory scheme for health, old age and unemployment, rather than merely the pretence of a flat tax on incomes, as recommended by the parliamentary committee. Over the 1937–8 new year, emphasis shifted towards a larger universal contributory pension of £1, supplemented by a means-tested 10s pension.

The final plan of February 1938, prepared by Ashwin, Reid and Maddex, proposed a subsidised contributory scheme as the only viable way of achieving a universal pension at an adequate level. An employer contribution of 6d and extension of the National Provident Fund was rejected. Contributions would be supplemented 2:1 from the consolidated fund, in order to extend the benefits enjoyed by those in the government scheme, the National Provident Fund and private superannuation schemes to the entire population.[143] This would provide a contributory pension, supplemented if necessary to make it up to a minimum of 30s. The plan tried to steer a course between fiscal realism and Labour's egalitarianism, with the bait of a redistributive loading in favour of lower income groups.

The Labour caucus would not have a bar of it. It put forward a pension of 30s a week at age 60 years, financed by taxation. It was to be termed the social security 'contribution'. There was to be an additional levy on adult males and a consolidated fund subsidy. Treasury remained very critical of such a proposal and doubted whether the country could afford it. The Farmers' Union, Chambers of Commerce and employers providing private schemes also voiced antagonism towards the proposal.[144] The government as a whole (including Savage and Nash) at this point closed ranks and would brook no opposition to its emerging scheme, whether by Treasury or interest groups. The Treasury would not be called in to report – 'the Government is making the decisions' – and Savage bluntly stated that 'we did not want the head of Treasury to tell us what our policy was to be'.[145]

The select committee blandly asserted that there was no distinction between a contributory pension and other benefits in the scheme: 'Each one is a social security benefit, which term implies that the community as a whole insures its individual members against part of the financial loss resulting from permanent invalidity, unemployment, widowhood, orphanhood, sickness, disability, and, in the case of superannuation, the attainment of old age without sufficient means of livelihood.'[146] It was confident that national production would be sufficiently increased in the future to provide revenue for the scheme.

Opposition members of the select committee put out a minority report underlining the uncertain financial basis, the failure to consider a contributory scheme, and the misuse of the emergency taxation measures of the depression.[147] They pointed out that the majority on the select committee refused their request to call the heads of Treasury and Labour to give evidence, and that they also refused to disclose details on methods of financing the scheme. They had little doubt that many other existing superannuation schemes would cease to operate and that friendly societies would go into decline. Officials continued to argue that the scheme was unsustainable, to no effect.

The government also ignored the friendly societies, who had entertained expectations that they might be involved in administration of the scheme. The Dominion Council of Friendly Societies had argued that the scheme should be comprehensive and contributory, and administered by approved friendly societies. Now it had to go down on bended knee before the special select committee, pointing out that the scheme 'would mean the slow strangling of the voluntary movements of this kind' and their eventual extinction.[148]

Minimal concessions were made. The Social Security Act included sections (47 and 50) that allowed payment of sickness benefits to members through their societies. Friendly society benefits could also be paid up to a combined total of £5 a week without affecting the state benefit.[149] But societies lost their National Provident Fund-related maternity benefit, and their agreements with hospital boards were terminated. They also failed in attempts over following years to gain exemptions, particularly in moving from a state sickness to an age benefit.

Subsequently, the refusal of the British Medical Association to accept a national health service based on capitation led the government in 1940 to offer a subsidy for friendly society medical benefits. The association urged termination of society contracts as a result and, when the Social Security Amendment Act (to establish the new medical services arrangements) went through in 1941, most friendly societies were forced to drop their medical benefits. The friendly society movement was no longer able to attract new members and soon went into decline.

In 1938, the task became one of making Labour's promises financially manageable by means-testing the old-age pension of 30s and providing a smaller supplementary universal pension.[150] Just before the Social Security Bill was introduced in August the government agreed that the pension should be supplemented by a small universal pension. This would be increased over time to reach parity eventually with the other pension, at which time there would be a more generous universal old-age pension. In this manner Labour found a compromise between universality and cost and was able to deliver on its promises.

The bill was little changed and was soon passed. The Social Security Act 1938 raised the means-tested old-age pension to 30s, which was now paid to both men and women at 60 years. It introduced a token universal 'superannuation' payment of £10 a year to those 65 years and over. Conditions for existing means-tested benefits were liberalised and rates were improved. New sickness, orphans, health and emergency benefits were introduced, which made the scheme notable for its comprehensiveness.

The scheme was to be administered by a new Social Security Department and funded by the employment tax, now termed the social security tax, supplemented by general revenue. The social security tax or 'contribution' entailed (a) a registration fee – adult males paying £1 per annum and those 16–20 years old and females 16 years and over paying 5s per annum; and (b) the social security charge – a tax of 1s in the pound on the income of those 16 years and over and of companies. The appearance of a contributory approach was maintained by means of this separate social security contribution.

Social security nonetheless represented a final rupture with social insurance that had been considered from the 1880s onwards. This form of welfare not only redistributed income, but also shifted the balance from groups predominantly saving to those who were spending, in a manner consistent with the secular trend identified earlier. There had been a general shift, favouring lending over saving, that emerged with advances to workers and was perpetuated by state advances lending.[151]

New Zealand's new and distinctive taxpayer-funded welfare state had advantages. The scheme was simple to administer; benefits were not related to the extent of contribution, and there was no need to delay payment while a fund was built up. Furthermore, no contributions were required before payment could be made, nor did the entitlement expire after a certain period. Most importantly, payments in principle could be far more generous and more related to the standard of living than was possible otherwise. But would the leap of faith be fulfilled? Could the New Zealand state meet its fiscal commitments?

Funding social security

Labour at the time had no way of telling whether and how the demands for social security benefits might be met from likely future economic capacity to generate revenue for the state. Indeed all advice, both within government and from outside, indicated that the scheme would be unsustainable.

The introduction of social security was in fact accompanied by a marked expansion in state revenue and the fortuitous circumstances of war. The measures of the depression provided the means for this expansion. In 1936 the basic and top rates of income tax had been increased, justified explicitly by the increased pension rates.[152] In 1939 both income tax and the employment tax (now the social security contribution) were raised considerably. The graduation of the upper part of the income tax scale was steepened and a supertax of 15 percent imposed across the scale. The exemption was lowered a little to a level approximating to the basic wage, so that virtually all wage and salary earners were included in the net.

The fiscal basis for the welfare state was now laid. Most wage and salary earners paid income tax, and the remainder contributed by means of the social security tax. In the decade from 1929 the basic income tax rate had increased

SHRINKING

The taxpayer realises that, commendable though the Government's national superannuation and health scheme may be, it will mean more taxation.

Savage and Nash retrieve their shrunken social security scheme through taxation. New Zealand Free Lance, *13 April 1938*

from 2.9 percent to 10 percent and the maximum rate from 22.5 percent to 42.9 percent, to which was added the supertax and the substantial social security tax. The number of income taxpayers had increased fourfold, and those with incomes of less than £300 now comprised more than 40 percent of income taxpayers.[153]

Labour was able to take further advantage of revenue opportunities when the Second World War gave a huge fillip to the state's fiscal capacity.[154] The government was determined not to repeat the experience of the First World War in increasing overseas debt. It financed war expenditure internally for the most part. Nearly 40 percent of war expenditure was met by internal borrowing and another 36 percent by special war taxation, which increased the tax take dramatically.

'*All fool's day'. Labour's social security scheme takes off on 1 April 1939, minus the key component of medical benefits*. Auckland Star, *1 April 1939*

In 1940 income tax was raised and a national security tax was imposed in parallel to the social security contribution.[155] The national security tax was raised in 1942 and the supertax increased to one-third. The bottom rate was now 16.7 percent of income, while at incomes of £3,700 and above the top marginal tax rate was 77.5 percent. To this had to be added the 12.5 percent of income levied in the form of social security and national security taxes. Taxation had reached levels undreamed of in the 1920s, when the country's taxable capacity was already thought to have been exceeded.

In 1946, after the war, the social security contribution was raised and the national security tax reduced, thereby shifting a substantial proportion of war-related revenue directly into the social security fund in order to cope with the cost of the new universal family benefit. The income supertax was reduced to 15 percent again, and in 1947 the residual national security tax was abolished. Now those on the basic income tax rate paid 14.6 percent of income and the top marginal rate was 72.4 percent. To this was added 7.5 percent of income for the social security charge.

Improved economic conditions, the war and the startling general expansion of fiscal capacity had funded much of the cost of social security with ease. But even so the social security fund was not self-supporting as intended. By 1951 it had relied upon transfers from the consolidated fund of more than £100 million since its inception. The necessity for transfer increased greatly after the war, particularly as a result of the cost of the universal family benefit.

After the war, inflation, rising incomes and the resulting fiscal drag that inexorably increased the tax take sufficed to fill the expanding coffers of the state. Income taxation took centre stage in state revenue and the welfare state became the lynchpin of postwar New Zealand. The taxpayer-funded welfare state, providing monetary benefits, formed an integral part of wider economic policy directed towards social ends.

The National Party when it came to power in 1949, although originally opposed to the Social Security Act, accepted its existence and administered its provisions with equanimity. As Oliver commented: 'Social welfare has become . . . so universally accepted that . . . Any attempt to improve the system by taking notice of better designed schemes elsewhere in the world would be too plausibly represented by the reformer's political opponents as sabotage. Such a charge could prove electorally disastrous.'[156] Welfare was extended – the general medical services benefit in 1941 was followed by a range of other medical benefits, a universal family benefit in 1946 and capitalisation of the family benefit in 1958. There was a more rapid convergence of superannuation and the old-age benefit than anticipated, a general liberalisation of qualification provisions (such as property and income tests) and increasing use of the emergency benefit.

By the 1970s, after some forty years of consolidation, the welfare state was coming under scrutiny. The Labour government's politically disastrous compulsory contributory superannuation scheme of 1973 was replaced by National's non-contributory National Superannuation scheme of 1976. This was fiscally unsustainable and became less generous as the economy experienced difficulties in the 1980s and 1990s. In the latter part of the 1990s there was again discussion of contributory superannuation. But the legacy of New Zealand's distinctive approach has been hard to shake off.

Conclusion

The welfare state had a long genesis stretching back to the mid nineteenth century in an experimental contract between state and citizens, which was guided by overseas models adapted to local circumstances. Along the way the focus of this contract moved from land to labour to welfare. State policies preceding the welfare state had the same objective – to give a good standard of living in this country for all – as the priority shifted from land to labour; that is, from land providing opportunities for wage-earning migrants, to wage earners emerging with their own distinct interests. The resolution of land reform closed the old settler world; state regulation, and control over labour and immigration, represented the opening of the new world.

The characteristic nineteenth-century separation of labour market policy from the 'dependent' population began to collapse under the weight of the 1880s depression. The old concept of self-reliance within the unfettered confines of the labour market was discredited, and state regulation of employment, working conditions, wages and industrial relations to protect the male breadwinner developed to a marked degree.

The state at first addressed the needs of labour directly, by means of strengthened legislation protecting workplace conditions, and new methods of protecting workers' much-vaunted standard of living through the arbitration system. These initiatives were supplemented by attempts to provide worker housing. Just as significantly, state welfare provisions began to shift from the margins to a place of considerable importance, in association with a general strengthening of the state's fiscal capacity.

By the late nineteenth century, with the payment of the old-age pension, the elderly had become the object of attention for central government, as a group supplementary to and outside of the labour market. This pension became a platform for the extension of pensions to others in need. The families of wage earners also became a legitimate focus for state assistance. This was first manifest in support for the male 'breadwinner', that recognised female and child dependents, and then in family allowances. Parallel policies protected the wage earner and those outside the labour market through the arbitration system and improvement to pensions respectively. These policies began to converge in the 1920s around the family wage and family allowances, breaking down the traditional barrier between the workforce and the dependent population outside the labour market.

From the 1880s contributory social insurance schemes that drew upon the long experience of friendly societies were considered. New Zealand's ultimate failure to go down the social insurance road was due to the uncertain and difficult economic conditions of the 1920s, which made such a departure in welfare policy extremely hard to promote politically, particularly after the non-contributory old-age pension had been brought into existence. The depression of the early 1930s confirmed the impossibility of social insurance and gave rise to a special unemployment tax. What had begun with the old-age pension now became firmly entrenched as a result of the emergency conditions. This tax proved decisive in cementing the non-contributory approach to state welfare provisions.

The emergence of a fully-fledged welfare state from the late 1930s, supported by the enormous expansion of state revenue and associated with the extension of the arbitration system, effectively replaced labour market mechanisms with state regulation and welfare provision.

During the passage of the Social Security Act in 1938, John A. Lee, one of the principal proponents of the legislation in the Labour caucus, quoted the verses from Bracken's 'The Emigrant's Welcome' and from Reeves' 'New Zealand' that preface Chapters 3 and 5 respectively.[157] These quotations were fitting for the occasion, in which the coping stone of the welfare state was set in place. New Zealand's social security system was based on the original promise held out to emigrants of 'building a new nation' free of old-world

'The first forty-four years are the worst'. Social security saddles New Zealand's younger generation with the cost of paying for the elderly. Auckland Star, 16 August 1938

evils, and subsequently related to the wide range of policies that would make 'labour lord'.

In the 1980s the dismantling of what Francis Castles terms 'the wage earners' welfare state' took place. Historically entrenched policies, such as state-based wage determination, employment promotion, immigration and protectionism, were challenged and abandoned. Protection was lifted, central state-regulated wage fixing and the objective of full employment were eliminated, and immigration and the labour market were freed up. New Zealand's generous benefits were cut back and targeted more closely. With the welfare state itself being challenged, and stronger links made between the labour market and welfare, the state's non-contributory fiscal underpinnings to welfare also became the subject of examination.[158]

There is a deeper dimension to this issue than the provision of welfare by the state itself. The welfare state relied upon a strong relationship between citizen and state – a historically forged social contract. The shift of emphasis towards market relationships and individual interest has diminished the state's role and destabilised this relationship, which was founded upon collective mechanisms of redistribution, provision of employment and security through welfare benefits.

Such concern has been expressed in a variety of forms – in the communitarian perspective, in the so-called 'Third Way' of the British Labour government, in the interest in the institutions of civil society, and in a realisation that a globalised economy will need socially integrating mechanisms to function effectively.[159] The common thread is that the centralised welfare state is no longer the pivotal mechanism for ensuring social cohesion and the central values of a modern democratic society – it is no longer the basis for a social contract with its citizens.

Many argue that sources of social cohesion have to be found in institutions and organisations that exist within society itself rather than via the central state, and further, that these institutions and organisations have to facilitate democratic participation, inclusion and fairness. The old antinomies of state and economy or state and society, with the state addressing the failures or inequities of a society or economy, no longer suffice in a world in which the nation state is being bypassed.

New Zealand possesses both advantages and disadvantages in the face of such international trends. Its small size and capacity to change and innovate have served it well in the past and may assist it in responding to the future. On the other hand it will be difficult to depart from a highly centralised state welfare system. The resounding rejection of compulsory, contributory private superannuation in the 1997 referendum suggested that New Zealanders' perceived welfare solutions have changed little even if the fiscal basis is looking shaky. The recently introduced KiwiSaver – a voluntary retirement savings scheme with state assistance and employer contributions – has been popular but is already under pressure from deteriorating economic conditions. For the same reason, the current government is not going to expand the Superannuation Fund, which was created to reduce the burden on the taxpayer of providing New Zealand Superannuation payments to an increasing number of people as the population ages.

The concept of an evolving social contract between wage earners and the state illuminates a wide range of policies that had their origins in colonisation and settlement on the land and which were eventually expressed in the twentieth-century welfare state. All such policies were impelled by the concern to provide a good standard of living in a 'new world' society that had been dependent on continued migration for its vitality.

These values are still held today, in the early years of the twenty-first century. But the means whereby they might be addressed are less certain than before. New Zealand has always been exposed to the whims of international markets, but the tension this creates between economic realities and social aspirations is particularly acute these days, when global migration has become relatively free of geographical barriers and historical cultural ties. This poses new challenges for the concept of citizenship and with it any notion of a social contract that might be forged between citizen and state.

NOTES

Chapter 1: 'A small nation on the move' – establishing the contract

1 Julius Vogel, 'Social politics in New Zealand', *The Fortnightly Review*, new series, vol 53, 1893, pp. 130, 143.

2 E.G. Wakefield and J. Ward, *The British Colonization of New Zealand*, London: John W. Parker, 1837, introduction, pp. iii, xiv–xv.

3 Thomas Cholmondley, *Ultima Thule, or Thoughts Suggested by a Residence in New Zealand*, London: Woodfall and Kinder, 1854, p. 43.

4 *The Times*, 5 July 1851. The writer also suggested that New Zealand would become a new Britain long before Macaulay's 'promised New Zealand chief [who] ruminates upon the decay of civilisation' in London. The image of a 'New Zealander' in front of the ruins of London soon became a common and powerful one. See Gustave Doré's *London, a Pilgrimage*, London: Grant and Co., 1872.

5 Cholmondley, *Ultima Thule*, pp. 1, 5, 18, 45–8, 87.

6 Frederick J. Turner, *The Frontier in American History*, New York: Holt, 1958, 'The significance of the frontier'.

7 Russel Ward, *The Australian Legend*, Melbourne: Oxford University Press, 1966, chapter 9.

8 Fred Alexander, *Moving Frontiers: An American Theme and its Application to Australian History*, Melbourne: Melbourne University Press, 1947. H.C. Allen, *Bush and Backwoods: A Comparison of the Frontier in Australia and the United States*, East Lansing: Michigan State University Press, 1959.

9 Geoffrey Blainey, *The Tyranny of Distance: How Distance Shaped Australia's History*, Melbourne: Sun Books, 1966.

10 Louis Hartz, *The Founding of New Societies: Studies in the History of the United States, Latin America, South Africa, Canada and Australia*, New York: Harcourt, Brace and World, 1964, especially pp. 40–4, and Richard N. Rosecrance, 'The radical culture of Australia'. See also Richard N. Rosecrance, 'The radical tradition in Australia: an interpretation', *Review of Politics*, vol 22, no 1, 1960.

11 Rosecrance, in Hartz, *Founding of New Societies*, p. 284.

12 A.W. Martin, 'Australia and the Hartz "fragment thesis"', *Australian Economic History Review*, vol 13, no 2, 1973.

13 J.B. Hirst, 'Keeping colonial history colonial: the Hartz thesis revisited', *Historical Studies*, vol 21, 1984. Also J.B. Hirst, 'Egalitarianism', *Australian Cultural History*, no 5, 1986. Martin, 'Australia and the Hartz "fragment thesis"', suggests that we need to allow for individualism as well as collectivism. See also Gary Cross, 'Comparative exceptionalism: rethinking the Hartz thesis in the settler societies of nineteenth-century United States and Australia', *Australasian Journal of American Studies*, vol 14, no 1, 1995. Gary Cross, 'Labour in settler-state democracies: comparative perspectives on Australia and the US, 1860–1920', *Labour History*, no 70, 1996.

14 Alexander Brady, *Democracy in the Dominions: A Comparative Study in Institutions*, Toronto: University of Toronto Press, 1947.

15 W.H. Oliver, *The Story of New Zealand*, London: Faber, 1960.

16 Keith Sinclair, *A History of New Zealand*, Auckland: Penguin, 1959. Michael Turnbull, *The New Zealand Bubble: The Wakefield Theory in Practice*, Wellington: Price Milburn, 1959.

17 Keith Sinclair, *A Destiny Apart: New Zealand's Search for National Identity*, Wellington: Allen and Unwin, 1986, chapter 1.

18   K.A. Pickens, 'The writing of New Zealand history: a Kuhnian perspective', *Historical Studies: Australia and New Zealand*, vol 17, 1977. P.J. Coleman, 'The New Zealand frontier and the Turner thesis', *Pacific Historical Review*, vol 27, no 3, 1958, questioned the applicability of the frontier to New Zealand.

19   See Erik Olssen, 'Where to from here? Reflections on the twentieth-century historiography of nineteenth-century New Zealand', *New Zealand Journal of History* (*NZJH*), vol 26, no 1, 1992, pp. 60–1.

20   See John E. Martin, 'Country report: labor history in New Zealand', *International Labor and Working-class History*, no 49, 1996.

21   Rollo Arnold, *The Farthest Promised Land: English Villagers, New Zealand Immigrants of the 1870s*, Wellington: Victoria University Press, 1981. Rollo Arnold, 'Community in rural Victorian New Zealand', *NZJH*, vol 24, no 1, 1990.

22   Tony Simpson, *The Immigrants: The Great Migration from Britain to New Zealand, 1830–1890*, Auckland: Godwit, 1997.

23   Erik Olssen, *Building the New World*, Auckland: Auckland University Press, 1995, p. 260.

24   Miles Fairburn, *The Ideal Society and its Enemies: The Foundation of Modern New Zealand Society, 1850–1900*, Auckland: Auckland University Press, 1989. Duncan Mackay, *Frontier New Zealand: The Search for Eldorado, 1800–1920*, Auckland: HarperCollins, 1992.

25   Miles Fairburn, 'Is there a good case for New Zealand exceptionalism?', in Tony Ballantyne and Brian Moloughney (eds), *Disputed Histories: Imagining New Zealand's Pasts*, Dunedin: Otago University Press, 2006.

26   James Belich, *Making Peoples – From Polynesian Settlement to the End of the Nineteenth Century*, Auckland: Penguin, 1996.

27   Michael King, *The Penguin History of New Zealand*, Auckland: Penguin, 2003, p. 10.

28   Pickens, 'Writing of New Zealand history'. Olssen, 'Where to from here?'.

29   Fairburn, 'New Zealand exceptionalism', pp. 165–6.

30   George Nadel, *Australia's Colonial Culture: Ideas, Men and Institutions in Mid Nineteenth Century Eastern Australia*, Melbourne: F.W. Cheshire, 1957.

31   Terry Irving, '1850–70', in Frank Crowley (ed), *A New History of Australia*, Melbourne: Heinemann, 1974, p. 126.

32   Stuart Macintyre, *A Colonial Liberalism: The Lost World of Three Victorian Visionaries*, Melbourne: Oxford University Press, 1991.

33   David Hamer, *The New Zealand Liberals*, Auckland: Auckland University Press, 1988, chapter 1. See also André Siegfried, *Democracy in New Zealand*, (second edition, intro. D. Hamer), Wellington: Victoria University Press, 1982, pp. 52–62; Victor S. Clark, *Report on Labour Conditions in New Zealand*, pp. 181–2, reprinted in Department of Labour, *Journal*, February–July 1904.

34   See James E. Cronin, 'The British state and the structure of political opportunity', *Journal of British Studies*, vol 27, 1988, pp. 207–10, for the British situation.

35   Hamer, *New Zealand Liberals*, p. 23.

36   W.H. Oliver, 'The origins and growth of the welfare state', in A.D. Trlin (ed), *Social Welfare and New Zealand Society*, Wellington: Methuen, 1977. M. Tennant, 'Duncan MacGregor and charitable aid administration, 1886–1896', *NZJH*, vol 13, no 1, 1979. M. Tennant, *Paupers and Providers: Charitable Aid in New Zealand*, Wellington: Allen and Unwin, 1989. P.J. Gibbons, '"Turning tramps into taxpayers": the Department of Labour and the casual labourer in the 1890s', MA, Massey University, 1970. See the criticisms of F.M.L. Thompson, 'Social control in Victorian Britain', *Economic History Review*, second series, vol 34, no 2, 1981.

37   Oliver, *Story of New Zealand*, pp. 272–3. Keith Sinclair, 'The significance of "the Scarecrow Ministry", 1887–1891', in Robert Chapman and Keith Sinclair (eds), *Studies of a Small Democracy*, Auckland: Blackwood and Janet Paul, 1963, p. 103.

38   D.A. Hamer, 'The Agricultural Company and New Zealand politics, 1877–1886', *Historical Studies: Australia and New Zealand*, vol 10, 1962. W.H. Oliver, 'Reeves, Sinclair and the social pattern', in Peter Munz (ed), *The Feel of Truth*, Wellington: Reed, 1969, p. 169. Victor S. Clark, *The Labour Movement in Australasia: A Study in Social Democracy*, London: Constable, 1907, p. 282.

39   For Australia, Hirst, 'Keeping colonial history colonial'; Hirst, 'Egalitarianism'; Martin, 'Australia and the Hartz "fragment thesis"'.

40   Robert Stout, 'New Zealand', *The Contemporary Review*, October 1899, pp. 541, 547. Also Robert Stout, *Politics and Poverty*, Dunedin: Otago Daily Times, 1883.

41   Siegfried, *Democracy in New Zealand*, pp. 54–5. See Michael Bassett, *The State in New Zealand, 1840–1984*, Auckland: Auckland University Press, 1998, generally.

42   *Appendices to the Journal of the House of Representatives (AJHR)*, A-1A, 1867, p. 76.

43   Oliver has stressed this broader conception of welfare. W.H. Oliver, 'Social policy in New Zealand: an historical overview', in Report of the Royal Commission on Social Policy, *The April Report, vol 1, New Zealand Today*, Wellington, 1988 (*AJHR*, 1988, H-2).

44   Clark, *Labour Movement in Australasia*, p. 121.

45   *The Times*, 27 June 1896. Asquith's comments were in endorsement of Chamberlain's imperial federation scheme. The British Empire was sustained by the free development of institutions in the colonies. Ralph C. Hayburn, 'William Pember Reeves, *The Times* and New Zealand's Industrial Conciliation and Arbitration Act, 1900–1908', *NZJH*, vol 21, no 2, 1987, pp. 254–5.

46   William Pember Reeves, *The Long White Cloud* (4th edition), London: Allen and Unwin, 1950, p. 260. *AJHR*, 1879, B-2A, Atkinson on land policy. W.D. Stewart, *William Rolleston*, Christchurch: Whitcombe and Tombs, 1940, pp. 117, 138, 164.

47   Hamer, *New Zealand Liberals*, chapter 2. F. Rogers, 'The influence of political theories in the Liberal period, 1890–1912: Henry George and John Stuart Mill', in Chapman and Sinclair (eds), *Studies of a Small Democracy*. F. Rogers, 'The single tax movement in New Zealand', MA, University of Auckland, 1949. P. Coleman, 'The spirit of New Zealand Liberalism in the nineteenth century', *Journal of Modern History*, vol 30, 1958.

48   Hamer, *New Zealand Liberals*, chapter 2. Sinclair, *A Destiny Apart*, pp. 74–6.

49   Jose Harris, 'Political thought and the welfare state, 1870–1940: an intellectual framework for British social policy', *Past and Present*, no 135, 1992.

50   Hirst, 'Egalitarianism', for similar comments on the Labor Party and Australia at the turn of the century. The change was more muted here because of the mediation of the Liberal and Reform governments.

51   Francis G. Castles, *The Working Class and Welfare*, Wellington: Allen and Unwin, 1985. Francis G. Castles, *Australian Public Policy and Economic Vulnerability*, Sydney: Allen and Unwin, 1988.

52   Castles, *Working Class and Welfare*, p. 103.

Chapter 2: The landed laboratory in a 'People's Farm'

1   Malcolm Chase, *The People's Farm: English Radical Agrarianism, 1775–1840*, Oxford: Clarendon, 1988, p. 1. Broadside ballads were popular music printed on a single sheet of paper.

2   Also see Erik Olssen, 'Mr Wakefield and New Zealand as an experiment in post-Enlightenment experimental practice', *NZJH*, vol 31, no 2, 1997.

3   Tom Brooking, *Lands for the People? The Highland Clearances and the Colonisation of New Zealand – A Biography of John McKenzie*, Dunedin: Otago University Press, 1996, p. 84.

4   Fairburn, *The Ideal Society and its Enemies*.

5   J.D.N. McDonald, 'New Zealand land legislation', *Historical Studies: Australia and New*

Zealand, vol 5, 1952. J.D.N. McDonald, 'A brief survey of land policy in New Zealand, 1876–1900', MA, University of Auckland, 1945.

6   *New Zealand Parliamentary Debates (NZPD)*, vol 57, 1887, p. 493.

7   *Lyttelton Times (LT)*, 15 January 1853.

8   For the United States, Roy M. Robbins, *Our Landed Heritage: The Public Domain, 1776–1970* (second edition), Lincoln: University of Nebraska Press, 1976, and B.H. Hibbard, *A History of the Public Land Policies*, Madison, Wisconsin: University of Milwaukee Press, 1965. For Australia, S.H. Roberts, *History of Australian Land Settlement*, Sydney: Macmillan, 1968.

9   *Dictionary of New Zealand Biography, 1769–1960 (DNZB)*, 5 vols, Wellington/Auckland: Allen and Unwin/Bridget Williams Books/Auckland University Press, 1990–2000, vol 1, entry on Binns.

10   Malcolm S. Chase, 'The land and the working classes: English agrarianism, c. 1775–1851', PhD, University of Sussex, 1984, especially appendix to chapter 7. See also Chase, *The People's Farm*, and Jamie L. Bronstein, *Land Reform and Working-class Experience in Britain and the United States, 1800–1862*, Stanford: Stanford University Press, 1999.

11   John E. Martin, 'A "small nation on the move": Wakefield's theory of colonisation and the relationship between state and labour in the mid-nineteenth century', in Friends of the Turnbull Library, *Edward Gibbon Wakefield and the Colonial Dream: A Reconsideration*, Wellington: GP Publications, 1997. Philip Temple, *A Sort of Conscience – The Wakefields*, Auckland: Auckland University Press, 2003, chapters 28, 29. Bernard Semmel, *The Rise of Free Trade Imperialism: Classical Political Economy, the Empire of Free Trade and Imperialism, 1750–1850*, Cambridge: Cambridge University Press, 1970.

12   R.S. Neale, 'Class and class consciousness in early nineteenth century England: three classes or five?', in R.S. Neale (ed), *History and Class*, Oxford: Blackwell, 1983.

13   J.S. Marais, *The Colonisation of New Zealand*, Oxford: Clarendon Press, 1927, p. 27.

14   Martin, 'A "small nation on the move"'. Olssen, 'Mr Wakefield and New Zealand'.

15   Paul Hudson, 'English emigration to New Zealand, 1839 to 1850 – an analysis of the work of the New Zealand Company', PhD, University of Lancaster, 1996, table 5.11, p. 146, and pp. 331–4.

16   Fairburn, *Ideal Society*, chapter 2. Neil J. Smelser, *Social Change in the Industrial Revolution*, London: Routledge and Kegan Paul, 1959, pp. 210–12.

17   R.S. Neale, *Class and Ideology in the Nineteenth Century*, London: Routledge and Kegan Paul, 1972, including 'The colonies and social mobility: governors and executive councillors in Australia, 1788–1856', and 'Class and ideology in a provincial city: Bath, 1800–50'.

18   Julian Harney, cited in Ray Boston, *British Chartists in America, 1839–1900*, Manchester: Manchester University Press, 1971, p. 33 and generally. A.L. Morton and George Tate, *The British Labour Movement*, London: Lawrence and Wishart, 1956, p. 99. Bronstein, *Land Reform*, especially chapter 5.

19   Archives New Zealand (ArchNZ), CO 208/2 (39/661), John Saint to Ward, 20 July 1839, regarding advertisement. Michael Turnbull, 'New Zealand labour politics, 1840–1843', *Political Science*, vol 4, no 2, 1952, p. 35.

20   Eugenio F. Biagini and Alastair J. Reid (eds), *Currents of Radicalism: Popular Radicalism, Organised Labour and Party Politics in Britain, 1850–1914*, Cambridge: Cambridge University Press, 1991. Eugenio F. Biagini, *Liberty, Retrenchment and Reform*, Cambridge: Cambridge University Press, 1992. John Belchem, *Popular Radicalism in Nineteenth-Century Britain*, London: Macmillan, 1996. Craig Calhoun, *The Question of Class Struggle: Social Foundations of Popular Radicalism During the Industrial Revolution*, Chicago: University of Chicago Press, 1982; Gareth Stedman Jones, 'Rethinking Chartism', in *Languages of Class: Studies in English Working Class History, 1832–1982*, Cambridge: Cambridge University Press, 1983. Margot C. Finn, *After Chartism: Class and Nation in English Radical Politics, 1848–1874*, Cambridge: Cambridge University Press, 1993. Brian Harrison and Patricia

Hollis, 'Chartism, Liberalism and the life of Robert Lowery', *English Historical Review*, vol 82, 1967. For discussion of the relationship between radicalism, liberalism and the labour movement in the USA, see David Montgomery, *Beyond Equality: Labor and the Radical Republicans, 1862–1872*, New York: Knopf, 1967.

21 Belchem, *Popular Radicalism*, chapters 6, 7. A.E. Musson, *British Trade Unions, 1800–1875*, London: Macmillan, 1972. Finn, *After Chartism*.

22 *DNZB*, vol 1, entry. Alexander Turnbull Library (ATL) Ms Papers 2294, J.C. Dakin, 'The background of the working-class pioneers'. ArchNZ, CO 208/298, surgeon's journal, *Birman*, 3 November 1841; H.F. Alston to James Phipson, 20 October 1841. *Wellington Independent* (*WI*), 24, 31 May 1845. *New Zealand Spectator* (*NZS*), 12 December 1846, 1 February 1851.

23 *DNZB*, vol 1, entry. ATL, Ms Papers 1859, M.G. Vincent, 'The inky way', (story of the Vincent family).

24 Ruth M. Allan, *Nelson – A History of Early Settlement*, Wellington: Reed, 1965, p. 113. *DNZB*, vol 1, entry. Stephen Roberts, *Radical Politicians and Poets in Early Victorian Britain: The Voices of Six Chartist Leaders*, New York: Edwin Mellen Press, 1994, chapter 2.

25 *DNZB*, vol 1, entry. Diana Beaglehole, 'Political leadership in Wellington, 1839–1853', in David Hamer and Roberta Nicholls (eds), *The Making of Wellington, 1800–1914*, Wellington: Victoria University Press, 1990. J.K. Hoar, 'A descriptive history of the major aspects of the friendly society movement in New Zealand, 1840–1900', MA, University of Idaho, 1963, p. 82. H.W. Gourlay, *Odd Fellowship in New Zealand, 1842–1942: A Century of Progress*, Christchurch: Andrews, Baty and Co., 1942, pp. 17, 64–5. ArchNZ, NZC 108/2, no 105, c. June 1842. *Wellington Spectator* (*WS*), 26 December 1840; 2, 9 January 1841; 19 October 1842. *NZS*, 12 December 1846; 5 February 1851. *LT*, 15 November 1851; 1, 8 January, 5 February, 30 April, 4 June, 16 July, 20 August 1853; 28 January 1854; 3 February 1855.

26 ATL, Ms Papers 2597, Diary of Isaac Mason Hill, 1843–4. *DNZB*, vol 1, entry. *Nelson Examiner* (*NE*), 14 May 1842; 27 March 1847; 8 March, 28 June 1851; 20 March, 10 July 1852; 12 March, 16 July (electoral roll) 1853. *Nelson Evening Mail*, 1 September 1885. *Press*, 23 September 1885.

27 *DNZB*, vol 1, entry. Jim McAloon, *Nelson – A Regional History*, Nelson: Cape Catley, 1997, pp. 60–70. *Otago Witness* (*OW*), 4 September 1858.

28 H.S. Chapman, 'Peasant proprietorship, the source of wealth for a colony', *WI*, 2 July 1851, reprinted in *NE*, 2 August 1851. John Miller, *Early Victorian New Zealand: A Study of Racial Tension and Social Attitudes, 1839–1852*, London: Oxford University Press, 1958, pp. 132–3. H.S. Chapman, *The New Zealand Portfolio*, London: Smith, Elder and Co., 1843, 'Some observations on the necessity for continuing to facilitate voluntary emigration', p. 105, also 'Observations on the advantages of a representative assembly' in same. G.H. Scholefield (ed), *A Dictionary of New Zealand Biography*, Wellington: Government Printer, 1940, entry. *DNZB*, vol 1, entry. R.S. Neale, 'H.S. Chapman and the "Victorian" ballot', *Historical Studies: Australia and New Zealand*, vol 12, 1967. Neale, 'Class and class consciousness'.

29 ATL, Vincent, 'The inky way', pp. 29–30. *DNZB*, vol 1, entry. Scholefield (ed), *Dictionary of Biography*, entry. Kathleen Coleridge, 'Thriving on impressions: the pioneer years of Wellington printing', in Hamer and Nicholls (eds), *Making of Wellington*, pp. 89, 94.

30 Richard Wakelin, *Small Farms and Small Farm Settlements*, Greytown: Standard Office, 1879, pp. 6–7. Scholefield (ed), *Dictionary of Biography*, entry.

31 *DNZB*, vol 2, entry. H. Roth, 'Charles Joseph Rae', *New Zealand Libraries*, vol 22, no 6, 1959.

32 Charles Rooking Carter, *Life and Recollections of a New Zealand Colonist*, 3 vols, London: R. Madley, 1866–75. *DNZB*, vol 1, entry. Alan Henderson, *Fortuitous Legacy: The*

Masterton Trust Lands Trust, 1872–1997, Masterton: Masterton Trust Lands Trust, 1997, pp. 16–20.

33 Hamer, *New Zealand Liberals*, p. 49ff. Timothy McIvor, *The Rainmaker: A Biography of John Ballance*, Auckland: Heinemann Reed, 1989. Keith Sinclair, *William Pember Reeves*, Oxford: Clarendon, 1965. Brooking, *Lands for the People?* David Hamer, 'Sir Robert Stout, 1844–1930', MA, University of Auckland, 1960. James Drummond, *The Life and Work of Richard John Seddon*, Christchurch: Whitcombe and Tombs, 1906. R.M. Burdon, *King Dick: A Biography of Richard John Seddon*, Christchurch: Whitcombe and Tombs, 1955. *DNZB*, vol 2, entry on Seddon.

34 *DNZB*, vol 2, entry.

35 Olssen, *Building the New World*, pp. 181, 186. Scholefield (ed), *Dictionary of Biography*, entry. *NZPD*, vol 79, 1893, p. 479.

36 *DNZB*, vol 2, entry on George Fisher. *Cyclopedia*, vol 1, Wellington, Wellington: Cyclopedia Co., 1897, pp. 552–3.

37 *DNZB*, vol 2, entry. Olssen, *Building the New World*, pp. 100–2.

38 *Cyclopedia*, vol 1, Wellington, 1897, p. 553. See others noted, pp. 554–5.

39 *Cyclopedia*, vol 1, Wellington, 1897, p. 547.

40 Arnold, *Farthest Promised Land*, pp. 77, 130–1, 168, 191–210, 329. Henry Tomlinson, *A Farm Labourer's Report of New Zealand*, Laceby, Grimsby: Burton and White, 1876. Alfred Simmons, *Old England and New Zealand*, London: Edward Stanford, 1879. *Canterbury Times*, 16 January 1890.

41 *The Times*, 20 December 1875.

42 Arnold, *Farthest Promised Land*, p. 329.

43 Edward Arnold, letter of 15 January 1879, printed in Julius Vogel (ed), *New Zealand: Land and Farming in New Zealand*, London: Waterlow and Sons, 1879, p. 60.

44 ArchNZ, CO 208/291, 'Regulations for labourers', issued 29 June, 5 December 1839; 22 May 1840; New Zealand Company posters, June 1840; contract for service with New Zealand Company, 1841. CO 208/84, quarterly returns of those employed and wages paid, 1841. NZC 231/2, April 1841, contracts in Nelson. NZC 3/30, W. Cargill to W. Wakefield, 15 May 1848, and enclosed address to immigrants, regarding Otago public works. M. Turnbull, 'The colonisation of New Zealand by the New Zealand Company, 1839–43', thesis, Oxford University, 1950, pp. 314, 317–18, 332–4. Raewyn Dalziel, 'Popular protest in New Plymouth: why did it occur?', *NZJH*, vol 20, no 1, 1986.

45 ArchNZ, NZC 208/2, petition, 14 January 1843, 'The working men of Nelson to Captain Wakefield'.

46 ArchNZ, NZC 3/1–4, 3/12–14, 3/18–19, 3/30–31, 104/2–4, 104/7, 108/2, 231/2. CO208/291, 'Regulations for labourers', 1 July 1843, no longer contains the guarantee. Miller, *Early Victorian New Zealand*, 1958, chapter 9. Dalziel, 'Popular protest'. Allan, *Nelson*, pp. 183–92. C.J. Colbert, 'The working class in Nelson under the New Zealand Company, 1841–1851', MA, Victoria University of Wellington, 1948. McAloon, *Nelson*, pp. 28–9, 37–9.

47 ArchNZ, CO208/2, H.A. Thompson to Captain Wakefield, 26 January 1843; Philip Valle et al., memorials on employment of labourers, July and September 1843; F. Tuckett to William Fox, 9 October 1843.

48 The purported mass emigration derives from a mistaken statistic that only 85 of the original 436 arrivals in Wellington remained by 1848 (Sinclair, *History of New Zealand*, p. 96; Turnbull, *New Zealand Bubble*, p. 58). The source of these figures is a misinterpretation in Turnbull, 'Colonisation of New Zealand', p. 384, citing CO 208/106, Fox to New Zealand Company, 24 November 1848. The numbers concern *resident land purchasers* compared to *absentees* and not the numbers leaving the settlement. Nelson was the worst affected by emigration but only about one-ninth of steerage passengers re-emigrated by mid 1844 (NZC 3/14, W. Fox to W. Wakefield, 9 July 1844). A more general demographically based

estimate gives a loss of around 1,000 people from the New Munster settlements at large in the period 1841–8 (*Great Britain, Parliamentary Papers* (*GBPP*), 1850, 1280, pp. 158–9; 'Statistics of New Munster down to 1848', *Journal of the Statistical Society*, vol 14, 1851). This was about one-eleventh of the assisted migrants who had arrived in that period, or even less if unassisted migrants are also taken into account.

49   ArchNZ, NZC 3/13, W. Fox report on Wakefield village to W. Wakefield, 1 December 1843. See also Motueka and Riwaka. SSD3, 1, Nelson census returns, 1845. ArchNZ, CO 208/106, statistics for Wellington, 1847, and W. Fox letter to New Zealand Company, 24 November 1848, and appended tables giving extent of cultivation by labourers in Wellington and Nelson, printed in *GBPP*, 1850, 1136, p. 219ff.

50   *NZPD*, 1854, pp. 347–8. *Votes and Proceedings* (*VP*), session 2, 31 August 1854. *Wellington Gazette*, 1857, pp. 191–4. *NE*, 5 January, 27 April 1850. *GBPP*, 1854, 1779, pp. 79–83, memorial, May 1850, enclosed with Governor Grey to Earl Grey, 11 March 1852. Nelson Provincial Council, *Proceedings,* session 4, 1857, report on compensation, and Compensation Act 1857; session 6, 1859, report on compensation. ArchNZ, NP2, Provincial Council papers, 19 April 1859, enclosures to message no 4, Land for Compensation Bill and report on compensation. The initiatives apparently came to nothing in New Plymouth.

51   J. Rutherford, *Sir George Grey K.C.B., 1812–1898: A Study in Colonial Government*, London: Cassell, 1961, pp. 38, 188–91. Edmund Bohan, *To Be A Hero – A Biography of Sir George Grey*, Auckland: HarperCollins, 1998, pp. 111–12, 124–5.

52   *LT*, 16 August 1851. *GBPP*, 1854, 1779, pp. 244–5, 259, 271–2, addresses to Grey. See W.L. Rees, *The Life and Times of Sir George Grey, KCB*, London: Hutchinson, 1892, vol 1, pp. 152–60, for Grey's view. Land regulations, *New Zealand Gazette*, 1853, pp. 13–18.

53   *VP*, session 4, 1856, C-12, return of lands sold, 1850–6. Auckland Provincial Council, *Proceedings*, session 1, 1853–4. *New Zealander*, 23 April, 21 May, 17 August, 3 September 1853. Rutherford, *Grey*, pp. 198–9, 202. W. David McIntyre (ed), *The Journal of Henry Sewell*, Christchurch: Whitcoulls, 1980, vol 1, p. 470.

54   A.G. Bagnall, *Wairarapa: An Historical Excursion*, Masterton: Hedley's Bookshop, 1976, pp. 100, 137ff. Henderson, *Fortuitous Legacy*, chapter 1.

55   *New Zealander*, 23 April, 21 May, 3 September 1853.

56   Peter Stuart, *Edward Gibbon Wakefield in New Zealand*, Wellington: Price Milburn, 1971, p. 160, and p. 54ff. Martin, 'A "small nation on the move"'. B.R. Patterson, 'Reading between the lines: people, politics and the conduct of surveys in the southern North Island, New Zealand, 1840–1876', PhD, Victoria University of Wellington, 1984, pp. 310–14. *NZPD*, 1854, pp. 233–5. Muriel F. Lloyd Prichard, *An Economic History of New Zealand to 1939*, Auckland: Collins, 1970, pp. 68, 80–1.

57   Rutherford, *Grey*, pp. 202–3. *LT*, 20 August 1853. F. Fuller, *Five Years' Residence in New Zealand*, London: Williams and Norgate, 1859, chapter 4. Patterson, 'Reading between the lines', chapters 5 and 6, especially pp. 307–10. R. Garnett, *Edward Gibbon Wakefield: The Colonisation of South Australia and New Zealand*, London: T. Fisher Unwin, 1898, p. 292. Stuart, *Wakefield*, pp. 137–43. *NZPD*, 1855, pp. 233–5.

58   *VP*, session 1, 1854, pp. 467–70.

59   *VP*, session 2, 20 July 1854, 31 August 1854. *NZPD*, 1855, pp. 347–8; vol 10, 1871, p. 696, E.J. Wakefield.

60   For provincial regulations, see W.R. Jourdain, *Land Legislation and Settlement in New Zealand*, Wellington: Government Printer, 1925, and W.P. Morrell, *The Provincial System in New Zealand, 1852–76*, Christchurch: Whitcombe and Tombs, 1964, pp. 105–6, 113. Grey's regulations were largely retained in Nelson and New Plymouth. The land regulations of Hawke's Bay and Marlborough strongly favoured runholders.

61   R.D. McGarvey, 'Local politics in the Auckland province, 1853–62', MA, University of Auckland, 1954. H.J. Whitwell, 'The forty acre system', MA, University of Auckland,

1954. Auckland Provincial Council, *Proceedings*, session 29, 1873–4, A-27. R.C.J. Stone, 'Auckland party politics in the early years of the provincial system, 1853–58', *NZJH*, vol 14, no 2, 1980. R.C.J. Stone, 'Auckland's political opposition in the Crown Colony period, 1841–53', in Len Richardson and W. David McIntyre (eds), *Provincial Perspectives*, Christchurch: Whitcoulls, 1980. John Young, 'The political conflict of 1875', *Political Science*, vol 13, no 2, 1961, pp. 69–72.

62 *New Zealander*, 20 April 1853. McGarvey, 'Local politics', pp. 23–4.

63 Auckland Provincial Council, *Proceedings*, 25 October, 19 December 1854. *DNZB*, vol 1, entry. H.J. Hanham, 'The political structure of Auckland, 1853–76', MA, University of Auckland, 1950, pp. 52, 119.

64 Whitwell, 'Forty acre system', especially p. 13 and table 1. *Statistics of New Zealand*, 1861–9.

65 Whitwell, 'Forty acre system', pp. 49–52.

66 Auckland Provincial Council, *Proceedings*, session 13, 1860–1, A-6; session 16, 1863–4, p. 142, and A-12, return of land orders; session 17, 1864, A-12. Guy H. Scholefield (ed), *The Richmond–Atkinson Papers*, Wellington: Government Printer, 1960, vol 1, pp. 481–2, E. Stafford to C.W. Richmond, 17 August 1859. Edmund Bohan, *Edward Stafford: New Zealand's First Statesman*, Christchurch: Hazard Press, 1994, pp. 132–3, 139–40.

67 R.C.J. Stone, *Makers of Fortune: A Colonial Business Community and its Fall*, Auckland: Auckland University Press, 1973, p. 8.

68 Auckland Provincial Council, *Proceedings*, session 19, 1866, p. 49; session 21, 1867, pp. 12–13.

69 Auckland Provincial Council, *Proceedings*, session 29, 1873–4, A-27.

70 *Wellington Gazette*, 20 July 1855. See Patterson, 'Reading between the lines', for large-scale acquisition of land. *WI*, 20 March–3 April, 25, 29 September 1858.

71 *NZS*, 20 March, 22 September 1858. Wellington Provincial Council, *Proceedings*, session 6, 17 March 1858. *WI*, 20 March–3 April, 25, 29 September 1858.

72 *NZS*, 11 August 1858.

73 *NZS*, 13 May 1863. Wellington Provincial Council, *Proceedings*, session 10, 1863, paper on land applications; session 13, 12 July 1865; session 14, 15, 19 June 1866; session 15, Superintendent's opening address, and council paper, and 14, 30 May 1867. *WI*, 10 August 1865; 9, 16 June 1866.

74 Wellington Provincial Council, *Proceedings*, session 22, 30 April 1871, Superintendent's opening address; session 22, 1871, appendix, Crown Commissioner's report on land revenue; session 27, 1874, C-7, Manchester block; session 28, 1875, appendix, report of Crown Lands Commissioner on special settlements and the Hutt Small Farm Association.

75 *WI*, 10 May 1873.

76 G.C. Hensley, 'Land policy and the runholders', in W.J. Gardner (ed), *A History of Canterbury*, vol 2, Christchurch: Whitcombe and Tombs, 1971. T.J. Hearn, 'South Canterbury: some aspects of the historical geography of agriculture, 1851–1901', MA, University of Otago, 1971, pp. 8–58. T.J. Hearn and G.W. Kearsley, 'Voting patterns in the Canterbury Provincial Council: an application of cluster analysis', *Proceedings of Ninth New Zealand Geography Conference*, Dunedin: New Zealand Geographical Society, 1977. Macintyre (ed), *Journal of Sewell*, vol 2, pp. 112–18.

77 Originally published 1858, reprinted in Pilgrim (C.L. Innes), *Canterbury Sketches, or Life From the Early Days*, Christchurch: Lyttelton Times, 1879, pp. 81–7.

78 Canterbury Provincial Council, *Proceedings*, session 4, opening address, 11 April 1855.

79 Canterbury Provincial Council, *Proceedings*, session 26, 1866–7, report on and returns of pre-emptive rights. The total homestead and improvement rights granted since 1858 comprised 3 percent of the total run area, largely granted for fencing. Very little land had been challenged.

80 Canterbury Provincial Council, *Proceedings*, session 35, 28 July 1871; session 39, printed

papers no 3, resolution, 11 June 1873.

81   *Otago Gazette*, 6 March 1855; 23 July 1856. A.H. McLintock, *The History of Otago: The Origins and Growth of a Wakefield Class Settlement*, Dunedin: Otago Centennial Historical Publications, 1949, pp. 337–404, 484–508, 526–54, 629–38. W.R. Jourdain, *Land Legislation and Settlement in New Zealand*, Wellington: Government Printer, 1925, pp. 86–9. Tom Brooking, *And Captain of their Souls: Cargill and the Otago Colonists*, Dunedin: Otago Heritage Books, 1984, pp. 109–15. G.W. Kearsley, T.J. Hearn and T.W.H. Brooking, 'Land settlement and voting patterns in the Otago Provincial Council, 1863–1872', *NZJH*, vol 18, no 1, 1984, pp. 32–3. Morrell, *Provincial System*, chapter 11.

82   Otago Provincial Council, *Proceedings*, session 9, 11, 17–19, 27 April 1860; session 10, 27 October 1860; session 12, 19 June 1861, Richardson.

83   Otago Provincial Council, *Proceedings*, session 15, 28 April 1862, message no 3 and report on message no 3. *Otago Ordinances*, 1862. *Otago Gazette*, 18 March 1863.

84   T.J. Hearn, 'Land, water and gold in Central Otago, 1861–1921: some aspects of resource use policy and conflict', PhD, University of Otago, 1981.

85   Hearn, 'Land, water and gold', pp. 27, 37–9, 95–6. Otago Provincial Council, *Proceedings*, session 24, 1868, council paper no 5. *AJHR*, 1869, C-1, F-10.

86   *AJHR*, 1870, C-6.

87   Otago Provincial Council, *Proceedings*, session 29, 1871, appendix, pp. 65–79, resolutions; session 33, 1874, appendix, p. 248; session 34, 1875, appendix, p. 303, departmental reports, 1875–6, Crown Lands, p. 4. *NZPD*, vol 15, 1873, pp. 1116–21; vol 16, 1874, pp. 528–46; vol 17, 1875, p. 116; vol 18, 1875, pp. 45–8; vol 19, 1875, pp. 312–14. *Journal of the House of Representatives* (*JHR*), 1875, p. 269. *AJHR*, 1878, C-1, p. 3.

88   Blair C. Shick and Irving H. Plotkin, *Torrens in the United States*, Lexington, Mass: Lexington Books, 1978. Theodore B.F. Ruoff, *An Englishman Looks at the Torrens System*, Sydney: Law Book Co., 1957. Douglas J. Whalan, 'The origins of the Torrens system and its role in New Zealand', in G.W. Hinde (ed), *The New Zealand Torrens System Centennial Essays*, Wellington: Butterworths, 1971.

89   H.J. Perkin, 'Land reform and class conflict in Victorian Britain', in J. Butt and I.F. Clarke (eds), *The Victorians and Social Protest*, Newton Abbot: David and Charles, 1973, pp. 184, 191–4. David Martin, 'Land reform', in Patricia Hollis (ed), *Pressure From Without in Early Victorian England*, London: Edward Arnold, 1974, especially pp. 139, 152–5. Malcolm Chase, 'Out of radicalism: the mid-Victorian freehold land movement', *English Historical Review*, vol 106, 1991, pp. 335–6.

90   *NZPD*, vol 9, 1970, p. 194, and pp. 195–200.

91   *NZPD*, vol 7, 1870, p. 442, and pp. 312–13, Rolleston.

92   Canterbury Museum (CM), William Rolleston, political correspondence, box 1, folder 3, letter from J.W. Treadwell, 24 February 1880, and enclosed clippings.

93   Charles W. Purnell, *Our Land Laws – What Should Be Their Basis?* Dunedin: Evening Star, 1876. Charles W. Purnell, *An Agrarian Law for New Zealand*, Wellington: Robert Burrett, 1874. H.J. Sealy, *Are We To Stay Here? A Paper on the New Zealand Public Works Policy of 1870*, Lyttelton: Lyttelton Times, 1881.

94   Reeves, *Long White Cloud*, pp. 261–5.

95   *NZPD*, vol 7, 1870, p. 345.

96   *NZPD*, vol 22, 1876, pp. 134–8. J. Bassett, *Sir Harry Atkinson, 1831–1892*, Auckland: Auckland University Press, 1975, pp. 49–50. *AJHR*, 1878, C-1, table 3.

97   *NZPD*, vol 25, 1877, p. 251; vol 26, 1877, pp. 168–76; vol 27, 1877, pp. 120, 187–8, 605.

98   *NZPD*, vol 27, 1877, p. 609, and pp. 511, 512, 604.

99   *NZPD*, vol 44, 1883, p. 627.

100   McIvor, *Rainmaker*, p. 94.

101 *NZPD*, vol 24, 1877, p. 501. Rutherford, *Grey*, chapter 39. *NZPD*, vol 52, 1885, pp. 92–3, Ballance. McIvor, *Rainmaker*, pp. 74–8.

102 ATL, Hall letters, MSX-912, J. Hall to F.D. Bell, 1 December 1881; MSX- 908, J. Hall to W. Rolleston, 17 February 1880. *NZPD*, vol 32, 1879, pp. 22, 434, 579–81. *AJHR*, 1879, Session II, D-4, p. 3; 1891, Session II, C-5. McIvor, *Rainmaker*, p. 98. George Oliver, *Homes for the People in the Provincial District of Otago*, Oamaru: North Otago Times, 1879. Sealy, *Are We To Stay Here?*.

103 *AJHR*, 1880, C-2; 1881, C-5; 1885, C-1; 1886, C-1; 1888, C-1; 1899, C-7.

104 *NZPD*, vol 44, 1883, p. 627. Stewart, *Rolleston*, pp. 142–8, especially p. 148, letter to Bell, 1 December 1882. W.J. Gardner, *A Pastoral Kingdom Divided: Cheviot, 1889–94*, Wellington: Bridget Williams Books, 1992, pp. 75–6.

105 Stewart, *Rolleston*, p. 149, letter to Wynne Williams, 27 September 1883. A.H. McLintock and G.A. Wood, *The Upper House in Colonial New Zealand*, Wellington: Government Printer, 1987, pp. 84–6. W.K. Jackson, *The New Zealand Legislative Council*, Dunedin: University of Otago Press, 1972, pp. 116–7.

106 *AJHR*, 1883, I-8; 1885, I-4A; 1890, I-5A. Brooking, *McKenzie*, pp. 60–1.

107 *NZPD*, vol 42, 1882, p. 334; vol 103, 1898, pp. 120–2. Jean Garner, *By His Own Merits: Sir John Hall – Pioneer, Pastoralist and Premier*, Hororata: Dryden Press, 1995, pp. 69–71. CM, Rolleston, correspondence, box 1, folder 7, letters 28 August, 3, 6, 9 September 1898.

108 *NZPD*, vol 52, 1885, p. 45. McIvor, *Rainmaker*, pp. 109–14, 121–5. Hamer, 'Agricultural company'. Victoria University Library, Stout pamphlets, vol 44, Company Prospectus.

109 CM, William Rolleston, political correspondence, box 1, folder 1, item 10, letter of 17 November 1879.

110 *AJHR*, 1886, C-9.

111 *NZPD*, vol 54, 1886, pp. 51–63, 144–5, 367–72; vol 56, 1886, pp. 527, 865–6.

112 *NZPD*, vol 52, 1885, pp. 45–6; vol 54, 1886, p. 145. *AJHR*, 1887, C-2; 1888, C-1; 1889, C-1, C-5; 1891, session II, C-5. McIvor, *Rainmaker*, pp. 130–5.

113 John E. Martin, 'Unemployment, government and the labour market in New Zealand, 1860–1890', *NZJH*, vol 29, no 2, 1995.

114 Bassett, *Atkinson*, p. 148. *NZPD*, vol 57, 1887, pp. 601–18.

115 *NZPD*, vol 54, 1886, p. 374. Brooking, *Lands For the People*, p. 68. Gardner, *Pastoral Kingdom Divided*, pp. 76–8. McIvor, *Rainmaker*, pp. 136–7.

116 Jourdain, *Land Legislation*, pp. 30–1. J.O. Bassett, 'Sir Harry Atkinson – a political biography, 1872–1892', MA, University of Auckland, 1966, p. 208.

117 *NZPD*, vol 59, 1887, pp. 132–7; vol 61, 1888, pp. 619–21; vol 66, 1889, pp. 101–2, 604–5; vol 67, 1890, pp. 10–12. *Evening Post* (*EP*), 8 May 1890. McIvor, *Rainmaker*, pp. 167, 170–2, 174. Brooking, *Lands For the People*, pp. 70–1.

118 John Woodward, *Jubilee Farms*, Christchurch: Union Office, 1888, pp. 20–4.

Chapter 3: 'The road to wealth is wide'? Enabling the contract

1 Thomas Bracken, *Musings in Maoriland*, Dunedin: Arthur T. Keirle, 1890.

2 Cronin, 'British state', pp. 207–10; P.H.J.H. Gosden, *Self-Help: Voluntary Associations in Nineteenth Century Britain*, London: Batsford, 1973.

3 ATL Ms Papers 2597, Diary of Isaac Mason Hill, 2 January 1844.

4 Miles Fairburn, *Nearly Out of Heart and Hope: The Puzzle of a Colonial Labourer's Diary*, Auckland: Auckland University Press, 1995, pp. 164–5. Brooking, *Lands for the People*, p. 85.

5 *NE*, 21 May 1842, Alfred Saunders letter.

6 P.H.J.H. Gosden, *The Friendly Societies in England, 1815–1875*, Manchester: Manchester University Press, 1961, p. 10.

7   Gourlay, *Odd Fellowship in New Zealand*. Manchester Unity IOOF, *New Zealand Centenary, Manchester Unity IOOF, 1842–1942*, Wellington: Manchester Unity IOOF, 1942, page from *Wairarapa Standard*, 1883, inside cover.

8   *NE*, 12 March, 23 April, 21 May 1842; 6 January 1843; 4 January 1845. *WS*, 23 May, 27 June, 4 July 1840.

9   *New Zealand Gazette*, 28 December 1840. *NE*, 26 March 1842. *New Zealander*, 7 March 1846. *LT*, 13 September, 20 December 1851; 1 January 1853; 24 July 1880. *AJHR*, 1881, H-7, p. 9 and table 1. Scholefield (ed), *Dictionary of Biography*, entry for McKenzie. *Cyclopedia*, vol 1, Wellington, pp. 296–7. Gourlay, *Odd Fellowship in New Zealand*, pp. 9–10.

10   *LT*, 3 September 1885.

11   Erik Olssen, 'Friendly societies in New Zealand, 1840–1990', in Marcel van der Linden et al. (eds), *Social Security Mutualism: The Comparative History of Mutual Benefit Societies*, Bern: Peter Lang, 1996. Hoar, 'Friendly society movement'. Heather Shepherd, 'The nature and role of friendly societies in later nineteenth century New Zealand', Massey University, history research essay, 1976. Jennifer Carlyon, 'Friendly societies, 1842–1938: the benefits of membership', *NZJH*, vol 32, no 1, 1998. David Thomson, *A World Without Welfare: New Zealand's Colonial Experiment*, Auckland: Auckland University Press, 1998, pp. 35–51.

12   Gourlay, *Odd Fellowship in New Zealand*, pp. 22, 27–8, 42–3.

13   Olssen, Friendly societies in New Zealand', p. 205. Thomson, *A World Without Welfare*, p. 40. Fairburn, *Ideal Society*, p. 178.

14   The figure should be at least doubled for registered societies not furnishing returns and those unregistered. *Census of Population and Dwellings*, 1871, tables 13, 30. I.S. Ewing, 'Public service reform in New Zealand, 1866–1912', MA, University of Auckland, 1979, p. 12.

15   ArchNZ, ABWL, series 7351, 4l, National Health Insurance Investigation Committee and friendly societies, 1894–1940, R. Sinel, review of friendly society registry, 1940. Susan Butterworth, 'Scholars, gentlemen and floppy disks', in Friends of the Turnbull Library (ed), *Edward Gibbon Wakefield and the Colonial Dream: A Reconsideration*, Wellington: GP Publications, 1997, p. 176. For involvement of Ballance and Stout, see McIvor, *Rainmaker*, p. 45; and Grand Lodge, Independent Order of Oddfellows, *Proceedings of fifteenth annual session*, Dunedin, 1877.

16   Macintyre (ed), *Sewell Journal*, 19 June 1854, p. 43. Shepherd, 'Friendly societies', p. 27.

17   ArchNZ, IA1, 1859/1254, letter to Colonial Secretary, 18 June 1859; 1860/1809, letter to Colonial Secretary, 10 September 1860. Gosden, *Friendly Societies*, p. 182, Act of 1850. The following Act of 1855 retained the certification requirement for societies offering annuities.

18   ArchNZ, IA1, 74/2335, appointment of Knight, 25 August 1874.

19   ArchNZ, LE1, 1869/118; 1870/109; 1871/123; 1873/117, returns of friendly societies, 1868–73. *AJHR*, 1872, G-52; 1878, H-14. These registrations were the basis for the Registrar's statement that 123 societies were registered in 1878. *Statistics of New Zealand*, 1873.

20   Gourlay, *Odd Fellowship in New Zealand*, p. 34, reductions in sick pay, 1854–79. ArchNZ, IA1, 75/2826A, L. Bagnall to W. Swanson, MHR, 9 August 1875; 76/1237.

21   ArchNZ, IA1, 73/903; 74/1339, 1340, 2317, 2335, 2773A, 2853, 3003, 3013, 3257, 3369, 3416, 3610; 75/1447, 1530, 1937, 2791, 2996, 3224; 76/1237. ABWL, series 7351, 1d, reports of Chief Registrar of Friendly Societies, England, 1876, Appendix I, report on Victoria. *NZPD*, vol 17, 1875, p. 267; vol 20, 1876, p. 235, Pollen.

22   *NZPD*, vol 17, 1875, pp. 195, 265–8. *JHR*, 1875, p. 51. *AJHR*, 1878, H-14, p. 4.

23   Bills Thrown Out, 1876. *NZPD*, vol 20, 1876, pp. 236–9, 552, 587. ArchNZ, IA1, 76/1237, 1377, 2054, 2953, 6721, 6859.

24   *NZPD*, vol 24, 1877, pp. 59–60, 176–8.

25   ArchNZ, IA1, 78/667, 1228, 1230. LE1, 1878/134. *New Zealand Gazette*, 1877, p. 1171; 1878, pp. 162, 326, 1143. *AJHR*, 1878, B-2B, H-14; 1879, H-14. Grand Lodge, Independent Order of Oddfellows, *Proceedings of fifteenth annual session*, Dunedin, 1877.

26   *AJHR*, 1880, H-19; 1881, H-7, p. 9. ArchNZ, IA1, 1878/1230, Solicitor General to Colonial Secretary, 29 January 1878, 250 friendly societies in New Zealand, 140 of which were registered. *NZPD*, vol 43, 1882, pp. 152, 331–2. Gourlay, *Odd Fellowship in New Zealand*, pp. 23, 34.

27   *AJHR*, 1878, H-14, p. 4; 1879, H-12, pp. 23–5; 1881, H-7, schedule II.

28   *WS*, 21 October 1843. *NZS*, 16 May, 12 December 1846; 13 January 1847. *New Munster Gazette*, 1849, p. 15. H. Oliver Horne, *A History of Savings Banks*, London: Oxford University Press, 1947, pp. 25–7. Gosden, *Self-Help*, chapter 8.

29   *Historical Sketch of the Auckland Savings Bank*, Auckland: Herald Office, 1884. *New Ulster Gazette*, 15 May 1848; 7 June 1850; *NZ Gazettes* for 1850–2. *NZH*, 3 June 1873. *LT*, 18 July, 11 August, 1, 12, 29 September, 13 October 1855; 10 March, 7 April, 5 May 1858.

30   CM, Tradesman's and Mechanics Loan Society, minute book, 1860–83. *LT*, 14 November 1860.

31   Horne, *History of Savings Banks*, pp. 76, 100, 106. G.R. Hawke, *The Making of New Zealand: An Economic History*, Cambridge: Cambridge University Press, 1985, p. 109.

32   For Britain, Horne, *History of Savings Banks*, chapters 8, 9.

33   Hawke, *Making of New Zealand*, pp. 109–10. *JHR*, 1870, pp. 152–3. *NZPD*, vol 6, 1869, pp. 191–2, 715; vol 7, 1870, p. 88; vol 8, 1870, pp. 93–4, 479–80, 564.

34   Bills Thrown Out, 1870.

35   ArchNZ, NZC 231/10; SSD 3/1, Nelson census, 1845. *New Zealander*, 21, 28 March 1846; 7, 11, 14, 18, 21 June, 9, 12, 16 August 1851; 29 June 1853. *Auckland Independent and Operatives Journal*, 14 June 1851. Gourlay, *Odd Fellowship in New Zealand*, p. 15. J.R. Phillips, 'A social history of Auckland, 1840–53', MA, University of Auckland, 1966, p. 113. ATL, Micro Ms 510, UMS 229 (Bett collection), Rules of the Nelson Co-operative Society, March 1863. *Press*, 10 September 1863.

36   *NZPD*, vol 1, part 1, 1867, p. 290; vol 24, 1877, p. 105. *New Zealand Gazette*, 1873, p. 669; 1874, p. 222; 1875, pp. 164, 205, 518. ArchNZ, IA1, 72/3111; 73/3473; 74/664, 1883, 2081, 2218; 75/506, 2257, 2298; 78/1230.

37   ArchNZ, IA1, 75/2783. LE1, 1870/109. *New Zealand Gazette*, 1869, p. 423. *LT*, 2 March 1872. *New Zealand Mail*, 15 January 1876.

38   ArchNZ, LE1, 1869/118. IA1, 69/1217; 70/912; 71/1020, 2690; 72/1555; 76/800, 2081. AAEC, 653, inwards correspondence record books, vol 1, (76/340; 77/4, 27, 229; 78/39, 93, 163, 185, 195; 79/201). *New Zealand Gazette*, 1869, p. 238. *Co-operation*, Dunedin: Mills, Dick and Co., c. 1871. *DNZB*, vol 2, entry on S.P. Andrews.

39   W.A. Poole, 'Co-operative retailing in New Zealand', research paper no 13, New Zealand Institute of Economic Research, 1969, p. 11.

40   Hawke, *Making of New Zealand*, p. 65, in an overview of New Zealand's economic history fails to recognise them.

41   *NZS*, 19 February 1862.

42   J.A. Dowie, 'The course and character of capital formation in New Zealand, 1871–1900', *New Zealand Economic Papers*, vol 1, no 1, 1966, pp. 45–6, 50, table 4.

43   T.H. Gregg, *New Zealand, its Climate, Work, Wages and Cost of Living*, London: Marlborough and Co., 1875, p. 9.

44   Raymond W. Goldsmith, *Financial Structure and Development*, New Haven: Yale University Press, 1969, table 5–12, p. 242. Robert Stout, *Notes on the Progress of New*

Zealand for Twenty Years, 1864–1884, Wellington: Government Printer, 1886, pp. 32–3. Neil C. Quigley, 'Monetary policy and the New Zealand financial system: an historical perspective', in Reserve Bank of New Zealand, *Monetary Policy and the New Zealand Financial System* (third edition), Wellington: Reserve Bank of New Zealand, 1992, table 1, p. 208. *OW*, 14 August 1858. C.G.F. Simkin, *The Instability of a Dependent Economy*, London: Oxford University Press, 1951, pp. 68–71. Keith Sinclair and W.F. Mandle, *Open Account: A History of the Bank of New South Wales in New Zealand, 1861–1961*, Wellington: Whitcombe and Tombs, 1961, pp. 26–7. In Australia there was not the same connection with the land; see N.G. Butlin, *Investment in Australian Economic Development, 1861–1900*, Cambridge: Cambridge University Press, 1964, pp. 211–12, 247.

45   Review of Arthur Stratchley, *Industrial Investment and Emigration, being a Treatise on Benefit Building Societies, and on the General Principles of Associations for Land Investment and Colonization*, 1851, *New Zealander*, 4 October 1851.

46   Gosden, *Self-Help*, chapter 6. Chase, 'Out of radicalism'. S.D. Chapman and J.N. Bartlett, 'The contribution of building clubs and freehold land societies to working-class housing in Birmingham', in S.D. Chapman (ed), *The History of Working Class Housing*, Newton Abbot: David and Charles, 1971.

47   *NZH*, 22 March 1866.

48   *NZH*, 17 February, 16, 22 March 1866.

49   *WS*, 20 February, 6 March, 10 July 1841; 16, 19 February 1842; 22 May 1844. *NZS*, 23 November 1844; 16 May, 12 December 1846. Scholefield (ed), *Dictionary of Biography*, entry for T.W. McKenzie. H.S. Chapman, 'Some observations on the necessity for continuing to facilitate voluntary emigration' in *The New Zealand Portfolio*, London: Smith, Elder and Co., 1843, p. 108.

50   *NE*, 30 March, 26 October 1850; 28 June, 5, 19 July, 2, 30 August 1851; 10 July 1852; 8 July 1854; 11 July 1855. *LT*, 17 July 1858. *Otago News*, 27 July 1850. *OW*, 6, 20 January, 3 February, 28 May 1855. James McIndoe, *A Sketch of Otago from the Initiation of the Settlement to the Abolition of the Province*, Dunedin: R.T. Wheeler, 1878, pp. 93, 98. *Timaru Herald*, 22 October 1864, advertisement, and following issues.

51   *NZS*, 12 July 1851. *New Zealander*, 23 August 1851; 21 May 1853.

52   Auckland Provincial Council, *Proceedings*, session 1, Building and Land Societies Ordinance Amendment Act, 1854.

53   *New Zealander*, 20, 30 August, 3, 6 September, 8 October 1851; 28 August 1852; 9 March, 17 August, 3 September, 9 November 1853; 20, 27 May 1857; 3, 7 September 1858. *AJHR*, 1870, D-45.

54   *New Zealander*, 16 August 1851. *NZS*, 12, 22, 26 March, 27 September 1851; 3 November 1852; 1 March, 29 October 1856; 29 April 1857; 6 November 1858; 22 March, 1 April 1865. Carter, *Life and Recollections*, vol 2, p. 13.

55   *NZS*, 6 November 1858; 4 January, 8 February 1860; 15 February 1862; 2 March 1864; 1 March, 1 April 1865. *AJHR*, 1881, H-7, p. 13. Stone, *Makers of Fortune*, pp. 51–4.

56   *LT*, 12 July 1851; 13 March 1852; 2, 16 July 1853. *Canterbury Almanack*, 1854; *Wellington and Canterbury Almanack*, 1855. Johannes C. Andersen, *Jubilee History of South Canterbury*, Christchurch: Whitcombe and Tombs, 1916, pp. 427–8.

57   *LT*, 30 September, 14, 17, 21 October 1857; 2 February 1859; 18 March 1865; 4, 24, 31 January, 8 February, 11, 30 May 1866. *Press*, 30 August 1866; 4 July, 11 October 1867; 8, 17 February, 18 June, 23 July 1868. *AJHR*, 1870, D-45. G. Wright, 'The petty bourgeoisie in colonial Canterbury', MA, University of Canterbury, 1999, pp. 123–36.

58   *OW*, 3 May, 20 December 1851; January–June 1855; 14 August 1858. McIndoe, *Sketch of Otago*, pp. 3, 57–8, 61, 63–4, 92, 96, 101, 104. Victoria University Library, Stout pamphlets, vol 16, Standard Property Investment Society, balance sheet and report, 1870.

Vogel, *New Zealand: Land and Farming*, p. 35. McIvor, *Ballance*, p. 24.

59   Lloyd Prichard, *Economic History*, tables pp. 105–6.

60   *AJHR*, 1870, D-45. ArchNZ, LE1, 1870/2369. *Census of Population and Dwellings*, *1874*, figures on societies. *Statistics of New Zealand*, 1870. Julius Vogel (ed), *The Official Handbook of New Zealand*, London: Wyman and Sons, 1875, notes societies around the country. McIndoe, *Sketch of Otago*, p. 58. See *Press*, 11 September 1879, for cases of embezzlement.

61   ArchNZ, IA1, 1876/2451, letter, John Lewis to Minister of Justice, 10 June 1876; also April 1876 to the Minister of Justice, together with James Brown, letter, 13 June 1876.

62   *Census of Population and Dwellings, 1878. Statistics of New Zealand*, 1885.

63   Vogel, *Official Handbook*, 1875, p. 112. See also *WI*, 6 February 1873, editorial; Arthur Clayden, *The England of the Pacific, or New Zealand as a English Middle-Class Emigration-Field*, London: Wyman and Sons, 1879, p. 27; and John Bathgate, *New Zealand: Its Resources and Prospects*, London: W. and R. Chambers, 1884, pp. 20–1.

64   H. Roth, *Trade Unions in New Zealand – Past and Present*, Wellington: Reed, 1973, pp. 3–4. Also see ATL, Roth papers, box 29, folder 1.

65   *WS*, 23 May, 27 June, 4 July, 26 December 1840; 2, 9 January 1841; 17 December 1842. *New Zealand Gazette*, 25, 28 May 1842. J.D. Salmond, *New Zealand Labour's Pioneering Days*, Auckland: Forward Press, 1950, p. 15.

66   B.G. Hardie et al., *Statistics of New Zealand for the Crown Colony Period, 1840–1852*, Auckland University, 1954, table 62. *Statistics of Nelson from 1843 to 1854*, Nelson, 1855, table 48.

67   John E. Martin, *The Forgotten Worker: The Rural Wage Earner in Nineteenth-Century New Zealand*, Wellington: Allen and Unwin, 1990, chapter 8.

68   Roth, *Trade Unions in New Zealand*, p. 4. Olssen, *Building the New World*, pp. 100–1. P. Franks, *Print and Politics*, Wellington: Victoria University Press, 2001, p. 26.

69   Bert Roth, *Wharfie*, Auckland: New Zealand Waterfront Workers Union, 1993, pp. 12–13.

70   *WI*, 3, 4, 6, 18 January; 6, 15, 22 May; 20, 21, 30 June 1873. Salmond, *Labour's Pioneering Days*, pp. 42, 75–7. Martin, *Forgotten Worker*, pp. 22–3; John E. Martin, *Tatau Tatau – One Big Union Altogether*, Wellington: New Zealand Workers' Union, 1987, chapter 1. John E. Martin, 'The struggle for £1: the emergence of the shearers' union in the 1870s', *NZJH*, vol 24, no 1, 1990. Len Richardson, *Coal, Class and Community: The United Mineworkers of New Zealand, 1880–1960*, Auckland: Auckland University Press, 1995, p. 29.

71   Musson, *British Trade Unions*, pp. 22–8. In 1861 an Auckland employer attempted to prosecute a group of tailors under the Act. ArchNZ Auckland, BADW, A130/23, Possenski v Stewart, Froude, Good and others, 22 July 1861.

72   *Southern Cross*, 26, 27, 28, 30 January, 2, 6 February 1871. ArchNZ, P1, 7, Inspector Broham to Commissioner of Armed Constabulary, 18 December 1871; P1, 166, 40/89, Inspector Broham to Commissioner of Police, 3 January 1889. Richard S. Hill, *The Colonial Frontier Tamed: New Zealand Policing in Transition, 1867–1886*, Wellington: Department of Internal Affairs, 1989, p. 242.

73   *EP*, 2, 4 January 1873. Arnold, *Farthest Promised Land*, p. 12. *New Zealand Mail*, 26 October, 2 November, 28 December 1872; 4 January 1873, Hill, *Colonial Frontier Tamed*, pp. 175, 251.

74   *LT*, 3, 4, 5 April, 2, 6 June 1872. Gardner (ed), *History of Canterbury*, vol 2, pp. 342–3. Canterbury Provincial Council, *Proceedings*, session 37, 1872, paper no 7. W.A. Pierre, *Canterbury Provincial Railways – Genesis of the NZR System*, Wellington: New Zealand Railway and Locomotive Society, 1964, pp. 14–15. Canterbury Provincial Council, *Proceedings*, session 36, report on general management of railways, 2 May 1872; session 37, 1872, report of committee into management of railways.

75   R.H. Eyton, 'Our representative system', *New Zealand Magazine*, no 2, April 1876, p. 174. Salmond, *Labour's Pioneering Days*, p. 77. CM, *The Makomako*, Christchurch, 6 May 1876. Bert Roth, *Along the Line: 100 Years of Post Office Unionism*, Wellington: New Zealand Post Office Union, 1990, chapter 1.

76   Hamer, 'Stout', pp. 50, 305–9. *NZPD*, vol 51, 1885, pp. 529, 597; vol 69, 1890, pp. 515–18. D.E. Macdonald, *The State and the Trade Unions* (second edition), London: Macmillan, 1976, p. 30ff. Henry Pelling, *A History of British Trade Unionism* (fifth edition), London: Macmillan, 1992, p. 58ff.

77   Raewyn Dalziel, 'Towards representative democracy: 100 years of the modern electoral system', in *Towards 1990*, Wellington: GP Books, 1989, p. 50. For a reassessment of political participation, see John E. Martin, 'Political participation and electoral change in nineteenth-century New Zealand', *Political Science*, vol 57, no 1, 2005.

78   *LT*, 14 March 1860, advertisement.

79   D.M. Wylie, 'Representation and the franchise in New Zealand, 1852–1879', MA, University of Otago, 1951, p. 81. Sinclair, 'Scarecrow Ministry', pp. 105–6. Tony Simpson, *A Vision Betrayed: The Decline of Democracy in New Zealand*, Auckland: Hodder and Stoughton, 1984, chapter 1. But see D.G. Herron, 'The structure and course of New Zealand politics, 1853–1858', PhD, University of Otago, 1959, pp. 96–9.

80   Leslie Lipson, *The Politics of Equality: New Zealand's Adventures in Democracy*, Chicago: University of Chicago Press, 1948, pp. 11, 20.

81   A.H. McLintock, *Crown Colony Government in New Zealand*, Wellington: Government Printer, 1958, pp. 310–11. *NE*, 26 June 1847, 1 September 1849. William Fox, *The Six Colonies of New Zealand*, London: John W. Parker and Son, 1851, pp. 158–9.

82   *GBPP*, 1850, 1136, pp. 9–14, Governor Grey to Earl Grey, 29 November 1848.

83   Herron, 'New Zealand politics', p. 80. *GBPP*, 1851, 1420, pp. 112, 116–17, 163–4, enclosures in letters from Governor Grey to Earl Grey, 29 January, 12 February 1851. *NZS*, 1, 5 February 1851. There were similar meetings in Canterbury and Otago and demands for 'popular' suffrage. McLintock, *Crown Colony Government*, pp. 314–15. *LT*, 16, 23 August 1851.

84   *GBPP*, 1851, 1420, p. 163.

85   *GBPP*, 1851, 1420, p. 116. *NE*, 18 January 1851; 7 August 1853.

86   *GBPP*, 1852, 1475, p. 6, Governor Grey to Earl Grey, 4 August 1851; pp. 18–33, Governor Grey to Earl Grey, 30 August 1851. *GBPP*, 1852, 1483, p. 10, enclosure 2, draft bill (Earl Grey to Governor Grey, 23 February 1852). *New Zealander*, 9 August 1851. For Earl Grey's proposal, see ArchNZ, G1/27, Earl Grey to Governor Grey, 19 February 1851.

87   Wylie, 'Representation and the franchise'. G.A. Wood, 'The 1878 Electoral Bill and franchise reform in nineteenth century New Zealand', *Political Science*, vol 28, no 1, 1976.

88   Martin, 'Political participation and electoral change', p. 41.

89   See J. Shephard, *NZPD*, vol 18, 1875, p. 611.

90   For the adoption of the secret ballot in Victoria in the 1850s, see Neale, 'Chapman and the "Victorian ballot"'.

91   *GBPP*, 1851, 1420, pp. 113–22, enclosed memorial in Governor Grey to Earl Grey, 29 January 1851.

92   ArchNZ, LE1, 1858/241. Nelson Provincial Council, *Proceedings*, session 5, 1858, pp. 48, 105. Wylie, 'Representation and the franchise', pp. 41–7, 74–92. Wellington Provincial Council, *Proceedings*, session 6, 28 April 1858.

93   *NZPD*, vol 4, 1868, p. 244.

94   *NZPD*, vol 5, 1869, p. 75.

95   ArchNZ, LE1, 1870/126, Nelson, 2 June 1870; 1870/130, Otago, 11, 12 May 1870.

96   *NZPD*, vol 23, 1876, p. 532. See Wylie, 'Representation and the franchise', pp. 92–170 *passim* for manhood suffrage.

97   *NZPD*, vol 7, 1870, p. 252; also see pp. 251–61; vol 9, 1870, pp. 328–9.

98   *NZPD*, vol 7, 1870, pp. 255, 257.

99   W.K. Jackson and G.A. Wood, 'The New Zealand parliament and Maori representation', *Historical Studies: Australia and New Zealand*, vol 2, 1964, pp. 388–9.

100 Dalziel, '100 years', p. 53.

101 *NZPD*, vol 14, 1873, p. 31; also vol 10, 1871, p. 122; vol 11, 1871, p. 329; vol 15, 1873, pp. 1297–8; vol 16, 1874, pp. 115, 276, 284.

102 Bills Thrown Out, 1873–5.

103 Bills Thrown Out, 1876.

104 *NZPD*, vol 24, 1877, p. 499ff.

105 *NZPD*, vol 26, 1877, p. 293.

106 Rutherford, *Grey*, pp. 613–15.

107 *NZPD*, vol 29, 1878, p. 607.

108 Atkinson, *NZPD*, vol 64, 1889, pp. 577, 579; also vol 39, 1881, pp. 471–2.

109 *NZPD*, vol 64, 1889, p. 453ff.

110 Bohan, *To Be A Hero*, pp. 290, 298, 301, 313.

111 Patricia Grimshaw, *Women's Suffrage in New Zealand*, Auckland: Auckland University Press, 1972. Patricia Grimshaw, 'Women's suffrage in New Zealand revisited: writing from the margins', in Caroline Daley and Melanie Nolan (eds), *Suffrage and Beyond: International Feminist Perspectives*, Auckland: Auckland University Press, 1994. Raewyn Dalziel, 'The colonial helpmeet. Women's role and the vote in nineteenth-century New Zealand', *NZJH*, vol 11, no 2, 1977, pp. 121–2.

112 Grimshaw, *Women's Suffrage*, chapter 11. Grimshaw, 'Women's suffrage revisited', p. 37.

113 *NZPD*, vol 71, 1891, pp. 29, 55, 57, 99, 103; vol 77, 1892, pp. 231–2, 572–83, 609–15; vol 78, 1892, pp. 281–2, 461–2, 523; vol 79, 1893, p. 129; vol 80, 1893, pp. 322–5, 477, 596–7, 616, 623–5; vol 82, 1893, p. 785.

114 *Political and Other Ballads*, Auckland Free Lance, Auckland, 1879.

115 *LT*, 24 January, 14 February, 1 March, 12 May, 13 June 1866. *DNZB*, vol 1, W.H. Barnes; vol 2, S.P. Andrews. Wright, 'The petty bourgeoisie in colonial Canterbury', pp. 80–101. The unemployed met in Auckland. *NZH*, 13 February 1866.

116 *LT*, 21, 23, 26, 28 January, 1, 10 February 1871. *Southern Cross*, 3, 16, 19, 20, 21, 27, 28 January, 3, 4, 17 February 1871. *NZH*, 19, 20 January 1871. *OW*, 11 February 1871. *DNZB*, vol 2, entry on James McPherson.

117 ArchNZ, IM4, 1/1, 76/243, petition, reproduced in *AJHR*, 1876, D-2, pp. 14–15. *The Times*, 20, 21 December 1875.

118 *WI*, 31 January 1873. *EP*, 6 February 1873; 27 November 1875. *New Zealand Times*, 27 November 1875. J.L. Hunt, 'The election of 1875–6 and the abolition of the provinces', MA, University of Auckland, 1961, pp. 233–4, 302.

119 Reeves, *Long White Cloud*, pp. 195, 259–60. *NZPD*, vol 29, 1879, pp. 190, 192. Rutherford, *Grey*, pp. 600–11. D. Corstophine, 'Grey's liberalism as a factor in the development of party government in New Zealand', MA, University of Canterbury, 1950, pp. 76, 97–100. L.R. Todd, 'Grey's liberal ministry, 1877–1879', MA, University of Auckland, 1942, p. 23ff.

120 *DNZB*, vol 2, entry on S.P. Andrews. Bohan, *To Be a Hero*, p. 280. Allwright argued subsequently that he had been elected to support liberal measures and not the man. *LT*, 17 October 1881. McLintock and Wood, *Upper House*, p. 138.

121 For example, *LT*, 10 July 1884. Generally, see A.M. Evans, 'A study of Canterbury politics in the early 1880s', MA, University of Canterbury, 1959; D.P. Millar, 'The general election of 1884 in Canterbury', MA, University of Canterbury, 1960, pp. 36, 39–40, 240–5, 254; and H.M.O. Coates, 'The labour movement in Canterbury, 1880–1895', MA, University of Canterbury, 1980.

122 Millar, 'General election of 1884', pp. 13, 61–2, 66, 184, 213. *LT*, 21, 30 June, 8, 10, 23 July 1884. *Timaru Herald*, 14, 16, 17, 23 July 1884.

123 J.H. Angus, 'City and country – change and continuity, electoral politics and society in Otago, 1877–1893', PhD, University of Otago, 1976.

124 Martin, 'Unemployment, government and the labour market'.

125 Bert Roth, *Advocate, Educate, Control: The History of the New Zealand Engineers' Union, 1863–1983*, Wellington: New Zealand Engineering Union, 1984, p. 14. Bert Roth, 'Labour day in New Zealand', in John E. Martin and Kerry Taylor (eds), *Culture and the Labour Movement*, Palmerston North: Dunmore Press, 1991. CM, Rolleston, correspondence, box 1, folder 1, letter, R.E. Evenden, 17 November 1879 and enclosed clipping. *Press*, 23 September 1879. *LT*, 15 November, 1 December 1881. For England, Jonathon Spain, 'The labour law reforms of 1875', in Biagini and Reid, *Currents of Radicalism*.

126 Victoria University Library, Stout pamphlets, vol 37, Rules of Otago Trades and Labour Council, 1881. Salmond, *Labour's Pioneering Days*, p. 98.

127 Eric Charman, 'Land tenure reform in New Zealand, 1875–1896', MA, University of Auckland, 1953. *DNZB*, vol 2, entry on Thomas Bracken. Victoria University Library, Stout unbound pamphlet no 183, Manifesto of Otago Trades and Labour Council, 1884.

128 ArchNZ Christchurch, Provincial Council papers, CH287, CP637c/4, memo for select committee on unemployed, 21 October 1870; CP113/941; CP115/1282, 1379, 1385.

129 *NZOYB*, 1963, 'The development of New Zealand's railway system, 1863–1963', p. 1179. *AJHR*, 1879, session I, D-5, p. 3; 1880, E-1, p. v. *NZPD*, vol 42, 1882, pp. 515–64. *LT*, 19, 26–8 September, 1, 3, 5, 11 October 1881. M.J. Stock, 'The development of the railway system of New Zealand, 1870–81', MA, Victoria University of Wellington, 1936, chapter 7. P.G. Macarthy, 'The living wage in Australia – the role of government', *Labour History*, no 18, 1970, discusses the state's relation to public sector labour in Australia similarly.

130 *LT*, 15, 16, 20 August, 10 November 1884; 6–11, 19–21 May, 2, 25 June 1885. *NZH*, 26–30 January, 22 February 1886. J.B. Condliffe, *New Zealand in the Making* (second revised edition), London: Allen and Unwin, 1959, p. 177. Salmond, *Labour's Pioneering Days*, pp. 42, 76. Neill Atkinson, 'The Auckland Seamen's Union, 1880–1914', in Pat Walsh (ed), *Trade Unions, Work and Society: The Centenary of the Arbitration System*, Palmerston North: Dunmore Press, 1994. Neill Atkinson, 'Auckland seamen and their union, 1880–1922', MA, University of Auckland, 1990, pp. 54–7.

131 ArchNZ, P1, 129, 2190/85; 130, 2546/85. Len Richardson, *The Denniston Miners' Union: A Centennial History, 1884–1984*, Westport: Denniston Miners' Union, 1984, pp. 10–15. Gavin McLean, *The Southern Octopus: The Rise of a Shipping Empire*, Wellington: New Zealand Ship and Marine Society, 1990, p. 89. *AJHR*, 1885, C-4, p. 7; 1886, C-4C, p. 3. *LT*, 21, 26 August, 14 October 1885.

132 *Press*, 19, 23 September 1885. *EP*, 19, 21 September 1885. *LT*, 20 August–26 October 1885. Roth, *Wharfie*, p. 15. ATL, Roth papers, box 29, folder 1.

133 *NZPD*, vol 53, 1885, pp. 978–9; vol 69, 1890, pp. 515–18. *NZH*, 29 January, 22 February 1886.

134 *NZPD*, vol 53, 1885, p. 978.

135 *NZH*, 29 January, 1, 22 February 1886, incl. Stout letter, telegram.

136 Salmond, *Labour's Pioneering Days*, pp. 76, 78. *LT*, 28–30 January, and April–June 1886, generally. Richardson, *Coal, Class and Community*, pp. 37–8. *NZPD*, vol 55, 1886, p. 557; vol 57, 1887, p. 346.

137 Bert Roth and Janny Hammond, *Toil and Trouble: The Struggle for a Better Life in New Zealand*, Auckland: Methuen, 1981, p. 28. Salmond, *Labour's Pioneering Days*, p. 77. Conrad Bollinger, *Against the Wind: The Story of the New Zealand Seamen's Union*, Wellington: New

Zealand Seamen's Union, 1968, pp. 14–22. Atkinson, 'Auckland Seamen's Union', pp. 59–71, 76–7.

138 Richardson, *Denniston Miners' Union*, pp. 15–19. Richardson, *Coal, Class and Community*, p. 39. Salmond, *Labour's Pioneering Days*, pp. 80–5.

139 Sinclair, 'Scarecrow ministry', p. 108. Sinclair, *Reeves*, p. 71. Victoria University of Wellington, Stout pamphlets, vol 68, Industrial Protection League, first annual conference, 6–12 June 1889. P.J. Lineham, 'Freethinkers in nineteenth-century New Zealand', *NZJH*, vol 19, no 1, 1985. McIvor, *Ballance*, pp. 115–17. Robert E. Weir, 'Whose left/who's left? The Knights of Labour and "radical progressivism"', in Pat Moloney and Kerry Taylor (eds), *On the Left: Essays on Socialism in New Zealand*, Dunedin: Otago University Press, 2002.

140 J.D. Salmond, 'The history of the New Zealand labour movement from the settlement to the Conciliation and Arbitration Act 1894', MA, University of Otago, 1924, p. 278.

Chapter 4: The 'duty of the state'? Extending the contract

1 The song '"A Land of Our Own" – the South Sea Colonists' Hymn' was composed in 1848 for those departing for Canterbury. Johannes C. Andersen, *Old Christchurch*, Christchurch: Capper Press reprint, 1975, pp. 216–17.

2 Harold Perkin, 'Individualism versus collectivism in nineteenth-century Britain: a false antithesis', in *The Structured Crowd*, Sussex: Harvester, 1981.

3 *NZPD*, vol 6, 1869, pp. 673–5.

4 D.A. Hamer, 'Sir Robert Stout and the labour question, 1870–1893', in Chapman and Sinclair (eds), *Studies in a Small Democracy*.

5 Robert Stout, *The Social Future of Labourers*, Napier: Hawke's Bay Observer, 1918, reprint of 1870 address.

6 Robert Stout, *Politics and Poverty*, Dunedin: Otago Daily Times, 1883.

7 *NZPD*, vol 42, 1882, pp. 183–4.

8 Stout, *Politics and Poverty*, p. 3.

9 *NZPD*, vol 56, 1886, pp. 612–13, 866; vol 57, 1887, pp. 715–17; vol 58, 1887, p. 492.

10 Robert Stout, 'State Experiments in New Zealand', *Journal of the Royal Statistical Society*, September 1892.

11 Hill, *Policing the Colonial Frontier*, p. 207.

12 Jon Henning, 'New Zealand: an antipodean exception to master and servant rules', *NZJH*, vol 41, no 1, 2007, provides other examples.

13 For example, *North Otago Times*, 4 March 1875.

14 CM, Charles Clifford papers, folder 10, employment agreement, 28 October 1852.

15 CM, [ARC 1988 14], employment agreement, 19 January 1884 (from Kaiapoi Museum).

16 Fairburn, *Ideal Society*, p. 228. Judith Bassett, 'Abstemious millhands and bush lawyers: the Te Kopuru magistrates' court, 1875–1878', *Australian Journal of Legal History*, vol 1, 1995. Richard Shires, 'Civil litigation in nineteenth century Wellington', History 316 research essay, Victoria University of Wellington, 1985. Jane Cunninghame, 'Litigation in the nineteenth century – Hokitika', History 316 research essay, Victoria University of Wellington, 1985. Roger Palairet, 'Litigation in Wanganui in the 1870s', History 316 research essay, Victoria University of Wellington, 1984. ATL, Micro Ms 800 (Bett collection), Nelson Petty Sessions, Registry of Criminal Matters, 1842–9, cases of 'refusal to pay wages due'.

17 *OW*, 2 June, 24 July 1855. *LT*, 18, 21 February 1857; 19 February, 5 March 1859. *Press*, 17 June 1863. *Timaru Herald*, 5 August 1865.

18 Douglas Hay, 'Patronage, paternalism and welfare: masters, workers and magistrates in eighteenth-century England', *International Labor and Working-class History*, no 53, 1998. *New Munster Gazette*, 1849, pp. 56, 120, 147. GBPP, 1850, 1136, p. 204. *Statistics of Nelson from 1843 to 1854, Compiled from Official Records*, Nelson, 1855, table 26,

offences, 1854. *WS*, 5 February 1842. *LT*, 25 January 1851. Olssen, *Building the New World*, p. 244.

19   *New Zealand Gazette*, 28 November 1840. For Australia, Adrian Merritt, 'The historical role of law in the regulation of employment – abstentionist or interventionist?', *Australian Journal of Law and Society*, vol 1, no 1, 1982.

20   Auckland Provincial Council, *Proceedings*, session 5, 15 February 1856. *New Zealander*, 16, 20, 23, 27 February 1856.

21   *Press*, 31 January 1863. Otago Provincial Council, *Proceedings*, session 18, 1864, pp. 18, 34, 83.

22   *NZPD*, 1864, pp. 69–70; 1865, 252–3, 352, 414, 630–2. Bills Thrown Out, 1865.

23   *Press*, 14 August 1865. Also *LT*, 12 August 1865.

24   *LT*, 27 December 1856; 7, 21 January, 14 February, 5 September 1857; 10 February 1858.

25   Auckland Provincial Council, *Proceedings*, session 1, 1853–4; Nelson Provincial Council, *Proceedings*, session 2, 1854–5, pp. 13, 22–3, 26, and report of select committee. *NZPD*, 1858, p. 400; vol 25, 1877, pp. 539–40. For offences, see *LT*, 7 January 1854; 2 June, 17 July 1858; 9, 18 March 1865. *New Zealand Mail*, 22, 29 January 1876. ATL, Micro Ms 800 (Bett collection), Nelson Petty Sessions, Registry of Criminal Matters, 1842–9. *Statistics of Nelson from 1843 to 1854, Compiled From Official Records*, Nelson, 1855, table 25, 1848, table 26, 1854.

26   *LT*, 12 April 1851; 3 October 1857; 31 December 1858; 14 May 1859.

27   *OW*, 2 June 1855. *NZPD*, 1865, p. 657.

28   *Southern Cross*, 3, 4 February 1871.

29   CM, Charles Clifford papers, folder 10, apprenticeship indenture, 1852.

30   CM, articles of apprenticeship, Arthur Johnston with John Anderson, 28 April 1873.

31   In the rural sector, see *Oamaru Times*, 16 December 1870. *Lake Wakatip Mail*, 7 February 1872. *Timaru Herald*, 28 February 1872. *North Otago Times*, 4 March 1875. *Tuapeka Times*, 2, 5 February 1876. *Canterbury Times*, 18 March 1887. From 1872 offences against the Masters and Servants Act were recorded in the *Statistics of New Zealand* series.

32   Arnold, *Farthest Promised Land*, chapter 1. *AJHR*, 1873, D-1, p. 19, I-5; 1881, I-1A. *Journal of the Legislative Council (JLC)*, 1873, no 12, pp. 40–1. *Marlborough Press*, 14, 21 August 1872. Letter, 'A Bebington navvy', *WI*, 18 January 1873.

33   *AJHR*, 1881, I-1A, p. 25. *EP*, 2 January 1873. *WI*, 10, 24 January 1873.

34   William Pember Reeves, *State Experiments in Australia and New Zealand* (2 vols), London: Allen and Unwin, 1902, vol 2, p. 207.

35   *NZPD*, vol 10, 1871, pp. 90, 132–3; vol 67, 1890, p. 129.

36   Bills Thrown Out, 1882.

37   *JHR*, 1883, petitions 114–16, 157, 240, 276. *JLC*, 1883, petitions 38, 66. *NZPD*, vol 44, 1883, pp. 95–6; vol 48, 1884, p. 400; vol 49, 1884, p. 420.

38   *NZPD*, vol 60, 1888, pp. 89, 164, 433; vol 64, 1889, p. 122; vol 66, 1889, p. 150; vol 67, 1890, p. 129; vol 68, 1890, pp. 22, 87–8.

39   Reeves, *State Experiments*, vol 2, p. 208. *NZPD*, vol 80, 1893, p. 631.

40   *WI*, 18 August 1873.

41   E.R. Martin, *Marine Department Centennial History, 1866–1966*, Wellington: Government Printer, 1969, pp. 107–12.

42   *NZPD*, vol 24, 1873, p. 546ff.; vol 25, 1873, p. 871ff.; vol 26, 1874, p. 67ff. *AJHR*, 1880, H-18; 1881, H-14. Richardson, *Coal, Class and Community*, pp. 27–8. Ian Campbell, *Compensation for Personal Injury in New Zealand: Its Rise and Fall*, Auckland: Auckland University Press, 1996, pp. 9–11.

43   *AJHR*, 1887, C-4, p. 10. *New Zealand Gazette*, 1887, pp. 1124–8. See Brian Wood, *Disaster at Brunner*, Greymouth: Bright Print, 1996, pp. 90–2 for subsequent lack of inspection in West Coast mines.

44 *NZPD*, vol 41, 1882, pp. 337–41. Campbell, *Compensation for Personal Injury*, p. 6. Wood, *Disaster at Brunner*, p. 165.

45 *NZPD*, vol 41, 1882, p. 340; vol 247, 1936, p. 23.

46 Campbell, *Compensation for Personal Injury*, p. 14. *NZPD*, vol 68, 1890, p. 74.

47 *NZPD*, vol 61, 1888, p. 554, also pp. 100–1, 553–4. Bassett, 'Harry Atkinson', pp. 207–8.

48 Otago Provincial Council, *Proceedings*, session 34, 19 June 1875. *New Zealand Mail*, 3 July 1875. ArchNZ, IA1, 87/744, directive, 6 December 1886, report of inspector, 19 February 1887. *NZPD*, vol 56, 1886, p. 136.

49 *NZPD*, vol 19, 1875, p. 305. John E. Martin, 'English models and antipodean conditions: the origins and development of protective factory legislation in New Zealand', *Labour History*, no 73, 1997. *DNZB*, vol 2, entry. A.B. Trezise, 'Factory conditions and legislation in New Zealand, 1873–1891', History research essay, Massey University, 1973. D.M. Unwin, 'Women in New Zealand industry – with specific reference to factory workers and to conditions in Dunedin', MA, University of Otago, 1944. J.E. Bartlett, 'Woven together: the industrial workplace in the Otago woollen mills, 1871–1930', BA (Hons), University of Otago, 1987.

50 *AJHR*, 1878, H-2; 1880, H-22; 1885, H-20; 1886, H-20, H-20A, H-20B; 1887, Session I, H-7. *NZPD*, vol 57, 1887, p. 24. W.B. Sutch, *The Quest for Security in New Zealand, 1840 to 1966*, Wellington: Oxford University Press, 1966, p. 67. Roth, *Trade Unions in New Zealand*, p. 5. Judith Bassett, 'Dark Satanic mills, 1880–1890', in Judith Binney, Judith Bassett and Erik Olssen, *An Illustrated History of New Zealand, 1820–1920*, Wellington: Allen and Unwin, 1990, pp. 190–1.

51 *Otago Daily Times*, 12 January 1885. *NZPD*, vol 51, 1885, p. 190; vol 54, 1886, p. 57; vol 57, 1887, pp. 24–5, 374–8; vol 64, 1889, pp. 37, 310; vol 66, 1889, pp. 313–14. See also Salmond, *Labour's Pioneering Days*, pp. 50–1.

52 ATL, Broadside, Wellington: Independent Office, 1850 (Bagnall, *National Bibliography*, 5879a). Also see *WI*, 2 November 1865.

53 J.G.S. Grant, *The Early Closing System*, Dunedin, 1880, pp. 1-2. J.A. Davis, 'Business is business', in *Plain Talks on Being Out of Work*, Dunedin: J. Horsburgh, 1880, p. 9. *ODT*, 13 January 1885.

54 Reeves, *State Experiments*, vol 2, pp. 182–91.

55 *NZPD*, vol 45, 1883, pp. 137–8. Bills Thrown Out, 1883.

56 Bills Thrown Out, 1886, 1887. *NZPD*, vol 57, 1887, pp. 24–5, 374–8; vol 58, 1887, p. 256; vol 60, 1888, p. 44; vol 64, 1889, pp. 493–501. *JHR*, session II, 1887, 5 petitions; 1888, 6 petitions. Bassett, 'Harry Atkinson', pp. 208, 212.

57 *NZ Punch*, 7 April 1888.

58 Martin, 'Unemployment, government and the labour market'. Dowie, 'Course and character of capital formation', pp. 45–6.

59 Salmond, *Labour's Pioneering Days*, p. 31.

60 Arthur Clayden, *A Popular Handbook to New Zealand – Its Resources and Industries*, London: Wyman and Sons, 1885, p. 21.

61 *Press*, 17 December 1883. *LT*, 17, 19, 21, 24 December 1883. ArchNZ, IM4, 1/2, 83/833, clippings from *LT*, mid December 1883. IA1/80/1401, petition.

62 Wellington Provincial Council, *Proceedings*, session 6, 1858, message no 12. Also session 3, Featherston, 27 December 1855; session 6, 1858, Featherston's opening address; session 7, 1859, memorial and petition. Otago Provincial Council, *Proceedings*, session 11, 12 December 1860, 400 men roadmaking; session 12, 1861, appendix, memorial signed by 1,010 people regarding public works employment.

63 ArchNZ, IA4, 14, 64/751, William Gisborne to J. Martin and J. May, 1 April 1864.

64 ArchNZ, Christchurch, CH287, CP637c/6, re. unemployed petition; CP637c/3, survey of employers, 20 October 1870.

65   *NZPD*, vol 7, 1870, pp. 344–5.

66   *NZPD*, vol 7, 1870, p. 395; also Fitzherbert, p. 438.

67   Martin, 'Unemployment, government and the labour market'.

68   *AJHR*, 1870, B-2, p. 19, Vogel; also 1872, D-1, p. 9; and *NZPD*, vol 7, 1870, p. 345.

69   *NZPD*, vol 35, 1880, p. 91.

70   *WI*, 28 February 1871.

71   *Census of Population and Dwellings*, 1874, occupational tables.

72   ArchNZ, Christchurch, CH287, CP637c/1–7, petition of unemployed, 4 October 1870, and related enquiry. *LT*, 11 August–30 September 1870. Andersen, *Jubilee History*, pp. 431–3. ArchNZ, Otago Province, 1/40/26, employer petition, 17 May 1870.

73   *OW*, 8 January 1870.

74   ArchNZ, IM4, 1/2, 87/143. *NZPD*, vol 35, 1880, pp. 70–1; vol 39, 1881, pp. 559–60. Martin, *Forgotten Worker*, chapter 2.

75   *AJHR*, 1879, Session II, D-1A, p. 2; 1880, E-1, p. 60; 1881, D-1, pp. 44–5.

76   *Press*, 16 September 1884.

77   CM, Rolleston, correspondence, box 1, folder 3, Treadwell letter, 24 February 1880.

78   Woodward, *Jubilee Farms*, p. 5.

79   Vogel (ed), *New Zealand: Land and Farming*, pp. 31–2. *Yeoman*, 5 March 1881, p. 9. Rollo Arnold, 'The opening of the great bush, 1869–1881', PhD, Victoria University of Wellington, 1972. CM, Rolleston, correspondence, box 1, folder 3, Treadwell letter, 24 February 1880, and enclosed clippings. ArchNZ, IM4, 1/2, 80/537, Rolleston to J.E. March, relief officer, 19 June 1880.

80   *AJHR*, 1881, D-1, H-36; 1882, D-1, I-1B; 1883, D-1; 1884, D-1; 1886, D-1; 1887, D-1. *Census of Population and Dwellings*, 1886. *NZPD*, vol 42, 1882, pp. 525, 544; vol 43, 1882, pp. 163–4; vol 49, 1884, p. 305. There was talk that this would affect 10,000 people. *LT*, 17 December 1883.

81   *NZPD*, vol 54, 1886, p. 145; vol 56, 1886, pp. 52, 229–31, 250–1, 305–6, 606–13, 865–66; vol 58, 1887, p. 488. ArchNZ, LE1, 1886/160.

82   *NZPD*, vol 56, 1886, p. 230; vol 58, 1887, p. 552.

83   ArchNZ, W1, 85/3100, J. Powell regarding settlement on the land in the North Island, 6 June 1885. *NZPD*, vol 51, 1885, pp. 48–50. *AJHR*, 1885, H-28, rules of the association. Christopher Campbell, 'Parties and special interests in New Zealand, 1890–1893', MA, Victoria University of Wellington, 1978, pp. 12–15.

84   *NZPD*, vol 56, 1886, pp. 250–1.

85   *LT*, 15 December 1883, editorial. Bassett, *Atkinson*, chapter 11. Rosslyn J. Noonan, *By Design: A Brief History of the Public Works Department/Ministry of Works, 1870–1970*, Wellington: Government Printer, 1975, chapter 3.

86   The rate was much greater than official figures suggested. Rollo Arnold, 'Family or strangers? Trans-Tasman migrants, 1870–1920', Australia-New Zealand: Aspects of a Relationship, Stout Research Centre Conference, 1991. R.J. Campbell, 'The black "Eighties": unemployment in New Zealand in the 1880s', *Australian Economic History Review*, vol 16, 1976, pp. 70–1. *NZOYB*, 1898, p. 98, table 'Increase of population'.

Chapter 5: The social laboratory – rebuilding the contract

1   This was Reeves' attempt at a national anthem. There appear to be different versions of the poem; this one is to be found in W.R. Alexander and A.E. Currie, *New Zealand Verse*, London: Walter Scott Publishing, 1906.

2   Hirst, 'Egalitarianism', for Australia.

3   D.A. Hamer, 'Centralization and nationalism (1891–1912)', in Keith Sinclair (ed), *The Oxford Illustrated History of New Zealand*, Auckland: Oxford University Press, 1990.

4   John E. Martin, '"Waging war on the labour market": the state and wage labour in late nineteenth-century New Zealand', *Turnbull Library Record*, nos 1, 2, 1993. John E. Martin, 'God made the country and man the town', in I. Shirley (ed), *Development Tracks*, Palmerston North: Dunmore Press, 1982.

5   Castles, *Working Class and Welfare*, pp. 94–5. Miles Fairburn, 'Why did the New Zealand Labour Party fail to win office until 1935?', *Political Science*, vol 37, no 2, 1985, pp. 120–4.

6   Brooking, *Lands for the People?*, p. 73.

7   Brooking, *Lands for the People?*, chapters 7, 9, 10, 13. McIvor, *Rainmaker*, chapters 9–11. Gardner, *Pastoral Kingdom Divided*. Hamer, *New Zealand Liberals*, pp. 64–75.

8   *NZPD*, vol 62, 1888, pp. 240–56; vol 63, 1888, pp. 51, 434–46; vol 66, 1889, p. 467. McIvor, *Rainmaker*, p. 130.

9   John E. Martin, *Holding the Balance: A History of New Zealand's Department of Labour, 1891–1995*, Christchurch: Canterbury University Press, 1996, pp. 32–7.

10   Martin, *Holding the Balance*, pp. 91–8, 128–35. *AJHR*, 1904, H-11B.

11   Sinclair, *Reeves*, pp. 149–50. Hamer, *New Zealand Liberals*, pp. 95–6.

12   Neil C. Quigley, 'The mortgage market in New Zealand, and the origins of the Government Advances to Settlers Act, 1894', *New Zealand Economic Papers*, vol 23, 1989.

13   *AJHR*, 1908, B-6, p. xii. *NZPD*, vol 144, 1908, p. 500. *NZOYB*, 1914, p. 741; 1918, p. 646; 1931, p. 625, figures on loans.

14   Fairburn, 'Why did the New Zealand Labour Party fail to win office?', p. 122. Miles Fairburn, 'The farmers take over', in Sinclair (ed), *Oxford Illustrated History*, p. 206. John E. Martin, 'The removal of compulsory arbitration and the depression of the 1930s', *NZJH*, vol 28, no 2, 1994, pp. 136–7.

15   *NZPD*, 1863, pp. 980–1, 1005, 1009; 1867, p. 306. *AJHR*, 1864, A-1, pp. 18–19.

16   *AJHR*, 1879, session I, A-3; 1880, A-1, pp. 56–7, A-2, p. 44, A-6; 1881, A-2, p. 8; 1882, A-1, pp. 2–3, 6–7, A-2, pp. 2, 5.

17   *AJHR*, 1880, A-1, pp. 46, 49–56, A-5.

18   *AJHR*, 1880, A-1, pp. 14–15, A-2, pp. 3–6.

19   *AJHR*, 1879, session II, D-1, p. 1.

20   *Censuses of Population and Dwellings*, 1864, 1874, 1891, 1896.

21   Brian Moloughney and John Stenhouse, '"Drug-besotten, sin-begotten fiends of filth": New Zealanders and the Oriental other, 1850–1920', *NZJH*, vol 33, no 1, 1999. Miles Fairburn, 'What best explains the discrimination against the Chinese in New Zealand, 1860s–1950s?', *Journal of New Zealand Studies*, new series 2–3, 2003–4.

22   W.D. Borrie, 'Immigration to New Zealand since 1854', MA, University of Otago, 1938, chapter 22. F.A. Ponton, 'Immigration restriction in New Zealand: a study of policy from 1908 to 1939', MA, Victoria University of Wellington, 1946. P.S. O'Connor, 'Keeping New Zealand white, 1908–1920', *NZJH*, vol 2, no 1, 1968. Bills Thrown Out, 1879. *NZPD*, vol 36, 1880, pp. 91–107, 615.

23   *AJHR*, 1881, A-3.

24   Reeves, *State Experiments*, vol 2, pp. 332–8, for Australia.

25   Reeves, *State Experiments*, vol 2, pp. 329, 330, 354, 355, 359–60 for following quotations.

26   *NZPD*, vol 93, 1896, pp. 465–72; vol 100, p. 125. *JLC*, 1896, pp. 98–9. John E. Martin, 'Refusal of assent – a hidden element of constitutional history in New Zealand', *Victoria University of Wellington Law Review*, vol 41, no 1, 2010.

27   Sean Brawley, '"No white policy" in New Zealand: fact and fiction in New Zealand's immigration record, 1946–1978', *NZJH*, vol 27, no 1, 1993.

28   John E. Martin, '1890: a turning point for labour', in Pat Walsh (ed), *Pioneering New Zealand Labour History*, Palmerston North: Dunmore Press, 1994. Martin, 'English models and antipodean conditions'. Sinclair, *Reeves*, p. 109. I.A. Merrett, 'A reappraisal of the 1890 Maritime strike in New Zealand', MA (Hons), University of Canterbury, 1970, p. 243.

29 *LT*, 5 August 1890. *NZPD*, vol 67, 1890, pp. 3, 10. For Hislop see *NZPD*, vol 209, 1926, pp. 15–18, 92–4. William Earnshaw went so far as to describe him as the 'father of the modern Labour movement'.

30 Reeves, *State Experiments*, vol 2, pp. 206–7. *WI*, 30 June, 21 August 1873. Donald Reid wanted payment of wages in public houses prohibited in the Regulation of Mines Act 1874. Brogden's contracts had such provisions written into them. *AJHR*, 1872, D-19, p. 10ff. *NZH*, 28 January 1886. *NZPD*, vol 68, 1890, p. 86, Seddon. Martin, *Forgotten Worker*, chapter 7.

31 *The Tomahawk*, 26 March 1870, p. 7.

32 ArchNZ, LE1, Labour Bills Committee, 1890/4.

33 C. Campbell, 'The "working class" and the Liberal party in 1890', *NZJH*, vol 9, no 1, 1975, p. 47.

34 William Pember Reeves ['Pharos'], *Some Historical Articles on Communism and Socialism*, Christchurch: Lyttelton Times, 1890. William Pember Reeves, *The State and its Functions in New Zealand*, Fabian Tract, no 74, 1896. Sinclair, *Reeves*, pp. 100–103. J. Harris, *Unemployment and Politics: A Study in English Social Policy, 1886–1914*, Oxford: Clarendon, 1972, chapter 3.

35 Martin, *Holding the Balance*.

36 John Blair, *Lays of the Old Identities*, Dunedin: R.T. Wheeler, 1889, pp. 73–7.

37 Martin, *Forgotten Worker*, pp. 151–4.

38 Campbell, *Compensation for Personal Injury*, pp. 11–19. Martin, *Holding the Balance*, pp. 65–6. *AJHR*, 1893, H-10, p. 3; 1897, H-6, pp. v–vi; 1897, H-2; 1898, H-6, p. iii. *JLC*, 1898, no 4, Wages Protection bill, pp. 51–4. *NZPD*, vol 110, 1899, p. 233.

39 F.W. Rowley, *The Industrial Situation in New Zealand*, Wellington: Harry H. Tombs, 1931, chapter 10. Campbell, *Compensation for Personal Injury*, chapter 3.

40 Martin, *Holding the Balance*, pp. 63–4, 80–2, 111–12, 143–4.

41 Sinclair, *Destiny Apart*, pp. 13, 72–3.

42 For example, *Letters from Emigrants Published by the New Zealand Company for the Information of the Labouring Classes*, London: G. McKewan, 1841. Arnold, *Farthest Promised Land*, chapter 11.

43 ATL, Ms Papers 2287, Thomas Kempton, letter, 11 April 1841. *Journal of the Early Settlers and Historical Association of Wellington*, vol 1, no 3, September 1913, pp. 146–7.

44 Bathgate, *New Zealand*, pp. 20–1, 35–6, 67.

45 Correspondent of *Daily News*, in Vogel (ed), *New Zealand – Land and Farming*, pp. 37–8.

46 *NZPD*, vol 57, 1887, p. 486, Garrick.

47 A.S. Thomson, *The Story of New Zealand* (2 vols), London: John Murray, 1859. Alfred K. Newman, 'Is New Zealand a healthy country? An enquiry (with statistics by F.W. Frankland)', *Transactions and Proceedings of the New Zealand Institute*, vol 15, 1882. Robert Stout, *Notes on the Progress of New Zealand for Twenty Years, 1864–1884*, Wellington: Government Printer, 1886, p. 8. George Leslie, *New Zealand Mortality Rates, 1881–1891*, Dunedin: Otago Daily Times, 1895, reprinted with revisions from *New Zealand Journal of Insurance, Mining and Finance*, September, November 1895. Fairburn, *Ideal Society*, p. 34. Campbell J. Gibson, 'Demographic history of New Zealand', PhD, University of California, Berkeley, 1971, p. 173. Ian Pool, 'Is New Zealand a healthy country?', *New Zealand Population Review*, vol 8, no 2, 1982. Pool, while questioning the conclusion of Newman and Franklin, partly supports them on non-Maori mortality for similar reasons – food, low population density and high incomes.

48 ArchNZ, IM4, 1/1, 76/793, circular to immigration officers, 11 December 1875. *AJHR*, 1871, D-3, p. 4; 1875, D-1, p. 15; 1876, D-1, p. 9.

49 *AJHR*, 1866, D-7B. J.A. Dowie, 'A century-old estimate of the national income of New Zealand', *Business Archives and History*, vol 6, 1966. Keith Rankin, 'Gross national product

estimates for New Zealand, 1859–1939', in L. Evans, J. Poot and N. Quigley (eds), *Long-run Perspectives on the New Zealand Economy*, Wellington: New Zealand Association of Economists, 1991, especially figure 3. Margaret Galt, 'Wealth and income in New Zealand, c.1870–c.1939', PhD, Victoria University of Wellington, 1985.

50   ArchNZ Christchurch, Provincial Council papers, CH287, CP637c/4, memo for select committee on unemployed, 21 October 1870. M.N. Arnold, 'Wage rates, 1873–1911', Victoria University of Wellington, Department of Economics discussion paper no 11, 1982.

51   *AJHR*, 1893, H-10. Department of Labour, 'Inquiry into the cost of living in New Zealand', *Journal*, April 1912.

52   John Burnett, *A History of the Cost of Living*, Harmondsworth: Penguin, 1969, pp. 250–4.

53   *AJHR*, 1871, D-3, p. 4; 1875, D-6, p. 2. *Statistics of New Zealand*, 1876. Vogel (ed), *Official Handbook of New Zealand*, pp. 150, 214, 262. James McIndoe, *Sketch of Otago*, Dunedin: R.T. Wheeler, 1878, pp. 59–61. Judith Elphick, 'Auckland 1870–74: a social portrait', MA, University of Auckland, 1974, pp. 102, 104. Clayden, *The England of the Pacific*, pp. 7, 37. Simmons, *Old England and New Zealand*, p. 92. Gregg, *New Zealand*, pp. 9, 13. Wakefield, *Taxes in New Zealand*, pp. 6–7. J. Brittain Pash, *Report on New Zealand*, Colchester: Essex Standard, 1883, p. 6. T. Mann, 'Conditions of labour in New Zealand', *Nineteenth Century*, vol 52, September 1902. Fairburn, *Nearly Out of Heart and Hope*, pp. 129–30. *Marlborough Press*, 14 August 1872. B.J.G. Thompson, 'The Canterbury farm labourers' dispute, 1907–1908', MA, University of Canterbury, 1967, pp. 64, 178. *Farmers' Union Advocate*, 14, 21 December 1907; 6, 11 January, 29 February, 14 March 1908.

54   Martin, 'Unemployment, government and the labour market', pp. 171–5. Hocken Library, J.T. Paul, New Zealand Pamphlets, vol 31, Canterbury Shearers' Union, annual report, 1908.

55   Salmond, *Labour's Pioneering Days*, pp. 7–14. Roth, *Trade Unions in New Zealand*, pp. 3–4. Roth, 'Labour day in New Zealand'.

56   *NZPD*, vol 49, 1884, p. 28, Smith; also vol 55, 1886, p. 560, Joyce. W.E. Murphy, *History of the Eight Hours' Movement*, Melbourne: Spectator Publishing Co., 1896, p. 13.

57   Martin, *Forgotten Worker*, p. 171. *NZPD*, vol 57, 1887, pp. 346–7.

58   *NZPD*, vol 16, 1874, p. 70. *JHR*, 1874, petition, 21 July.

59   Bills Thrown Out, 1882–90. *NZPD*, vol 41, 1882, pp. 170–8; vol 42, 1882, pp. 381–4; vol 44, 1883, p. 95; vol 49, 1884, pp. 21–33; vol 52, 1885, pp. 196–201; vol 55, 1886, pp. 556–66. Roth, 'Labour Day in New Zealand'.

60   *NZPD*, vol 55, 1886, p. 560, Menteath.

61   See *JHR*, 1883, petition nos 122, 123, 156, 310.

62   *NZPD*, vol 55, 1886, pp. 563–5; vol 57, 1887, pp. 343–8; vol 64, 1889, pp. 216–29.

63   Reprinted in *Samuel Duncan Parnell, Founder of Eight Hours System*, Wellington: Evening Post, 1891.

64   Lawrence B. Glickman, *A Living Wage: American Workers and the Making of Consumer Society*, Ithaca: Cornell University Press, 1997, chapter 5.

65   Macarthy, 'Living wage', for Australia.

66   E.H. Phelps Brown with Margaret H. Browne, *A Century of Pay: The Course of Pay and Production in France, Germany, Sweden, the United Kingdom, and the USA, 1860–1960*, London: Macmillan, 1968, p. 47. Clark, *Report on Labour Conditions in New Zealand*, p. 180. Clark, *Labour Movement in Australasia*, pp. 51–3. M.B. Hammond, 'Judicial interpretation of the minimum wage in Australia', pp. 570–1, reprinted in Department of Labour, *Journal*, August 1913.

67   Arnold, 'Wage rates, 1874–1911'. William Pember Reeves, 'Protective tariffs in Australia and New Zealand', *The Economic Journal*, vol 9, 1899, p. 41. James Holt, *Compulsory Arbitration in New Zealand – The First Forty Years*, Auckland: Auckland University Press, 1986,

p. 105. *Book of Awards*, vol 20, 1919, pp. 403–5. G.W. Clinkard, 'Wages and working-hours in New Zealand, 1897–1919', pp. 896–7, appendix E, *NZOYB*, 1919. N.S. Woods, 'A study of the basic wage in New Zealand prior to 1928', *Economic Record*, December 1933. E.J. Riches, 'The fair wage principle in New Zealand', *Economic Record*, December 1937.

68 Clark, *Report on Labour Conditions in New Zealand*, pp. 170–1, 182.

69 Clark, *Labour Movement in Australasia*, p. 299.

70 Hammond, 'Judicial interpretation'. For examples, see *Book of Awards*, vol 16, 1915, p. 354; vol 17, 1916, p. 418.

71 *AJHR*, session II, 1912, H-18, pp. xix, c–cii, 67–9. J.G. Findlay, *Labour and the Arbitration Act*, Wellington: New Zealand Times, 1908, p. 3.

72 Sinclair, *Destiny Apart*, pp. 72–3. Department of Labour, 'Inquiry into the cost of living in New Zealand', *Journal*, April 1912. Report of the Economic Commission, January 1914, *Printed Annexures to the Votes and Proceedings*, 4th session, House of Assembly, First Parliament, Union of South Africa, 1914.

73 Glickman, *Living Wage. AJHR*, 1890, H-5, p. v. *GBPP*, 1908, Cd 4167, Ernest Aves, 'Report on the wages boards and Industrial Conciliation Acts of Australia and New Zealand', pp. 100–101. Macarthy, 'Living wage', p. 18. Olssen, *Building the New World*, pp. 82–3. Holt, *Compulsory Arbitration*, pp. 44–5, 66–8.

74 *AJHR*, session II, 1891, H-48. *NZPD*, vol 69, 1890, pp. 124, 387–407, 892–907. Martin, *Holding the Balance*, pp. 84–90, 152–63. Reeves, *State Experiments*, vol 2, p. 85ff. Merrett, 'Reappraisal of the 1890 Maritime strike', pp. 125–7, 215–16.

75 Bills Thrown Out, 1890. *NZPD*, vol 69, 1890, pp. 118–33, 514–18.

76 *NZPD*, vol 78, 1892, p. 181.

77 J.E. Le Rossignol and W.D. Stewart, 'Compulsory arbitration in New Zealand', *Quarterly Journal of Economics*, vol 24, 1910, pp. 14–15. *Book of Awards*, vol 1, 1894–1900, pp. 304–7, judgement of Stout.

78 Historians have tended to take for granted the existence of a family wage in terms of males being paid higher wages than females. Stephen Robertson, 'Women workers and the New Zealand Arbitration Court, 1894–1920', *Labour History*, no 61, 1991, p. 40. Annabel Cooper and Maureen Molloy, 'Poverty, dependence and "women": reading autobiography and social policy from 1930s New Zealand', *Gender and History*, vol 9, no 1, 1997, pp. 45–6. Melanie Nolan, '"Politics swept under a domestic carpet"? Fracturing domesticity and the male breadwinner wage', *NZJH*, vol 27, no 2, 1993, pp. 199, 201. But also see Melanie Nolan, *Breadwinning: New Zealand Women and the State*, Christchurch: Canterbury University Press, 2000, pp. 22, 141–4.

79 Henry Broadhead, *State Regulation of Labour and Labour Disputes in New Zealand*, Christchurch: Whitcombe and Tombs, 1908, pp. 57–61. Woods, *Arbitration in New Zealand*, pp. 78–80, 95–6. Woods, 'Basic wage'. M.B. Hammond, 'The regulation of wages in New Zealand', *Quarterly Journal of Economics*, vol 31, 1917. John Child, 'Wages policy and wage movements in New Zealand, 1914–23', *Journal of Industrial Relations*, vol 13, 1971. Holt, *Compulsory Arbitration*, p. 68.

80 Rossignol and Stewart, 'Compulsory arbitration in New Zealand', pp. 24–6.

81 *Press*, 9 January 1907. *ODT*, 29 January 1907.

82 *NZOYB*, 1908, pp. 539–40, 'Estimated rise in wages and prices of necessary foods'. *NZPD*, vol 139, 1907, pp. 367–8.

83 *NZPD*, vol 139, 1907, p. 442, also p. 439. *Auckland Star*, 30 November 1905. J.C. Clarke, 'The New Zealand Liberal Party and government, 1895–1906', MA, University of Auckland, 1962, pp. 177–8. Alex Frame, *Salmond: Southern Jurist*, Wellington: Victoria University Press, 1995, pp. 83–7.

84 *NZPD*, vol 140, 1907, p. 594. The Harvester judgement is to be found in *Commonwealth*

Arbitration Reports, vol 2, pp. 1–3, November 1907. Woods, *Arbitration in New Zealand*, p. 95. Hammond, 'Regulation of wages', pp. 421–3, 426–7. Woods, 'Basic wage', pp. 263–4.

85   Findlay, *Labour and the Arbitration Act*, p. 11. Woods, *Arbitration in New Zealand*, p. 96. Nolan, *Breadwinning*, chapter 5.

86   *Book of Awards*, vol 9, 1908, p. 526.

87   ArchNZ, L1 (burnt files), box 85b, file 13/3/85, Arbitration Act amendment, 1912, outline of proposed amendments by Rowley, 22 July 1912. *AJHR*, session II, 1912, H-18.

88   *Book of Awards*, vol 16, 1915, pp. 157, 279, 431; vol 17, 1916, pp. 137–8.

89   *Book of Awards*, vol 19, 1918, pp. 1061–2.

90   A.J. Everton, 'Government intervention in the New Zealand economy, 1914–18 – its aims and effectiveness', MA, Victoria University of Wellington, 1995.

91   John E. Martin, 'Blueprint for the future? "National efficiency" and the First World War', in John Crawford and Ian McGibbon (eds), *New Zealand's Great War*, Auckland: Exisle, 2007.

92   J.G. Findlay, 'Industrial peace in New Zealand', *International Labour Review*, vol 4, 1921, pp. 39–40. ArchNZ, L9, unnumbered files, box 2, trade union disputes and matters, 1912–23, telegram, Allen to Massey, 6 May 1919; box 5, misc matters 1907–31, two pamphlets of 1921.

93   J.B. Condliffe, 'Experiments in state control in New Zealand', *International Labour Review*, vol 9, no 3, 1924, p. 353.

94   *Book of Awards*, vol 20, 1919, pp. 403–5. Riches, 'Fair wage principle '.

95   *Book of Awards*, vol 21, 1920, pp. 513–14, 2103–5, 2233–42; vol 22, 1921, pp. 804–6. Holt, *Compulsory Arbitration*, chapter 6 and especially p. 144.

96   *Book of Awards*, vol 23, 1922, pp. 333–55, 964–9. Department of Labour, *Pronouncements of the Court re Cost of Living and General Order Amending Awards, May 1922*, Wellington: Government Print, 1922, p. 9.

97   *Book of Awards*, vol 23, 1922, pp. 350–1. *NZH*, 1 May 1922.

98   *Book of Awards*, vol 25A, 1925, pp. 800–4. *NZH*, 12 September 1925. Such an approach was not formally recorded in the pronouncement. Bruce Brown, *The Rise of New Zealand Labour*, Wellington: Price Milburn, 1962, p. 82. *New Zealand Worker*, 5 August 1925. J. Robinson, *The Basic Wage in New Zealand*, Wellington: New Zealand Worker, 1926.

99   *NZPD*, vol 213, 1927, p. 860ff. *New Zealand Worker*, 14 August 1929, specimen budgets. *Book of Awards*, vol 29, 1929, pp. 695–705.

100 Woods, *Arbitration in New Zealand*, pp. 172–3. *Book of Awards*, vol 51, 1951, p. 14.

101 *Book of Awards*, vol 47, 1947, pp. 1363–4. Nolan, *Breadwinning*, chapter 8.

Chapter 6: The welfare laboratory and the social contract

1   H.E. Holland, *Red Roses on the Highways*, Sydney: Holland and Stephenson, 1924.

2   For Britain, see M.J. Daunton, 'Payment and participation: welfare and state-formation in Britain, 1900–1951', *Past and Present*, no 150, 1996. H.C.G. Matthew, 'Disraeli, Gladstone, and the politics of mid-Victorian budgets', *Historical Journal*, vol 22, no 3, 1979. Eugenio F. Biagini, 'Popular Liberals, Gladstonian finance and the debate on taxation, 1860–1874', in Biagini and Reid, *Currents of Radicalism*. James E. Cronin, *The Politics of State Expansion – War, State and Society in Twentieth Century Britain*, London: Routledge, 1991. Cronin, 'British state'. Sven Steinmo, *Taxation and Democracy: Swedish, British and American Approaches to Financing the Modern State*, New Haven: Yale University Press, 1993, 'Introduction'.

3   In Walter Jerrold (ed), *The Complete Poetical Works of Thomas Hood*, London: Henry Frowde, 1908.

4   *NZPD*, vol 35, 1880, p. 91.

5   Derek Fraser, *The Evolution of the British Welfare State* (second edition), London: Macmillan, 1984, pp. 50–1.

6   Tennant describes charitable aid as a form of poor law in *Paupers and Providers*, p. 31. David Thomson, in *A World Without Welfare – New Zealand's Colonial Experiment* (Auckland: Auckland University Press, 1998, p. 28), describes it as an alternative to the poor law.

7   Simmons, *Old England and New Zealand*, pp. 60–1.

8   W.H. Oliver, 'Social policy in the Liberal period', *NZJH*, vol 13, no 1, 1979, pp. 32–3. Castles, *The Working Class and Welfare*.

9   Bentley B. Gilbert, *The Evolution of National Insurance in Great Britain*, London: Joseph, 1966, chapter 3. Tennant, *Paupers and Providers*, pp. 98–9.

10   Tennant, *Paupers and Providers*, p. 13. Sutch, *Quest for Security*, p. 84. Thomson, *World Without Welfare*, pp. 22–7.

11   Tennant, *Paupers and Providers*, chapter 1. R.E. Wright-St Clair, *A History of the New Zealand Medical Association*, Wellington: Butterworths, 1987, p. 20, and chapter 10. *AJHR*, 1975, H- 23, pp. 12–14.

12   Thomson, *World Without Welfare*, p. 18. Martin Daunton, *Charity, Self-interest and Welfare in the English Past*, London: University College London Press, 1996, 'Introduction', especially p. 10. Derek A. Dow, 'Springs of charity? The development of the New Zealand hospital system, 1876–1910', in L. Bryder (ed), *A Healthy Country: Essays on the Social History of Medicine in New Zealand*, Wellington: Bridget Williams Books, 1991, p. 55. Iain Hay, *The Caring Commodity: The Provision of Health Care in New Zealand*, Auckland: Oxford University Press, 1989, appendix 1.

13   See Tennant, *Paupers and Providers*, pp. 13, 24, for an alternative interpretation of the ordinance.

14   Michael F. Chilton, 'The genesis of the welfare state: a study of hospitals and charitable aid in New Zealand, 1877–92', MA, University of Canterbury, 1968.

15   Stewart, *Rolleston*, p. 128.

16   *NZPD*, vol 24, 1877, pp. 144–9, 505.

17   Tennant, *Paupers and Providers*, pp. 24–5.

18   *NZPD*, vol 35, 1880, p. 77.

19   Thomson, *World Without Welfare*, p. 155. Brian Heenan, 'Population ageing among non-Maori New Zealanders in later Victorian times', *NZJH*, vol 35, no 2, 2001. R.J. Warwick Neville, 'Trends and differentials in age-sex structure', table 30, in *Population of New Zealand* (country monograph series no 12) vol 1, New York: United Nations, 1985.

20   Victoria University of Wellington, Stout pamphlets, vol 29, Grand Lodge, Independent Order of Oddfellows, 'Proceedings of fifteenth annual session', Dunedin, 1877, and Otago Manchester Unity Oddfellows, annual meeting, Dunedin, 1878. ArchNZ, LE1, 1894/9, evidence of Mark Cohen. *AJHR*, 1884, H-1.

21   Bassett, *Atkinson*, p. 109. Scholefield (ed), *Dictionary of Biography*, entry on Atkinson. Frankland had been appointed as revising barrister and actuary for friendly societies in the late 1870s. He provided mortality statistics in 1882; the only such study within New Zealand at the time. In 1884 he became Registrar of Friendly Societies and in 1886 Government Actuary and Statistician.

22   *NZPD*, vol 42, 1882, p. 183. H.A. Atkinson, *Speeches Delivered by the Colonial Treasurer*, Christchurch: Press Office, 1883. *AJHR*, 1882, B-2, pp. iii–v.

23   *New Zealand Times*, 22 March 1883. Bassett, *Atkinson*, pp. 109, 113.

24   Scholefield (ed), *Richmond–Atkinson Papers*, p. 512.

25   James H. Treble, 'The attitudes of friendly societies towards the movement in Great Britain for state pensions, 1878–1908', *International Review of Social History*, vol 15, 1970. *NZPD*,

vol 209, 1926, p. 94. *New Zealand Mail*, 14 April 1883. ArchNZ, LE1, 1894/9, evidence of Mark Cohen. Chilton, 'Genesis of the welfare state', pp. 125–6. *NZPD*, vol 95, 1896, pp. 642–3. Jenny Carlyon, 'New Zealand friendly societies, 1842–1941', PhD, University of Auckland, 2001, p. 185.

26   Stout, *Politics and Poverty*. *New Zealand Mail*, 7, 14, 21 April 1883.

27   Raymond Richards, *Closing the Door to Destitution: The Shaping of the Social Security Acts of the United States and New Zealand*, Pennsylvania: Pennsylvania University Press, 1994, chapter 2.

28   ArchNZ, LE1, 1894/9. *AJHR*, 1894, I-11; 1895, H-1A, memorandum on friendly society financial reform. Sutch, *Quest for Security*, pp. 88–9. Treble, 'Attitudes of friendly societies', for Britain.

29   Hamer, *New Zealand Liberals*, pp. 146–9. Drummond, *Seddon*, chapter 20. Burdon, *King Dick*, pp. 160–8.

30   *NZPD*, vol 95, 1896, p. 625. Drummond, *Seddon*, p. 331.

31   *NZPD*, vol 95, 1896, pp. 629–32; vol 100, 1897, pp. 328, 658; vol 103, 1898, pp. 541, 548–9; vol 104, 1898, pp. 567, 595–7. Stewart, *Rolleston*, pp. 196–7.

32   ArchNZ, U1, paper, 4 July 1905, and later estimates, papers, 1 July 1913, 22 July 1920.

33   *NZPD*, vol 103, 1898, p. 540. *EP*, 7 October 1904. *New Zealand Times*, 8 September 1906, citing Seddon letter of 15 May.

34   *New Zealand Times*, 24 April 1906. ArchNZ, SS7, Acc W2756, 9/5/8, National Provident Fund, 1899–1961. Nash papers, bundle 1022, evidence to National Health and Superannuation select committee, 1938, vol 4, evidence of R. Sinel, Superintendent NPF, re. memo 2 March 1906. See also, *EP*, 7, 18, 24, 25 April 1906, *New Zealand Times*, 11, 19 April 1906. *NZPD*, vol 176, 1916, pp. 658, 661–4. Burdon, *King Dick*, pp. 315–16. Drummond, *Seddon*, pp. 337–9, 360–1. Hamer, *New Zealand Liberals*, p. 253.

35   *AJHR*, 1889, H-50; 1893, H-17A; 1895, H-1. Hoar, 'Friendly society movement', p. 63ff.

36   Thomson, *World Without Welfare*, pp. 45–51. Carlyon, 'Friendly societies', argues that societies were more significant but makes little attempt to assess contributions, benefits or financial viability. See Gilbert, *Evolution of National Insurance*, chapter 4. Bentley B. Gilbert, 'The decay of nineteenth-century provident institutions and the coming of old age pensions in Great Britain', *Economic History Review*, second series, vol 17, no 3, 1965.

37   *AJHR*, 1911, H-1, pp. 1–3. See Gilbert, *National Insurance*, pp. 220–1, 293ff. Treble, 'Attitudes of friendly societies'.

38   Carlyon, 'New Zealand friendly societies, 1842–1941', pp. 190–4. *New Zealand Times*, 25 April, 28 August 1906. *AJHR*, session II, 1906, B-6, p. ix; 1907, B-6, pp. viii–ix; 1908, B-6, pp. xii–xiii; 1909, B-6, p. xviii; 1913, I-8, pp. 6, 58–9, Seddon's proposal to societies. *NZPD*, vol 153, 1910, pp. 276–7, 286, 510–15. ArchNZ, Nash, bundle 1022, evidence to select committee, vol 2, Z, p. 6.

39   *AJHR*, session II, 1912, H-17, and following NPF annual reports.

40   *AJHR*, 1911, H-1, p. 1.

41   *AJHR*, 1907, H-1, pp. 4–5; 1908, I-15, pp. 26–7; 1912, H-1, p. 4. *NZPD*, vol 148, 1909, p. 885. *New Zealand Times*, 25 April 1906.

42   The dispute related to the difference between the accumulated fund approach of the British friendly societies and the lateral or 'dividing out' approach of American societies. Gilbert, *National Insurance*, pp. 345–6.

43   *AJHR*, 1908, I-15. *NZPD*, vol 148, 1909, p. 882ff. Carlyon, 'New Zealand friendly societies, 1842–1941', pp. 172–7.

44   *AJHR*, 1910, H-1, pp. 1–2. *NZPD*, vol 154, 1911, p. 435; vol 156, 1911, pp. 815–16. ArchNZ, SS7, Acc W2756, 9/5/8. SS, Acc W1844, U1, E.F. Guinness to Parry, Minister of Pensions, 28 February 1936. Carlyon, 'New Zealand friendly societies, 1842–1941', pp. 200–7.

45   *AJHR*, 1975, H-23, pp. 38–9. Hay, *Caring Commodity*, pp. 50–5, 77–83, 122–3. Carlyon, 'New Zealand friendly societies, 1842–1941', pp. 141–52. Wright-St Clair, *History of the New Zealand Medical Association*, chapters 8 and 10.

46   Wright-St Clair, *History of the New Zealand Medical Association*, pp. 19–20.

47   ArchNZ, AACS 622/3b, R. Hayes (Registrar and Superintendent of National Provident Fund) to Ward, 8 February 1911.

48   *NZPD*, vol 158, 1912, p. 7; vol 159, 1912, pp. 671–4. ArchNZ, AACS 622/3b. LE1, 1913/309, 30 July 1913; 1913/310, 10 September 1913.

49   ArchNZ, AACS 622/3b, memo to Minister of Friendly Societies, 6 December 1912.

50   *NZPD*, vol 164, 1913, pp. 298–302, 592. *AJHR*, 1913, I-8.

51   ArchNZ, AACS 622/3b, Hayes to Hall, 7 August 1913. *NZPD*, vol 169, 1914, pp. 413–21, 643–4.

52   *AJHR*, 1915, I-2A. ArchNZ, AACS 622/3b, Heaton Rhodes to Lang, 20 April 1915.

53   ArchNZ, AACS 622/4b, reinsurance for friendly society members in Expeditionary Forces, 1914–21, Hayes, memo to Minister of Defence, 18 November 1919; 622/7b, sick pay after war effort, 1917–21. *AJHR*, 1917, H-1, p. 2; 1920, B-6, p. xix; 1921, B-6, p. xxvi.

54   Wright-St Clair, *History of the New Zealand Medical Association*, p. 84. *AJHR*, 1915, H-1, p. 1; 1916, B-6, p. xx, H-1, p. 1; 1917, H-1, p. 1. *NZPD*, vol 176, 1916, pp. 560–1. ArchNZ, ABWL, 7351, 4l, papers, reports, National Health Insurance Investigation Committee and friendly societies, 1894–1940. J.T. Strang, 'Welfare in transition: Reform's income support policy, 1912–28', MA, Victoria University of Wellington, 1992, p. 161.

55   Douglas E. Ashford, *The Emergence of the Welfare States*, Oxford: Blackwell, 1986, chapter 3. Bentley B. Gilbert, *British Social Policy, 1914–1939*, London: Batsford, 1970.

56   ArchNZ, SS, Acc W1844, U1, universal pensions, 1904–36. Strang, 'Welfare in transition', pp. 174–92. Martin, *Holding the Balance*, p. 168. *NZPD*, vol 203, 1924, pp. 822, 827–8.

57   Martin, *Holding the Balance*, pp. 101–2. J.K. Chilwell, 'Unemployment insurance in New Zealand, 1883–1929', MA, Victoria University of Wellington, 1947, chapter 1. *NZPD*, vol 147, 1909, p. 258; vol 149, 1910, p. 431; vol 153, 1910, p. 41. Barry Gustafson, *Labour's Path to Political Independence*, Auckland: Oxford University Press, 1980, pp. 18–23, 36–46.

58   Chilwell, 'Unemployment insurance in New Zealand', chapter 3.

59   *NZPD*, vol 193, 1921–22, pp. 860–3; vol 196, 1922, p. 931. Bills Thrown Out, 1921.

60   *NZPD*, vol 186, 1920, p. 436. ArchNZ, LE1, 1920/226.

61   ArchNZ, SS, Acc W1844, U1, Fache to Minister, 10 April 1922, 25 May 1922, J.J. Esson to Massey, 18 April 1922.

62   *NZPD*, vol 200, 1923, pp. 1134–5. ArchNZ, SS, Acc W1844, U1, Fache to Minister, 5 February 1924, Fache memo to Minister, 20 March 1924.

63   *NZPD*, vol 203, 1924, pp. 822–8; vol 204, 1924, pp. 405–7; vol 205, 1924, pp. 277, 398–402; vol 206, 1925, p. 668; vol 208, 1925, p. 248; vol 210, 1926, p. 622.

64   *Auckland Star*, 9 October 1925. *EP*, 3, 9 October 1925.

65   It would cost the state between £3 million and £5 million yearly to cover older workers. ArchNZ, SS, Acc W1844, U1, Fache to Minister, 28 July 1925.

66   Nolan, *Breadwinning*, chapter 5. Martin, *Holding the Balance*, p. 159.

67   *NZH*, 19 October 1925.

68   R.M. Campbell, 'Family allowances in New Zealand', *Economic Journal*, September 1927.

69   ArchNZ, T1, 52/479, part 1, 1925–36, Secretary to the Treasury to Anderson, 24 August 1925.

70   ArchNZ, SS, Acc W1844, U1, Fache to Minister, 25 February, 8 April 1926, memo to Government Actuary regarding draft bill, 9 June 1927, Fache to Minister, 16 June 1927, Government Actuary to Fache, 10 October 1927.

71   *NZPD*, vol 217, 1928, p. 3. Michael Bassett, *Coates of Kaipara*, Auckland: Auckland University Press, 1995, p. 107.

72 This section was written before publication of the first comprehensive history of taxation in New Zealand – Paul Goldsmith's *We Won, You Lost, Eat That: A Political History of Tax in New Zealand Since 1840* (Auckland: David Ling, 2008). His general theme is the 'consistent triumph of political calculation over sound economic and tax principles' against a background of the burden of taxation on the economy (p. 346). Here the focus is policy debates related to the social objectives of forms of revenue that led to the welfare state, but the broad outlines of the development of revenue are similar.

73 *NZOYB*, 1893, pp. 419–32. G.T. Bloomfield, *New Zealand: A Handbook of Historical Statistics*, Boston, Mass: G.K. Hall, 1984. Simkin, *Instability*, pp. 48–51. *AJHR*, 1888, B-12, 'balance-sheets of the colony, 1832–88'.

74 Atkinson suggested that the impact of customs duties on labourers and artisans was not unduly high (at 4–5 percent of income). *AJHR*, 1882, B-2, pp. ix–xi, table 9.

75 *NZPD*, 1858, p. 67. *VP*, 1858, p. 77, petition.

76 *AJHR*, 1866, B-8, p. 5. *NZPD*, vol 1, part 1, 1867, pp. 263, 470.

77 For tariffs, see *Taxation in New Zealand*, Wellington: Government Printer, 1967, 'Notes on the history of taxation in New Zealand'. Simkin, *Instability*, pp. 50–1.

78 *NZPD*, vol 17, 1875, pp. 154, 307–14; vol 19, 1875, pp. 269–85; vol 24, 1877, p. 227ff., 499ff., in particular Woolcock, Montgomery, Atkinson.

79 *NZPD*, vol 24, 1877, pp. 144–5, 505; vol 34, 1879, p. 984. *AJHR*, 1878, B-2, pp. 15–16.

80 *NZPD*, vol 28, 1878, pp. 2–3.

81 Wakefield, *Taxes in New Zealand*.

82 *AJHR*, 1878, B-2. See also *NZPD*, vol 28, 1878, pp. 604–5; vol 30, 1878, pp. 856, 863, 865; vol 31, 1879, pp. 319–21. McIvor, *Ballance*, pp. 72–8, 103.

83 *AJHR*, 1878, B-2, p. 19.

84 *AJHR*, 1878, B-2, pp. 15–16.

85 T.G. Wilson, *The Grey Government, 1877–9*, Auckland: University of Auckland, 1954, pp. 26–7. Edwin R.A. Seligman, *Essays in Taxation* (tenth edition revised), London: Macmillan, 1925, pp. 459, 464–6, 539.

86 *AJHR*, 1879, B-2A.

87 Bassett, *Atkinson*, pp. 62–3, 108–13.

88 *AJHR*, 1882, B-2, pp. ix–xi, table 9.

89 Sinclair, 'Scarecrow ministry', pp. 108–9.

90 Seligman, *Essays in Taxation*, p. 460.

91 Marion M. McEwing, 'The protection of manufacturing industries in New Zealand', MA, University of Otago, 1985, pp. 10–35. Martin, 'English models', pp. 55, 60–1. Condliffe, *New Zealand in the Making*, pp. 178–9. Sinclair, 'Scarecrow Ministry', p. 113. J. Kennedy Brown, *A Protective Policy in its Relations to Colonial Industries and Manufacturers*, Wellington: Lyon and Blair, 1880.

92 David Plowman, 'Forced march: the employers and arbitration', in Stuart Macintyre and Richard Mitchell (eds), *Foundations of Arbitration: The Origins and Effects of State Compulsory Arbitration, 1890–1914*, Melbourne: Oxford University Press, 1989, p. 146, citing V.S. Clark, 'Labor conditions in Australia', *Bulletin of the Bureau of Labor*, vol 10, Washington, Government Printer, 1905, p. 285.

93 *AJHR*, 1880, H-22, p. 4.

94 *NZPD*, vol 35, 1880, pp. 418, 618.

95 *LT*, 28 October 1885.

96 See Raewyn Dalziel, *Julius Vogel: Business Politician*, Auckland: Auckland University Press, 1986, pp. 261, 296–7. *AJHR*, 1885, B-1, pp. v–ix.

97 *NZPD*, vol 57, 1887, pp. 406, 422, 446, 455.

98 New Zealand Protection Association, *Proposed Changes in the Tariff*, Christchurch: Lyttelton Times, 1887. Drummond, *Seddon*, p. 94.

99   K. Sinclair, 'Scarecrow Ministry', pp. 110–11.

100   Marie E.S. Prentice, 'Some liberal measures of the continuous ministry, 1879–90', MA, University of Auckland, 1942, pp. 46–54. Sinclair, 'Scarecrow Ministry'.

101   *AJHR*, 1888, B-6. Drummond, *Seddon*, pp. 93–9.

102   *NZPD*, vol 60, 1888, p. 494, 497, Stuart-Menteath, Taylor. Seddon strongly favoured the free breakfast table. He made sure that the tariffs on tea and sugar were removed when he was Premier. Drummond, *Seddon*, p. 99.

103   *NZPD*, vol 60, 1888, p. 512. See also Reeves, *Long White Cloud*, pp. 258–9.

104   Reeves, 'Protective tariffs'.

105   Sinclair, *Destiny Apart*, p. 72. *AJHR*, 1866, D-7B. Income tax, applied to an estimated 5,000 taxpayers using the British exemptions and rates (7d per pound on incomes of £100–150 and 10d on £150 or more), could have raised almost £200,000 per annum.

106   *AJHR*, 1866, D-7B, p. 7.

107   Oliver, 'Problems and prospects of conservatism', p. 24. Carolyn Webber and Aaron Wildavsky, *A History of Taxation and Expenditure in the Western World*, New York: Simon and Schuster, 1986, chapters 6, 8. Seligman, *Essays in Taxation*, pp. 459–66, 539. For changes in taxation in New Zealand generally, see *Taxation in New Zealand*, appendix 1.

108   *NZOYB*, 1894, p. 244. *AJHR*, 1893, B-15, pp. 2–3.

109   *NZPD*, vol 152, 1910, p. 664. *AJHR*, 1911, B-22; 1915, B-22.

110   John E. Martin, 'War economy', in Ian McGibbon (ed), *The Oxford Companion to New Zealand Military History*, Auckland: Oxford University Press, 2000. *NZOYB*, 1919, pp. 744–8, 'taxation'. ArchNZ, Nash, bundle 1099, ff. 0015–0123, F.B. Stephens and B.R. Turner, 'Taxation and the economic depression in New Zealand, 1928–9 to 1935–6', tax revision papers, 1936–7.

111   *NZPD*, vol 176, 1916, p. 549; also vol 174, 1915, p. 799; vol 176, 1916, p. 555. *AJHR*, 1915, B-6, p. xxvi; 1916, B-6, p. xxiii; 1922, B-5, pp. 2, 10.

112   *NZOYB*, 1919, p. 744; 1921–2, pp. 418–19, income tax. Lloyd Prichard, *Economic History*, p. 256, table.

113   *AJHR*, 1917, B-6, p. xxviii; 1920, B-6, pp. xxxii, xli; 1921, B-6, p. xli. *NZPD*, vol 188, 1920, p. 234. Bloomfield, *New Zealand; a Handbook of Historical Statistics*, table VIII.7. Steinmo, *Taxation and Democracy*, chapter 4.

114   Lloyd Prichard, *Economic History*, pp. 304–5. Calculated from Bloomfield, table VIII and GNP figures in Rankin, 'Gross National Product estimates'.

115   *AJHR*, 1926, B-6.

116   *AJHR*, 1922, B-5. Colin Clark, 'Public finance and changes in the value of money', *The Economic Journal*, vol 55, 1945, for limit to taxation of 25 percent of national income.

117   *AJHR*, 1924, B-5, appendices B and C.

118   *AJHR*, 1924, B-5; 1927, B-6. *NZPD*, vol 213, 1927, pp. 928–9, 996–7. *Dominion*, 15 July 1926.

119   Martin, *Holding the Balance*, chapter 4.

120   *AJHR*, 1929, H-11B; 1930, H-11B.

121   *NZPD*, vol 217, 1928, p. 547. Bassett, *Coates of Kaipara*, pp. 107, 137–8. *Dominion*, 27 October 1928.

122   *NZPD*, vol 222, 1929, p. 1112.

123   *NZPD*, vol 224, 1930, p. 410, Veitch (ex Minister of Labour).

124   R.T. Robertson, 'Government responses to unemployment in New Zealand, 1929–35', *NZJH*, vol 16, no 1, 1982, suggests contrarily that the government avoided its responsibility.

125   *AJHR*, 1930, H-11B, p. 7.

126   Gilbert, *British Social Policy*, p. 54ff. A.I. Ogus, 'Great Britain', in Peter A. Köhler and Hans F. Zacher (eds), *The Evolution of Social Insurance*, London: Frances Pinter, 1982.

127   ArchNZ, L1, burnt files, box 79, file 9/1/-, part 3, 1935–6, Commissioner of

Unemployment, memo to Acting Minister of Employment, 1 April 1935. *AJHR*, 1930, H-11B.

128 *NZPD*, vol 224, 1930, pp. 404–13, 420. ArchNZ, LE1, 1930/17, Unemployment Bill committee, 1930, minutes of meetings, draft of bill, submissions.

129 Hawke, *Making of New Zealand*, pp. 149–50. Keith Sinclair, *Walter Nash*, Auckland: Auckland University Press, 1976, p. 92.

130 *AJHR*, 1933, B-6. ArchNZ, Nash, bundle 1099, ff. 0015–0123, Stephens and Turner, 'Taxation and the economic depression'. L1, burnt files, box 78, file 9/1/-, part 1, 1931–4, paper, Commissioner to Minister of Unemployment, 10 March 1932. Clark, 'Public finance'.

131 ArchNZ, T1, 52/479, correspondence regarding NPF and social insurance, 15 March 1932 to 4 October 1935. NZPD, vol 226, 1930, p. 811.

132 ArchNZ, T1, 52/479, Coates to Farmers' Union, 21 January 1935. *AJHR*, 1935, B-6, p. 6, H-30. *NZPD*, vol 241, 1935, pp. 252–5; vol 242, 1935, pp. 4, 135; vol 252, 1938, p. 536. For national health insurance, see Wright-St Clair, *History of the New Zealand Medical Association*, pp. 129–30, and D.G. Bolitho, 'Some financial and medico-political aspects of the New Zealand medical profession's reaction to the introduction of social security', *NZJH*, vol 18, no 1, 1984, pp. 38–9.

133 Bruce Farland, *Coates' Tale*, Wellington: Farland, 1995, p. 132.

134 Elizabeth Hanson, *The Politics of Social Security*, Auckland: Auckland University Press, 1980, pp. 43–5. ArchNZ, Nash, bundle 1076, budget 1936/7, proposals to increase pensions, Ashwin to Nash, 28 February, 19 March, 26 August 1936.

135 ArchNZ, Nash, bundle 1099, ff. 0015–0123, Stephens and Turner, 'Taxation and the economic depression', tax revision papers, 1936–7, especially draft report, and J.S. Reid, memo to Nash, 5 November 1936.

136 ArchNZ, Nash, bundle 1007/0089, notes meeting Nash's office, 23 September 1936.

137 ArchNZ, T1, 52/479, Ashwin to Director-General of Health, 18 August 1936. ABWL, 7351, 4k, papers, reports, national health insurance investigation committee, 1936–7. Barry Gustafson, *From the Cradle to the Grave: A Biography of Michael Joseph Savage*, Auckland: Penguin, 1988, pp. 118–19, 221. See Brian Easton, 'Bernard Ashwin: secretary to the nation building state', *New Zealand Studies*, vol 7, no 3, 1997, for information on Ashwin as a public servant.

138 ArchNZ, Nash, bundle 1007/0099, (First) report of departmental committee, 1 October 1936.

139 ArchNZ, Nash, bundle 1007/0333, notes of a combined meeting, 6 October 1936. ABWL, 7351, 4k, papers, reports, national health insurance investigation committee, 1936–7, address on English scheme, 27–28 October 1936. Carlyon, 'New Zealand friendly societies, 1842–1941', chapter 8.

140 ArchNZ, Nash, bundle 1007/0334, (Second) report of department committee, [3 February 1937]; bundle 1007/0108, (Third) report of department committee, 18 March 1937; bundle 1003, Reid to Nash 9 February, 15 March 1937. Hanson, *Politics of Social Security*, pp. 53–5.

141 ArchNZ, Nash, bundle 1003, minutes of meeting, 25 March 1937, Reid to Nash, 25 March 1937; bundle 1007/0109, (Fourth) report of department committee, 26 August 1937. T25, 19, national superannuation contributory proposals, 1937–8, 'suggested government subsidy to superannuation scheme' by Maddex, 28 October 1937, copy to Nash.

142 ArchNZ, ABWL, 7351, 5d, memoranda, notes and reports by Maddex, 1937; 5f, national superannuation, health and unemployment insurance, vol 1, 1936–7, no 4, preliminary report of departmental committee, c. late September 1937.

143 ArchNZ, T25, 19, national superannuation contributory proposals, 1937–8, 'finance of comprehensive national scheme', 18 February 1938. ABWL, 7351, 5d, Maddex paper to

Nash on NPF, 18 February 1938, memo, Ashwin, Reid, Maddex, health, superannuation, unemployment and sickness, 25 February 1938.

144 ArchNZ, T1, 52/479, Secretary of Treasury to Nash, 28 March 1938. Nash, bundle 1007 for vol 6, bundle 1022 for vols 1–5, evidence to select committee.

145 ArchNZ, Nash, bundle 1022, evidence to select committee, vol 1, P, p. 1. NZPD, vol 252, 1938, p. 421. Gustafson, *From the Cradle to the Grave*, p. 222.

146 *AJHR*, 1938, I-6, p. 16.

147 ArchNZ, Nash, bundle 1003, superannuation and health insurance – report on government's proposals, [August 1938]; minutes of meetings of select committee, 3, 28 May 1937; bundle 1017, S15/3, Ashwin memos to Nash, 27 May, 4 August 1938. SS7, Acc W2756, 10/1/1, part 1, 1939–50, Ashwin to Nash, 30 October 1939, 24 January 1940. NZPD, vol 252, 1938, pp. 537–8.

148 ArchNZ, Nash, bundle 1022, evidence to select committee, vol 2, 2A, p. 6; bundle 1007/ F18, 'friendly societies and national insurance', n.d. ABWL, 7351, 4k, draft report on friendly societies, n.d., covering note, 9 July 1937; papers, reports, national health insurance investigation committee, 1936–7, questionnaire, and Dominion Council of Friendly Societies response, February 1937.

149 ArchNZ, Nash, bundle 1007/F18, notes deputations to Nash, 22, 24 August, Nash to Friendly Societies Council, 25 August 1938. SS7, W2756, 9/5/4, friendly society benefits, 1901–60. T1, 52/479, 1952–7, Secretary to Treasury to Minister, 1 September 1955.

150 ArchNZ, ABWL, 7351, 5g, social security, (National Superannuation, Health and Unemployment Insurance, vol 2), 1938, Beckingsale, memos throughout May, June and August 1938, largely to Reid, and especially to Secretary for Treasury, 10, 11 August regarding superannuation.

151 J.V.T. Baker, *War Economy*, Wellington: Department of Internal Affairs, 1965, pp. 111–12, 544.

152 *AJHR*, 1936, B-6, p. 15.

153 John E. Martin, 'Income, inequality and the welfare state in New Zealand', Proceedings of Inequality and Ideology conference, Massey University, 1982.

154 Martin, 'War economy'.

155 *AJHR*, 1940–6, B-6; 1967, B-18.

156 Oliver, *Story of New Zealand*, pp. 196–7.

157 *NZPD*, vol 252, 1938, p. 566.

158 Michael Jones, *Reforming New Zealand Welfare: International Perspectives*, Centre for Independent Studies: St Leonards, 1997, chapter 3. David Thomson, *Selfish Generations? The Ageing of New Zealand's Welfare State*, Wellington: Bridget Williams Books, 1991. Castles, *Working Class and Welfare*, pp. 93–5.

159 See for example, Amitai Etzioni, *The Spirit of Community: Rights, Responsibilities and the Communitarian Agenda*, New York: Crown, 1993. Anthony Giddens, *The Third Way: The Renewal of Social Democracy*, Cambridge: Polity, 1998. OECD, *Societal Cohesion and the Globalising Economy – What Does the Future Hold?*, OECD: Paris, 1997. Lester Thurow, *The Future of Capitalism – How Today's Economic Forces Will Shape Tomorrow's World*, St Leonards, NSW: Allen and Unwin, 1996. Francis Fukuyama, *Trust: The Social Virtues and the Creation of Prosperity*, London: Penguin, 1995.

BIBLIOGRAPHY

Abbreviations

AJHR	*Appendices to the Journal of the House of Representatives*
ArchNZ	Archives New Zealand
ATL	Alexander Turnbull Library
CM	Canterbury Museum
DNZB	*Dictionary of New Zealand Biography*
EP	*Evening Post*
GBPP	*Great Britain, Parliamentary Papers*
JHR	*Journal of the House of Representatives*
JLC	*Journal of the Legislative Council*
LT	*Lyttelton Times*
NE	*Nelson Examiner*
NZH	*New Zealand Herald*
NZJH	*New Zealand Journal of History*
NZOYB	*New Zealand Official Yearbook*
NZPD	*New Zealand Parliamentary Debates*
NZS	*New Zealand Spectator*
OW	*Otago Witness*
WI	*Wellington Independent*
WS	*Wellington Spectator*

A. Primary sources

1. Archives

Alexander Turnbull Library
Archives New Zealand
Canterbury Museum

2. Newspapers

Canterbury Times
Dominion
Evening Post
Lyttelton Times
Nelson Examiner
New Zealand Herald
New Zealand Mail
New Zealand Spectator
New Zealand Times
New Zealand Worker

New Zealander
North Otago Times
Otago Daily Times
Otago Witness
Press (Christchurch)
Southern Cross
The Times (London)
Timaru Herald
Wellington Independent
Wellington Spectator

3. Other

Victoria University of Wellington Library, Stout pamphlets
Provincial *Almanac[k]s*

B. Official Publications

Appendices to the Journal of the House of Representatives
Bills Thrown Out (Parliamentary Library)
Books of Awards
Census of Population and Dwellings
Great Britain, Parliamentary Papers
Journals of the House of Representatives
Journals of the Legislative Council
New Munster and New Ulster *Gazettes*
New Zealand Gazette
New Zealand Official Yearbook
New Zealand Parliamentary Debates
Provincial Council *Gazettes*
Provincial Council *Ordinances*
Provincial Council *Proceedings*
Statistics of New Zealand
Votes and Proceedings, 1854–56

C. Contemporary literature

Alexander, W.R. and Currie, A.E., *New Zealand Verse*, London: Walter Scott Publishing, 1906

Atkinson, H.A., *Speeches Delivered by the Colonial Treasurer*, Christchurch: Press Office, 1883

Bathgate, John, *New Zealand: Its Resources and Prospects*, London: W. and R. Chambers, 1884

Blair, John, *Lays of the Old Identities*, Dunedin: R.T. Wheeler, 1889

Bracken, Thomas, *Musings in Maoriland*, Dunedin: Arthur T. Keirle, 1890

Brown, J. Kennedy, *A Protective Policy in its Relations to Colonial Industries and Manufactures*, Wellington: Lyon and Blair, 1880

Carter, Charles Rooking, *Life and Recollections of a New Zealand Colonist*, 3 vols, London, 1866, 1875

Chapman, H.S., *The New Zealand Portfolio*, London: Smith, Elder and Co., 1843

Cholmondley, Thomas, *Ultima Thule, or Thoughts Suggested by a Residence in New Zealand*, London: Woodfall and Kinder, 1854

Clark, Victor S., 'Labor conditions in Australia', *Bulletin of the Bureau of Labor*, vol 10, Washington, Government Printer, 1905

Clark, Victor S., *Report on Labour Conditions in New Zealand*, reprinted in Department of Labour *Journal*, February–July 1904

Clark, Victor S., *The Labour Movement in Australasia: A Study in Social Democracy*, London: Constable, 1907

Clayden, Arthur, *A Popular Handbook to New Zealand – Its Resources and Industries*, London: Wyman and Sons, 1885

Clayden, Arthur, *The England of the Pacific, or New Zealand as a English Middle-Class Emigration-Field*, London: Wyman and Sons, 1879

Co-operation, Dunedin: Mills, Dick and Co., c. 1871

Cyclopedia, vol 1, Wellington, Wellington: Cyclopedia Co., 1897

Davis, J.A., *Plain Talks on Being Out of Work*, Dunedin: J. Horsburgh, 1880

Doré, Gustave, *London, a Pilgrimage*, London: Grant and Co., 1872

Eyton, R.H., 'Our representative system', *New Zealand Magazine*, no 2, April 1876

Findlay, J.G., *Labour and the Arbitration Act*, Wellington: New Zealand Times, 1908

Findlay, J.G., 'Industrial peace in New Zealand', *International Labour Review*, vol 4, 1921

Fox, William, *The Six Colonies of New Zealand*, London: John W. Parker and Son, 1851

Fuller, F., *Five Years' Residence in New Zealand*, London: Williams and Norgate, 1859

Gisborne, William, *New Zealand Rulers and Statesmen – From 1840 to 1897*, London: Sampson, Low Marston and Co., 1897

Grant, J.G.S., *The Early Closing System*, Dunedin, 1880

Gregg, T.H., *New Zealand, its Climate, Work, Wages and Cost of Living*, London: Marlborough and Co., 1875

Historical Sketch of the Auckland Savings Bank, Auckland: Herald Office, 1884

Holland, H.E., *Red Roses on the Highways*, Sydney: Holland and Stephenson, 1924

Jerrold, Walter (ed), *The Complete Poetical Works of Thomas Hood*, London: Henry Frowde, 1908

Labour, Department of, 'Inquiry into the cost of living in New Zealand', *Journal*, April 1912

Labour, Department of, *Pronouncements of the Court re Cost of Living and General Order Amending Awards, May 1922*, Wellington: Government Print, 1922

Leslie, George, *New Zealand Mortality Rates, 1881–1891*, Dunedin: Otago Daily Times, 1895

Leslie, Walter, *Parliamentary Portraits*, 2 vols, 1887

Letters from Emigrants Published by the New Zealand Company for the Information of the Labouring Classes, London: G. McKewan, 1841

McIndoe, James, *A Sketch of Otago from the Initiation of the Settlement to the Abolition of the Province*, Dunedin: R.T. Wheeler, 1878

Mann, T., 'Conditions of labour in New Zealand', *Nineteenth Century*, vol 52, September 1902

Murphy, W.E., *History of the Eight Hours' Movement*, Melbourne: Spectator Publishing Co., 1896

New Zealand Protection Association, *Proposed Changes in the Tariff*, Christchurch: Lyttelton Times, 1887

Newman, Alfred K., 'Is New Zealand a healthy country? An enquiry (with statistics by F.W. Frankland)', *Transactions and Proceedings of the New Zealand Institute*, vol 15, 1882

Oliver, George, *Homes for the People in the Provincial District of Otago*, Oamaru: North Otago Times, 1879

Pash, J. Brittain, *Report on New Zealand*, Colchester: Essex Standard, 1883

Pilgrim (C.L. Innes), *Canterbury Sketches, or Life From the Early Days*, Christchurch: Lyttelton Times, 1879

Political and Other Ballads, Auckland Free Lance, Auckland, 1879

Purnell, Charles W., *An Agrarian Law for New Zealand*, Wellington: Robert Burrett, 1874

Purnell, Charles W., *Our Land Laws – What Should Be Their Basis?* Dunedin: Evening Star, 1876

Rees, W.L., *The Life and Times of Sir George Grey, KCB* (2 vols), London: Hutchinson, 1892

Reeves, William Pember, *The Long White Cloud* (4th edition), London: Allen and Unwin, 1950

Reeves, William Pember, 'Protective tariffs in Australia and New Zealand', *The Economic Journal*, vol 9, 1899

Reeves, William Pember ['Pharos'], *Some Historical Articles on Communism and Socialism*, Christchurch: Lyttelton Times, 1890

Reeves, William Pember, *The State and its Functions in New Zealand*, Fabian Tract, no 74, 1896

Robinson, J., *The Basic Wage in New Zealand*, Wellington: New Zealand Worker, 1926

Rowley, F.W., *The Industrial Situation in New Zealand*, Wellington: Harry H. Tombs, 1931

Samuel Duncan Parnell, Founder of Eight Hours System, Wellington: Evening Post, 1891

Sealy, H.J., *Are We To Stay Here? A Paper on the New Zealand Public Works Policy of 1870*, Lyttelton: Lyttelton Times, 1881

Siegfried, André, *Democracy in New Zealand* (2nd edition), Wellington: Victoria University Press, 1982

Simmons, Alfred, *Old England and New Zealand*, London: Edward Stanford, 1879

Stout, Robert, 'New Zealand', *The Contemporary Review*, October 1899

Stout, Robert, *Notes on the Progress of New Zealand for Twenty Years, 1864–1884*, Wellington: Government Printer, 1886

Stout, Robert, *Politics and Poverty*, Dunedin: Otago Daily Times, 1883

Stout, Robert, *The Social Future of Labourers*, Napier: Hawke's Bay Observer, 1918

Stout, Robert, 'State Experiments in New Zealand', *Journal of the Royal Statistical Society*, September 1892

Thomson, A.S., *The Story of New Zealand* (2 vols), London: John Murray, 1859

Tomlinson, Henry, *A Farm Labourer's Report of New Zealand*, Laceby, Grimsby: Burton and White, 1876

Vogel, Julius (ed), *New Zealand: Land and Farming in New Zealand*, London: Waterlow and Sons, 1879

Vogel, Julius (ed), *The Official Handbook of New Zealand*, London: Wyman and Sons, 1875

Vogel, Julius, 'Social politics in New Zealand', *The Fortnightly Review*, new series, vol 53, 1893

Wakefield, E.G. and Ward, J., *The British Colonization of New Zealand*, London: John W. Parker, 1837

Wakelin, Richard, *Small Farms and Small Farm Settlements*, Greytown: Standard Office, 1879

Woodward, John, *Jubilee Farms*, Christchurch: Union Office, 1888

D. Secondary literature

1. Books

Alexander, Fred, *Moving Frontiers: An American Theme and its Application to Australian History*, Melbourne: Melbourne University Press, 1947

Allan, Ruth M., *Nelson – A History of Early Settlement*, Wellington: Reed, 1965

Allen, H.C., *Bush and Backwoods: A Comparison of the Frontier in Australia and the United States*, East Lansing: Michigan State University Press, 1959

Andersen, Johannes C., *Jubilee History of South Canterbury*, Christchurch: Whitcombe and Tombs, 1916

Andersen, Johannes C., *Old Christchurch*, Christchurch: Capper Press reprint, 1975

Arnold, Rollo, *The Farthest Promised Land: English Villagers, New Zealand Immigrants of the 1870s*, Wellington: Victoria University Press, 1981

Ashford, Douglas E., *The Emergence of the Welfare States*, Oxford: Blackwell, 1986

Bagnall, A.G., *Wairarapa: An Historical Excursion*, Masterton: Hedley's Bookshop, 1976

Baker, J.V.T., *War Economy*, Wellington: Department of Internal Affairs, 1965

Bassett, J., *Sir Harry Atkinson, 1831–1892*, Auckland: Auckland University Press, 1975

Bassett, Michael, *Coates of Kaipara*, Auckland: Auckland University Press, 1995

Bassett, Michael, *The State in New Zealand, 1840–1984*, Auckland: Auckland University Press, 1998

Belchem, John, *Popular Radicalism in Nineteenth-Century Britain*, London: Macmillan, 1996

Belich, James, *Making Peoples – From Polynesian Settlement to the End of the Nineteenth Century*, Auckland: Penguin, 1996

Biagini, Eugenio F., *Liberty, Retrenchment and Reform*, Cambridge: Cambridge University Press, 1992

Biagini, Eugenio F. and Reid, Alastair J. (eds), *Currents of Radicalism: Popular Radicalism, Organised Labour and Party Politics in Britain, 1850–1914*, Cambridge: Cambridge University Press, 1991

Blainey, Geoffrey, *The Tyranny of Distance: How Distance Shaped Australia's History*, Melbourne: Sun Books, 1966

Bloomfield, G.T., *New Zealand: A Handbook of Historical Statistics*, Boston, Mass: G.K. Hall, 1984

Bohan, Edmund, *Edward Stafford: New Zealand's First Statesman*, Christchurch: Hazard Press, 1994

Bohan, Edmund, *To Be A Hero – A Biography of Sir George Grey*, Auckland: HarperCollins, 1998

Bollinger, Conrad, *Against the Wind: The Story of the New Zealand Seamen's Union*, Wellington: New Zealand Seamen's Union, 1968

Boston, Ray, *British Chartists in America, 1839–1900*, Manchester: Manchester University Press, 1971

Brady, Alexander, *Democracy in the Dominions: A Comparative Study in Institutions*, Toronto: University of Toronto Press, 1947

Broadhead, Henry, *State Regulation of Labour and Labour Disputes in New Zealand*, Christchurch: Whitcombe and Tombs, 1908

Bronstein, Jamie L., *Land Reform and Working-class Experience in Britain and the United States, 1800–1862*, Stanford: Stanford University Press, 1999

Brooking, Tom, *And Captain of their Souls: Cargill and the Otago Colonists*, Dunedin: Otago Heritage Books, 1984

Brooking, Tom, *Lands for the People? The Highland Clearances and the Colonisation of New Zealand – A Biography of John McKenzie*, Dunedin: Otago University Press, 1996

Brown, Bruce, *The Rise of New Zealand Labour*, Wellington: Price Milburn, 1962

Brown, E.H. Phelps with Browne, Margaret H., *A Century of Pay: The Course of Pay and Production in France, Germany, Sweden, the United Kingdom, and the USA, 1860–1960*, London: Macmillan, 1968

Burdon, R.M., *King Dick: A Biography of Richard John Seddon*, Christchurch: Whitcombe and Tombs, 1955

Burnett, John, *A History of the Cost of Living*, Harmondsworth: Penguin, 1969

Butlin, N.G., *Investment in Australian Economic Development, 1861–1900*, Cambridge: Cambridge University Press, 1964

Calhoun, Craig, *The Question of Class Struggle: Social Foundations of Popular Radicalism During the Industrial Revolution*, Chicago: University of Chicago Press, 1982

Campbell, Ian, *Compensation for Personal Injury in New Zealand: Its Rise and Fall*, Auckland: Auckland University Press, 1996

Castles, Francis G., *Australian Public Policy and Economic Vulnerability*, Sydney: Allen and Unwin, 1988

Castles, Francis G., *The Working Class and Welfare*, Wellington: Allen and Unwin, 1985

Chase, Malcolm, *The People's Farm: English Radical Agrarianism, 1775–1840*, Oxford: Clarendon, 1988

Condliffe, J.B., *New Zealand in the Making* (second revised edition), London: Allen and Unwin, 1959

Cronin, James E., *The Politics of State Expansion – War, State and Society in Twentieth Century Britain*, London: Routledge, 1991

Dalziel, Raewyn, *Julius Vogel: Business Politician*, Auckland: Auckland University Press, 1986

Daunton, Martin, *Charity, Self-interest and Welfare in the English Past*, London: University College London Press, 1996

Dictionary of New Zealand Biography, 1769–1960, 5 vols, Wellington/Auckland: Allen and Unwin/Bridget Williams Books/Auckland University Press, 1990–2000

Drummond, James, *The Life and Work of Richard John Seddon*, Christchurch: Whitcombe and Tombs, 1906

Etzioni, Amitai, *The Spirit of Community: Rights, Responsibilities and the Communitarian Agenda*, New York: Crown, 1993

Evans, L., Poot, J., and Quigley, N. (eds), *Long-run Perspectives on the New Zealand Economy*, Wellington: New Zealand Association of Economists, 1991

Fairburn, Miles, *The Ideal Society and its Enemies: The Foundation of Modern New Zealand Society, 1850–1900*, Auckland: Auckland University Press, 1989

Fairburn, Miles, *Nearly Out of Heart and Hope: The Puzzle of a Colonial Labourer's Diary*, Auckland: Auckland University Press, 1995

Farland, Bruce, *Coates' Tale*, Wellington: Farland, 1995

Finn, Margot C., *After Chartism: Class and Nation in English Radical Politics, 1848–1874*, Cambridge: Cambridge University Press, 1993

Frame, Alex, *Salmond: Southern Jurist*, Wellington: Victoria University Press, 1995

Franks, P., *Print and Politics*, Wellington: Victoria University Press, 2001

Fraser, Derek, *The Evolution of the British Welfare State* (second edition), London: Macmillan, 1984

Fukuyama, Francis, *Trust: The Social Virtues and the Creation of Prosperity*, London: Penguin, 1995

Gardner, W.J., *A Pastoral Kingdom Divided: Cheviot, 1889–94*, Wellington: Bridget Williams Books, 1992

Garner, Jean, *By His Own Merits: Sir John Hall – Pioneer, Pastoralist and Premier*, Hororata: Dryden Press, 1995

Garnett, R., *Edward Gibbon Wakefield: The Colonisation of South Australia and New Zealand*, London: T. Fisher Unwin, 1898

Giddens, Anthony, *The Third Way: The Renewal of Social Democracy*, Cambridge: Polity, 1998

Gilbert, Bentley B., *British Social Policy, 1914–1939*, London: Batsford, 1970

Gilbert, Bentley B., *The Evolution of National Insurance in Great Britain*, London: Joseph, 1966

Glickman, Lawrence B., *A Living Wage: American Workers and the Making of Consumer Society*, Ithaca: Cornell University Press, 1997

Goldsmith, Paul, *We Won, You Lost, Eat That: A Political History of Tax in New Zealand Since 1840*, Auckland: David Ling, 2008

Goldsmith, Raymond W., *Financial Structure and Development*, New Haven and London: Yale University Press, 1969

Gosden, P.H.J.H., *The Friendly Societies in England, 1815–1875*, Manchester: Manchester University Press, 1961

Gosden, P.H.J.H., *Self-Help: Voluntary Associations in Nineteenth Century Britain*, London: Batsford, 1973

Gourlay, H.W., *Odd Fellowship in New Zealand, 1842–1942: A Century of Progress*, Christchurch: Andrews, Baty and Co., 1942

Grimshaw, Patricia, *Women's Suffrage in New Zealand*, Auckland: Auckland University Press, 1972

Gustafson, Barry, *From the Cradle to the Grave: A Biography of Michael Joseph Savage*, Auckland: Penguin, 1988

Gustafson, Barry, *Labour's Path to Political Independence*, Auckland: Oxford University Press, 1980

Hamer, David, *The New Zealand Liberals*, Auckland: Auckland University Press, 1988

Hanson, Elizabeth, *The Politics of Social Security*, Auckland: Auckland University Press, 1980

Hardie, B.G., et al., *Statistics of New Zealand for the Crown Colony Period, 1840–1852*, Auckland University, 1954

Harris, J., *Unemployment and Politics: A Study in English Social Policy, 1886–1914*, Oxford: Clarendon, 1972

Hartz, Louis, *The Founding of New Societies: Studies in the History of the United States, Latin America, South Africa, Canada and Australia*, New York: Harcourt Brace and World, 1964

Hawke, G.R., *The Making of New Zealand: An Economic History*, Cambridge: Cambridge University Press, 1985

Hay, Iain, *The Caring Commodity: The Provision of Health Care in New Zealand*, Auckland: Oxford University Press, 1989

Henderson, Alan, *Fortuitous Legacy: The Masterton Trust Lands Trust, 1872–1997*, Masterton: Masterton Trust Lands Trust, 1997

Hibbard, B.H., *A History of the Public Land Policies*, Madison, Wisconsin: University of Milwaukee Press, 1965

Hill, Richard S., *The Colonial Frontier Tamed: New Zealand Policing in Transition, 1867–1886*, Wellington: Department of Internal Affairs, 1989

Holt, James, *Compulsory Arbitration in New Zealand – The First Forty Years*, Auckland: Auckland University Press, 1986

Horne, H. Oliver, *A History of Savings Banks*, London: Oxford University Press, 1947

Jackson, W.K., *The New Zealand Legislative Council*, Dunedin: University of Otago Press, 1972

Jones, Michael, *Reforming New Zealand Welfare: International Perspectives*, Centre for Independent Studies: St Leonards, 1997

Jourdain, W.R., *Land Legislation and Settlement in New Zealand*, Wellington: Government Printer, 1925

King, Michael, *The Penguin History of New Zealand*, Auckland: Penguin, 2003

Lipson, Leslie, *The Politics of Equality: New Zealand's Adventures in Democracy*, Chicago: University of Chicago Press, 1948

Lloyd Prichard, Muriel F., *An Economic History of New Zealand to 1939*, Auckland: Collins, 1970

McAloon, Jim, *Nelson – A Regional History*, Nelson: Cape Catley, 1997

Macdonald, D.E., *The State and the Trade Unions* (second edition), London: Macmillan, 1976

Macintyre, Stuart, *A Colonial Liberalism: The Lost World of Three Victorian Visionaries*, Melbourne: Oxford University Press, 1991

McIntyre, W. David (ed), *The Journal of Henry Sewell*, Christchurch: Whitcoulls, 1980

McIvor, Timothy, *The Rainmaker: A Biography of John Ballance*, Auckland: Heinemann Reed, 1989

Mackay, Duncan, *Frontier New Zealand: The Search for Eldorado, 1800–1920*, Auckland: HarperCollins, 1992

McLean, Gavin, *The Southern Octopus: The Rise of a Shipping Empire*, Wellington: New Zealand Ship and Marine Society, 1990

McLintock, A.H., *Crown Colony Government in New Zealand*, Wellington: Government Printer, 1958

McLintock, A.H., *The History of Otago: The Origins and Growth of a Wakefield Class Settlement*, Dunedin: Otago Centennial Historical Publications, 1949

McLintock, A.H. and Wood, G.A., *The Upper House in Colonial New Zealand*, Wellington: Government Printer, 1987

Manchester Unity IOOF, *New Zealand Centenary, Manchester Unity IOOF, 1842–1942*, Wellington: Manchester Unity IOOF, 1942

Marais, J.S., *The Colonisation of New Zealand*, Oxford: Clarendon Press, 1927

Martin, E.R., *Marine Department Centennial History, 1866–1966*, Wellington: Government Printer, 1969

Martin, John E., *Holding the Balance: A History of New Zealand's Department of Labour, 1891–1995*, Christchurch: Canterbury University Press, 1996

Martin, John E., *Tatau Tatau – One Big Union Altogether*, Wellington: New Zealand Workers' Union, 1987

Martin, John E., *The Forgotten Worker: The Rural Wage Earner in Nineteenth-Century New Zealand*, Wellington: Allen and Unwin, 1990

Miller, John, *Early Victorian New Zealand: A Study of Racial Tension and Social Attitudes, 1839–1852*, London: Oxford University Press, 1958

Montgomery, David, *Beyond Equality: Labor and the Radical Republicans, 1862–1872*, New York: Knopf, 1967

Morrell, W.P., *The Provincial System in New Zealand, 1852–76*, Christchurch: Whitcombe and Tombs, 1964

Morton, A.L. and Tate, George, *The British Labour Movement*, London: Lawrence and Wishart, 1956

Musson, A.E., *British Trade Unions, 1800–1875*, London: Macmillan, 1972

Nadel, George, *Australia's Colonial Culture: Ideas, Men and Institutions in Mid Nineteenth Century Eastern Australia*, Melbourne: F.W. Cheshire, 1957

Neale, R.S., *Class and Ideology in the Nineteenth Century*, London: Routledge and Kegan Paul, 1972

Nolan, Melanie, *Breadwinning – New Zealand Women and the State*, Christchurch: Canterbury University Press, 2000

Noonan, Rosslyn J., *By Design: A Brief History of the Public Works Department/Ministry of Works, 1870–1970*, Wellington: Government Printer, 1975

OECD, *Societal Cohesion and the Globalising Economy – What Does the Future Hold?*, OECD: Paris, 1997

Oliver, W.H., *The Story of New Zealand*, London: Faber, 1960

Olssen, Erik, *Building the New World*, Auckland: Auckland University Press, 1995

Pelling, Henry, *A History of British Trade Unionism* (fifth edition), London: Macmillan, 1992

Pierre, W.A., *Canterbury Provincial Railways – Genesis of the NZR System*, Wellington: New Zealand Railway and Locomotive Society, 1964

Reeves, W. Pember, *State Experiments in Australia and New Zealand* (2 vols), London: Allen and Unwin, 1902

Richards, Raymond, *Closing the Door to Destitution: The Shaping of the Social Security Acts of the United States and New Zealand*, Pennsylvania: Pennsylvania University Press, 1994

Richardson, Len, *Coal, Class and Community: The United Mineworkers of New Zealand, 1880–1960*, Auckland: Auckland University Press, 1995

Richardson, Len, *The Denniston Miners' Union: A Centennial History, 1884–1984*, Westport: Denniston Miners' Union, 1984

Robbins, Roy M., *Our Landed Heritage: The Public Domain, 1776–1970*, (second edition), Lincoln: University of Nebraska Press, 1976

Roberts, S.H., *History of Australian Land Settlement*, Sydney: Macmillan, 1968

Roberts, Stephen, *Radical Politicians and Poets in Early Victorian Britain: The Voices of Six Chartist Leaders*, New York: Edwin Mellen Press, 1994

Roth, Bert, *Advocate, Educate, Control: The History of the New Zealand Engineers' Union, 1863–1983*, Wellington: New Zealand Engineering Union, 1984

Roth, Bert, *Along the Line: 100 Years of Post Office Unionism*, Wellington: New Zealand Post Office Union, 1990

Roth, H., *Trade Unions in New Zealand – Past and Present*, Wellington: Reed, 1973

Roth, Bert, *Wharfie*, Auckland: New Zealand Waterfront Workers Union, 1993

Roth, Bert and Hammond, Janny, *Toil and Trouble: The Struggle for a Better Life in New Zealand*, Auckland: Methuen, 1981

Ruoff, Theodore B.F., *An Englishman Looks at the Torrens System*, Sydney: Law Book Co., 1957

Rutherford, J., *Sir George Grey K.C.B., 1812–1898: A Study in Colonial Government*, London: Cassell, 1961

Salmond, J.D., *New Zealand Labour's Pioneering Days*, Auckland: Forward Press, 1950

Scholefield, G.H. (ed), *A Dictionary of New Zealand Biography*, Wellington: Government Printer, 1940

Scholefield, Guy H. (ed), *The Richmond-Atkinson Papers*, Wellington: Government Printer, 1960

Seligman, Edwin R.A., *Essays in Taxation* (tenth edition revised), London: Macmillan, 1925

Semmel, Bernard, *The Rise of Free Trade Imperialism: Classical Political Economy, the Empire of Free Trade and Imperialism, 1750–1850*, Cambridge: Cambridge University Press, 1970

Shick, Blair C. and Plotkin, Irving H., *Torrens in the United States*, Lexington, Mass.: Lexington Books, 1978

Simkin, C.G.F., *The Instability of a Dependent Economy*, London: Oxford University Press, 1951

Simpson, Tony, *The Immigrants: The Great Migration from Britain to New Zealand, 1830–1890*, Auckland: Godwit, 1997

Simpson, Tony, *A Vision Betrayed: The Decline of Democracy in New Zealand*, Auckland: Hodder and Stoughton, 1984

Sinclair, Keith, *A Destiny Apart: New Zealand's Search for National Identity*, Wellington: Allen and Unwin, 1986

Sinclair, Keith, *A History of New Zealand*, Auckland: Penguin, 1959

Sinclair, Keith, *Walter Nash*, Auckland: Auckland University Press, 1976

Sinclair, Keith, *William Pember Reeves*, Oxford: Clarendon, 1965

Sinclair, Keith and Mandle, W.F., *Open Account: A History of the Bank of New South Wales in New Zealand, 1861–1961*, Wellington: Whitcombe and Tombs, 1961

Smelser, Neil J., *Social Change in the Industrial Revolution*, London: Routledge and Kegan Paul, 1959

Steinmo, Sven, *Taxation and Democracy: Swedish, British and American Approaches to Financing the Modern State*, New Haven: Yale University Press, 1993

Stewart, W.D., *William Rolleston*, Christchurch: Whitcombe and Tombs, 1940

Stone, R.C.J., *Makers of Fortune: A Colonial Business Community and its Fall*, Auckland: Auckland University Press, 1973

Stuart, Peter, *Edward Gibbon Wakefield in New Zealand*, Wellington: Price Milburn, 1971

Sutch, W.B., *The Quest for Security in New Zealand, 1840 to 1966*, Wellington: Oxford University Press, 1966

Taxation in New Zealand, Wellington: Government Printer, 1967

Temple, Philip, *A Sort of Conscience – The Wakefields*, Auckland: Auckland University Press, 2003

Tennant, M., *Paupers and Providers: Charitable Aid in New Zealand*, Wellington: Allen and Unwin/Historical Branch, 1989

Thomson, David, *Selfish Generations? The Ageing of New Zealand's Welfare State*, Wellington: Bridget Williams Books, 1991

Thomson, David, *A World Without Welfare – New Zealand's Colonial Experiment*, Auckland: Auckland University Press, 1998

Thurow, Lester, *The Future of Capitalism – How Today's Economic Forces Will Shape Tomorrow's World*, St Leonards, NSW: Allen and Unwin, 1996

Turnbull Library, Friends of (ed), *Edward Gibbon Wakefield and the Colonial Dream: A Reconsideration*, Wellington: GP Publications, 1997

Turnbull, Michael, *The New Zealand Bubble: The Wakefield Theory in Practice*, Wellington: Price Milburn, 1959

Turner, Frederick J., *The Frontier in American History*, New York: Holt, 1958

Ward, Russel, *The Australian Legend*, Melbourne: Oxford University Press, 1966

Webber, Carolyn and Wildavsky, Aaron, *A History of Taxation and Expenditure in the Western World*, New York: Simon and Schuster, 1986

Wilson, T.G., *The Grey Government, 1877–9*, Auckland, 1954

Wood, Brian, *Disaster at Brunner*, Greymouth: Bright Print, 1996

Wright-St Clair, R.E., *A History of the New Zealand Medical Association*, Wellington: Butterworths, 1987

2. Articles

Arnold, Rollo, 'Community in rural Victorian New Zealand', *NZJH*, vol 24, no 1, 1990

Atkinson, Neill, 'The Auckland Seamen's Union, 1880–1914', in Pat Walsh (ed), *Trade Unions, Work and Society: The Centenary of the Arbitration System*, Palmerston North: Dunmore Press, 1994

Bassett, Judith, 'Abstemious millhands and bush lawyers: the Te Kopuru magistrates' court, 1875–1878', *Australian Journal of Legal History*, vol 1, 1995

Bassett, Judith, 'Dark Satanic mills, 1880–1890', in Judith Binney, Judith Bassett and Erik Olssen, *An Illustrated History of New Zealand, 1820–1920*, Wellington: Allen and Unwin, 1990

Beaglehole, Diana, 'Political leadership in Wellington, 1839–1853', in David Hamer and Roberta Nicholls (eds), *The Making of Wellington, 1800–1914*, Wellington: Victoria University Press, 1990

Biagini, Eugenio F., 'Popular Liberals, Gladstonian finance and the debate on taxation, 1860–1874', in Eugenio F. Biagini and Alastair J. Reid (eds), *Currents of Radicalism: Popular Radicalism, Organised Labour and Party Politics in Britain, 1850–1914*, Cambridge: Cambridge University Press, 1991

Bolitho, D.G., 'Some financial and medico-political aspects of the New Zealand medical profession's reaction to the introduction of social security', *NZJH*, vol 18, no 1, 1984

Brawley, Sean, '"No white policy" in New Zealand: fact and fiction in New Zealand's immigration record, 1946–1978', *NZJH*, vol 27, no 1, 1993

Butterworth, Susan, 'Scholars, gentlemen and floppy disks', in Friends of the Turnbull Library (ed), *Edward Gibbon Wakefield and the Colonial Dream: A Reconsideration*, Wellington: GP Publications, 1997

Campbell, C., 'The "working class" and the Liberal party in 1890', *NZJH*, vol 9, no 1, 1975

Campbell, R.J., 'The black "Eighties": unemployment in New Zealand in the 1880s', *Australian Economic History Review*, vol 16, 1976

Campbell, R.M., 'Family allowances in New Zealand', *Economic Journal*, September 1927

Carlyon, Jennifer, 'Friendly societies, 1842–1938: the benefits of membership', *NZJH*, vol 32, no 1, 1998

Chapman, S.D. and Bartlett, J.N., 'The contribution of building clubs and freehold land societies to working-class housing in Birmingham', in S.D. Chapman (ed), *The History of Working Class Housing*, Newton Abbot: David and Charles, 1971

Chase, Malcolm, 'Out of radicalism: the mid-Victorian freehold land movement', *English Historical Review*, vol 106, 1991

Child, John, 'Wages policy and wage movements in New Zealand, 1914–23', *Journal of Industrial Relations*, vol 13, 1971

Clark, Colin, 'Public finance and changes in the value of money', *The Economic Journal*, vol 55, 1945

Clinkard, G.W., 'Wages and working-hours in New Zealand, 1897–1919', *NZOYB*, 1919

Coleman, P., 'The spirit of New Zealand Liberalism in the nineteenth century', *Journal of Modern History*, vol 30, 1958

Coleman, P.J., 'The New Zealand frontier and the Turner thesis', *Pacific Historical Review*, vol 27, no 3, 1958

Coleridge, Kathleen, 'Thriving on impressions: the pioneer years of Wellington printing', in David Hamer and Roberta Nicholls (eds), *The Making of Wellington*, Wellington: Victoria University Press, 1990

Condliffe, J.B., 'Experiments in state control in New Zealand', *International Labour Review*, vol 9, no 3, 1924

Cooper, Annabel and Molloy, Maureen, 'Poverty, dependence and "women": reading autobiography and social policy from 1930s New Zealand', *Gender and History*, vol 9, no 1, 1997

Cronin, James E., 'The British state and the structure of political opportunity', *Journal of British Studies*, vol 27, 1988

Cross, Gary, 'Comparative exceptionalism: rethinking the Hartz thesis in the settler societies of nineteenth-century United States and Australia', *Australasian Journal of American Studies*, vol 14, no 1, 1995

Cross, Gary, 'Labour in settler-state democracies: comparative perspectives on Australia and the US, 1860–1920', *Labour History*, no 70, 1996

Dalziel, Raewyn, 'The colonial helpmeet. Women's role and the vote in nineteenth-century New Zealand', *NZJH*, vol 11, no 2, 1977

Dalziel, Raewyn, 'Popular protest in New Plymouth: why did it occur?', *NZJH*, vol 20, no 1, 1986

Dalziel, Raewyn, 'Towards representative democracy: 100 years of the modern electoral system', in *Towards 1990*, Wellington: GP Books, 1989

Daunton, M.J., 'Payment and participation: welfare and state-formation in Britain, 1900–1951', *Past and Present*, no 150, 1996

Dow, Derek A., 'Springs of charity? The development of the New Zealand hospital system, 1876–1910', in L. Bryder (ed), *A Healthy Country: Essays on the Social History of Medicine in New Zealand*, Wellington: Bridget Williams Books, 1991

Dowie, J.A., 'A century-old estimate of the national income of New Zealand', *Business Archives and History*, vol 6, 1966

Dowie, J.A., 'The course and character of capital formation in New Zealand, 1871–1900'. *New Zealand Economic Papers*, vol 1 no 1, 1966

Easton, Brian, 'Bernard Ashwin: secretary to the nation building state', *New Zealand Studies*, vol 7, no 3, 1997

Fairburn, Miles, 'The farmers take over', in Keith Sinclair (ed), *The Oxford Illustrated History of New Zealand*, Auckland: Oxford University Press, 1990

Fairburn, Miles, 'Is there a good case for New Zealand exceptionalism?', in Tony Ballantyne and Brian Moloughney (eds), *Disputed Histories: Imagining New Zealand's Pasts*, Dunedin: Otago University Press, 2006

Fairburn, Miles, 'What best explains the discrimination against the Chinese in New Zealand, 1860s–1950s?', *Journal of New Zealand Studies*, new series 2–3, 2003–4

Fairburn, Miles, 'Why did the New Zealand Labour Party fail to win office until 1935?', *Political Science*, vol 37, no 2, 1985

Gilbert, Bentley B., 'The decay of nineteenth-century provident institutions and the coming of old age pensions in Great Britain', *Economic History Review*, second series, vol 17, no 3, 1965

Grimshaw, Patricia, 'Women's suffrage in New Zealand revisited: writing from the margins', in Caroline Daley and Melanie Nolan (eds), *Suffrage and Beyond: International Feminist Perspectives*, Auckland: Auckland University Press, 1994

Hamer, D.A., 'The Agricultural Company and New Zealand politics, 1877–1886', *Historical Studies*, vol 10, no 38, 1962

Hamer, D.A., 'Centralization and nationalism (1891–1912)', in Keith Sinclair (ed), *The Oxford Illustrated History of New Zealand*, Auckland: Oxford University Press, 1990

Hamer, D.A., 'Sir Robert Stout and the labour question, 1870–1893', in Robert Chapman and Keith Sinclair (eds), *Studies of a Small Democracy*, Auckland: Blackwood and Janet Paul, 1963

Hammond, M.B., 'Judicial interpretation of the minimum wage in Australia', reprinted in Department of Labour, *Journal*, August 1913

Hammond, M.B., 'The regulation of wages in New Zealand', *Quarterly Journal of Economics*, vol 31, 1917

Harris, Jose, 'Political thought and the welfare state, 1870–1940: an intellectual framework for British social policy', *Past and Present*, no 135, 1992

Harrison, Brian and Hollis, Patricia, 'Chartism, Liberalism and the life of Robert Lowery', *English Historical Review*, vol. 82, 1967

Hay, Douglas, 'Patronage, paternalism and welfare: masters, workers and magistrates in eighteenth-century England', *International Labor and Working-class History*, no. 53, 1998

Hayburn, Ralph C., 'William Pember Reeves, *The Times* and New Zealand's Industrial Conciliation and Arbitration Act, 1900–1908', *NZJH*, vol 21, no 2, 1987

Hearn, T.J. and Kearsley, G.W., 'Voting patterns in the Canterbury Provincial Council: an application of cluster analysis', *Proceedings of Ninth New Zealand Geography Conference*, Dunedin: New Zealand Geographical Society, 1977

Heenan, Brian, 'Population ageing among non-Maori New Zealanders in later Victorian times', *NZJH*, vol 35, no 2, 2001

Henning, Jon, 'New Zealand: an antipodean exception to master and servant rules', *NZJH*, vol 41, no 1, 2007

Hensley, G.C., 'Land policy and the runholders', in W.J. Gardner (ed), *A History of Canterbury*, vol 2, Christchurch: Whitcombe and Tombs, 1971

Hirst, J.B., 'Egalitarianism', *Australian Cultural History*, no 5, 1986

Hirst, J.B., 'Keeping colonial history colonial: the Hartz thesis revisited', *Historical Studies*, vol 21, 1984

Irving, Terry, '1850–70', in Frank Crowley (ed), *A New History of Australia*, Melbourne: Heinemann, 1974

Jackson, W.K. and Wood, G.A., 'The New Zealand parliament and Maori representation', *Historical Studies: Australia and New Zealand*, vol 2, no 5, 1964

Jones, Gareth Stedman, 'Rethinking Chartism', in *Languages of Class: Studies in English Working Class History, 1832–1982*, Cambridge: Cambridge University Press, 1983

Kearsley, G.W., Hearn, T.J. and Brooking, T.W.H., 'Land settlement and voting patterns in the Otago Provincial Council, 1863–1872', *NZJH*, vol 18, no 1, 1984

Le Rossignol, J.E. and Stewart, W.D., 'Compulsory arbitration in New Zealand', *Quarterly Journal of Economics*, vol 24, 1910

Lineham, P.J., 'Freethinkers in nineteenth-century New Zealand', *NZJH*, vol 19, no 1, 1985

Macarthy, P.G., 'The living wage in Australia – the role of government', *Labour History*, no 18, 1970

McDonald, J.D.N., 'New Zealand land legislation', *Historical Studies: Australia and New Zealand*, vol 5, 1952

Martin, A.W., 'Australia and the Hartz "fragment thesis"', *Australian Economic History Review*, vol 13, no 2, 1973

Martin, David, 'Land reform', in Patricia Hollis (ed), *Pressure From Without in Early Victorian England*, London: Edward Arnold, 1974

Martin, John E., '1890: a turning point for labour', in Pat Walsh (ed), *Pioneering New Zealand Labour History*, Palmerston North: Dunmore Press, 1994

Martin, John E., 'A "small nation on the move": Wakefield's theory of colonisation and the relationship between state and labour in the mid-nineteenth century', in Friends of the Turnbull Library (ed), *Edward Gibbon Wakefield and the Colonial Dream: A Reconsideration*, Wellington: GP Publications, 1997

Martin, John E., 'Blueprint for the future? "National efficiency" and the First World War', in John Crawford and Ian McGibbon (eds), *New Zealand's Great War*, Auckland: Exisle, 2007

Martin, John E., 'Country report: labor history in New Zealand', *International Labor and Working-class History*, no 49, 1996

Martin, John E., 'English models and antipodean conditions: the origins and development of protective factory legislation in New Zealand', *Labour History*, no 73, 1997

Martin, John E., 'God made the country and man the town', in I. Shirley (ed), *Development Tracks*, Palmerston North: Dunmore Press, 1982

Martin, John E., 'Political participation and electoral change in nineteenth-century New Zealand', *Political Science*, vol 57, no 1, 2005

Martin, John E., 'Refusal of assent – a hidden element of constitutional history in New Zealand', *Victoria University of Wellington Law Review*, vol 41, no 1, 2010

Martin, John E., 'The removal of compulsory arbitration and the depression of the 1930s', *NZJH*, vol 28, no 2, 1994

Martin, John E., 'The struggle for £1: the emergence of the shearers' union in the 1870s', *NZJH*, vol 24, no 1, 1990

Martin, John E., Unemployment, government and the labour market in New Zealand, 1860–1890', *NZJH*, vol 29, no 2, 1995

Martin, John E., '"Waging war on the labour market": the state and wage labour in late nineteenth-century New Zealand', *Turnbull Library Record*, nos 1 and 2, 1993

Martin, John E., 'War economy', in Ian McGibbon (ed), *The Oxford Companion to New Zealand Military History*, Auckland: Oxford University Press, 2000

Matthew, H.C.G., 'Disraeli, Gladstone, and the politics of mid-Victorian budgets', *Historical Journal*, vol 22, no 3, 1979

Merritt, Adrian, 'The historical role of law in the regulation of employment – abstentionist or interventionist?', *Australian Journal of Law and Society*, vol 1, no 1, 1982

Moloughney, Brian and Stenhouse, John, '"Drug-besotten, sin-begotten fiends of filth": New Zealanders and the Oriental other, 1850–1920', *NZJH*, vol 33, no 1, 1999

Neale, R.S., 'Class and class consciousness in early nineteenth century England: three classes or five?', in R.S. Neale (ed), *History and Class*, Oxford: Blackwell, 1983

Neale, R.S., 'H.S. Chapman and the "Victorian" ballot', *Historical Studies: Australia and New Zealand*, vol 12, 1967

Neville, R.J. Warwick, 'Trends and differentials in age-sex structure', in *Population of New Zealand* (country monograph series no 12), vol 1, New York: United Nations, 1985

Nolan, Melanie, '"Politics swept under a domestic carpet"? Fracturing domesticity and the male breadwinner wage', *NZJH*, vol 27, no 2, 1993

NZOYB, 1963, 'The development of New Zealand's railway system, 1863–1963'

O'Connor, P.S., 'Keeping New Zealand white, 1908–1920', *NZJH*, vol 2, no 1, 1968

Ogus, A.I., 'Great Britain', in Peter A. Köhler and Hans F. Zacher (eds), *The Evolution of Social Insurance*, London: Frances Pinter, 1982

Oliver, W.H., 'The origins and growth of the welfare state', in A.D. Trlin (ed), *Social Welfare and New Zealand Society*, Wellington: Methuen, 1977

Oliver, W.H., 'Reeves, Sinclair and the social pattern', in Peter Munz (ed), *The Feel of Truth*, Wellington: Reed, 1969

Oliver, W.H., 'Social policy in New Zealand: an historical overview', in Report of the Royal Commission on Social Policy, *The April Report, vol 1, New Zealand Today*, Wellington, 1988

Oliver, W.H., 'Social policy in the Liberal period', *NZJH*, vol 13, no 1, 1979

Olssen, Erik, 'Friendly societies in New Zealand, 1840–1990', in Marcel van der Linden et al. (eds), *Social Security Mutualism: The Comparative History of Mutual Benefit Societies*, Bern: Peter Lang, 1996

Olssen, Erik, 'Mr Wakefield and New Zealand as an experiment in post-Enlightenment experimental practice', *NZJH*, vol 31, no 2, 1997

Olssen, Erik, 'Where to from here? Reflections on the twentieth-century historiography of nineteenth-century New Zealand', *NZJH*, vol 26, no 1, 1992

Perkin, H.J., 'Land reform and class conflict in Victorian Britain', in J. Butt and I.F. Clarke (eds), *The Victorians and Social Protest*, Newton Abbot: David and Charles, 1973

Perkin, Harold, 'Individualism versus collectivism in nineteenth-century Britain: a false antithesis', in Harold Perkin, *The Structured Crowd*, Sussex: Harvester, 1981

Pickens, K.A., 'The writing of New Zealand history: a Kuhnian perspective', *Historical Studies: Australia and New Zealand*, vol 17, 1977

Plowman, David, 'Forced march: the employers and arbitration', in Stuart Macintyre and Richard Mitchell (eds), *Foundations of Arbitration: The Origins and Effects of State Compulsory Arbitration, 1890–1914*, Melbourne: Oxford University Press, 1989

Pool, Ian, 'Is New Zealand a healthy country?', *New Zealand Population Review*, vol 8, no 2, 1982

Quigley, Neil C., 'Monetary policy and the New Zealand financial system: an historical perspective', in Reserve Bank of New Zealand, *Monetary Policy and the New Zealand Financial System* (third edition), Wellington: Reserve Bank of New Zealand, 1992

Quigley, Neil C., 'The mortgage market in New Zealand, and the origins of the Government Advances to Settlers Act, 1894', *New Zealand Economic Papers*, vol 23, 1989

Rankin, Keith, 'Gross national product estimates for New Zealand, 1859–1939', in L. Evans, J. Poot and N. Quigley (eds), *Long-run Perspectives on the New Zealand Economy*, Wellington: New Zealand Association of Economists, 1991

Riches, E.J., 'The fair wage principle in New Zealand', *Economic Record*, December 1937

Robertson, R.T., 'Government responses to unemployment in New Zealand, 1929–35', *NZJH*, vol 16, no 1, 1982

Robertson, Stephen, 'Women workers and the New Zealand Arbitration Court, 1894–1920', *Labour History*, no 61, 1991

Rogers, F., 'The influence of political theories in the Liberal period, 1890–1912: Henry George and John Stuart Mill', in Robert Chapman and Keith Sinclair (eds), *Studies of a Small Democracy*, Auckland: Blackwood and Janet Paul, 1963

Rosecrance, Richard N., 'The radical culture of Australia', in Louis Hartz, *The Founding of New Societies: Studies in the History of the United States, Latin America, South Africa, Canada and Australia*, New York: Harcourt Brace and World, 1964

Rosecrance, Richard N., 'The radical tradition in Australia: an interpretation', *Review of Politics*, vol 22, no 1, 1960

Roth, H., 'Charles Joseph Rae', *New Zealand Libraries*, vol 22, no 6, 1959

Roth, Bert, 'Labour day in New Zealand', in John E. Martin and Kerry Taylor (eds), *Culture and the Labour Movement*, Palmerston North: Dunmore Press, 1991

Sinclair, Keith, 'The significance of "the Scarecrow Ministry", 1887–1891', in Robert Chapman and Keith Sinclair (eds), *Studies of a Small Democracy*, Auckland: Blackwood and Janet Paul, 1963

Spain, Jonathon, 'The labour law reforms of 1875', in Eugenio F. Biagini and Alastair J. Reid, (eds), *Currents of Radicalism: Popular Radicalism, Organised Labour and Party Politics in Britain, 1850–1914*, Cambridge: Cambridge University Press, 1991

Stone, R.C.J., 'Auckland party politics in the early years of the provincial system, 1853–58', *NZJH*, vol 14, no 2, 1980

Stone, R.C.J., 'Auckland's political opposition in the Crown Colony period, 1841–53', in Len Richardson and W. David McIntyre (eds), *Provincial Perspectives*, Christchurch: Whitcoulls, 1980

Tennant, M., 'Duncan MacGregor and charitable aid administration, 1886–1896', *NZJH*, vol 13, no 1, 1979

Thompson, F.M.L., 'Social control in Victorian Britain', *Economic History Review*, second series, vol 34, no 2, 1981

Treble, James H., 'The attitudes of friendly societies towards the movement in Great Britain for state pensions, 1878–1908', *International Review of Social History*, vol 15, 1970

Turnbull, Michael, 'New Zealand labour politics, 1840–1843', *Political Science*, vol 4, no 2, 1952

Weir, Robert E., 'Whose left/who's left? The Knights of Labour and "radical progressivism"', in Pat Moloney and Kerry Taylor (eds), *On the Left: Essays on Socialism in New Zealand*, Dunedin: Otago University Press, 2002

Whalan, Douglas J., 'The origins of the Torrens system and its role in New Zealand', in G.W. Hinde (ed), *The New Zealand Torrens System Centennial Essays*, Wellington: Butterworths, 1971

Wood, G.A., 'The 1878 Electoral Bill and franchise reform in nineteenth century New Zealand', *Political Science*, vol 28, no 1, 1976

Woods, N.S., 'A study of the basic wage in New Zealand prior to 1928', *Economic Record*, December 1933

Young, John, 'The political conflict of 1875', *Political Science*, vol 13, no 2, 1961

3. Theses and papers

Angus, J.H., 'City and country – change and continuity, electoral politics and society in Otago, 1877–1893', PhD, University of Otago, 1976

Arnold, M.N., 'Wage rates, 1873–1911', Victoria University of Wellington, Department of Economics discussion paper no 11, 1982

Arnold, Rollo, 'Family or strangers? Trans-Tasman migrants, 1870–1920', Australia-New Zealand: Aspects of a Relationship, Stout Research Centre Conference, 1991

Arnold, Rollo, 'The opening of the great bush, 1869–1881', PhD, Victoria University of Wellington, 1972

Atkinson, Neill, 'Auckland seamen and their union, 1880–1922', MA, University of Auckland, 1990

Bartlett, J.E., 'Woven together: the industrial workplace in the Otago woollen mills, 1871–1930', BA (Hons), University of Otago, 1987

Bassett, J.O., 'Sir Harry Atkinson – a political biography, 1872–1892', MA, University of Auckland, 1966

Borrie, W.D., 'Immigration to New Zealand since 1854', MA, University of Otago, 1938

Campbell, Christopher, 'Parties and special interests in New Zealand, 1890–1893', MA, Victoria University of Wellington, 1978

Carlyon, Jenny, 'New Zealand friendly societies, 1842–1941', PhD, University of Auckland, 2001

Charman, Eric, 'Land tenure reform in New Zealand, 1875–1896', MA, University of Auckland, 1953

Chase, Malcolm S., 'The land and the working classes: English agrarianism, c. 1775–1851', PhD, University of Sussex, 1984

Chilton, Michael F., 'The genesis of the welfare state: a study of hospitals and charitable aid in New Zealand, 1877–92', MA, University of Canterbury, 1968

Chilwell, J.K., 'Unemployment insurance in New Zealand, 1883–1929', MA, Victoria University of Wellington, 1947

Clarke, J.C., 'The New Zealand Liberal Party and government, 1895–1906', MA, University of Auckland, 1962

Coates, H.M.O., 'The labour movement in Canterbury, 1880–1895', MA, University of Canterbury, 1980

Colbert, C.J., 'The working class in Nelson under the New Zealand Company, 1841–1851', MA, Victoria University of Wellington, 1948

Corstophine, D., 'Grey's liberalism as a factor in the development of party government in New Zealand', MA, University of Canterbury, 1950

Cunninghame, Jane, 'Litigation in the nineteenth century – Hokitika', History 316 research essay, Victoria University of Wellington, 1985

Elphick, Judith, 'Auckland 1870–74: a social portrait', MA, University of Auckland, 1974

Evans, A.M., 'A study of Canterbury politics in the early 1880s', MA, University of Canterbury, 1959

Everton, A.J., 'Government intervention in the New Zealand economy, 1914–18 – its aims and effectiveness', MA, Victoria University of Wellington, 1995

Ewing, I.S., 'Public service reform in New Zealand, 1866–1912', MA, University of Auckland, 1979

Galt, Margaret, 'Wealth and income in New Zealand, c.1870–c.1939', PhD, Victoria University of Wellington, 1985

Gibbons, P.J., '"Turning tramps into taxpayers": the Department of Labour and the casual labourer in the 1890s', MA, Massey University, 1970

Gibson, Campbell J., 'Demographic history of New Zealand', PhD, University of California, Berkeley, 1971

Hamer, David, 'Sir Robert Stout, 1844–1930', MA, University of Auckland, 1960

Hanham, H.J., 'The political structure of Auckland, 1853–76', MA, University of Auckland, 1950

Hearn, T.J., 'Land, water and gold in Central Otago, 1861–1921: some aspects of resource use policy and conflict', PhD, University of Otago, 1981

Hearn, T.J., 'South Canterbury: some aspects of the historical geography of agriculture, 1851–1901', MA, University of Otago, 1971

Herron, D.G., 'The structure and course of New Zealand politics, 1853–1858', PhD, University of Otago, 1959

Hoar, J.K., 'A descriptive history of the major aspects of the friendly society movement in New Zealand, 1840–1900', MA, University of Idaho, 1963

Hudson, Paul, 'English emigration to New Zealand, 1839 to 1850 – an analysis of the work of the New Zealand Company', PhD, University of Lancaster, 1996

Hunt, J.L., 'The election of 1875–6 and the abolition of the provinces', MA, University of Auckland, 1961

McDonald, J.D.N., 'A brief survey of land policy in New Zealand, 1876–1900', MA, University of Auckland, 1945

McEwing, Marion M., 'The protection of manufacturing industries in New Zealand', MA, University of Otago, 1985

McGarvey, R.D., 'Local politics in the Auckland province, 1853–62', MA, University of Auckland, 1954

Martin, John E., 'Income, inequality and the welfare state in New Zealand', Proceedings of Inequality and Ideology conference, Massey University, 1982

Merrett, I.A., 'A reappraisal of the 1890 Maritime strike in New Zealand', MA (Hons), University of Canterbury, 1970

Millar, D.P., 'The general election of 1884 in Canterbury', MA, University of Canterbury, 1960

Palairet, Roger, 'Litigation in Wanganui in the 1870s', History 316 research essay, Victoria University of Wellington, 1984

Patterson, B.R., 'Reading between the lines: people, politics and the conduct of surveys in the southern North Island, New Zealand, 1840–1876', PhD, Victoria University of Wellington, 1984

Phillips, J.R., 'A social history of Auckland, 1840–53', MA, University of Auckland, 1966

Ponton, F.A., 'Immigration restriction in New Zealand: a study of policy from 1908 to 1939', MA, Victoria University of Wellington, 1946

Poole, W.A., 'Co-operative retailing in New Zealand', research paper no 13, New Zealand Institute of Economic Research, 1969

Prentice, Marie E.S., 'Some liberal measures of the continuous ministry, 1879–90', MA, University of Auckland, 1942

Rogers, F., 'The single tax movement in New Zealand', MA, University of Auckland, 1949

Salmond, J.D., 'The history of the New Zealand labour movement from the settlement to the Conciliation and Arbitration Act 1894', MA, University of Otago, 1924

Shepherd, Heather, 'The nature and role of friendly societies in later nineteenth century New Zealand', history research essay, Massey University, 1976

Shires, Richard, 'Civil litigation in nineteenth century Wellington', History 316 research essay, Victoria University of Wellington, 1985

Stock, M.J., 'The development of the railway system of New Zealand, 1870–81', MA, Victoria University of Wellington, 1936

Strang, J.T., 'Welfare in transition: Reform's income support policy, 1912–28', MA, Victoria University of Wellington, 1992

Thompson, B.J.G., 'The Canterbury farm labourers' dispute, 1907–1908', MA, University of Canterbury, 1967

Thompson, G.F., 'The politics of retrenchment: the origin and some aspects of the politics of the Hall ministry, 1879–82', MA, Victoria University of Wellington, 1967

Todd, L.R., 'Grey's liberal ministry, 1877–1879', MA, University of Auckland, 1942

Trezise, A.B., 'Factory conditions and legislation in New Zealand, 1873–1891', History research essay, Massey University, 1973

Turnbull, M., 'The colonisation of New Zealand by the New Zealand Company, 1839–43', thesis, Oxford University, 1950

Unwin, D.M., 'Women in New Zealand industry – with specific reference to factory workers and to conditions in Dunedin', MA, University of Otago, 1944

Whitwell, H.J., 'The forty acre system', MA, University of Auckland, 1954

Wright, G., 'The petty bourgeoisie in colonial Canterbury', MA, University of Canterbury, 1999

Wylie, D.M., 'Representation and the franchise in New Zealand, 1852–1879', MA, University of Otago, 1951

INDEX

Page numbers in **bold** indicate illustrations